OXFORD IB DIPLOMA PROGRAM

ENGLISH B

COURSE COMPANION

Kawther Saa'd AlDin
Jeehan Abu Awad
Tiia Tempakka
Kevin Morley

OXFORD
UNIVERSITY PRESS

OXFORD
UNIVERSITY PRESS

Great Clarendon Street, Oxford OX2 6DP

Oxford University Press is a department of the University of Oxford.
It furthers the University's objective of excellence in research, scholarship,
and education by publishing worldwide in

Oxford New York

Auckland Cape Town Dar es Salaam Hong Kong Karachi
Kuala Lumpur Madrid Melbourne Mexico City Nairobi
New Delhi Shanghai Taipei Toronto

With offices in

Argentina Austria Brazil Chile Czech Republic France Greece
Guatemala Hungary Italy Japan Poland Portugal Singapore
South Korea Switzerland Thailand Turkey Ukraine Vietnam

© Oxford University Press 2012

British Library Cataloguing in Publication Data

Data available

ISBN 978-0-19-912968-3

10 9 8 7 6 5 4 3 2 1

Printed in Malaysia by Vivar Printing Sdn. Bhd.

Paper used in the production of this book is a natural, recyclable product made
from wood grown in sustainable forests. The manufacturing process conforms to
the environmental regulations of the country of origin.

ACKNOWLEDGMENTS

The author and publisher would like to thank the following for their kind permission to reproduce photographs and other copyright material:

Cover photo: William Robinson/Alamy.

P1: Wavebreakmedia Ltd/Shutterstock; **P2:** Irena Misevic/Shutterstock; **P13:** Journey Pictures; **P17:** Polina Maltseva/Shutterstock; **P19:** Copyright © 1999 by Laurie Halse Anderson. Reprinted by permission of Farrar, Straus and Giroux, LLC; **P19:** C.Showtime/Everett/Rex Features; **P23:** Design Pics Inc./Alamy; **P25:** Michael Jung/Shutterstock; **P26:** Image Courtesy Of The Advertising Archives; **P27:** Seanpavonephoto/Shutterstock.Com; **P29:** PVDE/Rue Des Archives/Mary Evans; **P30:** R. Twining And Company Ltd; **P31:** Serg64/Shutterstock; **P32:** Hulton Archive/Stringer; **P42:** Henry Beeker/Alamy; **P44:** Ayimages/Istock; **P44:** AVAVA/Shutterstock; **P44:** Beboy/Shutterstock; **P44:** Quinten Massys, An Old Woman ('The Ugly Duchess') © The National Gallery, London. Bequeathed By Miss Jenny Louisa Roberta Blaker, 1947; **P54:** Mustafa Arican/Istock; **P56:** Stocksnapper/Shutterstock; **P60:** Lenetstan/Shutterstock; **P67:** Patrimonio Designs Limited/Shutterstock; **P70:** Denis Vrublevski/Shutterstock; **P72:** Kraska/Shutterstock; **P74:** Peter Menzel/Science Photo Library; **P78:** Wdstock/Istock; **P79:** John E. Davidson/Aurora Photos/Corbis; **P81:** Alexander Mcclearn/Alamy; **P83:** Andrew Fox/Corbis; **P85:** Christopher Elwell/Shutterstock.Com; **P87:** © Paul Hostetler, 2009; **P88:** Josh Resnick/Shutterstock; **P90:** Ken Banks, Kiwanja.Net; **P110:** Best View Stock/Alamy; **P110:** Pamela Chandler/Topfoto; **P110:** Bettmann/CORBIS; **P129:** D. Hurst/Alamy; **P131:** Sean Spencer/Alamy; **P136:** Zoom-Zoom/Istock; **P138:** Gartshore & Associates Advertising Pte Ltd; **P140:** Tupungato/Shutterstock.Com; **P141:** Anna Lee; **P143:** Minfong Ho; **P146:** Rod Edwards/Alamy; **P151:** Gunnar Pippel/Shutterstock; **P157:** NASA Goddard Space Flight Center Image By Reto Stöckli; **P161:** Epa European Pressphoto Agency B.V./Alamy; **P162:** Christopher Felver/CORBIS; **P163:** Getty Images; **P168:** Reginald W. Bibby; **P172:** Martin Twomey Photography; **P176:** Getty Images/Staff; **P177:** Jonathan Larsen/Diadem Images/Alamy; **P179:** Richard Wareham Fotografie (Nieuws)/Alamy; **P180:** Getty Images; **P181:** Royston Robertson/Www.Cartoonstock.Com; **P183:** Farrar Straus, New York; **P188:** AKV/Shutterstock; **P191:** Li Kim Goh/Istock; **P195:** Edward Simons/Alamy; **P195:** Malcolm Freeman/Alamy; **P196:** Joe Gough/Shutterstock; **P197:** Cultura RM/Alamy; **P200:** Matias Rafael Mendiola/Istock; **P201:** AFH/Shutterstock; **P202:** Andersen Ross/Getty; **P205:** Everett Collection/Rex Features; **P205:** Moviestore Collection Ltd/Alamy; **P210:** James Cauty and Son/L-13; **P210:** John E Davidson/Aurora Photos/Corbis; **P210:** David Grossman/Alamy; **P215:** Amana Images Inc./Alamy; **P217:** Golden Pixels LLC/Shutterstock; **P225:** David Bagnall/Alamy; **P233:** Mark David; **P233:** Diana Lundin/Istock; **P234:** Image Courtesy Ethan Persoff, Http://Www.Ep.Tc; **P244:** Ducu59us/Shutterstock; **P245:** © Museum of The City of New York, USA/The Bridgeman Art Library ; **P248:** Mike Baldwin/Www.Cartoonstock.Com; **P282:** M4OS Photos/Alamy; **P286:** SDM Images/Alamy; **P304:** © David Levenson/Alamy; **P306:** Chris Willson/Alamy; **P306:** David Pearson/Alamy; **P306:** Steve Bly/Alamy; **P306:** Philipus/Alamy; **P306:** Kumar Sriskandan/Alamy; **P311:** Randy Glasbergen; **P314:** Photoalto/Alamy; **P316:** Randy Glasbergen; **P318:** Photos 12/Alamy; **P321:** Randy Glasbergen; **P326:** Naval History And Heritage Command; **P326:** David Jones/PA Archive/Press Association Images; **P327:** Imagezoo/Alamy; **P329:** Toyo Engineering Corporation; **P330:** David R. Frazier Photolibrary, Inc./Alamy; **P330:** Martin Shields/Alamy; **P337:** Pete Saloutos/Corbis; **P345:** Brian Derenzi; **P344:** The Arterial Network; **P347:** Eric Lafforgue/Alamy; **P347:** Mike Hutchings/Reuters/Corbis; **P347:** Mike Hutchings/Reuters/Corbis; **P348:** Mark Kelly/Getty Images; **P348:** Cliff Parnell/Istock; **P352:** Mipan/Istock; **P354:** Popperfoto/Getty Images; **P354:** Jack Sullivan/Alamy; **P365:** Oskarwells/Veer.Com; **P366:** Iofoto/Veer.Com; **P368:** Courtesy Of Twentieth Century Fox/Bureau L.A. Collection/Corbis; **P368:** Bureau L.A. Collection/Sygma/Corbis; **P368:** Bureau L.A. Collection/Sygma/Corbis; **P375:** FIFA Via Getty Images; **P376:** Tomislav Pinter/Shutterstock.Com; **P388:** Login/Shutterstock.

Illustrations by Paul Hostetler and Tony Randell.

We have made every effort to trace and contact all copyright holders before publication but this has not been possible in all cases. If notified, the publisher will rectify any errors or omissions at the earliest opportunity.

Course Companion definition

The IB Diploma Programme Course Companions are resource materials designed to support students throughout their two-year Diploma Programme course of study in a particular subject. They will help students gain an understanding of what is expected from the study of an IB Diploma Programme subject while presenting content in a way that illustrates the purpose and aims of the IB. They reflect the philosophy and approach of the IB and encourage a deep understanding of each subject by making connections to wider issues and providing opportunities for critical thinking.

The books mirror the IB philosophy of viewing the curriculum in terms of a whole-course approach; the use of a wide range of resources, international mindedness, the IB learner profile and the IB Diploma Programme core requirements, theory of knowledge, the extended essay, and creativity, action, service (CAS).

Each book can be used in conjunction with other materials and indeed, students of the IB are required and encouraged to draw conclusions from a variety of resources. Suggestions for additional and further reading are given in each book and suggestions for how to extend research are provided.

In addition, the Course Companions provide advice and guidance on the specific course assessment requirements and on academic honesty protocol. They are distinctive and authoritative without being prescriptive.

IB mission statement

The International Baccalaureate aims to develop inquiring, knowledgable and caring young people who help to create a better and more peaceful world through intercultural understanding and respect.

To this end the IB works with schools, governments and international organizations to develop challenging programmes of international education and rigorous assessment.

These programmes encourage students across the world to become active, compassionate, and lifelong learners who understand that other people, with their differences, can also be right.

The IB learner profile

The aim of all IB programmes is to develop internationally minded people who, recognizing their common humanity and shared guardianship of the planet, help to create a better and more peaceful world. IB learners strive to be:

Inquirers   They develop their natural curiosity. They acquire the skills necessary to conduct inquiry and research and show independence in learning. They actively enjoy learning and this love of learning will be sustained throughout their lives.

Knowledgable   They explore concepts, ideas, and issues that have local and global significance. In so doing, they acquire in-depth knowledge and develop understanding across a broad and balanced range of disciplines.

Thinkers   They exercise initiative in applying thinking skills critically and creatively to recognize and approach complex problems, and make reasoned, ethical decisions.

Communicators They understand and express ideas and information confidently and creatively in more than one language and in a variety of modes of communication. They work effectively and willingly in collaboration with others.

Principled They act with integrity and honesty, with a strong sense of fairness, justice, and respect for the dignity of the individual, groups, and communities. They take responsibility for their own actions and the consequences that accompany them.

Open-minded They understand and appreciate their own cultures and personal histories, and are open to the perspectives, values, and traditions of other individuals and communities. They are accustomed to seeking and evaluating a range of points of view, and are willing to grow from the experience.

Caring They show empathy, compassion, and respect towards the needs and feelings of others. They have a personal commitment to service, and act to make a positive difference to the lives of others and to the environment.

Risk-takers They approach unfamiliar situations and uncertainty with courage and forethought, and have the independence of spirit to explore new roles, ideas, and strategies. They are brave and articulate in defending their beliefs.

Balanced They understand the importance of intellectual, physical, and emotional balance to achieve personal well-being for themselves and others.

Reflective They give thoughtful consideration to their own learning and experience. They are able to assess and understand their strengths and limitations in order to support their learning and personal development.

A note on academic honesty

It is of vital importance to acknowledge and appropriately credit the owners of information when that information is used in your work. After all, owners of ideas (intellectual property) have property rights. To have an authentic piece of work, it must be based on your individual and original ideas with the work of others fully acknowledged. Therefore, all assignments, written or oral, completed for assessment must use your own language and expression. Where sources are used or referred to, whether in the form of direct quotation or paraphrase, such sources must be appropriately acknowledged.

How do I acknowledge the work of others?
The way that you acknowledge that you have used the ideas of other people is through the use of footnotes and bibliographies.

Footnotes (placed at the bottom of a page) or endnotes (placed at the end of a document) are to be provided when you quote or paraphrase from another document, or closely summarize the information provided in another document. You do not need to provide a footnote for information that is part of a 'body of knowledge'. That is, definitions do not need to be footnoted as they are part of the assumed knowledge.

Bibliographies should include a formal list of the resources that you used in your work. 'Formal' means that you should use one of the several accepted forms of presentation. This usually involves separating the resources that you use into different categories (e.g. books, magazines, newspaper articles, Internet-based resources, CDs and works of art) and providing full information as to how a reader or viewer of your work can find the same information. A bibliography is compulsory in the extended essay.

What constitutes malpractice?
Malpractice is behaviour that results in, or may result in, you or any student gaining an unfair advantage in one or more assessment component. Malpractice includes plagiarism and collusion.

Plagiarism is defined as the representation of the ideas or work of another person as your own. The following are some of the ways to avoid plagiarism:

- Words and ideas of another person used to support one's arguments must be acknowledged.

- Passages that are quoted verbatim must be enclosed within quotation marks and acknowledged.

- CD-ROMs, email messages, web sites on the Internet, and any other electronic media must be treated in the same way as books and journals.

- The sources of all photographs, maps, illustrations, computer programs, data, graphs, audio-visual, and similar material must be acknowledged if they are not your own work.

- Works of art, whether music, film, dance, theatre arts, or visual arts, and where the creative use of a part of a work takes place, must be acknowledged.

Collusion is defined as supporting malpractice by another student. This includes:

- allowing your work to be copied or submitted for assessment by another student

- duplicating work for different assessment components and/or diploma requirements.

Other forms of malpractice include any action that gives you an unfair advantage or affects the results of another student. Examples include, taking unauthorized material into an examination room, misconduct during an examination, and falsifying a CAS record.

About the authors

Kawther Saa'd AlDin is a senior examiner for English B, a workshop leader and a DP consultant. She has worked as an English B teacher and DP coordinator for a good number of years and was a member of the Language B curriculum review committee. Kawther's dedication to the field of education has earned her the European Council of International Schools (ECIS) Award for the Promotion of International Education, and the Stanford University Teacher Tribute.

Jeehan Abu-Awad is an IB DP English B assistant and senior examiner, an online workshop facilitator, a face-to-face active workshop leader and a standardizer. She has been teaching English B for the past 9 years in different schools in Amman, Jordan and has engaged in local schools curriculum development, headship positions, teacher coaching and training as well as university advising.

Tiia Tempakka has been involved in the world of International Baccalaureate since 1995, as a teacher, assistant and senior examiner, workshop leader, paper setter and standardizer, member of curriculum review, OCC faculty member, and consultant. She has taught in the language and literature programmes at universities and at several international schools in the UK and Finland. She is currently based in Helsinki. She is passionate about words and meaning and enjoys the global village of international education.

Kevin Morley has held a number of posts of responsibility at United World College of South East Asia in Singapore since 1992. Currently he is Head of Gap Year Projects. He has taught English A and B, schools supported self-taught languages and, occasionally, TOK. He is a workshop leader for Languages A and English B and is an IB English examiner for various components including internal assessment. In conjunction with the British Council, Kevin has written and teaches an introductory English Language Teaching scheme for IB diploma students. He is also a pro bono director of Bridges Across Borders South East Asia Community Legal Education Initiative and leads teacher–training workshops with regional community action groups and child protection agencies.

Contents

Introduction

This Course Companion has been written specifically for students of English B at higher or standard level of the International Baccalaureate Diploma Programme. This book supports the syllabus introduced in 2011 for first examinations in 2013. It presents texts and activities for all the three core topics and the five options. There are also specific chapters designed to introduce the literature requirements of the HL course. The authentic material in the English B Course Companion has been selected to reflect the diversity of anglophone culture in the 21st century with texts from five continents. These texts also reflect the different registers and language genres needed for English B.

Each chapter is structured around the core and the option topics. In each you will find a wealth of practical advice to improve your communication skills and linguistic competence in English. There are also integrated links to the theory of knowledge (TOK), creativity, action and service (CAS) and the IB learner profile as well as specific chapters on Paper 1 (receptive skills) and Paper 2 (written productive skills) and the Extended Essay in English B. By using this multi-faceted approach the Course Companion allows you to examine in depth some fascinating issues being debated in contemporary anglophone cultures. In each chapter you will also find tips to develop appropriate skills for the assessment activities.

In English B you will need to employ a very wide range of reading strategies. The Course Companion is designed to help you. To focus your attention on the subject matter each text is introduced with a 'Before You Read' activity. These questions and visuals encourage you to bring your prior linguistic and factual knowledge to the subject matter of the text. You are also encouraged to predict the content of the texts. During your initial reading of the texts you will have opportunities to practise a wide variety of while-reading strategies at varying degrees of complexity designed to help you to develop the skills to analyse surface features such as vocabulary and referencing within the texts.

Furthermore, in order to help you satisfy the intellectual requirements of the course, each text has activities to encourage inferential reading and critical thinking. For example, there are exercises that require you to offer explanations or draw conclusions from explicit or implicit ideas in a text. Moreover, you are encouraged to develop an intercultural perspective by reflecting on the similarities and differences between specific aspects of anglophone culture and the ones with which you are familiar. Further post-reading stimuli can assist you to engage actively in more extensive research into the subject matter. Additionally each chapter contains closely integrated writing tasks that allow you to respond to the issues raised in the chapters.

The new English B course also requires you to demonstrate a wide variety of listening and speaking skills. This Course Companion offers you a range of ideas for interactive group activities requiring you to examine, discuss and present core topics in a variety of formats. Such exercises are designed to enable you to practise the topic-specific language of the module and simultaneously to gain self-assurance and fluency in English in an atmosphere of cooperation and mutual support. Consequently, the option modules contain both single photographs and captions for practice at HL, and pairs of photographs and accompanying captions for SL. In each case the Course Companion offers you practical advice about how to analyse the content of photographs and gives you tips for doing the individual oral itself.

The Course Companion can help you to develop a repertoire of writing styles appropriate to the text types prescribed by the course and offers tips on the processes of drafting and rewriting. You will also find useful information about the particular characteristics of the prescribed text types, and hints and advice on how to use English creatively and appropriately for a specific audience and purpose. For example, you can make use of the specialist language of the stimulus text and integrate it with your own ideas. With a specific purpose and audience in mind, you can then create your own text using the stylistic and linguistic features of a given text type. This approach to writing has also been integrated into practice material for the other English B assessment components: the personal response for Section B of Paper 2 (HL) and the written assignment. Within the relevant sections on the core and option topics and within the literature chapters you will find guidelines and exercises to practise these features of the course.

English B can provide you with many opportunities to examine critically several aspects of anglophone culture. It can also help you to develop fluency and accuracy in one of the world's global languages. If you have been intrigued by the topics in the course and wish to undertake a more extensive piece of work, the book contains a final chapter to help you with the practical research and writing skills required for a successful Extended Essay.

The writers hope you find the texts and concepts in this Course Companion provocative and stimulating and that the book helps you to develop communicative competence both for the English B examination and as a skill for life in the wider world beyond the International Baccalaureate.

Social relationships

BEFORE YOU READ

→ How important is learning English nowadays?

→ As a language learner, what do you enjoy about learning English? What do you find difficult?

→ When you use English, do you think in your own language and translate your thoughts into English?

→ Would anyone be able to speak English fluently and accurately simply by learning its rules?

→ When you are using your first language, do you use English words like email, the Internet, CD, etc., or do you use their alternatives in your own language?

→ Which languages do you predict will be most used in fifty years from now?

→ David Crystal is one of the world's leading experts on languages. Listen to Crystal's podcast on the disappearance and preservation of languages: http://vimeo.com/6677955. What are Crystal's main arguments?

→ What evidence have you got from your local communities that certain languages are dying out? Alternatively what are local communities doing to preserve their languages?

The group over there seems nice.
Would they understand my English?

Linguistic dominance

English – a Global Language?

IN THE 21st century, English 1. (has been/is/is being) regarded as the major international language. Nowadays many people wonder 2. (whether/about/as) it is not the world

5 language. Population experts believe between 300 million and 400 million now speak 3. (this/it/that) as their mother tongue. However, it is also recognized 4. (as/by/for) an official language in about 100 countries.

10 In India, for example, English is 5. (so/such/so much) important that it is a national language.

The rise of English was 6. (nearly/almost/first) linked to the history of colonialism.

15 For example, when the British Empire was expanding in the 19th century, many languages in Africa 7. (were/was/have) submerged because of English. Later, the dominance of the USA after the second world

20 war ensured that this expansion of English 8. (continuing/continued/continues).

However, this spread 9. (to/in/of) English is relatively recent. In Shakespeare's time, it 10. (was being spoken/was spoken/

25 had been spoken) by just under five million people. Originally English was brought to Britain 11. (through/ by/ from) the Anglo-Saxons from north-west Europe. The modern language was also

30 12. (nearly/partly/frequently) shaped by the Viking and Norman invasions from Scandinavia and France.

Nowadays English is 13. (considered/used/taken) by communities on all five

35 continents. International organizations 14. (have adopted/adopt/will adapt) English to improve communication. For the past 60 years, multinational companies have communicated in English, even though

40 15. (all/some/few) of their employees have English as an official mother tongue.

But what 16. (with/about/for) the future? Some argue that English will become dominant. In the next century, 17. (as/ when/

45 if) we become an increasingly globalized and wired society, everyone will speak the same global language. Consequently, it is feared 18. (much/many/few) other languages will

50 disappear as they will not be able to compete with English.

A more optimistic point of view 19. (will suggest/ has suggested/suggests) that the world will become multilingual with

55 most people becoming competent in several languages, including English. At the other end of the debate some experts argue that English will disappear, 20. (divide/divides/dividing) into several different local versions

60 such as Spanglish, Hinglish and Chinglish.

Kevin Morley, 2011

1 For each of the numbered options in the text, choose one word or phrase which renders the sentence meaningful.

2 Answer the following questions.

a Approximately how many countries use English as their official language?

b What does the term official language mean?

c What, in your opinion, is the difference between an official language and a national one?

d To whom does the word 'their' in 'as their mother tongue' (line 7) refer?

e What caused English to spread in the 19th century? How has this rise affected many African countries?

f To what does 'this spread' (line 22) refer?

g Which languages have helped shape modern English?

h Give three predictions about the future of English as mentioned in the text. Which of those predictions do you find most plausible (likely to happen)? Why?

3 The following statements are all false. Give the exact quotes from the text which prove that these statements are false.

a English has been regarded as a major language since the 1950s.

b Approximately half a million people speak English as a first language.

c The British impact on the world after the second world war has helped in spreading the use of English.

d English is an original creation of the residents of the British Isles.

e The majority of employees in international organizations speak English as a first language.

Grammar

How did you do in question 1? What did you think helped you make the right choices? You may want to consider revising the following:
- Verb tenses
- Countable and uncountable nouns, and their quantifiers
- Linking words.

TIP

For any text to be coherent, the words used must form meaning. For example, a sentence like 'Peter is a car', while grammatically correct, does not have a logical meaning. Therefore, when you read a text, examine how the words are used to make meaningful statements.

Interactive oral activity

Work in pairs. Imagine that you are a linguist researching the impact of English.

1 In class, discuss and design a questionnaire to find out as much as possible about the impact of English in the country in which you go to school, either as an official language or as an unofficial language: in government, in education, in the traditional media, in popular culture and on the Internet.

2 Present the impact of English in your selected country. You may wish to use ICT (Information Communication Technologies) to show your results. Conclude by imagining how English will affect the country and its national language 20 years from now.

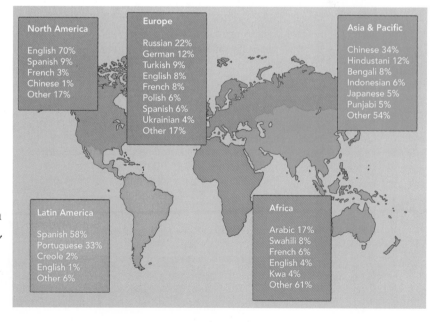

North America
English 70%
Spanish 9%
French 3%
Chinese 1%
Other 17%

Europe
Russian 22%
German 12%
Turkish 9%
English 8%
French 8%
Polish 6%
Spanish 6%
Ukrainian 4%
Other 17%

Asia & Pacific
Chinese 34%
Hindustani 12%
Bengali 8%
Indonesian 6%
Japanese 5%
Punjabi 5%
Other 54%

Latin America
Spanish 58%
Portuguese 33%
Creole 2%
English 1%
Other 6%

Africa
Arabic 17%
Swahili 8%
French 6%
English 4%
Kwa 4%
Other 61%

12:43 PM 99%

International Herald Tribune

As English's dominance continues, linguists see few threats to its rule

Riding the crest of globalization and technology, English dominates the world as no language ever has, and some linguists now say it may never be dethroned as the king of languages.

Others see pitfalls, but the factors they cite only underscore the grip English has on the
5   world: such cataclysms as nuclear war or climate change or the eventual perfection of a translation machine that would make a common language unnecessary.

Some insist that linguistic evolution will continue to take its course over the centuries and that English could eventually die as a common language as Latin did, or Phoenician or Sanskrit or Sogdian before it.

10 "If you stay in the mind-set of 15th-century Europe, the future of Latin is extremely bright," said Nicholas Ostler, the author of a language history called *Empires of the Word* who is writing a history of Latin. "If you stay in the mind-set of the 20th-century world, the future of English is extremely bright."

That scepticism seems to be a minority view. Such specialists on the English
15 language as David Crystal, author of *English as a Global Language*, say the world has changed so drastically that history is no longer a guide.

"This is the first time we actually have a language spoken genuinely globally by every country in the world," he said. "There are no precedents to help us see what will happen."

20 John McWhorter, a linguist at the Manhattan Institute, a research group in New York, and the author of a history of language called *The Power of Babel* was more unequivocal.

"English is dominant in a way that no other language has ever been before," he said. "It is vastly unclear to me what actual mechanism
25 could uproot English given conditions as they are."

As a new millennium begins, scholars say that about one-fourth of the world's population can communicate to some degree in English.
30 It is the common language in almost every endeavour, from science to air traffic control. It has consolidated its dominance as the language of the Internet, where 80 percent of the world's electronically stored information is in English
35 according to David Graddol, a linguist and researcher.

Seth Mydans, *International Herald Tribune*, 2007

1 Answer the following questions.

   a Which three occurrences, as mentioned in the text, will make it unnecessary for human beings to communicate using one language?

   b Name at least three languages which are no longer spoken.

   c According to the text, what does the sentence "If you stay in the mind-set of the 20th-century world, the future of English is extremely bright" (lines 12–13) imply about the future of English?

   d On the other hand, why might it be difficult to predict the future of the English language?

2 Below are selected words from the text. In each case choose the word or phrase from the options provided that could best replace the word given.

   a dethroned (line 2)
      A undone
      B replaced
      C withdrawn
      D moved away

   b underscore (line 4)
      A write
      B weaken
      C emphasize
      D narrate

   c cataclysms (line 5)
      A stories
      B events
      C accidents
      D disasters

   d continue to take its course (line 7)
      A change direction
      B slow down
      C accelerate
      D carry on

   e scepticism (line 14)
      A anger
      B optimism
      C doubt
      D certainty

   f precedents (line 18)
      A better examples
      B other examples
      C later examples
      D earlier examples

   g unequivocal (line 21)
      A certain
      B opinionated
      C quoted
      D angry

   h uproot (line 25)
      A spread
      B replace
      C defeat
      D transport

   i endeavour (line 31)
      A work
      B activity
      C difficulty
      D attempt

   j consolidated (line 32)
      A changed
      B held
      C made stronger
      D developed

3 From statements A to I select the four that are true according to the text on page 4.

   A Latin, like English, has dominated the world.
   B It is predicted that English will not remain a lingua franca.
   C Latin was the lingua franca in the 15th century.
   D English was a dominant language in the 20th century.
   E Many linguists believe English will ultimately die.
   F Some linguists believe we cannot predict the future of English based on history.
   G The use of English as a global language is unprecedented.
   H Almost 25% of the world's population can communicate in English to an extent.
   I A small percentage of electronic information is in English.

English won't dominate as world language

More bilingual people expected in future, expert says

THE WORLD faces a future of people speaking more than one language, with English no longer seen as likely to become dominant, a British language expert says in a new analysis.

"English is likely to remain one of the world's most important languages for the foreseeable future, but its future is more problematic, and complex, than most people appreciate," said language researcher David Graddol.

He sees English as likely to become the "first among equals" rather than having the global field to itself.

"Monolingual speakers of any variety of English — American or British — will experience increasing difficulty in employment and political life, and are likely to become bewildered by many aspects of society and culture around them," Graddol said.

The share of the world's population that speaks English as a native language is falling, Graddol reports in a paper in Friday's issue of the journal *Science*.

The idea of English becoming the world language to the exclusion of others "is past its sell-by date," Graddol says. Instead, it's major contribution will be in creating new generations of bilingual and multilingual speakers, he reports.

Multi-lingual homes

A multi-lingual population is already the case in much of the world and is becoming more common in the United States. Indeed, the Census Bureau reported last year that nearly one American in five speaks a language other than English at home, with Spanish leading, and Chinese growing fast. And that linguistic diversity, in turn, has helped spark calls to make English the nation's official language.

Yale linguist Stephen Anderson noted that multilingualism is "more or less the natural state. In most of the world multilingualism is the normal condition of people."

"The notion that English shouldn't, needn't and probably won't displace local languages seems natural to me," he said in a telephone interview.

While it is important to learn English, he added, politicians and educators need to realize that doesn't mean abandoning the native language.

Graddol, of the British consulting and publishing business The English Company, anticipates a world where the share of people who are native English speakers slips from 9 percent in the mid-twentieth century to 5 percent in 2050.

Chinese in the lead

As of 1995, he reports, English was the second most-common native tongue in the world, trailing only Chinese.

By 2050, he says, Chinese will continue its predominance, with Hindi-Urdu of India and Arabic climbing past English, and Spanish nearly equal to it.

Swarthmore College linguist K. David Harrison noted, however, that "the global share of English is much larger if you count second-language speakers, and will continue to rise, even as the proportion of native speakers declines."

Harrison disputed listing Arabic in the top three languages, "because varieties of Arabic spoken in say, Egypt and Morocco are mutually incomprehensible."

Even as it grows as a second language, English may still not ever be the most widely spoken language in the world, according to Graddol, since so many people are native Chinese speakers and many more are learning it as a second language.

English has become the dominant language of science, with an estimated 80 percent to 90 percent of papers in scientific journals written in English, notes Scott Montgomery in a separate paper in the same issue of Science. That's up from about 60 percent in the 1980s, he observes.

"There is a distinct consciousness in many countries, both developed and developing, about this dominance of English. There is some evidence of resistance to it, a desire to change it," Montgomery said in a telephone interview.

More languages on the web

For example, he said, in the early years of the Internet it was dominated by sites in English, but in recent years there has been a proliferation of non-English sites, especially Spanish, German, French, Japanese and others.

Nonetheless, English is strong as a second language, and teaching it has become a growth industry, said Montgomery, a Seattle-based geologist and energy consultant.

Graddol noted, though that employers in parts of Asia are already looking beyond English. "In the next decade the new 'must learn' language is likely to be Mandarin."

"The world's language system, having evolved over centuries, has reached a point of crisis and is rapidly restructuring," Graddol says. In this process as many as 90 percent of the 6,000 or so languages spoken around the world may be doomed to extinction, he estimated.

Graddol does have words of consolation for those who struggle to master the intricacies of other languages.

"The expectation that someone should always aspire to native speaker competence when learning a foreign language is under challenge," he comments.

The Associated Press, 2012

1 The sentences below are either true or false according to the text. Choose the correct response and then justify it with a relevant brief quotation from the text.

   a In the future, it will be usual for people to be able to speak more than one language.

   b English will remain the most significant global language.

   c Monolingual speakers will soon be a minority of the world's population.

   d Soon more people in the US will speak Spanish and Chinese than English.

   e Most experts agree that it is hard to become bilingual.

   f In the 20th century there were more first language speakers of English than Chinese.

   g David Graddol expects a 9% drop in the number of English speakers by 2050.

   h In the next 40 years the number of people with English as a first language will increase compared to speakers of English as a second language.

   i Graddol predicts that by 2050 there will be a rise in the number of Spanish and Hindi speakers.

   j Arabic will also become a new world language.

2 Write down to whom or to what the following words or phrases refer in the text.

   a it (line 83)   d he (line 122)
   b it (line 97)   e it (line 131)
   c it (line 118)   f this process (line 144)

3 Match each of the opinions listed to one of these speakers:

   David Graddol   Stephen Anderson
   K. David Harrison   Scott Montgomery

   a English dominates in the world of scientific research.

   b It can be hard to learn a new language.

   c Learning English does not mean abandoning community languages.

   d Soon more people will speak English as a second language than as a first language.

   e Teaching English is a growth industry.

   f The vast majority of the world's languages will not survive.

Interactive oral activity

1 Imagine that you are taking part in a debate about the future of English and other languages.

   a Group 1 argues that English will remain the lingua franca.

   b Group 2 argues that modern variations of English (Hinglish, Chinglish, etc.) will replace the English language.

2 Take 10 minutes to prepare your argument, strengthen it with examples and strengthen it with rebuttal points. You should try to predict how the other group will justify itself and try to refute their arguments.

3 Take part in the debate.

Remember

- All group members should take part in the debate.
- Listening is as important as speaking. In order to convince your audience, you should listen carefully to the other group's arguments and then try to refute them.
- Use linking words to present your ideas coherently: add (in addition, to add, etc.), contrast (but, nevertheless, however, etc.), or show consequence (therefore, consequently, etc.)

7

Beyond the text...

➤ English is originally a Germanic language but it was influenced by many languages such as French, Dutch, Spanish and Arabic to name a few. Conduct a simple search and find examples of English words and expressions which have their roots in other languages. What does this reveal about the English language?

➤ Standard English is defined as the form of English used by scholars or educated people. Is there one standard variation of English? Why? Why not?

➤ **Bloggable** and **onliner** are two newly created terms which have been recently added to the Oxford English Dictionary. Conduct a simple online search and find more examples of words which have been recently recognized. What does their recognition imply about the evolution of languages?

➤ Denotation is the literal meaning of a word or an expression while connotation is their implied association. Can you think of English words or expressions whose connotation is completely different from their denotation? Is it possible to be considered fluent in a language if one is incapable of understanding or using language connotations?

CAS

As one of your CAS activities, organize a translation campaign at your school. Your aim is to translate the English words and phrases which have infiltrated your first languages into the different languages you and your classmates speak. The newly-translated words should be easy to remember and to use. Promote your campaign by putting the translations on the school's bulletin boards.

The personal response

For the personal response (HL Paper 2 Section B) there is no one right answer. You are asked to write a reasoned argument in which you respond to a written stimulus using any text type of your choice. You will be assessed on your ability to take a systematic approach to the stimulus. So, you must be able to supply a logical, reasoned and coherent response. To do this, you must form a clear idea of how you wish to respond. You must support your ideas with evidence. The personal response exercises in this section aim to help you decide on an approach and develop a reasoned argument. In future sections, you will be asked to choose a specific type of text.

Based on the following stimulus, give a personal response and justify it. Write between 150–250 words.

"Riding the crest of globalization and technology, English dominates the world as no other language ever has, and some linguists now say it may never be dethroned as the king of languages."

1   Do you agree with the statement? Are you unsure? Do you prefer to analyse the arguments before you mention your opinion? Start by deciding on an approach from the ones listed in the Exam tip box below.

2   Divide your response into a series of supporting points. Each of these points should help you to prove your argument. Each point will focus on a single idea that supports your approach. You should express each point clearly in a topic sentence, which can be at the beginning or end of a paragraph. You should use details and specific examples to make your ideas clear and convincing. Make sure that each paragraph has a topic sentence, supporting examples and explanation.

3   Having decided on an approach, plan your response.

4   Write your personal response.

Exam tip

HL Paper 2 Section B

Here are three different approaches for tackling the personal response.

- The 'one-sided' approach

Either support or attack the main idea in the stimulus text. Give reasons for each point you make. Do not include the other side of the argument. Write a strong conclusion about what should be done.

- The 'balanced but undecided' approach

There is no single right answer to a problem. Give both sides of the argument. State that both sides have equally valid arguments. Alternatively, show how both sides have weak arguments. Give reasons for supporting or criticizing each point of view. Conclude by saying that the different sides should recognize that each has valid points and they need further discussion.

- The 'analytical' approach

Evaluate the argument/s in the stimulus text. Put your argument/s in order of strength. You can start with the weakest and finish with the strongest or the other way round. Explain why some points in your analysis are stronger than others. Which arguments are better supported by examples? Conclude by stating which ideas you would support and which you would not.

Half of world's 7000 languages to become extinct by turn of century

Hundreds of languages around the world are teetering on the brink of extinction, and eastern Siberia, northern Australia, central South America, Oklahoma, and the
5 US Pacific Northwest are among the worst affected zones, a new research has revealed.

[1]

"Languages are undergoing a global extinction crisis that greatly exceeds the pace of species extinction," said Prof. Harrison.

10 Prof. Harrison and Gregory Anderson, both affiliated to the Living Tongues Institute for Endangered Languages in Oregon, travelled across the world to interview the last speakers of critically endangered languages
15 as part of the National Geographic Society's Enduring Voices Project.

[2]

In the Northern Territory of Australia, the scientists found three speakers of Magati Ke. In Western Australia, they found
20 three speakers of the little-known Yawuru language, while deep in the outback, they located a single man with rudimentary knowledge of Amurdag, a language previously declared extinct.

25 In Bolivia, the duo found language diversity twice that of Europe. However, dominant languages such as Spanish were threatening that diversity, the findings revealed. "This is a radically new way of looking at language
30 diversity globally," said Prof. Harrison.

[3]

"Most of what we know about species and ecosystems is not written down anywhere: it's only in people's heads. We are seeing in front of our eyes the erosion of the human
35 knowledge base," said Prof. Harrison.

[4]

In Bolivia, the scientists came across the Kallawaya people who have been traditional herbalists since the time of the Inca Empire.

In daily life, the Kallawaya used the more
40 common Quechua language. But they also maintained a secret language to encode information about thousands of medicinal plants, some previously unknown to science that the Kallawayas use as remedies, they
45 said.

[5]

"There are people who may have a special set of terms … which enable them to navigate thousands of miles of uncharted ocean … without any modern instruments of
50 navigation," Prof. Harrison said.

Prof. Harrison said that while in the last 500 years an estimated half of the world's languages, from Etruscan to Tasmanian, had become extinct, the vanishings now were
55 taking place at a faster rate.

[6]

Hindustan Times, 2007

1 From sentences A to H below, choose which one best fits each of the spaces **[1]–[6]** in the text.

A "We're throwing away centuries' worth of knowledge and discoveries that they have been making all along," he said.

B At some places, the situation is so bad that only a single person knows the language, said David Harrison, a linguistics professor at Pennsylvania's Swarthmore College.

C Fewer than ten people probably spoke more than 500 languages, he said.

D Similarly, the navigational skills of peoples in Micronesia, was also encoded in small, vulnerable languages, the researchers found.

E The institute works with local communities and tries to help by developing teaching materials and by recording the language.

F "The key to getting a language revitalised," he said, "is by motivating a new generation of speakers."

G The researchers further found that more than half of the world's 7,000 languages would die out by the end of the century, often taking with them irreplaceable knowledge about the natural world.

H They found that while in some places, languages had disappeared instantly with small, vulnerable communities wiped out by natural disasters, in most cases languages died a slow death as people simply abandoned their native tongues when they became surrounded by people speaking a more common language.

2 Find a word in the text which is similar in meaning to each of the following:

a	annihilation	**f**	disappearance
b	surpass	**g**	cures
c	connected to	**h**	find the way
d	basic	**i**	unknown
e	variety	**j**	died out

Interactive oral activity

In this section, you touched on two fundamental questions: What is the future of English as a global language? What is the future for other minority languages in the face of globalization?

Having read the texts which explored linguistic dominance, what is your opinion of the future of English? Does the use of English seem to be growing or declining? Are there local versions of English developing in the country where you are studying? Can visitors and tourists understand local English? In order to do this, you may like to undertake individual research and find out what other linguists and journalists think.

Below are some interactive oral ideas.

Whole-class activities:

1 A discussion:
   a How should the government in an anglophone country support minority languages?
   b How can the government improve English competence in your country?

2 A presentation on English as a global language followed by a whole-class discussion

Group activity:

3 Role play involving some element of decision making or problem solving regarding funding minority languages in your school.

Remember

An effective presentation
To make an effective presentation, always focus on:

- the message you are communicating: The main purpose of any presentation is communication, and in oral presentations, you are delivering a message. You should do this in a simple, coherent, concise yet interesting way.
- the time you take to deliver your message: Your time is limited; therefore, always plan your presentation well. Make sure that your ideas flow smoothly, and that you do not concentrate only on listing facts. Give examples, justify points of view, and try to link your topic to your daily life and experience.
- the need to address your audience directly and involve them.
- the need to avoid reading from your notes or learning your presentation by heart.

The personal response

Based on the following stimulus, give a personal response and justify it. Write between 150 and 250 words.

"The key to revitalizing a language is by motivating a new generation of speakers."

1   Read a classmate's personal response. What do you like about your classmate's response? Why? What do you not like? Why?

2   In writing, tell your classmate how s/he can improve his or her personal response. Base your comments on your classmate's performance against the HL Paper 2 Section B assessment criteria (Language B Guide, pp. 46–47).

The SL Written Assignment

The written assignment is a piece of writing (300–400 words) which is based on an aspect related to one of the core topics that you have studied in class: communication and media, global issues, and social relationships. The assignment requires that you read three texts, understand them, and synthesize the ideas which appear in them in the form of a continuous piece of writing. This synthesis involves ability to identify key points in the three texts and join them in a new form. To do this, you need to:

● decide on an aim. Why are you using this information in your written assignment? How will you shed light on the topic the three texts share?

● decide on the text type you will use. Which type of text best delivers your message?

● decide on an audience. Whom does your piece of writing address? Why?

1   Begin by re-reading the texts on pages 2, 4, 6 and 10. What does each text discuss? Do the texts have anything in common?

2   Which ideas in the texts do you like best? Why? How can you use these ideas? What type of text do you think best delivers your message? Who is your audience? Why?

3   In pairs, discuss your answers to questions 1 and 2. How logical is your partner's approach? How applicable?

In addition to writing the assignment, you are required to submit a rationale in which you specify your aims and show how you achieved them.

4   After discussing the assignment with your partner, write your rationale.

Cultural diversity

→ How important is it to be able to practise your English in real-life situations with native speakers? How does this exposure compare to doing interactive oral activities in the classroom?

→ When does the ability to speak a second language become essential?

→ How does a nation's ability to speak English affect its economic prospects?

Language & cultural identity

▶ IN**CINEMAS**

MAD ABOUT ENGLISH

A fascinating tour of the English madness engulfing China

Movie Rating: ★ ★ ★

a Have you ever seen 10,000 students learning English from one teacher – all at the same time? Have you ever met a detective whose mission impossible is to arrest bad grammar? Or encountered a 74 year-old retiree who thinks nothing of ambushing foreigners on the streets just so he can practise his English? Or heard a Chinese policeman speak English in a New York Bronx accent?

b If you haven't, catch Mad About English! – the amazing story of 1,000,000,000 people and their MAD MAD MAD rush to learn English! As the clock ticks down to next month's Olympics, China's love affair with the English language has reached feverish proportions. With half a million or more visitors descending on Beijing for the Games, can the Chinese pull it off with their newly-acquired English? Mad About English! follows the inspiring and heart-warming efforts of a city preparing to host the world by learning a once-forbidden tongue.

c Having won the bid to host the Olympics, China began an extensive foray of preparation to usher the new found glory of welcoming international guests to their land. Having built massive architectural marvels like the National Aquatics Center ("Water cube") and the National Stadium ("Bird's nest"), one major hurdle faced the majority of its population: language. What are the hosts to do if they can't communicate with their own guests?

d One might be a little weary of such matters. Culture aside, we've seen countless viral emails or sites ridiculing the inappropriateness of some rather peculiar English usage in the region from menus to store signs and instructions. Admit it,

we've laughed at them too and then came this little documentary that we thought was going to aggravate the situation with never-ending satire. Well, that was the vibe I was getting from the trailer. But, I can't help but smile a little at the effort and determination they (Beijingers) demonstrate to upgrade their English and make sure they do their country proud. And it's not only just about the upcoming event, it's also about the fact that China is catching up with the rest of the world.

e Labeled as a docu-comedy, Lian Pek, once one of the most recognizable broadcast journalists, steps into the seat of director and does a great job capturing the charm and quirkiness of the people. Beautifully captured by Tong Zhijian, the ever changing landscape of urban Beijing lets us take a look from the native point of view. And many points did they cover, from retiree Jason Yang (who set up Golden Years English Salon), Li Yang (nicknamed, Crazy English Teacher, who became the spokesperson for English learning in China), Qi Qi (eleven year old student in English boot camp), Meng (the taxi driver, trying to earn a pass for his English test so he could drive during the Olympic duration), Dr David Tool (the grammar cop, who goes around inspecting bad English signs) and lastly Lui Wenli (a policemen who loves to master different accents, his favorite – Brooklyn New York!).

f We see each colorful character struggle to make ends meet. Learning English for them doesn't just mean better communication, it also means a livelihood. Documentaries like these are one in a million and capturing the essence of it all on film, priceless.

B S Lokman, 2011

Developing writing skills: Review

Answer the following questions. You must justify your answer by giving evidence from the text.

1   What is the subject matter of the review?

2   What audience do you think B S Lokman is writing for?

3   What is the reviewer's relationship with the readers?

4   What is the writer's attitude to the film?

5   How does the start of the review get our attention?

6   Write appropriate headings for each paragraph labelled **a–f** of the review.

Writing a review

Imagine you have to write a film, video game, restaurant or book review linked to cultural diversity. A review is a form of journalism and can be found in magazines, newspapers and in blogs. In a popular review you share an opinion about a new book, a new film, a CD or recent concert. Here are three pieces of advice about writing a review:

- Communicate a clear opinion about the subject matter
- Make sure you sound knowledgeable
- Make sure your language is appropriate to your audience

1   An opinion should be based on evidence: facts and details. This means the reviewer has to **summarize** the key information. In order to make your review reliable and authoritative, you need to think about what your reader will want to know. To achieve this, copy and complete the table below, deciding which details you would choose to include in each category. By using these different criteria to judge the product, your review will sound informed and informative.

Video Game	Book	Film	CD	Concert	Restaurant or Café
				Atmosphere	Food
				Songs	Service
				Quality of the performance	Price
				Length of show	Atmosphere

2   In addition to summarizing the key points, you also need to **evaluate**. A review emphasizes an opinion which can be positive or negative. However, an opinion should be based on evidence: facts and details. So before you start writing, decide what your overall opinion is and make sure you express this clearly to your audience.

3   Finally, think about the audience and the type of publication you are writing for. If you are writing for a school magazine or for your peer group, you will probably want to sound familiar and still show that you have some expert inside knowledge.

     If your task involves writing for a magazine where you do not know the audience or readership personally, then you have to be more formal. We know that English has different registers. These registers or levels of familiarity go from formal, to informal and familiar: "A most enjoyable musical experience" or "A totally cool show – a total blast!"

     If your review is to sound authentic you need to get the register right. However, this does not mean that you have to lose your sense of humour! You can still sound smart and clever and yet be quite formal.

4   Write a review for one these: video game, book, film, CD, concert, restaurant or café. Remember that you have to link your choice to cultural diversity. Before writing, use the table below to help you to plan your ideas.

Before you write	Notes
What kinds of detail do you need to include?	
Think about the kind of publication you are writing for.	
What is your role as writer: superior, expert, peer, friend, advisor?	
Think about the kind of audience you are writing for.	
Figure out your attitude: clever, humorous, intelligent, opinionated, balanced?	
What rating system are you going to use?	
How to start? What will be a good lead-in or attention grabber?	
Figure out the key points to write about and their order.	
How much background and context do you need?	

Beyond the text...

➤ Define cultural identity in your own words. How does language affect one's cultural identity?

➤ How is the cultural identity of a monolingual person different from that of a bilingual or multilingual one? Is it true that bilinguals enjoy the best of both 'worlds'? Do you think that the people mentioned in the review would suffer from a loss of cultural identity by learning English?

➤ In his book *The Silent Language*, Edward T. Hall argues that 'one of the most effective ways to learn about oneself is by taking seriously the cultures of others. It forces you to pay attention to those details of life which differentiate them from you'. Do you agree? Why?

➤ In your own culture, is non-verbal communication as important as verbal communication? Do people from different cultures use the same gestures to mean the same things? Look at the gestures on the left which are used in some English-speaking countries. How are they similar to, or different from, the gestures used in your own culture?

TOK

The Sapir Whorf Hypothesis

In the early twentieth century, Edward Sapir and his colleague and student Benjamin Whorf put forward the idea that there was a systematic relationship between the grammar and vocabulary of a language and how that person both understands the world and behaves in it.

The hypothesis states that people see and communicate ideas differently depending on the language. This idea challenges the possibility of perfectly representing the world with language because it suggests that each language conditions the thoughts of its speaker community. For example, it is said that in Japanese there is no distinction between green and blue and the Eskimos have over 50 words for snow.

In a certain part of New Guinea, people are hunter-gatherers and subsequently have little concept of material wealth and no reason to count things. Their

language has a word for one and another word for two. Today, because of contact with the outside world, they have had to adapt their language. They use the word for dog to indicate the number four (possibly because a dog has four legs). So, here is how the system works (using English equivalents):

One = 1
Two = 2
One and two = 3
Dog = 4
Dog and one = 5
Dog and two = 6
Dog and one and two = 7
Dog dog = 8
Dog dog and one = 9

Is perception in your own language encoded differently from that in English, for example colour and spatial relationships? What do these differences tell us about the relationships between perception, culture, reality and truth?

If certain languages are dying out because of globalization, what else is lost along with the language?

Self-identity

➤ Are there 'clans' at your school? If so, describe some of the social groups there are. How do they distinguish themselves?

➤ Why do you think teenagers want to belong to certain groups?

Welcome to Merryweather High

It is my first morning of high school. I have seven new notebooks, a skirt I hate, and a stomach-ache.

The school bus wheezes to my corner. The door opens and I step up. I am the first pickup of the day. The driver pulls away from the curb while I stand in the aisle. Where to sit? I've never been a backseat waste case. If I sit in the middle, a stranger could sit next to me. If I sit in the front, it will make me look like a little kid, but I figure it's the best chance I have to make eye contact with one of my friends, if any of them have decided to talk to me yet.

The bus picks up students in groups of four or five. As they walk down the aisle, people who were my middle-school lab partners or gym buddies glare at me. I close my eyes. This is what I've been dreading. As we leave the last stop, I am the only person sitting alone.

The driver downshifts to drag us over the hills. The engine clanks, which makes the guys in the back holler something obscene. Someone is wearing too much cologne. I try to open my window, but the little latches won't move. A guy behind me unwraps his breakfast and shoots the wrapper at the back of my head. It bounces into my lap–a Ho-Ho.

We pass janitors painting over the sign in front of the high school. The school board has decided that "Merryweather High–Home of the Trojans" didn't send a strong abstinence message, so they have transformed us into the Blue Devils. Better the Devil you know than the Trojan you don't, I guess. School colors will stay purple and gray. The board didn't want to spring for new uniforms.

Older students are allowed to roam until the bell, but ninth- graders are herded into the auditorium: We fall into clans: Jocks, Country Clubbers, Idiot Savants, Cheerleaders, Human Waste, Eurotrash, Future Fascists of America, Big Hair Chix, the Marthas, Suffering Artists, Thespians, Goths, Shredders. I am clanless. I wasted the last weeks of August watching bad cartoons. I didn't go to the mall, the lake, or the pool, or answer the phone. I have entered high school with the wrong hair, the wrong clothes, the wrong attitude. And I don't have anyone to sit with.

I am Outcast.

There is no point looking for my ex-friends. Our clan, the Plain Janes, has splintered and the pieces are being absorbed by rival factions. Nicole lounges with the Jocks, comparing scars from summer league sports. Ivy floats between the Suffering Artists on one side of the aisle and the Thespians on the other. She has enough personality to travel with two packs. Jessica has moved to Nevada. No real loss. She was mostly Ivy's friend, anyway.

The kids behind me laugh so loud I know they're laughing about me. I can't help myself. I turn around. It's Rachel, surrounded by a bunch of kids wearing clothes that most definitely did not come from the East Side Mall. Rachel Bruin, my ex-best friend. She stares at something above my left ear. Words climb up my throat. This was the girl who suffered through Brownies with me, who taught me how to swim, who understood about my parents, who didn't make fun of my bedroom. If there is anyone in the entire galaxy I am dying to tell what really happened, it's Rachel. My throat burns.

Her eyes meet mine for a second. "I hate you," she mouths silently. She turns her back to me and laughs, with her friends. I bite my lip. I am not going to think about it. It was ugly, but it's over, and I'm not going to think about it. My lip bleeds a little. It tastes like metal. I need to sit down.

I stand in the center aisle of the auditorium, a wounded zebra in a National Geographic special, looking for someone, anyone, to sit next to. A predator approaches: gray jock buzz cut, whistle around a neck thicker than his head. Probably a social studies teacher, hired to coach a blood sport.

Mr. Neck: "Sit."

I grab a seat. Another wounded zebra turns and smiles at me. She's packing at least five grand worth of orthodontia, but has great shoes. "I'm Heather from Ohio," she says. "I'm new here. Are you?" I don't have time to answer. The lights dim and the indoctrination begins.

From *Speak* by Laurie Halse Anderson, 1999

Melinda, the narrator, describes her first day as a high school student. Read the text and answer the following questions.

1   Why is Melinda worried about her appearance?

2   How can we tell that Melinda feels nervous on the school bus?

3   How many examples of aggressive behaviour towards Melinda can you find in the passage?

4   What thoughts does Melinda have about:

    a   her former friends?

    b   her new school?

5   Why do you think Melinda calls Heather 'another wounded zebra' (line 80)?

6   Melinda mentions a whole variety of different clans or peer groups, each making its own fashion statement. The groups she lists are: 'Jocks, Country Clubbers, Idiot Savants, Cheerleaders, Human Waste, Eurotrash, Future Fascists of America, Big Hair Chix, the Marthas, Suffering Artists, Thespians, Goths, Shredders'.

    In pairs, imagine what some teenagers would look like. They could be Americans from Merryweather High or clans from your own school. Use the chart below to help you create your descriptions.

10th ANNIVERSARY EDITION
LAURIE HALSE ANDERSON

NATIONAL BOOK AWARD FINALIST

speak

CONTAINS ALL-NEW MATERIAL FROM THE AUTHOR

Name of clan	Clothes	Interests	Facial appearance (e.g. make up or piercings)	Attitude to school	Behaviour and attitudes to others

7   In groups, discuss the following questions.

    a   If Merryweather High had had a school uniform, would Melinda's first day have been easier? Do you think she would have fitted in more easily?

    b   What reasons can you imagine for everyone's aggressive behaviour towards Melinda?

Writing activity

Watch the film *Speak* then write a film review in which you highlight how students relate to different social or cultural groups. Write between 250 and 400 words.

Beyond the text...

➤ Do you think belonging to a certain clan is a fashion statement or one of individuality?

➤ Conduct some research and find out if teenagers in other countries join the same clans as teenagers in the US. What do you conclude? Are clans representative of a certain social status or culture?

➤ What is the difference between a clan and a clique? Is there a relationship between being a clique member and bullying?

➤ Peruse some online sources to find out if belonging to a certain clique or clan affects a person's language. Give specific examples drawn from an anglophone culture. What does this show about the relationship between culture and language?

> ## Remember
>
> When you write a review:
> - communicate a clear opinion about the subject matter.
> - make sure you sound knowledgeable.
> - make sure your language and style are appropriate to your audience.

The HL Written Assignment

The written assignment is a piece of creative writing (500–600 words) which is based on one of the two literary works you are reading in class. In your assignment, you have to show understanding and appreciation of the literary work. To achieve this, you have to:

- reflect on the literary work: What is the works main theme? How does the author present his or her theme? How does the plot support the theme? How are the characters portrayed? What have you learned?
- decide on the aim of your assignment. For example, you may believe a certain event should be further explored. Why are you writing your assignment? Are you writing to highlight how a character feels at a certain point?
- decide on the text type you will use. Which type of text best delivers your message?
- decide on an audience. Whom does your writing address?

1 Begin by re-reading *Welcome to Merryweather High*. What is the text about? How are the characters portrayed? What would you like to explore further?

2 Which idea/s in the texts do you like best? Why? How can you use these ideas? What type of text do you think best delivers your message? Who is your audience? Why?
    The following are examples of possible assignments based on the text:
    a Melinda's diary entry for the remainder of the day.
    b A review of the opening chapter of the novel.
    c As a reporter for the Merryweather High School magazine, you interview Heather and Melinda and they discuss their impressions of the new school.
    d A feature article on teenage fashions at schools like Merryweather High.

In addition to writing the assignment you are required to submit a rationale in which you specify your aims and show how you achieved them. With a partner discuss your answers to questions 1 and 2. Ask your partner if your answers are logical and appropriate. Use the information gained to help you to write your rationale.

Customs & traditions

21

→ Do you wear school uniform? Do you like it? Why? If your school does not have a uniform, would you prefer one?

→ What, in your opinion, is the relationship between uniform and individuality? Can someone wear a uniform and still be themselves?

→ Do you think wearing uniform is a cultural issue? Why?

→ Is it essential that certain social or professional groups wear uniform? Why?

Uniforms

1 USA: Why schools should maintain the use of school uniforms in Arkansas

The question of whether students should wear school uniforms has raged on for quite a while. Some people argue that it doesn't help to stop indiscipline in schools. However, many schools all

5 over the world are adopting school uniforms and for good reasons too.

School uniforms are a perfect way to identify students within the school compound. This increases the safety of students since any intruder

10 would stand out. Uniforms also reduce the occurrences of theft of clothing items. It is common to hear of a child being beaten and having their shoes or other clothing taken away from them. This kind of violence is checked by the use of school

15 uniforms.

School uniforms are a perfect way to promote equality amongst the students. In other schools, you will find the affluent coming to school in expensive clothes and clothing accessories. School uniforms

20 make all students dress the same and removes this bias. This then creates an opportunity for the students to form friendships that overlook their backgrounds.

It is cheaper for you to buy school uniform for

25 your child than it is to buy branded clothing. This is an advantage to parents who may not have access to money to buy new clothes for their children every new season or term.

School uniforms also provide an atmosphere where

30 the students are not distracted from their studies. In other schools, provocative dressing and the concern about fashion create a distraction during class.

Most opponents to the idea of school uniforms argue that it affects the individual expression of the

35 child. They claim that the choice of what to wear falls on the students and their parents and should not be decided by the schools administration. These people should look at the benefits of school uniforms and realise that they outweigh the issue of

40 individuality. There are other ways of self-expression other than expression through fashion. The advantages of school uniforms have prompted many schools to adopt them rather than a casual dress code. These schools do realize the positive influence

45 that school uniforms can be.

School uniforms bring a sense of identity to the students. Just as is the case in sports, school uniforms provide students with pride especially when they perform well. Public schools have already

50 started introducing school uniforms in America so as to improve the safety and discipline of the students. It is time for parents, too, to support the move by encouraging more schools to adopt the school uniform policy.

US Military School Information & Directory, 2011

2 South Africa: Unique vs. Uniform

A few years ago I wrote an article on simplifying school uniforms and got this response from a fan: "Mr Potterton, I read everything you write and I must say this is the biggest load of rubbish you have ever
5   written."

The school uniform topic is one of those debates that generate a lot of heat and no one seems able to approach the topic with a cool head.

The school uniform has its roots in English public
10 schools 200 years ago when it was an indicator of social standing both inside and outside school. They became mandatory by the mid-20th century in England and were generally abandoned in the 1960s and 1970s.

15 Now uniforms are back in fashion and are once again an indicator of social attitudes. Since the uniform's origins in England, the idea has been taken to bizarre extremes around the world; one posh school in Johannesburg has 80 different
20 coloured ties.

Most people argue that a uniform gives learners a sense of belonging. It makes everyone equal and prevents children from being made fun of because of what they wear. One of the strongest arguments
25 put forward is that wearing school uniform improves behaviour and instils a sense of pride in the school. School uniforms are also thought to improve student attendance. Another argument is that uniforms are practical and made to last and that in the long run it
30 works out cheaper than ordinary clothes.

A few sociologists believe that those who wear school uniforms perform better academically in school. They argue that learners are often so focused on their wardrobe that it distracts them
35 from their school work. However, there is no data to prove that uniforms are conducive to learning and can improve student performance.

My own argument is that ties, acrylic jerseys and Teflon-coated blazers are uncomfortable and not

40 very warm in winter. Uniforms are expensive and don't last. They also stifle individuality. We already know that learners who are forced to wear uniforms will find other ways to express themselves, possibly through the inappropriate use of make-up, piercings
45 or jewellery. Schools spend a lot of time and energy on getting learners to wear their uniforms properly. Untucked shirts, loosened ties, missing belts, unbuttoned blazers and other infringements keep teachers very busy enforcing a uniform dress code.
50 This can affect teaching and learning time.

So what are the real motives behind this uniform craze? The industry is essentially a money-making one. British research shows that the 145 year-old company, Trutex, supplies 1000 schools and sells
55 around 2.5 million garments each year. Do the maths. Here in South Africa the average uniform in a middle-income school costs around R9000. If you have 400 learners buying uniforms, you're looking at a total of R3.6 million being spent on looking alike.

60 I'm not calling for the complete abolition of uniforms. Heaven forbid -- I don't want staunch supporters coming after me. I'm calling for the simplification of uniforms, a project also espoused by the previous minister of education. We need to
65 do away with those expensive blazers, the tracksuits with the unique school designs and colours, as well as socks with stripes that cost 10 times more than plain grey socks.

If schools want a unique identity, they ought to
70 have iron-on badges that parents can affix to shirts and other items of clothing. We already have some reputable chain stores selling high-quality school clothing made right here in South Africa.

Also, if schools want their children to wear
75 uniforms they should establish a fund to provide assistance to poorer families.

Mark Potterton, *The Teacher,* **2011**

1   Find the six arguments in favour of school uniform in the first text.

2   Read the second text. How does Mark Potterton refute the arguments you identified in question 1? Write them down. List any points that Potterton makes which are not explored in the first text.

3   Copy the table below and write all the arguments in favour of school uniform and all the arguments against it as outlined in the texts.

Arguments for school uniform	Mark Potterton's counter-arguments

Writing activity

You are taking part in a school debate on the importance (or lack of) of school uniform. Write an introduction to the debate in which you state your point of view (either for or against school uniform). Write between 250 and 400 words.

CAS

In groups, design a uniform which reflects your school's vision and the IB mission statement as defined in the Learner Profile. The uniform should be comfortable to wear, trendy and appealing to all students. It should also be acceptable in the culture in which you live.

Remember

The opening speech, or the debate's introduction, allows each speaker to express his or her ideas without being interrupted. In addition, it gives the speaker the chance to connect with the audience. However, just like presentations, time is limited. Therefore, your introduction has to be interesting, precise and concise (Revisit the effective presentation guidelines on page 11).

TOK

Read the summaries of the arguments in favour of and against school uniforms.

Summary: Arguments in favour of school uniforms

- In some countries almost all schools impose a school uniform.
- Students need to dress appropriately depending on the culture in which they go to school.
- Schools do not want their students to turn up in clothes that are too short or wearing clothes with inappropriate language or insignia, such as gang colours.
- It may be easier to have a uniform than to list and enforce what students can and cannot wear.
- Some families cannot afford to spend much on fashionable clothes and teenage fashions.
- Peer pressure can lead families to spend money that they cannot afford on teenagers' clothes.
- The wearing of a school uniform prevents the formation of cliques who are defined by their clothes and appearance.
- The wearing of school uniforms helps to create a sense of group identity and a school spirit.
- If everyone's uniform is identical, intruders and outsiders can be more readily identified.
- Students on field trips and out of school are more easily identified.
- The wearing of school uniforms helps students to realize people's talents are not defined by the clothes they wear.
- It removes the feeling of envy and jealousy between peers.
- Students are less likely to be mocked for their appearance.
- It helps impose obedience to school rules, improves attendance and makes students take school seriously.
- A uniform helps students achieve better academically. Students focus more on their education rather than on their appearance.
- Consequently, uniforms decrease social clashes in the schools.

Summary: Arguments against school uniforms

- Uniforms interfere with students' freedom of self-expression.
- Students should be free to create their own sense of identity so that they feel unique and distinctive.
- Students who are forced to wear school uniforms may develop extreme tastes in clothes out of school.
- Uniforms are an unnecessary expense.
- Uniforms are an unfair use of power by schools.
- Teenagers form cliques whether they wear a uniform or not.
- Students can still express unpopular or inappropriate views in ways other than clothing.
- School uniforms can be ugly and/or unflattering and no good for students' self-image.
- The wearing of uniforms will prevent students from developing a good dress sense.
- The wearing of school uniforms may give students the false message that conformity is a way to prevent conflict.
- Uniforms are associated with the military and the police and schools should not be seen in the same light.
- The pressure on a uniform dress code in school counters the spirit of unity in diversity.
- School uniforms prove to be ineffectual and futile once the pupil is out of school.
- This uneasiness at having to wear uniform might reflect unfavourably upon the academic performance of the student.
- Students wearing school uniform can be easily identified and bullied out of school.

Discussion

The debate about uniforms has been raging for ages. Above is a summary of both sides of the argument with 16 points on each side. Group the arguments into categories in a table like the one below.

Categories of argument	Arguments for keeping school uniform	Arguments against school uniform	Are the arguments used based on: logic , sense perception, language or emotion?
Academic			
Behavioural			
Cultural			
Economic			
Personal			
Social			
Other			

- Which arguments are the most convincing? Why?
- Can you add any arguments to the list?
- Do you agree with your school's policy on uniform? Why? On which ways of knowing (logic , sense perception, language or emotion) would you base your arguments?

The individual oral (HL/SL)

In groups, choose one of the photographs below and in 15 minutes, prepare a presentation on the photograph. Taking the photograph's caption into consideration, link your presentation to **customs and traditions**. Be prepared to answer your classmates' questions on your presentation.

Exam tip

HL/SL Individual Oral
For the individual oral, you will only receive a photograph and a caption. You will not be told to which option the photograph is linked

Is school uniform relevant in the 21st century?

School uniform is just training for the army

Beyond the text...

➤ The school uniform debate has been raging in the UK and elsewhere for a good number of years. However, rarely do we notice people arguing the necessity of a medical practitioner's lab coat or a nurse's uniform. Why do you think this is the case?

➤ What is a dress code? Where are dress codes adhered to? Why? Search for information about dress codes in an anglophone culture. Are people obliged to wear specific items of clothing to work, weddings, funerals, and certain cultural festivities?

➤ Can school uniforms be replaced by dress codes? Is this applied anywhere in the English-speaking world? If so, where? Why?

➤ Do uniforms and dress codes reinforce some positive and/or negative stereotypes? How?

Reflection point

● In this chapter, you have looked at linguistic dominance, language and cultural identity, self-identity and uniforms. You have also explored how these topics and issues are perceived in a number of English-speaking countries. What has this section taught you about how related the topics you have explored are?

● What determines our cultural identity? What do we gain from learning a second or a third language?

● How do languages develop?

● How is language used to convey meaning?

● What do you have to do to write a review? Why do we need reviews?

● Re-read the notes on presentations on page 11. How will you make your presentation effective?

Communication & media

→ Marshall McLuhan said: "The modern Little Red Riding Hood, reared on singing commercials, has no objections to being eaten by the wolf." What do you think the statement means? Why do you think McLuhan made such a statement?

→ Look at the advertisement below. Which stereotypical ideas does it convey?

→ What stereotypes about women have you come across? Are these stereotypes, in your opinion, similar to or different from those in the anglophone world?

→ How do the media usually deal with stereotypical issues?

→ Think of radio or television programmes which dispel stereotypes in your culture. How do they do it?

→ How responsible should the media be when representing certain issues?

→ What type of advertisements do you usually find in newspapers and magazines?

→ Do your local advertisements differ from those which are found in an English-speaking culture?

→ How can advertising affect one's health?

You mean a **woman** can open it?

Advertising

Making sense of advertisements

Over a century ago, *Harper's Weekly* commented that advertisements were "a true mirror of life, a sort of fossil history from which the future chronicler,
5 if all other historical monuments were to be lost, might fully and graphically rewrite the history of our time." Few, if any, historians today would claim that they could compose a complete history
10 of an era from its advertisements, but in recent years, scholars have creatively probed advertisements for clues about the society and the business environment that produced them. The
15 presence of many excellent online collections of advertisements provides learners as well as established scholars with the opportunity to examine these sources in new ways. The experience
20 can be tantalizing and frustrating, since advertisements don't readily proclaim their intent or display the social and cultural context of their creation. Yet, studying advertisements can also be
25 fascinating and revealing.

[1]

Usually the ad is trying to sell a product, but this is only an initial response to the question. Does it aim to persuade readers to buy something for the first
30 time or to switch brands? The tobacco industry, for example, has consistently maintained that its ads are aimed at maintaining brand loyalty or inducing smokers to switch. Hence, a prominent
35 campaign a generation ago for a now-forgotten cigarette brand featured models with bruises and black eyes saying "I'd rather fight than switch." Yet, critics have noted the themes of youth,
40 vitality, and pleasure in these ads and have exposed documents in which marketers strategize about attracting new smokers.

What does the ad want the reader
45 ### to do?

Ultimately, of course, commercial advertising aims to win sales, but some advertisements seek primarily to gain the reader's attention or stimulate interest in
50 hopes that purchases will follow. On the other hand, repetitive ads for familiar products often aim to short-circuit the conscious consideration of purchase decisions. They try to stimulate the
55 consumer to pick up the soft drink or the toothpaste or the detergent as s/he moves down the shopping aisles.

[2]

In the first half of the twentieth century, most American advertising portrayed
60 and promoted a world of mass produced, standardized products. Advertising and mass consumption would erase social differences. "We are making a homogeneous people out of
65 a nation of immigrants," proclaimed agency executive Albert Lasker in the 1920s. In more recent decades, however, marketing's emphasis has been on segmentation – fitting a
70 product and its marketing strategy to the interests and needs of a distinct subgroup. The historian Robert Wiebe has even suggested that the divisions – by economic, social, cultural and
75 even psychological characteristics – now mark the United States as a "segmented society." Few advertisers try to sell the same thing to everybody today; too often that has meant selling
80 to nobody.

[3]

After we have a sense of what the advertiser is trying to **[a]**, we can ask how they go about achieving their marketing goals. Does the
85 advertisement offer a "reason why" to buy the product? Or is it **[b]** more to emotional appeals? Does the ad feature the product or does it focus on the people using it? Does it address the
90 reader directly with **[c]** or commands? Does the ad offer a reduced price or a premium? Does a celebrity provide an **[d]**? Does it play on fear or anxiety or make positive appeals?
95 Most of the ads you examine will contain both illustrations and text. Advertising researchers devote large sums to testing consumers' responses to different colors, shapes,
100 and layouts. Especially in recent decades, advertisements often have been composed with minute attention to detail and extensive pre-testing, so even the smallest facet of an ad
105 may reflect a marketing strategy. But deliberate or unintentional, details of an advertisement may reveal something about the assumptions and perceptions of those who created it. A
110 hairstyle, a print font, a border design all may have something to teach us.
How does the ad attract the reader's attention? What route do your eyes follow through the ad? How do styles
115 fit with **[e]** trends? Do earth tones in recent advertising support "green" marketing strategies of companies hoping to appeal to environmentally-**[f]** buyers?

[4]

120 Ads are highly selective in their depiction of the world. Notably, historical and contemporary studies abound showing that advertising's depiction of American society has
125 been highly skewed in its portrayal of race, class, and gender.
Until a generation ago, African Americans and other people of colour were virtually invisible in mainstream
130 advertising, except when they were portrayed as servants or as exemplifying racially stereotyped behaviour. Images of women in advertising have hardly been uniform, but several themes recur: the
135 housewife ecstatic over a new cleaning product; the anxious woman fearing the loss of youthful attractiveness; the subservient spouse dependent on her assertive husband; the object of
140 men's not-so-innocent gaze and desire. Advertising also gives false testimony about the actual class structure of American society. Advertising images consistently show scenes of prosperity,
145 material comfort, and even luxury well beyond the conditions of life of most Americans. The advertising industry prefers to picture the world that consumers aspire to, not the one they
150 actually inhabit.

[5]

As we see the ads, we may also be able to "see through" them to broader social and cultural realities. We can note three contexts for these documents. First of
155 all, they are selling tools and reflect the business needs of the corporations that pay for them. Posing the questions about purposes and methods will give us insights into the role of advertising in
160 business. Second, advertisements are cultural indicators, although distorted ones. Finally, bear in mind that ads emerge from a professional culture of the advertising industry and suggest the
165 aspirations and anxieties of the men and women who create them.

Daniel Pope, 2003
www.historymatters.gmu.edu

READING is a receptive skill, and interactive reading, although still defined as receptive, emphasises interaction between the reader and the text. This interaction allows the reader to grasp the intricacies of the written text and it results in comprehension. To develop your ability to comprehend written text, you need to apply certain reading techniques, like skimming the text to develop a general understanding of the main ideas it presents, and scanning the text to find answers to specific questions by searching for key words and phrases.

1 Skim the text. What is the focal idea in the text? How does the author support this idea?

2 Scan the text to find answers to the following questions.
   a What might 'graphically rewrite the history of our time' mean (lines 6–7)?
   b Which word between lines 1 and 23 is closest in meaning to 'explored'?
   c For studying purposes, what type of advertisements have scholars found accessible?
   d How is the attempt to analyse advertisements described in lines 1 to 23?
   e What types of models have been used in smoking advertisements in the past?
   f Give two advertising aims as mentioned in lines 26 to 43.
   g How is the United States described in lines 58 to 80?
   h How has advertising changed between the 1920s and more recent decades in the United States?
   i Before finalizing an advertisement, what do advertising researchers do as suggested in lines 97 to 111?
   j Which word between lines 120 and 150 is closest in meaning to 'biased'?
   k How were African Americans represented in advertisements in the past?
   l Which word between lines 151 and 166 is closest in meaning to 'imprecise'?

3 Match each of the following questions to a section in the text numbered **[1]**–**[5]**. Which reading technique is required to complete this matching exercise: skimming the text, scanning the text or a combination of both? Why?
   a What strategies are used to sell the product?
   b What has the ad done?
   c What else do you need to know to analyse an ad?
   d Does the ad promote standardized products?
   e Do ads contain text?
   f What do ads reveal and conceal about an era?
   g Who is the intended audience?
   h When did African Americans start appearing in ads?
   i Are ads cultural indicators?
   j What is the ad's purpose?

4 Sometimes, even if you do not know the meaning of a certain word, identifying its part of speech will help you place it in a sentence. Choose a word from the box below to go in each of the gaps **[a]**-**[f]** between lines 81 and 119 in the text.

accomplish	actor	suggestions	endorsement	route
assumptions	awareness	use	lines	literary
conscious	cultural	oriented	focused	

In addition to knowing which part of speech the word belongs to, what do you need to place a word correctly in a sentence?

Remember

Scanning the text revolves around identifying key words and phrases not only in the text but also in the question. Therefore, read the question carefully and, before you scan the text to find an answer, underline what the question is asking you to do. For example, if the question asks you to find a word, you need to look for one word in the text. Similarly, if the question asks you to find a phrase, copying the whole sentence does not show that you have understood the question or the text.

Grammar

In order to comprehend a text fully, you need to identify how different parts of speech are combined to form meaning. Parts of speech are categorized into groups of nouns, verbs, adjectives, adverbs, pronouns, prepositions, conjunctions and articles. Use the Internet to find the definitions, subcategories and examples of the different parts of speech.

Beyond the text...

➤ Discrimination takes different shapes and forms. Read the advertising regulations in an English-speaking society, which can be found online. How can these regulations curb social, ethnic or gender discrimination?

➤ Most anglophone countries prohibit advertising tobacco products. Why do you think this is the case? Do you think advertising cigarette brands plays a role in increasing the numbers of smokers? Look at the advertisement on the left. In your opinion, would such an advertisement be published in any magazine in the UK? Why?

➤ In 1994, and under its Regulation and Prevention of Misuse Act, the Indian government prohibited the publication of advertisements relating to the use of prenatal diagnostic techniques to determine the gender of a foetus. Such advertisements are not prohibited in other English-speaking countries like the United Kingdom. Why do you think it is crucial for India to prohibit the publication of such advertisements? Do you think this prohibition addresses gender discrimination in India?

➤ Examine a few advertisements online. How is advertising on the Internet different from 'mainstream' advertising? Why?

Interactive oral activity

In pairs, find an advertisement that appeared in one of the magazines that are published in the anglophone world and analyse it based on your understanding of advertising techniques in English-speaking countries. Present your findings to your classmates. You may use ICT (Information Communication Technologies) in your presentation.

Developing writing skills: Set of instructions or guidelines

As a productive skill, writing communicates a message to the reader. Therefore, before you start writing it is very important to determine the communicative purpose of your written piece: are you writing to inform, persuade, argue or describe?

The text *Making Sense of Advertisements* on page 27 provides a set of guidelines which could be given to media students to help them 'see through' advertisements. A set of guidelines, or instructions, is usually written to inform its audience about how to do, approach or fix something.

When you write a set of instructions or guidelines, it is recommended that you:

• capture the reader's attention with the use of headings
• directly address your audience
• use bullet points or write your guidelines in note form
• be precise and concise.

1 In groups, imagine that you are designing an advertisement for a new mobile phone that will appear in one of the following magazines:

- *Time*
- *Seventeen*
- *Women's Weekly*

  a Begin by determining your audience. Who, in your opinion, is the targeted audience of each of the magazines above? Why?

  b Read the following statement, and keeping your advertisement in mind, list a number of words, expressions and phrases you can use in your advertisement to appeal to the audience of the magazine you have chosen.

  "The very first law in advertising is to avoid the concrete promise and cultivate the delightfully vague."

  Bill Cosby

  c Design your advertisement.

  d Share your advertisement with the other groups. Which do you think is the most effective ad? Why?

  e As the editor of your school's magazine, write a set of guidelines to be given to advertisers on how to create good ads.

The personal response

Read the following stimulus text:

"Advertising is everywhere you look, whether it is in the newspaper you pick up daily or on that billboard you see while driving down the highway. Some people may say that they are not in fact influenced by the advertising that is thrown at them each day, and that they do not fall into it, but everyone does."

Based on the stimulus, give a personal response and justify it. Choose any text type. Write between 150 and 250 words.

Before you write, answer the following questions:

1 What is the communicative purpose of your response? Are you writing to inform, describe, persuade or analyse?

2 Which approach will you adopt to respond to the stimulus?

- The 'one-sided' approach, arguing that advertising either negatively affects people or does not affect them at all.
- The 'balanced but undetermined' approach, arguing that advertising affects people negatively but not all the time.
- Or the 'analytical' approach, analysing how advertisements affect people.

3 Which text type best communicates your purpose?

TOK

- Can a study of cultures be free of bias?
- **Political correctness** is defined as 'the avoidance of forms of expression or action that are perceived to exclude, marginalize, or insult groups of people who are socially disadvantaged or discriminated against' (*Oxford English Dictionary Online*). Do you endorse the use of politically correct terms in advertisements?
- Would it be possible to publish the advertisement below in a magazine in any English-speaking country today?
- What does the advertisement below tell us about the ways in which the standards of language, culture and gender have changed since the publication of the advertisement in 1945?
- Is it ethical to apply tight control over the advertising of some products?

Radio & television

"Wires and Lights in a Box"

This just might do nobody any good. At the end of
this discourse, a few people may accuse this reporter
of fouling his own comfortable nest, and
your organization may be accused of having given
5 hospitality to heretical and even dangerous thoughts.
But the elaborate structure of networks, advertising
agencies and sponsors will not be shaken or
altered. It is my desire, if not my duty, to try to talk
to you journeymen with some candor about what is
10 happening to radio and television.

I have no technical advice or counsel to offer those of you who labour in this vineyard
that produces words and pictures. You will forgive me for not telling you that instruments
with which you work are miraculous, that your responsibility is unprecedented or that your
aspirations are frequently frustrated. It is not necessary to remind you that the fact that your
15 voice is amplified to the degree where it reaches from one end of the country to the other
does not confer upon you greater wisdom or understanding than you possessed when your
voice reached only from one end of the bar to the other. All of these things you know.

Our history will be what we make it. And if there are any historians about fifty or a
hundred years from now, and there should be preserved the kinescopes for one week of
20 all three networks, they will there find recorded in black and white, or colour, evidence
of decadence, escapism and insulation from the realities of the world in which we live. I
invite your attention to the television schedules of all networks between the hours of 8 and
11 p.m., Eastern Time. Here you will find only fleeting and spasmodic reference to the fact
that this nation is in mortal danger. There are, it is true, occasional informative programs
25 presented in that intellectual ghetto on Sunday afternoons. But during the daily peak
viewing periods, television in the main insulates us from the realities of the world in which
we live. If this state of affairs continues, we may alter an advertising slogan to read: LOOK
NOW, PAY LATER.

I am entirely persuaded that the American public is more reasonable, restrained and more
30 mature than most of our industry's program planners believe. Their fear of controversy is
not warranted by the evidence. I have reason to know, as do many of you, that when the
evidence on a controversial subject is fairly and calmly presented, the public recognizes it
for what it is – an effort to illuminate rather than to agitate.

One of the basic troubles with radio and television news is that both instruments have
35 grown up as an incompatible combination of show business, advertising and news. Each
of the three is a rather bizarre and demanding profession. And when you get all three
under one roof, the dust never settles. The top management of the networks, with a few
notable exceptions, has been trained in advertising, research, sales or show business.
But by the nature of the corporate structure, they also make the final and crucial decisions
40 having to do with news and public affairs. Frequently they have neither the time nor the
competence to do this. It is not easy for the same small group of men to decide whether

to buy a new station for millions of dollars, build a new building, alter the rate card, buy a new Western, sell a soap opera, decide what defensive line to take in connection with the latest Congressional inquiry, how much money to spend on promoting a new
45 program, what additions or deletions should be made in the existing covey or clutch of vice-presidents, and at the same time – frequently on the same long day – to give mature, thoughtful consideration to the manifold problems that confront those who are charged with the responsibility for news and public affairs.

So far as radio – that most satisfying and rewarding instrument – is concerned, the
50 diagnosis of its difficulties is rather easy. And obviously I speak only of news and information. In order to progress, it need only go backward: to the time when singing commercials were not allowed on news reports, when there was no middle commercial in a 15 minute news report, when radio was rather proud, alert and fast. I recently asked a network official, "Why this great rash of 5 minute news reports (including three
55 commercials) on weekends?" He replied, "Because that seems to be the only thing we can sell."

I began by saying that our history will be what we make it. If we go on as we are, then history will take its revenge, and retribution will not limp in catching up with us.

We are to a large extent an imitative society. If one or two or three corporations would
60 undertake to devote just a small fraction of their advertising appropriation along the lines that I have suggested, the procedure would grow by contagion; the economic burden would be bearable, and there might ensue a most exciting adventure: exposure to ideas and the bringing of reality into the homes of the nation.

To those who say people wouldn't look; they wouldn't be interested; they're too complacent,
65 indifferent and insulated, I can only reply: There is, in one reporter's opinion, considerable evidence against that contention. But even if they are right, what have they got to lose? Because if they are right, and this instrument is good for nothing but to entertain, amuse and insulate, then the tube is flickering now and we will soon see that the whole struggle is lost.

This instrument can teach, it can illuminate; yes, and it can even inspire. But it can do so
70 only to the extent that humans are determined to use it to those ends. Otherwise it is merely wires and lights in a box. There is a great and perhaps decisive battle to be fought against ignorance, intolerance and indifference. This weapon of television could be useful.

Stonewall Jackson, who knew something about the use of weapons, is reported to have said, "When war
75 comes, you must draw the sword and throw away the scabbard." The trouble with television is that it is rusting in the scabbard during a battle for survival.

Edward R. Murrow

Radio & Television News Directors Association (RTNDA) Convention

October 15, 1958

1 Read the text and write down to whom or to what the following words or phrases refer.

a this (line 1)
b this reporter (line 2)
c it (line 18)
d they (line 20)
e here (line 23)
f their (line 30)
g three (line 36)
h they (line 39)
i we (line 59)
j that contention (line 66)

2 For each of the words given below, choose a word from the table on the right that could meaningfully replace it.

a heretical (line 5)
b unprecedented (line 13)
c peak (line 25)
d agitate (line 33)
e manifold (line 47)

disconcert	prime
extraordinary	regular
few	religious
mountain	unorthodox
pacify	various

3 Choose the correct answer from A, B, C, or D.

a The word 'discourse' (line 2) means:
  A action   C conversation
  B interview   D speech

b The word 'candor' (line 9) means:
  A levity   C evasiveness
  B frankness   D gravity

c The phrase 'LOOK NOW, PAY LATER' (lines 27–28) means that:
  A the American public will adopt a new advertising slogan.
  B networks will lose money because people will pay later.
  C the Americans will pay the price of being kept ignorant.
  D news reporters will be sued for keeping people ignorant.

d The phrase 'the dust never settles' (line 37) means that:
  A networks and TV stations will always have problems.
  B networks and TV stations will be put out of business.
  C networks and TV stations will be very busy.
  D networks and TV stations will not have many problems.

➤ Peruse the evening schedules of at least three TV networks in an English-speaking country. Do these schedules support Murrow's claim that 'television in the main insulates us from the realities of the world in which we live'?

➤ 'Sensationalism' and 'bias' are two terms that are sometimes used to describe the media. What do these terms mean? Find examples of TV shows, radio shows or newspaper articles which support your definition.

➤ How do mainstream newspapers and tabloids differ? Find examples of both in an anglophone country. Examine the language used in both. How sensational are the reports? How biased? What evidence do you have to support your argument?

➤ News media are affected by the political views of the journalists or the networks. Do you agree? Find examples drawn from an anglophone culture that support your answer.

Developing writing skills: Speech

1 Any written text revolves around a major idea, or a thesis statement. In the text on pages 31–32, what is Murrow's thesis statement?

2 Which of the ideas below does Murrow use to support his thesis statement? You can choose more than one.
  a The RTNDA has asked the wrong person to give a speech.
  b The purpose of the speech is not to give advice on how to be good reporters.

c   Radio and television programmes are not up to the required standards.
d   The American public is wrongly perceived.
e   Controversial issues should be avoided by the media.
f   The news should be separated from advertising and show business.
g   Radio is not as important as television.
h   History will tell people how television was managed at a certain time.
i   The solution to radio and television problems lies in imitation.
j   It only takes one network to change its policy for the others to follow.
k   There's a lot at stake if networks change their 'insulation' policy.
l   If used appropriately, television is a powerful, illuminating tool.

3   Think of specific examples (TV shows, radio programmes) which support Murrow's argument. Come up with at least three and be prepared to tell your classmates why you believe your examples support Murrow's ideas.

Rhetoric is 'the art of effective or persuasive speaking or writing, especially the exploitation of figures of speech and other compositional techniques' (*Oxford English Dictionary Online*). The Greek philosopher Aristotle (384 BC–322 BC) identified three modes of persuasion in rhetoric: ethos, pathos and logos.

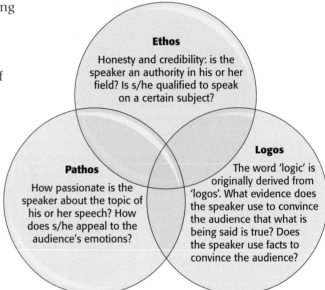

4   Reflect on Murrow's speech. Do you think Murrow makes use of Aristotle's modes of persuasion? Justify your answer by using specific examples drawn from Murrow's speech.

5   A good speaker uses a number of stylistic and rhetorical devices to strengthen his or her pathos. Re-read Murrow's speech and find examples of the devices defined in the table below. Murrow may not have used them all.

Alliteration	the occurrence of the same letter or sound at the beginning of adjacent or closely connected words: *the alliteration of 'sweet birds sang'*
Assonance	resemblance of sound between syllables of nearby words, arising particularly from the rhyming of two or more stressed vowels, but not consonants (e.g. *sonnet, porridge*), but also from the use of identical consonants with different vowels (e.g. *killed, cold, culled*)
Allusion	an expression designed to call something to mind without mentioning it explicitly; an indirect or passing reference
Hyperbole	exaggerated statements or claims not meant to be taken literally
Metaphor	a figure of speech in which a word or phrase is applied to an object or action to which it is not literally applicable: *'she's a rose'*
Onomatopoeia	the formation of a word from a sound associated with what is named (e.g. *cuckoo, sizzle*)
Personification	the attribution of a personal nature or human characteristics to something non-human, or the representation of an abstract quality in human form
Rhetorical question	[a question] asked in order to produce an effect or to make a statement rather than to elicit information
Simile	a figure of speech involving the comparison of one thing with another thing of a different kind, used to make a description more emphatic or vivid (e.g. *as brave as a lion*)
Synecdoche	a figure of speech in which a part is made to represent the whole or vice versa, as in *England lost by six wickets* (meaning 'the English cricket team')

(Definitions from Oxford English Dictionary Online)

6 How can a speaker strengthen his or her ethos and logos?

7 What determines the level of formality used in a speech? How does a speech usually begin and end? In groups, discuss the characteristics of a good speech. Write them down in point form. Remember to include comments on audience, level of formality, use of stylistic and rhetorical devices, greetings, etc.

The personal response

Based on the following stimulus, give a personal response and justify it. Write a speech using 150 to 250 words.

> *"This instrument can teach, it can illuminate; yes, and it can even inspire. But it can do so only to the extent that humans are determined to use it to those ends. Otherwise it is merely wires and lights in a box. There is a great and perhaps decisive battle to be fought against ignorance, intolerance and indifference. This weapon of television could be useful."*

Before you start writing, ask yourself the following questions:

- What is the topic that I am writing about?
- Which approach will I adopt? The one-sided? The balanced but undetermined? Or the analytical?
- To whom am I writing?
- How will I support my thesis statement?
- How will I organize my speech?
- Which stylistic and rhetorical devices will I use?

Interactive oral activity

In pairs, choose one of the following media-related topics and do some research on it. Present your findings to your classmates in a form of your choice: presentation, dialogue, sketch, interview, etc. Remember that you need to include specific examples related to your topic and drawn from an anglophone culture. You may use electronic material in your presentation. The topics are:

- Media ownership
- Bias
- Sensationalism
- Propaganda
- Documentaries
- Reality shows
- Talk shows
- Mainstream media
- Tabloids and broadsheets
- Political correctness

Remember

Interactive oral activity

1 The purpose of this exercise is not just to present the ideas you have found as you have found them. You need to use at least three sources, read them, choose the ideas you want to include in your oral activity and present your understanding of these ideas. In other words, you need to synthesize the information you find and reflect on it before you decide on the points to include in your oral.

2 Be precise and concise. The topics are too broad as they are. You need to narrow down your topic in order for you to be able to include all the points you would like to emphasize in 10 minutes.

3 Remember to include specific examples drawn from an English-speaking culture. If you decide to include examples from your own culture, these should be used only to compare how the issue is perceived in your culture as opposed to your chosen anglophone one.

Advertising effects

Should thin be "in"?

IMAGES OF female bodies are everywhere. Women – and their body parts – sell everything from food to cars. Popular film and
5 television actresses are becoming younger, taller, and thinner. Some have even been known to faint on the set from lack of food. Women's magazines are full of articles urging
10 that if they can just lose those last twenty pounds, they'll have it all – the perfect marriage, loving children, great relationships, and a rewarding career.

15 Why are standards of beauty being imposed on women, the majority of whom are naturally larger and more mature than any of the models? The roots, some
20 analysts say, are economic. By presenting an ideal difficult to achieve and maintain, the cosmetic and diet product industries are assured of growth and profits.
25 And it's no accident that youth is increasingly promoted, along with thinness, as an essential criterion of beauty.

The stakes are huge. On the one
30 hand, women who are insecure about their bodies are more likely to buy beauty products, new clothes, and diet aids. It is estimated that the diet industry
35 alone is worth anywhere from 40 to 100 billion dollars (US) a year selling temporary weight loss (90 to 95% of dieters regain the lost weight). On the other hand,
40 research indicates that exposure to images of thin, young, air-brushed female bodies is linked to depression, loss of self-esteem and the development of unhealthy
45 eating habits in women and girls.

Media activist Jean Kilbourne concludes that, "Women are sold to the diet industry by the
50 magazines we read and the television programs we watch, almost all of which make us feel anxious about our weight."

The Culture of Thinness

Researchers report that women's
55 magazines have ten and one-half times more ads and articles promoting weight loss than men's magazines do, and over three-quarters of the covers of women's
60 magazines include at least one message about how to change a woman's bodily appearance – by diet, exercise or cosmetic surgery.

Television and movies reinforce
65 the importance of a thin body as a measure of a woman's worth. Canadian researcher Gregory Fouts reports that over three-quarters of the female characters
70 in TV situation comedies are underweight, and only one in twenty is above average in size. Heavier actresses tend to receive negative comments from male
75 characters about their bodies ("How about wearing a sack?"), and 80 per cent of these negative comments are followed by canned audience laughter.

80 Advertising rules the marketplace and in advertising thin is 'in'. Twenty years ago, the average model weighed 8 per cent less than the average woman – but
85 today's models weigh 23 per cent less. Advertisers believe that thin models sell products. When the Australian magazine *New Woman* recently included a picture of a
90 heavy-set model on its cover, it received a truckload of letters from grateful readers praising the move. But its advertisers complained and the magazine returned to featuring
95 bone-thin models. *Advertising Age International* concluded that the incident "made clear the influence wielded by advertisers who remain convinced that only thin models
100 spur the sales of beauty products".

Self-Improvement or Self-Destruction?

The barrage of messages about thinness, dieting and beauty tells
105 'ordinary' women that they are always in need of adjustment – and that the female body is an object [a] perfected.

Jean Kilbourne [b] that the
110 overwhelming presence of media images of painfully thin women means that real women's bodies have become invisible in the mass media. The real tragedy, Kilbourne
115 [c], is that many women internalize these stereotypes, and judge themselves by the beauty industry's standards. Women learn to compare themselves to
120 other women, and [d] with them for male attention. This focus on beauty and desirability "effectively destroys any awareness and action that [e] to change that climate".

Media Awareness Network, 2010

1   Answer the following questions:

   a   According to the article, what is standing between women and the perfect life?

   b   How do cosmetic manufacturers make money?

   c   Which main measures of beauty are presented in ads?

   d   That are the effects on women of presenting a beauty ideal that is 'difficult to achieve and maintain'?

   e   What is meant by 'thin is 'in'' (line 82)?

   f   Why did *New Woman* receive many compliments?

   g   Why did *New Woman* revert to using underweight models?

   h   Why is the word 'ordinary' (line 105) put between inverted commas?

2   Find words from the text which are similar in meaning to the following:

   a   approximate   **e**   occurrence

   b   apprehensive   **f**   exercised

   c   emphasis   **g**   prompt

   d   recorded in advance

3   Which words go in the gaps **[a]–[e]** between lines 105 and 124 in the text? Choose from the box below.

argues	concludes	to compete	be	to be
compete	might help	argued	concluded	will help

4   Decide whether each of the sentences below is true or false according to the text and justify your choice with a relevant quotation from the text. The brief quotation is the word or the phrase that helped you determine the validity of the statement.

   a   Some actresses are endangering their health with their obsession with losing weight.

   b   Most women are larger in size than their representation in ads.

   c   The beauty ideal can be attained.

   d   It is easy to maintain weight loss.

   e   Females might suffer from eating disorders when exposed to images of thin models.

   f   Heavy-set actresses are usually ridiculed in TV shows.

Beyond the text...

➤ Consumerism is defined as the desire to purchase products in great quantities. How can advertising affect consumers? What are governments in the English-speaking world doing to protect their citizens from the adverse effects of advertising?

➤ Is advertising always negative? Can advertisements be used to increase public awareness of social and cultural issues like discrimination and health problems? Watch *Equals?* which features Daniel Craig and was commissioned to support gender equality (*www.weareequals.org*). What social problems does the short clip elucidate?

How many of these problems affect women in anglophone countries? Are women in Britain and the Philippines, Mauritius or Kenya, for example, equally affected by the same problems?

➤ Oxfam is a conglomerate of 15 like-minded charity organizations that aim to eradicate poverty and suffering. Visit the Oxfam website (*www.oxfam.org*). How is advertising used? Compare Oxfam's use of the media compared to a charity organization in your culture. How are they similar? How are they different? Why?

Developing writing skills

1   Answer the following questions based on the text on page 36:
    a   Is the title eye-catching? Why? Why not?
    b   Who is the intended audience? Provide examples from the
        text that support your answer.
    c   What is the main purpose of the text? Does it aim to inform,
        persuade, argue or explain? Provide examples from the text
        that justify your answer.

2   In three groups, re-write lines 1–45 of the text. Your target
    audience is:
    ● Group A: schoolgirls aged 8–12
    ● Group B: advertisers
    ● Group C: housewives

    Share your 'modified' section of the article with the other two
    groups. Be prepared to explain if and why your title and style
    have changed. In which magazine or newspaper would your
    'modified' article appear?

The personal response

Choose one of the following stimuli. Give a personal response and
justify it. Choose one of the text types that you have studied in this
section: set of instructions or guidelines, speech and article. Write
150 to 250 words. Remember that in the external examination, you
will only get one stimulus and you are free to choose any text type
you have practised writing in class.

*"Advertising is the art of convincing people to spend money they don't
have for something they don't need."*

Will Rogers

*"Good advertising does not just circulate information. It penetrates the
public mind with desires and belief."*

Leo Burnett

"In our factory, we make lipstick. In our advertising, we sell hope."
Peter Nivio Zarlenga

Interactive oral activity

In pairs, choose one of the following contexts and enact the scenario
reflecting your understanding of how advertising affects society.
Remember that your setting is an English-speaking one; therefore,
any examples used (shows, magazines, newspapers, advertisements)
need to be drawn from an English-speaking culture or country.

Context 1	Mother and daughter are watching TV. Daughter sees an advertisement promoting a new lipstick.
Context 2	Two friends go shopping. They see a huge billboard featuring a skinny model in a bikini promoting the latest hybrid car.
Context 3	A talk show host interviews an advertiser to discuss the latest advertising techniques.
Context 4	Two friends are browsing the Internet and are upset by the number of pop-up advertisements.

Remember

Before you start writing, ask
yourself the following questions:
● What is the topic I am writing
  about?
● Which approach will I adopt?
  The one-sided? The balanced
  but undetermined? Or the
  analytical?
● Which text type will I use?
● To whom am I writing?
● How will I support my thesis
  statement?
● How will I organize ideas?
● Which stylistic devices will I
  use?

CAS

As one of your CAS activities,
organize a full-day advertisement
awareness campaign in which
you collect advertisements from
your local community and show
younger students how to avoid
being swayed by them.

The SL written assignment

The written assignment is an integral part of your English B course. It is a 300–400 word piece of writing that is based on your synthesis of the information that appears in three thematically linked reading texts. You are required to read the texts carefully, determine what they have in common, reflect on how the topic affects an English-speaking society and decide on an approach with which to elucidate your understanding of the topic. The instructions below aim to clarify how the written assignment at **standard** level can be approached.

1   Re-read *Making Sense of Advertisements* (p. 28) and *Should Thin Be "In"* (p. 36).

2   What is the main idea in each text?
     Summarize the main idea in 30 words.

3   How do the authors support their ideas? List the examples, justifications and explanations they use. Use your own words.

4   Choose the idea that you would like to explore further in your written assignment. For example, how advertisements aim to sell irrespective of the effect on society. This is your aim or objective.

5   Choose the points that will support your argument.

6   Determine which text type you would like to use in your written assignment. Do not just choose a text type you would love to write. Think in terms of which text type would best deliver the message you have chosen. For example, an opinion column to be published in a newspaper is not the best type of text through which to explore the pros and cons of advertising. For this particular exercise, choose one of the text types explored in this section: a speech, a set of guidelines or a magazine article.

7   After you have chosen your type of text, determine who your audience is. Identifying your audience is very important, for it determines your style, tone and register. For example, if you are writing a speech about how advertising promotes products irrespective of the effect on society, you may want to address fellow advertisers or anti-advertising activists. You will then write to convince your audience by either ignoring the effect of advertising on society and highlighting advertising strategies (if you are addressing fellow advertisers), or emphasizing the negative effects of advertising and using emotive language to convince activists of your point of view.

8   Discuss your ideas with your teacher.

9   Write your rationale. Your aim and how you are going to achieve it must appear in your rationale. In other words, your rationale should consist of your answers to steps 4–7 above. Remember that the rationale should be clear and short; your ideas should be presented coherently and succinctly.

10   Write your assignment (300–400 words).

11   Revisit your rationale and include examples from your assignment that support your choice of topic and text type.

> **TIP**
>
> **SL written assignment**
> For the external written assignment, you will read three previously unseen texts chosen by your teacher.

Health

→ What is considered healthy in your culture?
→ What effect can daily practices, beliefs and societal norms have on people's mental health?
→ How is beauty defined in your culture?
→ How are eating disorders perceived in your culture?
→ Why do people develop eating disorders?
→ Are eating disorders linked to our perception of beauty? How?
→ "Becoming the new feminine ideal requires just the right combination of insecurity, exercise, bulimia and surgery" (G.B. Trudeau). Do you agree? Does the combination Trudeau mentions apply to men as well as women?

Mental health

Ladies and Gentlemen of the class of '97

WEAR SUNSCREEN

If I could offer you only one tip for the future, sunscreen would be it. The long-term benefits of sunscreen have been proved by scientists, whereas the rest of my advice has no basis more reliable
5 than my own [1] experience. I will dispense this advice now.

Enjoy the power and beauty of your youth. Oh, never mind. You will not understand the power and beauty of your youth until they've [2]. But
10 trust me, in 20 years, you'll look back at photos of yourself and [3] in a way you can't grasp now how much possibility lay before you and how fabulous you really looked. You were not as fat as you imagined.

15 Don't worry about the future. Or worry, but know that worrying is as [4] as trying to solve an algebra equation by chewing bubble gum. The real troubles in your life are apt to be things that never crossed your worried mind, the kind that [5] you
20 at 4 pm on some idle Tuesday.

Do one thing every day that scares you.

Sing.

Don't be [6] with other people's hearts. Don't put up with people who are reckless with yours.

25 Floss.

Don't waste your time on jealousy. Sometimes you're ahead, sometimes you're behind. The race is long and, in the end, it's only with yourself.

Remember compliments you receive. Forget the
30 insults. If you succeed in doing this, tell me how.

Keep your old love letters. Throw away your old bank statements.

Stretch.

Don't feel guilty if you don't know what you
35 want to do with your life. The most interesting people I know didn't know at 22 what they wanted to do with their lives. Some of the most interesting 40-year-olds I know still don't.

Get plenty of calcium. Be kind to your knees.
40 You'll miss them when they're gone.

Maybe you'll marry, maybe you won't. Maybe you'll have children, maybe you won't. Maybe you'll divorce at 40, maybe you'll dance the funky chicken on your 75th wedding anniversary.
45 Whatever you do, don't congratulate yourself too much, or [7] yourself either. Your choices are half chance. So are everybody else's.

Enjoy your body. Use it every way you can. Don't be afraid of it or of what other people think
50 of it. It's the greatest [8] you'll ever own.

Dance, even if you have nowhere to do it but your living room.

Read the directions, even if you don't follow them.

Do not read beauty magazines. They will only
55 make you feel [9].

Get to know your parents. You never know

when they'll be gone for good. Be nice to your siblings. They're your best link to your past and the people most likely to stick with you in the future.

60 Understand that friends come and go, but with a precious few you should hold on. Work hard to bridge the gaps in geography and lifestyle because the older you get, the more you need the people who knew you when you were young.

65 Live in New York City once, but leave before it makes you hard. Live in Northern California once, but leave before it makes you soft.

Travel.

Accept certain [10] truths: Prices will rise.
70 Politicians will philander. You, too, will get old. And when you do, you'll fantasize that when you were young, prices were reasonable, politicians

were noble, and children respected their elders.

Respect your elders.

75 Don't expect anyone else to support you. Maybe you have a trust fund. Maybe you'll have a wealthy spouse. But you never know when either one might run out.

Don't mess too much with your hair or by the
80 time you're 40 it will look 85.

Be careful whose advice you buy, but be patient with those who supply it. Advice is a form of nostalgia. Dispensing it is a way of fishing the past from the disposal, wiping it off, painting over the
85 ugly parts and recycling it for more than it's worth.

But trust me on the sunscreen.

Mary Schmich, 1997

Developing writing skills

It is really important to get a feel for the text in order to understand it. What glues the words and lines together? Why is a certain piece of writing effective while others are not? How is language used to form meaning? Is clear and succinct writing more effective than writing that is long and overly detailed? The secret lies in knowing what you want to write, to whom, and how to put your thoughts into words.

1 **Getting a feel for the text:**

a Choose from the options below the word which best fits in each of the gaps [1]–[10] in the text. Be prepared to defend your choice.

	Word 1	Word 2	Word 3	Answer
1	meandering	successful	bad	
2	greyed	faded	disappeared	
3	recall	remind	think	
4	possible	good	effective	
5	blindside	hit	slapped	
6	irresponsible	careless	reckless	
7	blame	berate	praise	
8	machine	instrument	tool	
9	bad	down	ugly	
10	challengeable	inalienable	controversial	

b List the pieces of advice that are given in the text in relation to:
  - Physical health
  - Mental health
  - Relationships
  - Lifestyle

c In pairs, discuss the pieces of advice you listed in part **b**. Do you think the author's message is clear? Why? Why not?

d Explain the analogy in 'Advice is a form of nostalgia. Dispensing it is a way of fishing the past from the disposal, wiping it off, painting over the ugly parts and recycling it for more than it's worth' (lines 82–85) in your own words.

> **Definition**
>
> **AN ANALOGY** is 'a comparison between one thing and another, typically for the purpose of explanation or clarification.'
> (*Oxford English Dictionary Online*)

41

2 **Putting thoughts into words:**

a Answer the following questions:
  i Which type of text is used?
  ii Who is the audience?
  iii What is the context (occasion, situation, etc.)?
  iv What strikes you as effective? Why?

b Work in pairs. Add another part to the text in which you:
  i introduce a topic which has not been broached in the original text.
  ii do not use any examples similar to those used in the text.
  iii use at least one analogy.
  iv emulate (copy) the author's style in terms of use of language and use of rhetorical devices. (Revisit p. 34.)

c Share your contribution with your classmates. Which of these additional parts do you think best fits in the text? Why?

Beyond the text...

➤ Mental health denotes emotional and cognitive well-being. What affects mental health? Who is considered mentally 'unhealthy'?

➤ Anxiety disorders, mood disorders and Schizophrenia disorders are examples of mental health problems or illnesses. Peruse sources which discuss such problems in an anglophone culture. How are they dealt with? Which institutions, be they public or private, help in solving mental health problems?

➤ Holden Caulfield, a character in *The Catcher in the Rye* by J.D. Salinger, is an adolescent who finds it difficult to 'come of age' and to accept how hypocritical people are. The novel was published in 1951. Find more about Holden Caulfield's problems in *The Catcher in the Rye* and compare them to the problems adolescents face in an anglophone culture today. Should society interfere to ensure that all adolescents are mentally healthy or are the problems they face part of growing up?

The individual oral (HL/SL)

For your individual oral, your teacher will choose a photograph for you which is based on one of the options you have studied in class. You will then have 15 minutes to prepare for your presentation, which is followed by discussion on the topic with your teacher.

The art of presentation, just like writing, revolves around being clear and succinct. Therefore, when you prepare for your presentation, you need to organize your ideas in a coherent manner. Your presentation also needs to be well mapped. The photograph on the right is linked to the idea of reading beauty magazines, which was mentioned in the text on page 36. Examine the photograph and answer the following questions:

- What do you see? Describe what you see in a sentence or two and link it to the Health option.
- Think of an English-speaking culture. What does the photograph tell us about this culture?
- Reflect on the photograph. What do you think? If this were your child or your little sister, for example, what would you do?
- Plan your presentation just like you plan your writing. Make sure that your ideas are well expressed and that you include examples or justifications for your opinion. Clearly mark your introduction and your conclusion using discourse markers ('in addition', 'however', 'therefore', etc.). Do not overuse those markers though.

Individual oral activity

1 The text on pages 40-41 highlights important concepts in people's lives, one of which is the concept of human beauty. How does the speaker describe human beauty?

2 Choose one of the concepts of human beauty which are mentioned in the text. Search for a photograph which exemplifies this concept and prepare a 3–4 minute presentation on the photograph. Present your chosen concept to your classmates.

Eating disorders

Manorexia: Men with eating disorders on the rise

When we think about eating disorders we rarely picture men starving or purging themselves to be thin, but a 2007 Harvard University study revealed that men account for 25 per cent of people suffering from anorexia or bulimia. That's more than double the previously reported statistic of 1 in 10, proving that manorexia, or men with eating disorders, is on the rise and much more common than most people think.

WHY THE HUGE INCREASE?

5 No one knows for sure why the numbers have increased so much, but several factors could be to blame. For one, men may finally 10 be feeling the pressure of physical perfection that women have been dealing with for decades. With every image of a waif-thin female in the media is an equally unattainable 15 image of a man sporting chiseled abs and a super-lean physique. Even if they don't want to admit it, some men feel pressure either from within or from society to achieve the 20 same lean, muscular look.

This leads to the second contributing factor, which is that more and more men are finally opening up about their struggle 25 with physical perfection. Women have been discussing their body-image issues for years, but men are often too embarrassed to admit they suffer from similar issues and 30 therefore rarely seek treatment or help of any kind. As more men come forward and are properly diagnosed, the statistics of men with eating disorders will inevitably rise.

35 Finally, another big reason the numbers are increasing is that men are now being properly diagnosed. A huge obstacle for doctors has been that the symptoms of eating disorders 40 among men are slightly different than for women, which are so well known by now that it can be fairly easy to diagnose women. Since the symptoms doctors measure eating 45 disorders by aren't tailored to men, many slip through the diagnostic crack. In addition, many men might not even realize they have an eating disorder because they don't fit the 50 stereotypical symptoms and so they think they are simply engaging in 'normal' male activities.

WHAT ARE THE CAUSES OF MANOREXIA AND OTHER 55 EATING DISORDERS IN MEN?

While it's true that men develop eating disorders for the same reasons women will — genetics, low self-esteem, trauma, and 60 cultural influences — many develop symptoms that are motivated by different emotional factors and are thus harder to diagnose.

THIN VS. MUSCULAR

65 It can be easier to diagnose females with eating disorders because their obsession with weight results in recognizable symptoms such as not eating, purging, and dramatic 70 weight loss. With men it's a different story. Men's obsession with weight usually manifests itself in 'normal male behavior' such as excessive exercise and steroid use. Instead 75 of striving to be super thin, men will often strive to appear lean and muscular by dramatically decreasing their percentage of body fat. Losing weight and trying to bulk up are 80 not bad goals, but they become

unhealthy behaviors once it turns into a desire for physical perfection. This preoccupation with perfection is a big indicator of body dysmorphic 85 disorder, one of the leading causes of eating disorders.

THE FAT KID AND THE ATHLETE

Certain risk factors for developing an eating disorder are specific to men. 90 Men who were teased as children for being overweight and athletes who must maintain a certain weight for enhanced performance are more at risk of developing eating disorders. 95 Dieting is often the primary trigger and symptoms usually develop later in life than they do for women.

GETTING HELP

Men face unique self-esteem 100 and emotional issues that require specific treatment for an eating disorder. Luckily, treatment tailored to men exists. By finding a treatment facility dedicated to 105 your specific needs, your chances of recovery will be very high.

Casa Palmera, **California 2009**

1 Find words or phrases in the text which are similar in meaning to:

a   vomiting
b   out of reach
c   clear cut
d   body
e   necessarily
f   impediment
g   customized
h   conventional

i   fixation (find 2 words)
j   making every effort
k   increase in size
l   sign
m   better
n   prompt
o   distinctive

2 Using your own words, answer the following questions.

a   What is manorexia?
b   In 50 words, summarize the reasons why manorexia is on the rise.
c   Why is it difficult to identify manorexics?
d   What does the text say about overweight children and athletes in relation to eating disorders?

TOK

- What does this section on health tell us about the relationship between perception, culture, reality and truth? Is it likely that different cultures have the same concepts of beauty?
- There is a proverb in English: 'Beauty is in the eye of the beholder'. What do you think the proverb means? Justify your answer by giving concrete examples.
- In your opinion, are men and women 'beautiful' in the same ways?
  - ▶ What makes a beautiful man?
  - ▶ What makes a beautiful woman?
- How do you perceive the people in the pictures below?

- 'The Ugly Duchess', painted by the Flemish artist Massys in 1513, is on display in the National Gallery in London. What does the painting reveal about human beauty?

Beyond the text...

➤ Anorexia and manorexia are only two examples of the eating disorders affecting people worldwide. Do some research about eating disorders in an anglophone country. What does the data reveal?

➤ Are eating disorders the only body image problem adolescents suffer from? What other body image and self-esteem problems affect Canadian or Australian teenagers? How are these problems similar to or different from the problems which Liberian, Ethiopian or Nigerian teenagers, for example, suffer from?

➤ Peruse other sources and find examples of how the media can help adolescents overcome developing a negative body image in an anglophone culture. Think in terms of advertisements, TV shows, radio shows, films, songs, etc.

➤ 'Obesity in America' is an organization which helps spread awareness about the dangers of obesity. Peruse their website (www.obesityinamerica.org) and choose one of their latest news topics. Study the topic to determine if the issue affects obese people in other anglophone countries. What do the statistics reveal?

Developing writing skills: Article

Articles are written for a variety of purposes. They usually aim to inform, persuade or entertain the reader. The aim of the article determines the style that writers use to achieve their aim. Articles, like essays, opinion columns, etc., follow a certain structure: an eye-catching title (headline), an introduction, a main body and a conclusion.

Re-read the text on page 43 and:

1   write down what the main purpose of the article is.

2   write down the headline the article uses. What is the article about? Is this clarified in the headline? How effective do you think the headline is?

3   mark the beginning and end of the following: introduction, main body and conclusion.

4   discuss why the writer uses subheadings in the body of the article. How is this related to the purpose of the article?

5   write down the general ideas which are used to support the writer's thesis statement.

6   identify the examples or explanations the writer uses to strengthen his or her argument.

Language and style

One very important feature in articles is that the writer's voice is always 'heard'. The writer applies his or her personal touch and style when writing an article. Look at the mindmap below and find examples in the text of each of the elements listed in the mindmap. You may not find examples of all of them.

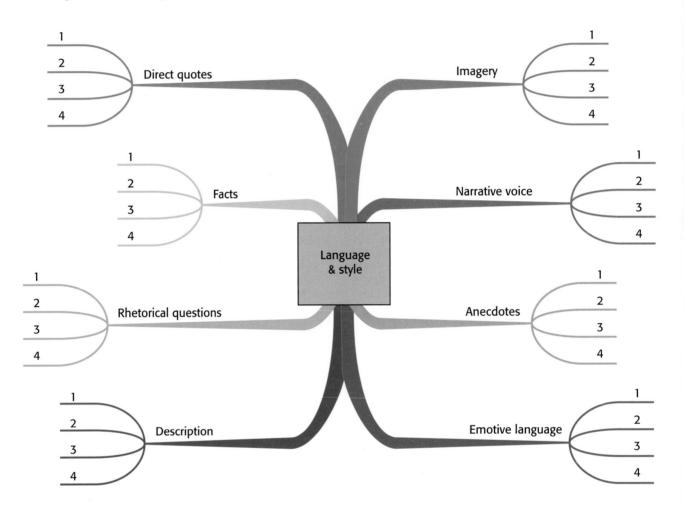

CAS

In cooperation with one of the health agencies in your town, organize a campaign which aims to inform adolescents at your school and in your local community about a health problem that has a negative effect on your community.

Cultural diversity

→ What youth subcultures are there in your culture? How do people in your culture react to these subcultures?
→ How do you perceive certain subcultures? How are those subcultures represented in the media?
→ How tolerant should people be of certain subcultures?
→ In your opinion, why would a person join a certain group or subculture?
→ Do the youth in your community use unique terms and expressions?

Subcultures

I have seen the future – and it's Goth

We mocked their make-up and giggled over their gloom. But the goths are taking over the country.

It's every parent's nightmare. Their apparently well-adjusted child suddenly comes home with hair the colour of a
5 coalface, a face whiter than anything, and [1], "Mummy, I'm a goth." However, according to a new study, parents of goths will probably end up boasting about their son or daughter the doctor, lawyer or bank manager.

That is the surprising finding of Sussex University's Dunja
10 Brill, whose doctorate in media and cultural studies looked at people with funny hair and eyeliner in London, Brighton and Cologne, and who is herself a former goth.

"Most youth subcultures [2] people to drop out of school and do illegal things," she says. "Most goths are well
15 educated, however. They hardly ever drop out and are often the best pupils. The subculture encourages interest in classical education, especially the arts. I'd say goths are more likely to make careers in web design, computer programming ... even journalism."

20 Perhaps she has a point. Long before finding gainful employment at the *Guardian*, I too was a goth. For at least six months in the 80s, I reached for the hair crimpers, [3] my bedroom black and scrawled the name of a gothy band, the Birthday Party, on the door so it looked like blood.
25 Hours were spent adopting the requisite air of mysterious gloom, reading the spines of Dostoevsky novels, and gazing forlornly at spots.

"Goths are like masons," I have been told. "They're everywhere." But rather than blaming some sinister
30 conspiracy, let us look at the reasons people become goths in the first place. According to Choque Hosein, formerly of goth band Salvation but now running a record label, "Goths tend to be the weirdo intellectual kids who have started

to view the world differently." Cathi Unsworth is now a
35 successful author, but she [4] that her own dark gothic past gave her an outlet for alienation. "I loved the bands, especially Siouxsie and the Banshees, but it wasn't a pose – I felt authentically depressed," she says. Unsworth was a teenager in Great Yarmouth, where she felt that "people [5]
40 me. It got to a point where I wanted to stop fighting against being different and embrace it."

Gillian Porter is now a successful PR but remembers a misspent youth of "electric-blue hair extensions, big boots with great big skulls, more crimped hair than Pete Burns.
45 Totally and utterly ridiculous." Porter wasn't depressed, although she [6] that "listening to a lot of Sisters of Mercy doesn't exactly cheer you up."

It could be tough, but being a goth [7] a world where art, current affairs and literature are embraced and openly
50 discussed, perhaps paving the way for future networking. Unsworth remembers debates about "current affairs, Oscar Wilde, decadence, hairspray ..."

Some took the whole thing very far. Hosein once lived in Headingley, Leeds; he remembers that students [8] at
55 Leeds University specifically because the town housed gothic kingpins (and his neighbours) the Sisters of Mercy. One night, Hosein saw a fog descending over the area and commented that lead singer Andrew Eldritch was around – then looked up to see him entering his doorway.

60 Brill insists that goth is a non-violent subculture. "They're like hippies. I [9] any goths who are into graveyard destruction or cat slaughtering. They like their graveyards and they love their cats."

So perhaps parents [10] too worried that a new generation
65 of goths is cropping up again.

David Simpson, 2006

1 The following statements are all false. Quote the phrases in the text which prove these statements false.

    a Parents always rue the day their children became Goths.

    b Dunja Brill is a Goth.

    c Goths, like some other subcultures, are school dropouts.

    d Goths usually become engineers.

    e Goths are feisty.

    f Becoming Goth does not allow adolescents to separate themselves from others.

    g Goths enjoy being brutal.

2 Which words go in the gaps **[1]–[10]** in the text? Choose from the table below.

announces	painted	didn't like	can open up	don't know
announced	paints	hadn't liked	could have opened up	wouldn't be
didn't know	conceded	should enrol	had remembered	should encourage
encourage	remembers	concedes	would enrol	shouldn't be

3 In less than 100 words, describe or paint a verbal portrait of a Goth. Your description should be vivid and in line with the evidence provided in the text.

Beyond the text...

➤ Are subcultures necessarily ethnic?

➤ Is a culture pure or do all cultures contain elements of other cultures? What examples drawn from the anglophone world can you use to support your point of view? Think of national dress, national dishes, cultural practices, festivals and lifestyles.

➤ Conduct some research on subcultures within anglophone culture/s. How similar are they? How different? Why?

➤ How is a citizen of a certain anglophone country similar to or different from a member of a certain subculture? Do subcultures transcend geographic and other cultural boundaries?

➤ In *Theorizing Nationalism*, Judith Lichtenberg states that 'within cultures we find subcultures whose members have a distinct sense of identity and belonging […]; the relationship between cultures and subcultures and between the loyalties of members to each may be subtle and complicated' (p. 169). Reflect on Lichtenberg's words. What do they show about the relationship between the anglophone culture and its subcultures?

Developing writing skills

Compare *Manorexia: Men with Eating Disorders on the Rise* (p. 43) and *I have seen the future – and it's Goth* (p. 47) in terms of structure and language and style. Use a table like the one below.

Structure	Manorexia	Goth Future
Purpose		
Introduction		
Main body		
Conclusion		
Language & Style	**Manorexia**	**Goth Future**
Anecdotes		
Descriptions		
Direct quotes		
Emotive language		
Facts		
Imagery		
Narrative voice		
Rhetorical questions		

Writing activity

1   Choose one of the following British youth subcultures or another one you know or have heard about:

   - Chavs
   - Greebos
   - Sk8ers
   - Punks

2   Find more information about the subculture you have chosen and summarise your findings in note form.

3   Write an article about the subculture you have chosen. The article will be published in a teen magazine. Write between 250 and 400 words.

4   Reflect on your article and the choices you have made. Pay attention to the structure, language and style of your writing.

TOK

A Goth Dictionary

- What do you learn about Goths from reading the following definitions?
- What do your reactions to the Goth dictionary tell you about your own attitudes to such subcultures?
- To what extent does the slang of a group such as the Goths affect our understanding of them and ourselves?

Babybat – A younger Goth (usually in their teens). Sometimes used derogatively to refer to younger Goths less familiar with the scene and more influenced by media portrayals of Goths.

Batcave – An infamous early Goth club in London, and more widely a term used for the sort of music played by the bands that used to perform there, such as Specimen, Alien Sex Fiend and Sex Gang Children.

Candygoth – A cheerful Goth who favours bright or 'candy' colours.

Corp Goth – A Goth who works in the business sector, but also the types of clothing they adopt (e.g. pinstripe suits, pencil skirts) which some Goths now wear at clubs.

Crowface – Make-up inspired by the comic book and movie franchise *The Crow*. Not usually considered a good look.

Cyberfalls – Synthetic dreadlocks worn by Cybergoths, usually made of brightly coloured yarn and varying types of plastic and attached to the hair around a ponytail or bunchies.

Darkwave – Genre of music that developed in the late 70s, best described as a combination of New Wave and Post Punk.

Deathrock – A genre of music that combines punk and Goth, originally from the west coast of America and using horror elements (and lyrics about zombies).

Doom Cookie – A derogative term used for a Goth (usually a man) who takes the angsty and depressive stereotype a little too far.

Eldergoth – An older Goth, especially one who remembers the early days of the scene, and especially one who moans about the state of the scene today.

Goth points – Fictitious reward points for doing something suitably gothic, again usually part of a friendly joke, e.g. "Reading Dracula by candlelight and listening to Bauhaus at the same time? Wow, how many Goth points is that?"

Gothwalk (or Goth Two Step) – A style of dance popular in clubs in the 90s.

Insta-goth – A Goth whose wardrobe came as off-the-shelf from a shop like *Hot Topic*.

Kindergoth – A younger Goth (sometimes used derogatively).

Normals – Derogative term for non-Goths (usually used by younger Goths).

CAS

Having gained permission from your school principal, organize a fashion show which aims to encourage your peers to accept others regardless of their ethnicity, gender, social status or looks. Proceeds from the show will go to one of your local anti-discrimination organizations.

"NOT MY ALMA MATER"...
A VITRIOLIC PROLOGUE

Montreal, May 1984

I got kicked out of high school today. I can't believe it. I have an A average and I've never gotten a detention or even so much as a demerit point and those morons go and kick
5 me out. Stupid morons.

It isn't that I was doing anything that I don't usually do. I was hanging out at my locker wearing my spray painted "Eat Dirt and Die" shirt that I made and the vice principal
10 walks by and tells me not to wear That Shirt anymore. Totally out of the blue. I've been wearing this shirt two, maybe three times a week for the past six months, and today he decides I can't wear it anymore.

15 Then later I'm in technical drawing and he comes back and takes me out of class. He makes me go to the principal's office and they tell me not to come to school anymore looking like this. I tell them to call my mom
20 and she shows up and totally supports them. I mean, I know she hates the way I look, but this has NONSENSE written all over it in mile-high letters and everyone's acting like it's totally my fault.

25 The v.p. tells me that I'm distracting the other students. Sure, when I got my mohawk, the lady who runs the cosmetology department asked me not to hang around there because I scare the old ladies who come
30 in to get their hair dyed blue (now, that's a joke) by the girly-girls. So I try, but it's kind of hard to do with my locker right down the hall and my technical drawing class right across from cosmetology. Still, I sit in the back of
35 the class all the time, so there's no reason

why they should say I'm distracting everybody. Besides which, my hair's been like this for six, seven months now. Get over it already.

40 Then the v.p. says that I'm just trying to be like this girl whose picture's in my locker. Really? The only reason Ms. Wendy O. Williams of the Plasmatics graces my locker door is because she looks like me, not the other way
45 around. I had a big, blonde fin way before I'd ever seen one on anybody else. And when's the last time they saw me standing on a tank wearing nothing but leather underwear? Please. "Besides," I tell them, "if anyone's
50 going to be like anyone else, you should want your other students to be like me. I'm the one who gets straight A's and has never got a detention." Right, imbeciles?

Okay. That didn't go over so well. The
55 principal says that the way I dress is indecent. Like, the first time I came to school in ripped fishnets, spike heels, thigh-high red mini, spiked belt, ripped-up T-shirt (no skin, though), lace gloves, full geisha make-up
60 and full-up fin, I brought a pair of jeans. I knew I was pushing it. Did they say anything then? No. But everyone else did. For some reason, the little dense boys in this school thought I was trying to be appealing, just like
65 these dim-wits are thinking now. Guess again. I'm just taking what they and their society think is attractive and I'm making it ugly. Because that's what it is. Get it? Guess not.

So I'm out of here. I got one year of
70 high school left and they've just kicked their smartest student out of their ugly, stupid building. They just don't get it. Well, damn them if they can't take a joke.

Atlanta, March 1998

Although these events occurred half a
75 lifetime ago, their effects linger in my life,
their repercussions defining my present and
shaping my future. Had I not been expelled
from Rosemere High School, I would probably
be a draftsperson, maybe even an architect
80 or civil engineer, today. This particular
episode remains a fresh and vivid memory.
I can still recall the precise shade of the
brown carpet in the principal's office, the
placement of the cheap office furniture.
85 Even more distinctly, I remember how I felt:
bewildered, frustrated, angry, powerless. It
was like a bad anxiety dream, the kind where
you talk or scream but no sound comes out.
Of course, in reality, I was talking out loud.
90 But no one heard me.

If you had asked me, then, who I was, what
I was doing, and what I had to say, I would have
told you that I was protesting 'The Injustice
of The System'. I would have told you that I
95 was not trying to anger people, but to scare
them, to wake them up. I would have told you,
maybe not in these words, that I was not
trying to be attractive or indecent, but that
I was mocking female sexuality through parody.
100 I would have told how becoming a punk was, for
me, the ultimate in self-empowerment — that
I had moved from a position of victimization,
as the smartest, dorkyest, most persecuted
girl in school, to one of agency, as a person in
105 control of my self-presentation. I would have
told you how I had gone from being a social
outcast to being a core member of a marginal
group, that it was no longer the case that
the world was against me, but rather that I
110 was against the world.

I would have told you how punk saved
my life. I recall, ever since the elementary
school, being told by boys - often, and to
my face - that I was ugly. A smart, myopic,
115 working-class girl, I was all the wrong things
in my school's social circles. Not only did I
wear large glasses, but my parents could not
afford to dress me in the latest designer
jeans or Lacoste shirts that denoted mid-
120 eighties preppie cool. Before I became a punk,
my 'ugliness' humiliated me. I walked hunched
over, staring at the floor, so ashamed of my
appearance that I did not dare look anyone
in the face. The tough, older kids in the back
125 of the school bus taunted me, threatened
me, and threw rotten lunch remains at me
as I got off the bus in the afternoon. This
was in part what precipitated my rejection
of social norms and my entry into the world
130 of punk. Of course, none of these objective
circumstances changed when I became a punk:
I stopped wearing my glasses and shaved
my head, but, in fact, my persecution only
increased. What did change was how I felt
135 about myself. After I became a punk, when I
was confronted with negative evaluations of
my supposed ugliness, I had the strength to
turn the tables on these assailants, to reply,
"Yeah, but at least I'm ugly on purpose."

140 My peers, the other punks in my high
school, understood this, and didn't have to
ask what I was doing, or what I had to say.
With ease and simplicity, they adopted me
as one of their own, just another rebel in
145 the ranks of the high school rejects. As a
matter of fact, no one ever asked me, not
even the administrators of my high school on
the day they expelled me for transgressing

their (gender?) norms. I distinctly recall
150 sitting in the principal's office that day,
listening to their declarations that my
hairstyle was disrupting class and that I was
a bad influence on the other students. As
much as I tried to defend my appearance
155 and my actions, they tried to force their
interpretation on me. It made no sense to me
then, and it doesn't to this day. To tell you
the truth, it still makes me mad.
    It seemed at the time that everyone had
160 a theory about who I was, what I was doing,
and what I was declaring, and people often
'shared' these with me in a most unpleasant

and confrontational manner. No one ever
asked me, or really listened to what I was
165 saying. I was dying (dyeing?) to tell people
what was on my mind. My adoption of the
punk style was an attempt at communicating
what I thought and felt about nuclear war,
religion, language, politics, racism, classism, or
170 any other topic, but no one wanted to hear
it. I was a fifteen-year-old girl challenging
the entire world on a number of fronts, but
no one cared to listen.

Adapted from Pretty in Punk
by Lauraine LeBlanc

1 Look at the first diary entry (Montreal, May 1984) and answer
the following questions
  a Why is LeBlanc surprised she was expelled from school?
  b The words 'vice principal' and 'principal' are written using
small instead of capital letters. What does this show about
LeBlanc's feelings towards her school's principal and vice
principal?
  c What does LeBlanc mean when she says 'this has
NONSENSE written all over it in mile-high letters' (lines
22–23)?
  d Explain the irony in 'to get their hair dyed blue' (line 30).
  e What is the most obvious similarity between LeBlanc, the
teenager, and Wendy O. Williams?
  f When LeBlanc says 'I brought a pair of jeans' (line 60), what
does this tell the reader about how she perceived what she
was wearing?

2 Look at the second diary entry (Atlanta, March 1998) and choose
the correct answer from A, B, C, or D.
  a 'repercussions' (line 76) is closest in meaning to:
    A consequences   **C** resolutions
    B allusions   **D** breakthroughs
  b LeBlanc's expulsion resulted in:
    A her becoming an artist
    B her not becoming an architect
    C her hating the educational system
    D her remembering everything about the incident
  c 'parody' (line 99) is similar in meaning to:
    A imitation   **C** irony

B mockery D caricature

d Becoming a punk was for LeBlanc:

A a way to prove herself C a way to control her life

B a way to stand out D a way to realize herself

e 'myopic' (line 114) is closest in meaning to:

A shortsighted C narrow-minded

B prejudiced D broad-minded

3 Answer the following questions:

a "I'm ugly on purpose" (line 139). How does this differ from being ugly according to LeBlanc?

b 'no one ever asked me' (line 146). What wasn't LeBlanc asked about?

c What is LeBlanc still upset about?

d 'dying (dyeing?) to tell people what was on my mind' (lines 165-166). What is the significance of the use of the words 'dying' and 'dyeing'?

Developing writing skills: Diary entry

1 Re-read the text and note down five examples from part 1 (Montreal, May 1984) and five from part 2 (Atlanta, March 1998) which prove that the text could have come from LeBlanc's diary. Think in terms of:

- the date/s
- the narrative voice
- anecdotes
- feelings and reflections.

2 How do the language and style LeBlanc uses in part 2 (Atlanta, March 1998) differ from those used in part 1 (Montreal, May 1984)? Give concrete examples. Why have LeBlanc's choice of words and style changed?

> **Remember**
>
> The beauty of a diary entry is that it is personal; it is about you. It is your personal journal, the place where you jot down your feelings, reflections and ideas about the world around you, specific events, etc. Therefore, the most important rule when writing a diary entry is voice... **your voice**.

3 Write a set of instructions to be given to your classmates on how to write a diary entry. Use the examples you have identified to clarify your instructions.

Writing activity

You have just witnessed a fellow student being bullied because he or she looked different and did not belong to any of the school's 'cool' cliques. Write a diary entry in which you reflect on the event. Write 250–400 words.

The individual oral (HL/SL)

Choose one of the photographs on the right and, in 15 minutes, prepare a presentation on the photograph. Taking the photograph's caption into consideration, link your presentation to one of the options you have studied in this chapter: Health or Cultural diversity. Be prepared to answer your classmates' questions on your presentation.

I am different, therefore I exist!

Too fat! Go damned inches, go I say!

The HL Written Assignment

The written assignment is an integral part of your English B course. It is a 500–600 word creative piece of writing which is based on one of the literary works you have read in class. This creative piece of writing could be a different ending to a novel, a parody or a pastiche of a poem, etc. You have to demonstrate your understanding of the literary work in your written assignment. You are required to reflect on the literary works you have read in class, determine which one you will use in your written assignment and decide on an approach with which to show your understanding of the literary work. The instructions below aim to clarify how the written assignment at higher level can be approached.

1   Re-read *"Not my alma mater"... A vitriolic prologue* (p. 51–53).

2   What is the main theme in the text? Summarize the main theme in 30 words. Use your own words.

3   Think of a different perspective from which to approach the text and explore the main theme. For example, we are only privy to LeBlanc's point of view in the text. What about the principal? The old ladies? LeBlanc's mother? Classmates? Write your ideas down.

4   Focus on one idea and think of how you can expand it. This will be your aim.

5   Determine which text type you would like to use in your written assignment. Do not merely choose a text type you would love to write. Think in terms of which text type would best deliver the message you have chosen. For example, a speech by LeBlanc's mother in which she publically denounces her daughter's behaviour may not be a good idea, for why would the mother want to do that? For this particular exercise, choose one of the text types you have studied in this chapter: speech, set of guidelines, magazine article or diary entry.

6   After you have chosen your type of text, determine who your audience is. Identifying your audience is very important since it determines your style, tone and register.

7   Discuss your ideas with your teacher.

8   Write your rationale. Your aim and how you are going to achieve it appear in your rationale. In other words, your rationale is your answers to steps 4–6 above. Remember that the rationale should be clear and short; your ideas should be presented coherently and succinctly.

9   Write your assignment (500–600 words).

10   Revisit your rationale and include examples from your assignment that support your choice of topic and text type.

TIP

HL Written Assignment
Your external written assignment must be based on one of the literary works you read in class.

Reflection point

- In chapter 2, you have looked at advertising, radio and television, health issues and subcultures in some anglophone cultures. What has this chapter taught you about how related the topics you have explored are?
- What role do advertising, radio and television play in shaping our understanding of certain issues? How can the media be used to lend support to certain causes?
- Are human beings affected by what the media project? Or do the media reflect humans' cultural and behavioural stances?
- How can a learner of a second language become a better reader?
- How is language used to get the message across? What do you have to do to deliver a speech and write a set of guidelines, a magazine article or a diary entry?

Global issues

→ What images come to your mind when the topic of climate change comes up in discussion?

→ Think of the impacts of climate change you have witnessed in your own country.

→ Whose responsibility is it to help alleviate the effects of climate change?

→ What do you think **geoengineering** involves?

→ Is it possible to solve climate change problems using solar technologies?

→ Do people in your own culture support manipulating nature to help with climate change effects?

→ How is it possible to conserve energy at home?

→ Are people in your own culture aware of the importance of energy conservation? If yes, what methods are used to do so?

→ Do you think the issue of energy reserves is adequately highlighted in the media?

USAID's Global Climate Program

Addressing the causes and effects of climate change has been a key focus of USAID's development assistance for over a decade. USAID has funded environmental programs that have reduced greenhouse gas emissions while promoting energy efficiency, forest protection, biodiversity conservation, and other development goals. This "multiple benefits" approach to climate change helps developing and transition countries achieve economic development without sacrificing environmental protection. To help countries address domestic and international climate change priorities, USAID's Global Climate Change Program is active in more than 40 countries.

USAID places particular emphasis on partnerships with the private sector and on working with local and national authorities, communities, and nongovernmental organizations to create alliances that build on the relative strengths of each. Bringing together a diverse range of stakeholders helps avoid unnecessary duplication and lays the foundation for a sustained, integrated approach. Through training, tools, and other means of capacity building, USAID helps developing and transition countries address climate-related concerns as a part of their development goals.

[1]

New technologies and practices offer the prospect for continued economic growth with reduced greenhouse gas emissions. Recognizing that increased productivity and efficiency are critical to economic growth, USAID supports the commercialization, dissemination, and widespread adoption of environmentally sound technologies. Attracting private investment is essential to popularizing such technologies. Recognizing that energy is one of the major expenditures for poor families living in urban townships, USAID promotes the use of low- cost solar water heating units in South Africa, which reduce household energy consumption and costs while providing hot water to households that could not otherwise afford it. USAID/India's Greenhouse Gas Pollution Prevention Project reduces emissions through efficient power generation and increased use of clean energy technology, including electric cars, clean coal, and energy generation with sugar cane waste (bagasse).

[2]

Promoting biodiversity conservation, improved forest management, and sustainable agriculture, USAID programs in more than 25 countries help mitigate climate change by absorbing and storing carbon dioxide from the atmosphere. They also help reduce the vulnerability of ecosystems to climate change. Reduced-impact logging of forests minimizes loss of vegetative cover, for instance, which helps stabilize the soil and prevent it from eroding away during rain and windstorms. Reduced tillage and contour planting by farmers increases soil organic carbon and therefore enhances soil fertility, which helps increase food security in developing countries. To better understand the carbon effects of such land management strategies, scientists, policymakers, and landowners in the international community need improved methods for monitoring carbon sequestration in soil-plant ecosystems.

Thus, USAID is not only promoting activities that preserve carbon stocks but is also helping to develop methodologies for measuring changes in carbon stocks in USAID's land use and forestry projects in areas such as the Congo Basin.

[3]

USAID supports activities to help developing countries lessen their vulnerability and adapt to climate variability and change. These activities are intended to build more resilience into economic sectors that may be affected by climatic stresses, including agriculture, water, and key livelihood sectors in coastal areas. In Indonesia, USAID's Coastal Resources Management Project (CRMP) helps coastal communities to sustainably manage fisheries, reefs, and other coastal resources. Participating villages and communities develop long-term plans to protect resources, such as ensuring that their coastline is protected from floods and storm damage by healthy stands of mangroves.

[4]

USAID is involved in U.S. and international climate change research to [a] that science addresses information needed for global development challenges and that scientific [b] are used to guide development planning. Informed policy decisions are essential to sustainable natural resource management and economic development, [c] priorities of USAID. For example, USAID supports long-term research [d] between U.S. universities, developing country research institutions, U.S. agribusiness, and private voluntary organizations through Collaborative Research Support Programs (CRSPs). CRSPs research issues of agricultural productivity and sustainability, food quality, and natural resource management that benefit [e] developing countries and the U.S.

For further information, contact us at

U.S. Agency for International Development

Bureau for Economic Growth, Agriculture and Trade

Office of Environment and Science Policy

Global Climate Change Team

1300 Pennsylvania Avenue, NW

Washington, DC 20523

Email: esp@usaid.gov

Tel: (202) 712-1672

www.usaid.gov/our_work/

environment/climate/index.html

Last Updated, October 2006

Cover Photo Credits Captions (top to bottom):

Photovoltaic system provides electricity for a community school in Alagoas, Brazil (Alexandre Mancuso, USAID/Brazil)

Local Communities in Guinea learn to manage valuable forest resources through reforestation and sustainable agro-forestry practices. (Laura Lartigue, USAID/Guinea)

Heat rate efficiency in power plants improved under the Greenhouse Gas Pollution Prevention (GEF) Project in India. (John Smith-Sreen, USAID/India)

USAID
FROM THE AMERICAN PEOPLE

GLOBAL CLIMATE CHANGE PROGRAM

1   Answer the following questions.

   a   Who is the target audience of this brochure?

   b   What is the aim of the brochure?

   c   Mention the three development goals USAID has to reduce greenhouse gas emissions.

   d   Why has USAID been interested in partnerships between private and local sectors?

   e   Find the phrase used between lines 28 and 37 to describe the type of technology adopted by USAID.

   f   What are the benefits of the low-cost solar water heating units used in South Africa?

2   Read the brochure again and choose a heading from the list below for each of the paragraphs marked **[1]–[4]**.

   A   Climate science for decision-making

   B   Collaborations with private and public sectors

   C   Monitoring carbon dioxide techniques

   D   Sustainable land use and forestry

   E   Installation of the low-cost solar water system

   F   Adaptation to climate change

   G   Fund-raising activities

   H   Clean energy technology

   I   Worrying obstacles

   J   Reservation of coastal areas

3   Complete the following sentences using information given between lines 49 and 65.

   a   The absorption and storing of carbon dioxide from the atmosphere leads to ....

   b   When vegetative cover is minimized, the soil .... and ....

   c   The increased food security results from ....

4   For each of the following words from the text, choose a word from the table which is closest in meaning.

   a   conservation (line 7)

   b   prospect (line 28)

   c   dissemination (line 33)

   d   mitigate (line 52)

   e   resilience (line 79)

distribution	maintain	increase
alleviate	preservation	flexibility
hope	resistance	rigidity

Grammar

A **phrase** is a group of words that does not form a meaningful sentence. For example, 'walking in the street' is a phrase, while 'The police officer is walking in the street' is a complete **sentence**.

In the exam:
- Read the question carefully.
- Decide if a **phrase**, a **sentence** or a **word** is required.

Remember

To identify the meaning of a word in the text, you need to consider the context in which it is used. Avoid basing your answer on any prior knowledge. One word has several meanings in different contexts.

5   Some of the words have been removed between lines 91 and
    107. From the table below, choose the word which best fits each
    gap labelled **[a]–[e]**. Do not use the same word more than once.

both	findings	communication	partnerships
ensure	either	researches	missions
minor	promote	key	

6   In each of the following phrases, to whom or to what does the
    underlined word refer?

In the phrase...	The word refers to...
...the relative strengths of <u>each</u> (lines 20–21)	
...as a part of <u>their</u> development goals (line 27)	
<u>They</u> also help reduce... (line 54)	
...ensuring that <u>their</u> coastline (line 88)	

Beyond the text...

➤ Are all anglophone countries aware of the increasing threats caused by climate change? Resort to statistics and find out, if possible, which country is most endangered by this global issue and why.

➤ Several climate change organizations are based in Australia. Peruse the official website of at least two of those and consider the methods they follow to raise awareness and alleviate the adverse effects of such global issues. Can you find any differences between those and the methods used by USAID?

➤ It is argued that people can do nothing about climate change. Find viewpoints used to support this argument in different anglophone countries.

➤ Examine how climate change affects the ecosystem in the US. Find articles on the Internet to provide supporting details.

Interactive oral activity

In groups, choose one of the following global issues, do some research on it and then present your findings to your classmates. Remember that you need to include specific examples drawn from an anglophone culture which are relevant to your topic. The topics are:

a Climate change

b Global warming

c Renewable energy

Remember

To conduct a good group presentation:
- Prepare as a TEAM.
- Decide on who says what.
- Make sure your voice is heard by the audience.
- Maintain eye contact with your audience.
- Don't panic if you forget something.
- Leave your audience with something to discuss or think about.

Developing writing skills: Brochure

1 In groups, examine the USAID brochure on page 57 carefully and write down the features that distinguish a brochure from any other writing style.

2 Describe the **tone** and **register** used in the brochure.

3 Share your observations with the rest of the class.

4 At home, search for another type of brochure to share with your group in the following lesson. Identify similarities and differences. Comment on rhetorical and stylistic devices of each. Remember to look for brochures about global issues in English-speaking countries.

Definition

- **Tone** is the writer's attitude towards the subject or audience.
- **Register** is a '…variety of a language or a level of usage, as determined by degree of formality and choice of vocabulary, pronunciation, and syntax, according to the communicative purpose, social context, and standing of the user' (*Oxford English Dictionary*)

CAS

Organize a full-day awareness campaign in which you prepare statistics and factual details about the effect of climate change on your local community. Suggest to students ways to deal with such hazardous impacts.

Global warming & science

Public support geoengineering research, survey finds

THE BRITISH, American and Canadian public is largely in favour of research into engineering the planet's climate to combat global warming, according to a study published on Monday. But critics said the paper was "not exactly disinterested science" because one of the authors is the founder and president of a geoengineering company.

The first international survey on the perception of geoengineering, published in the Environmental Research Letters of the Institute, comes at a critical stage as a major UK test project was recently postponed.

Scientists from Cambridge, Oxford, Reading and Bristol universities had planned to send a balloon with a hose attached 1km into the sky above Norfolk within months, to test the future feasibility of pumping hundreds of tonnes of minute chemical particles a day into the thin stratospheric air to reflect sunlight and cool the planet. But late in September, they delayed the test, citing the need to "allow time for more engagement with stakeholders".

The new 18-question, internet-based survey, was "designed to ascertain how widespread public knowledge of geoengineering was and how the public actually perceived it".

Some 72% of the 3,105 participants in the UK, US and Canada said they "somewhat" or "strongly" supported general research when asked: "Do you think scientists should study solar radiation management?"

But there was also significant support for views such as: "The Earth's temperature is too complicated to fix with one technology", "Humans should not be manipulating nature in this way", or "Research into solar radiation management will lead to a technology that will be used no matter what the public thinks."

Prof David Keith of Harvard University, one of the authors, said: "Some reports have suggested that opposition to geoengineering is associated with environmentalists, but our results do not support this view. We found that geoengineering divides people along unusual lines. Support for geoengineering is spread across the political spectrum and is linked to support for science concern about climate change. The strongest opposition comes from people who self-identify as politically conservative, who are distrustful of government and other elite institutions, and who doubt the very idea that there is a climate problem."

But Jim Thomas from the Ottawa-based technology watch ETC Group, that campaigns against geoengineering, said: "This commissioned survey by a commercial company is not exactly disinterested science – it's more like a marketing exercise by a high profile geoengineering advocate and his students."

Thomas said that Keith was "consistently on the record as a supporter of real world geoengineering experiments". He added: "Keith has designed 'self levitating' nanoparticles to be released in the upper atmosphere and managed a multi-million dollar private fund from Bill Gates from which he distributed monies to technicians developing geoengineering hardware to be used by private companies in experiments."

Keith is also the founder and president of Carbon Engineering, a geoengineering company with 10 employees funded with around $6m by Gates and tar sands oil magnate Murray Edwards.

Keith told the Guardian: "To be clear, starting two years ago I did organise a commercial activity in CO_2 removal [another form of geoengineering], but I believe that commercial activity in solar geoengineering [1]

He said that ETC Group was "attacking the messenger, not the message".

"We are happy to make all the survey materials publicly available. If the survey is wrong then [2] to produce a survey that contradicts these results. Our survey was reviewed by Nick Pidgeon, a leading expert on studying public reception," he said.

Ashley Mercer, co-author of the study at the Institute for Sustainable Energy, Environment and Economy at the University of Calgary, said: "I can assure you the funding sources [3] The goal was to simply assess current understanding and provide baseline data on emerging attitudes."

Earlier this October, the Washington-based thinktank Bipartisan Policy Center published a major report calling for the United States and other countries to move forward on "climate remediation". Prof John Shepherd, chair of the Royal Society's Working Group on Geoengineering, wrote in the *Guardian* in September that research would be "sadly necessary" because current greenhouse gas emission cuts and political will [4]

Hanna Gersmann,
The Guardian, **2011**

1   Answer the following questions.

    a **i**   Who conducted the UK test project referred to in line 17?
        ii What was the aim of the test project?
       iii Why was it postponed afterwards?

    b How was the new survey conducted?

    c How many questions did it include?

    d What was its main purpose?

    e Which question in the new survey was answered with a majority of approvals?

    f According to Prof David Keith,
       i   who disapproves of geoengineering?
      ii who endorses geoengineering?

    g To whom does the word 'advocate' (line 83) refer?

    h Why does Jim Thomas consider Keith's experiment 'commercial'?

    i In 'attacking the messenger, not the message' (lines 113 & 114), what or whom does Thomas refer to by
       i   'messenger'?
      ii 'message'?

    j Which detail does Keith give to lend reliability to his survey results?

    k Based on your understanding of the whole text, to whom does each of the following words refer:
       i   'critics' (line 6)
      ii 'one of the authors' (line 57)

    l In no more than 70 words, summarize both Jim Thomas' and David Keith's view points with regard to geoengineering as presented in the *Guardian* article. Use your own words.

2   Some of the sentences or phrases have been removed between lines 110 and 144. From the list below, choose the sentence or phrase which best suits each gap labelled **[1]–[4]**.

    A did not bias this research or its design

    B were not standard benchmark measurements

    C should be restricted or, where feasible, prohibited

    D could solve climate change problems

    E partially approve of the new research

    F ETC should work with a survey firm or academic

    G were not sufficient to stop global warming

    H promote new strategies to reduce climate change effects

Beyond the text...

➤ Conduct a quick search to find out about David Keith's latest contributions to the field of geoengineering.

➤ Do you agree that science should be cautiously trusted in saving the world? Support your argument with examples and facts drawn from online sources.

➤ What are some of the problems facing the future of geoengineering as an emergency solution for climate change? Look at several surveys and articles published in anglophone countries.

Developing writing skills

Write a news report that offers some solutions to global warming based on the facts in the table below.

You need to:

1 incorporate the conventions of an effective news report.

2 write between 250 and 400 words.

3 expand the information given, using relevant details from the previous two texts in this chapter.

The evidence that humans are causing global warming is strong, but the question of what to do about it remains controversial.
Even if humans stopped emitting greenhouse gases (GHGs) today, the Earth would still warm by another degree Fahrenheit or so.
Scientists predict that the Earth could eventually warm by as little as 2.5 degrees or as much as 10 degrees Fahrenheit.
Researchers at Princeton University have suggested 'stabilization wedges' which means reducing GHG emissions from a variety of sources with technologies available in the next few decades. Seven wedges could each reduce emissions, and all of them together could hold emissions at approximately current levels for the next 50 years, putting us on a potential path to stabilize around 500 ppm (parts per million).
There is also the potential to capture the carbon dioxide emitted from fossil fuels and store it underground – a process called 'carbon sequestration'.
The amount of gases we take out of the atmosphere can be increased. Plants and trees absorb CO_2 as they grow, 'sequestering' carbon naturally.
Increasing forest lands and making changes to the way we farm could increase the amount of carbon we are storing.

(*Adapted from:* http://environment.nationalgeographic.com/)

The personal response

Based on the following stimulus, give a personal response and justify it, using between 150 and 250 words. Choose any text type you have studied.

"There is still time to avoid the worst impacts of climate change if we take strong action now."

Sir Nicholas Stern

CAS

You are asked to organize a two-hour session led by an eminent scientist in your local community about using geoengineering to solve climate change. How would you go about organizing such an event? Consider where the event will take place and who will attend.

Remember

When you write a news report, remember that:

- it is highly formal
- personal opinions or feelings are not directly expressed
- the passive voice, reported or direct speech are usually used
- the report's aim/s and recommendations are stated clearly.

Exam tip

HL P2 Section A/ SL P2

In the external examination, HL P2 Section A / SL P2 is based on options. This is only a class activity to develop news report writing skill.

Remember

Ask yourself:

- What is the topic about which I am writing?
- Which approach will I adopt? The one-sided? The balanced but undetermined? The analytical?
- Which text type will I use?
- To whom am I writing?
- How will I support my thesis statement?
- How will I organize ideas?
- Which stylistic devices will I use?

Energy conservation

CLECO

Save money!
Save energy!
Tips inside!

ENERGY CONSERVATION GUIDE

*You have the **power** to save.*

78° SET IT FOR SUMMER

Warm Weather

- For maximum efficiency, set your thermostat at 78° or higher if comfort allows.
- Raise your thermostat 4° or more when you leave your home for several hours or more. And simply return it to its normal setting when you return. Drastically lowering the thermostat will not cool your home faster; it will only make your system work harder and run longer.
- Use fans to move the air. This will make you feel cooler and allow you to raise the setting on your thermostat.
- Don't run heat-producing appliances during the hottest part of the day.
- If you have drapes or shades, close them during the day to keep out the heat and open them at night to let the heat escape through the glass. Solar shades or screens are a cost-effective method to reduce the heat from sunlight coming in through your windows.
- Plant trees or shrubs to shade air conditioning units but don't block the airflow. A unit operating in the shade uses as much as 10 percent less electricity than the same one operating in the sun.
- If possible, locate window AC units on the north or shady side of your home. Direct sunlight falling on the unit will make it work harder.

68° SET IT FOR WINTER

Cold Weather

- For maximum efficiency set your thermostat at 68° or lower if comfort allows.
- Selectively open and close drapes and blinds during the day to maximize heat gain from the sun. Close them at night to keep the warm air inside.

Appliance use

In the chart on the right, you'll find average monthly kWh use amounts for a variety of appliances and equipment. Your actual use will depend on your individual usage habits and age and type of equipment.

A typical hair dryer uses approximately 7 kilowatts of electricity each month to operate.

Appliances	kWh used per month
Central air unit (2.5 tons)	848*
Water heater (electric)	290
Interior lighting	219
Electric range	104
Clothes dryer	87
Freezer (auto defrost)	82.5
Refrigerator-freezer (auto defrost)	67
Standard TV	15
Standard large screen TV	26
High-definition large screen TV	38
Stereo equipment	25
Computer	8.3
Clothes washer	8
Microwave oven	7.1
Hair dryer	7
Coffee maker	7
DVD/VCR	5
Vacuum cleaner	4

* Average usage May–October. The kWh figures are estimates based on a family of three living in a 1,500 sq. ft. home.

Adding or replacing appliances

Be sure to look for the Energy Star label when purchasing new appliances. Energy Star labels appear on appliances and home electronics that meet strict energy efficiency criteria established by the U.S. Department of Energy and U.S. Environmental Protection Agency.

If you are considering a used appliance, know that older models are less efficient and can end up costing you more due to higher energy use.

Air conditioners

Air conditioners come with a SEER rating. SEER stands for Seasonal Energy Efficiency Ratio and the number describes how well air conditioning equipment works. A higher SEER means better efficiency and lower energy bills. Proper matching of your inside and outside equipment is essential to achieving the desired SEER rating. A professional can help you choose the right air conditioning system for your home.

Reading your meter

You can keep track of your monthly electricity usage by reading your meter. Digitals are easy to read. If you have a meter with dials, read the numbers left to right and write the numbers down the same way. When the pointer is between two numbers always record the smaller number. Subtract last month's reading from this month's to get the number of kilowatt hours used.

Reading: 6,372

NOTE: Your reading will be different from the reading actually used to calculate your bill. Your meter may be read on different days each month, or your bill may include more or fewer days in the billing period.

1 From statements A to I below, select the ones that are true according to the first part of the *Energy Conservation Guide* given above.

A It is recommended to raise the thermostat all day long to maximize reservation.

B Solar screens are costly methods of energy conservation.

C AC appliances consume more electricity when working in the sun.

D Energy Star Label appliances are designed to conserve the maximum energy possible.

E Seasonal Energy Efficiency Ratio (SEER) ratings are structured to suit all domestic designs.

F A meter reading and the reading used to calculate the electricity bill are incompatible.

G Professional help is required upon estimating the average use of certain electrical appliances.

H Freezers and refrigerators function less effectively in non-air conditioned corners.

I Household electric devices consume less electricity when turned off.

Saving energy every day

Programmable thermostats

Programmable thermostats can reduce energy use by automatically raising or lowering the temperature in your home when it's vacant. They are inexpensive and easy to install. For each degree you raise or lower your thermostat from the recommended setting for each season, you can save up to 3 percent on your heating or cooling expense.

Insulation

Proper insulation helps keep your house cool in summer and warm in winter. Experts recommend R-30 (about 9.5 inches) of insulation for our part of the country. Increasing your attic insulation can reduce energy used to heat and cool your home by up to 10 percent.

Experts Recommend
INSULATION
R-30
9.5 inches

Water heating

Set your water heater's thermostat at the lowest temperature that meets your needs. Experts recommend 120°. Wrapping your electric water heater in an insulating blanket will also save energy used to keep the water warm in the tank.

Experts Recommend
WATER HEATER
120°
Setting

Lighting

Compact fluorescent bulbs (CFBs) use 75 percent less energy than standard incandescent bulbs and can last up to 10 times longer. Use CFBs in your most frequently used lights to reduce your lighting costs.

Refrigeration

Clean condenser coils at least once a year and replace worn door gaskets to ensure a tight fit for efficient operation.

Don't place refrigerators or freezers in garages, carports and other places that are not air conditioned. This puts strain on the motors and causes them to run continuously.

Experts Recommend
SET FRIDGE
37-40°F
Freezer 5° F

Swimming pools

Placing a timer on your pool pump can reduce energy use. Check with a professional to determine the amount of pump time needed for your size and type of pool.

Keep your pool filtration system clean. A dirty system will cause the motor to run longer and at higher back pressures in the pump, consuming more energy.

Use this formula to estimate your appliances' energy use:

Wattage x Hours Used Per Day ÷ 1,000 = Daily Kilowatt-hour (kWh) consumption

(1 kilowatt (kW) = 1,000 Watts)

Multiply this by the number of days you use the appliance during the year for the annual consumption. You can then calculate the annual cost to run an appliance by multiplying the kWh per year by your local utility's rate per kWh consumed.

Electronics

Computers, printers and attached devices are not big energy users. However, if left on for long periods of time, energy use can add up. In the average home, 75 percent of the electricity used to power home electronics is consumed while the products are turned off. This can be avoided by unplugging the appliance or using a power strip and using the switch on the power strip to stop all power to the appliance.

Notes: You can usually find the wattage of most appliances stamped on the bottom or back of the appliance or on its nameplate.

To estimate the number of hours a refrigerator actually operates at its maximum wattage, divide the total time the refrigerator is plugged in by three. Refrigerators, although turned "on" all the time, actually cycle on and off as needed to maintain interior temperatures.

Air leaks

Eliminate air leaks by caulking around windows and doorframes and install weather stripping around exterior doors. Check for air leaks where pipes enter your home from the outside and fill with expanding spray foam. Eliminating air leaks can save you as much as 10 to 20 percent on your heating and cooling costs.

Eliminate Air Leaks
HEATING/COOLING
10-20%
Savings

Filters and lint traps

Change or clean the filters in your home's air returns monthly. This also applies to window AC units. And clean your dryer's lint trap after each load. Clogged filters and lint traps can dramatically affect efficiency of the appliance.

Fill it up

Run dishwashers, clothes washers and dryers only when loads are full to maximize energy use.

Trees

Properly positioned trees can save up to 25 percent of a household's energy use for heating and cooling, according to the U.S. Department of Energy. In fact, the correct placement of only three trees will save an average household $100-$250 in energy costs in a single year.

Properly Positioned Trees
HEATING/COOLING
25%
Savings

CLECO

1.800.622.6537 · WWW.CLECO.COM

2 Copy and complete the table below based on the information given in the second part of the pamphlet given above:

Action	Result
Increasing attic insulation	
Using CFBs	The water in the tank remains warm
	and
Replacing worn gaskets in refrigerators	
Running washing machines at a full load	The motor pump runs longer and with greater pressure
Correctly positioning three trees in a house	

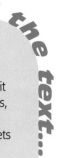

Beyond the text...

➤ How can energy conservation result in increasing national and personal security? Examine this issue in two different anglophone countries.

➤ Energy Efficiency and Conservation Authority is a New Zealand agency concerned with promoting energy conservation and proficiency. Search the several methods used by this agency and how effective they have been in New Zealand.

➤ In an article published by *The Economist* on 8 May, 2008, the writer mentions that 'it is a time-consuming chore for someone to identify the best energy-saving equipment, buy it and get it installed. It does not help that the potential savings, although huge when added up across the world, usually amount to only a small share of the budgets of individual firms and households.' Reflect on the statement above and examine how valid it is in anglophone countries.

 Developing writing skills

1 A friend of yours needs practical methods to conserve the maximum energy during winter and asks you for a set of guidelines to help him or her do so.

In groups:

  a Scan the *Energy Conservation Guide* again and identify relevant information.

  b Decide how you are going to send your friend the guidelines. Which text type are you going to incorporate these guidelines into? You must provide a **rationale** explaining why this has been chosen.

  c Write your guidelines.

2 In groups, examine the pamphlet again and:

  a list the features and conventions of a pamphlet as shown in the guide.

  b discuss what pamphlets are used for.

  c share your observations with the rest of the class.

  d refer to *USAID's Global Climate Change Program* brochure (p. 57) to copy and complete the table below:

	Brochure	**Pamphlet**
Communicative purpose		
Audience targeted		
Register		
Type of language		

The personal response

Based on the following stimulus, give a personal response and justify it. Write a newspaper article, using between 150 and 250 words.

"And I'm asking you for your good and for your nation's security to take no unnecessary trips, to use carpools or public transportation whenever you can, to park your car one extra day per week, to obey the speed limit, and to set your thermostats to save fuel. Every act of energy conservation like this is more than just common sense – I tell you it is an act of patriotism."

Jimmy Carter, 39th U.S. President,
Speech to the Nation, "Energy and the National Goals – A Crisis of Confidence", 15 July 1979

Exam tip

HL P2 Section B
In the external examination, you will be free to choose any text type you have practised in class.

Interactive oral activity

1 Search for other pamphlets discussing one of the following:
   - energy conservation in factories or schools
   - energy saving products
   - energy saving or conservation group(s).

2 Share the information you have with the class. Identify any new or additional features of pamphlets to add to your list.

CAS

As part of an awareness campaign on the International Conservation Day, invite a guest speaker to your school who will explain the necessity of energy conservation and possible ways to conserve energy in your community.

The SL Written Assignment

1 Read the following text about climate change.

Thank climate change for the rise of humans

Some claim climate change will destroy our species; now it seems it also helped forge it. The rapid fluctuations in temperature that characterized the global climate between 2 and 3 million years ago coincided with a golden age in human evolution. The fossil record shows that eight distinct species emerged from one hominin species, *Australopithecus africanus*, alive 2.7 million years ago. The first members of our genus appeared between 2.4 and 2.5 million years ago, while *Homo erectus*, the first hominin to leave Africa, had evolved by 1.8 million years ago.

To work out whether climate had a hand in the speciation spurt, Matt Grove of the University of Liverpool in the UK turned to a global temperature data set compiled by Lorraine Lisiecki at the University of California, Santa Barbara. Lisiecki analysed oxygen isotopes in the shells of fossilized marine organisms called *foraminifera*. During glacial periods, the forams' shells contain more of the heavier of two oxygen isotopes, as the lighter one is preferentially accumulated in snow and ice rather than the ocean.

Grove found that the mean temperature changed suddenly on three occasions during the last 5 million years. Each change was equivalent to the difference between glacial and interglacial temperatures – but none of these episodes coincided with the hominin 'golden age'. What marked out this period was a greater range of recorded temperatures, suggesting it was a time of rapid but short-lived fluctuations in climate. Grove says such conditions would have favoured the evolution of adaptability that is a hallmark of the genus *Homo* (*Journal of Archaeological Science*, DOI: 10.10 16/j. jas.2011.07.002).

Grove says the classic survival traits of *H. erectus*, forged during this period of change, include teeth suited for generalized diets and a large brain – both of which should have been advantageous at a time of swift climate change.

Andy Coghlan, 2011

2 Refer to *USAID's Global Climate Change Program* brochure (p. 57) and *The Guardian*'s news report (p. 61) and follow the instructions below.

Read the three texts and:

a Underline or note down the similarities and differences in the texts' approaches/ideas about global warming/climate change.
  - What do the texts have in common?
  - How are the texts different?

b Choose some points you would like to emphasize or explore further in your written assignment.

c Clearly state your aim/s and note down the ways in which you are going to achieve them by answering the following questions:

a	WHY am I writing about this issue?	(**Your AIM/s** should appear here)
b	WHAT am I writing?	(**TEXT TYPE**, for example – magazine article, letter to the editor of a newspaper, diary entry)
c	TO WHOM am I writing?	(**AUDIENCE**, for example – general public, a friend, a classmate)
d	WHY have I chosen this text type and audience?	**Link** your choice to your aim/s and mention **how the use of this specific test type and audience will help you achieve your aims**.

d Discuss ideas with your teacher.

e Write your **rationale** (100 words). In your rationale, you must state your aims and how you have achieved them in the assignment. Refer to step **c**.

f Write your assignment (300–400 words).

> ## TIP
>
> **SL Written Assignment**
> For the external written assignment, you will read three previously unseen texts chosen by your teacher.

Exam tip

The assessment of the task emphasizes content and organization over format.

You should:

- demonstrate understanding of the core topic.
- organize the information from the sources in a manner appropriate to the text.
- use the information from the sources to form a new text without copying.
- use language appropriate to the text type and purpose.

Language B Guide, page 34

TOK

Some geographical topics, such as climate change, are controversial. How does the scientific method attempt to address them? Are such topics always within the scope of the scientific method? What scientific or social factors might influence the study of a complex phenomenon such as global warming?

Some tests and statistics regarding climate change and pollution are controversial. Conservationists argue that gas emissions from cars contribute to global warming. Individual drivers feel that they are not to blame. An emission test measures the polluting gases produced by car engines under normal driving conditions. In order to do so, the test will examine the car's use of fuel when the engine starts up, accelerates, and runs normally. This allows test centres to compare the emissions of vehicles with the same engine capacity. This seems to be scientific. However, consider the following:

Problem	Result	Ways to improve engine performance
Cold weather means the engine will have to run for a greater period of time.	The engine oil, coolant and the catalytic converter will need extra time to get warm and will produce more emissions.	Drivers who know these facts take the test on a warm day.
A weak car battery can cause the fuel ejector to work badly.	The engine releases greater emissions of gas.	Drivers can change the battery just before the test.
The engine oil is dirty.	The car engine will produce more harmful emissions.	Drivers can change the oil before the test.
A car uses cheap petrol.	The car engine will produce more harmful emissions.	Drivers buy better fuel just for the test.
A driver lives close to the test centre.	A newly started engine produces more harmful emissions.	The driver drives around for 20–30 minutes before arriving at the test centre.

- Can such tests be fair?
- Can we trust the results of these tests?
- Is it ethical to make adjustments like the ones stated in the table prior to an emission test?

69

Science & technology

→ How dependent are today's youth on computers? Is this a curse or a blessing?
→ How would our lives be without technology?
→ Who is mostly affected by the adverse effects of technology in your own culture?
→ Is it possible to use mobile phones for educational purposes?
→ What images come to your mind when 'poetry in the age of technology' is brought up?
→ Should old weapons be perfected instead of developing new ones?
→ Apart from weapons, what guarantees victory in wars?
→ Describe one of the most technologically advanced weapons you have heard about.

Computers

Our Lives On A Chip

1 Our lives on a chip,
   Then fed through a wire,
   Computers control us
   And try to conspire.

| What is the comparison presented in the first stanza?

2 The way that we live
   And the things that we do,
   They always have answers,
   But nothing that's new.

| 1. To what does 'They' refer?
| 2. What does the poet mean by the last two lines?

3 We give them our trust
   And we give them our time,
   They soon take control
   Of our 'rhythm and rhyme'.

| What is referred to by 'rhythm and rhyme'?

4 Like puppets and robots,
   We follow their lead,
   But they are not human;
   Can't feel and don't bleed.

| Human beings are compared to puppets and robots. What does this imply?

5 Like all things man-made,
   They start to break down,
   Then where does that leave us
   And where are we bound?

| What does 'bound' mean?

6 When things that we trust
   And feel that we need,
   Soon start to reject us
   And give us no heed.

| Think of a word that is similar in meaning to 'heed'.

7 It's time that we started
   To think on our own,
   Take charge of our kingdom
   And take back the throne,

| Explain the image presented in stanzas 6 and 7.

8 For now we can see
   That this cold metal box,
   Which was once full of promise,
   Is nothing but talk.

| What did the 'cold metal box' once promise us?

9 Let's get back to basics
   Before it's too late,
   And look back and know
   That we made a mistake.
   David Ronald Bruce Pekrul

| 1. What would be 'too late'?
| 2. What is the mistake that we made?

Writing activity

Einstein's quote, *"It has become appallingly obvious that our technology has exceeded our humanity"*, triggered a heated discussion in one English B lesson. You have been asked to give a speech to your classmates, explaining your views and whether you agree or disagree with the quote above. Write between 250 and 400 words.

Remember

- **What am I writing?**
  (Conventions, rhetorical and stylistic devices, layout)
- **Who is my audience?**
  (Tone, register, diction)
- **Why am I writing?**
  (Agree? Disagree? re-read the quote)

Mobile phones

Quick access to poetry in the age of technology

THERE ARE probably people who have read *War and Peace* on their smartphones, but just the thought of spending that much time squinting at a little screen makes my eyes hurt.

A little haiku, on the other hand? A snippet of E.E. Cummings? Whitman's Leaves of Grass even? That's another matter.

Smartphones are arguably the best thing to hit poetry since the printing press, as even the most casual lovers of verse can read a poem whenever the spirit moves them, not just when they are in the vicinity of a book or computer.

Case in point: a friend hosted a dinner party, and after dessert we sat on the couch thumbing through some of his poetry books. We had trouble finding Litany, by Billy Collins, until I pulled out my iPhone and delivered a Web version in 30 seconds. Apps are even better.

And it's free, thanks to an app that is called, simply, Shakespeare. (On Amazon, I could score a print version of Shakespeare's complete works for around $30, with shipping.) Bear that price tag in mind when you grumble about the app's imperfect search technology. I tried to find one of my favorite passages – the 'Winter' song from Act 5 of *Love's Labour's Lost* – by entering a precise quote into the search box ('Greasy Joan doth keel the pot'). Nothing.

I tried 'greasy Joan' and 'keel the pot' as well, with similar results. Only when I tried another phrase from the song ('roasted crabs') did I succeed.

Another essential app is Poetry, from the Poetry Foundation (free for Apple devices). The app is a slot machine of verse: hit the Spin button, and themes like joy, passion, frustration and nostalgia race across the screen before the app settles on two.

If the app pairs passion and love, you've hit a jackpot of 367 poems on the topic, including *Deaf Republic: 10* by Ilya Kaminsky. If the app pairs anger and family, you are left with a meager six choices, including *Revenge* by Letitia Elizabeth Landon.

Would-be poets can get a considerable boost from Instant Poetry HD ($2 for Apple devices), which is similar to the popular magnetic poetry kits that covered refrigerator doors in the last decade. Drawing on words that the app's developers deemed especially profound, you can compose your work on top of a photo of your choosing, then e-mail your masterpiece or save it for later. Instant Poetry also splits up word lists by theme for poets who are in a hurry.

If you don't want that much help, lesser crutches await. B-Rhymes is a free iPhone app that helps you find words that almost rhyme. You can build tighter lines with Perfect Rhyme ($1) or RhymeBook ($2), both of which work when you do not have an Internet connection.

Android users also have great choices, in part because Feelsocial, an app developer, has flooded the Android Market with inexpensive or free poetry apps. Death Poems, Philosophical Poems and Graduation Poems, among others, cost $1, and sit alongside many more free apps that are tied to birthdays, love, proverbs, numbers, broken families and the like.

The Father's Day Poems app, by the way, costs $1, while its Mother's Day counterpart is free. Go figure.

The free Shakespeare Sonnets app lets you browse the bard's 154 poems, mark your favorites and e-mail them to friends. With the $1 version of the app, you can search the sonnets or browse them by first line or chronologically, and post them to your Facebook page.

Other author-specific apps await, including Frostisms, a free app that lets users share their favorite Robert Frost quotes via Twitter and Facebook. The Shmoop series of literature tutorials will help you parse specific poems for $2 apiece. These are especially good for students, but casual literature buffs will find them useful as well.

There is one app specifically linked to poetry: the Hafez Sonnets ($3). That will come as a great relief to the Hafez fans who happen to read Farsi, since the app comes only in that language.

It did not escape me that my friend who hosted the dinner party was the not-so-proud owner of a certain device which does not support poetry apps, and who all but mocked the app-related chatter among his friends earlier in the evening. He is about to trade in his device for an Android phone. Next time he hosts a party, I'm guessing there will be more poetry readings enhanced by the warm glow of the screen.

Bob Tedeschi, 2010

Had I the heavens' embroidered cloths,
Enwrought with golden and silver light,
The blue and the dim and the dark cloths
Of night and light and the half light,
I would spread the cloths under your feet:
But I, being poor, have only my dreams;
I have spread my dreams under your feet;
Tread softly because you tread on my dreams.

W.B. Yeats ·

1 Answer the following questions.
   a How can 'would-be' poets benefit from the Instant Poetry HD app?
   b What does the writer imply about Father's Day and Mother's Day poems by 'Go figure' (line 100)?
   c What is the significance of the anecdote given at the beginning of the article?

2 For each of the following, choose the correct answer from A, B or C.
   a 'That's another matter' (line 10) suggests that:
      A it is less strenuous to read poetry than novels on smartphones.
      B it is more important to discuss poetry than novels.
      C the writer is not in favour of using smartphones to read novels.
   b 'Smartphones are arguably the best thing to hit poetry since the printing press' (lines 11–13) indicates that:
      A there is evidence of other good devices than smartphones.
      B smartphones are better than the printing press.
      C smartphones appear to be the most efficient alternative these days.
   c The word 'vicinity' (line 17) means:
      A presence
      B area
      C realm
   d The writer believes that the imperfection of the 'Shakespeare' search technology:
      A is justifiable
      B should be disregarded
      C is unacceptable
   e The word 'deemed' (line 69) means:
      A proposed
      B reckoned
      C recommended

3 Copy and complete the following table by indicating to whom or to what the underlined word refers.

In the phrase…	The word refers to…
1 …after dessert <u>we</u> sat (lines 19–20)	
2 …some of <u>his</u> poetry books (line 21)	
3 …or save <u>it</u> for later (lines 73–74)	
4 If you don't want <u>that much help</u> (line 77)	
5 …and e-mail <u>them</u> to friends (line 104)	
6 …and post <u>them</u> to your Facebook page (line 108)	
7 …will find <u>them</u> useful as well (line 118)	

Beyond the text...

➤ Some people argue that mobile phones are gradually replacing computers. Support or refute this argument, providing supporting details from online articles pertinent to an anglophone country.

➤ In one of the public polls conducted, it was approximately estimated that 70% of Americans have become too dependent on computers and other electronic devices. Research the positive and negative impacts of this dependency on the American individual.

➤ How much has using computers and mobile phones reduced personal communication in anglophone countries?

➤ Many believe that education is improved when technology is used. Investigate the use(s) of a certain technological device to enhance education in an anglophone country.

➤ How much have scientific and technological advancements affected people's morals, attitudes and values? Support your answer by providing details drawn from an anglophone country.

The individual oral (HL/SL)

Examine the photograph and read the caption given.

1 Describe what you see in a sentence or two and link it to the option of science and technology.

2 Read the caption and use it to prepare your ideas.

3 Think of an English-speaking culture.

4 Reflect on the photograph. What do you think?

5 Plan your presentation. Your presentation should:

- last 3–4 minutes.

- be within the context of the option referred to.

- must not be memorized or rehearsed.

- include examples or justifications.

6 During the presentation, you should:

- use no more than 10 brief points as talking notes.

- be spontaneous.

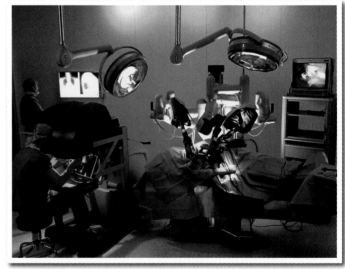

Using robots in surgeries is becoming a growing trend nowadays despite the various worries surrounding it.

CAS

Organize a campaign in your local community which aims to highlight the negative effects of over-using computers and mobile phones.

Weapons

Superiority

Part 1

IN MAKING THIS STATEMENT – which I do of my own free will – I wish first to make it perfectly clear that I am not in any way trying to gain sympathy, nor do I expect any mitigation of whatever sentence the Court may pronounce. I am writing this in an attempt to refute some of the lying reports broadcast over the prison radio and

5 published in the papers I have been allowed to see. These have given an entirely false picture of the true cause of our defeat, and as the leader of my race's armed forces at the cessation of hostilities I feel it my duty to protest against such libels upon those who served under me.

I also hope that this statement may explain the reasons for the application I have twice

10 made to the Court, and will now induce it to grant a favor for which I can see no possible grounds of refusal. The ultimate cause of our failure was a simple one: despite all statements to the contrary, it was not due to lack of bravery on the part of our men, or to any fault of the Fleet's. We were defeated by one thing only – by the inferior science of our enemies. I repeat – *by the inferior science of our enemies*.

15 When the war opened we had no doubt of our ultimate victory. The combined fleets of our allies greatly exceeded in number and armament those which the enemy could muster against us, and in almost all branches of military science we were their superiors. We were sure that we could maintain this superiority. Our belief proved, alas, to be only too well founded.

20 At the opening of the war our main weapons were the long-range homing torpedo, dirigible ball-lightning and the various modifications of the Klydon beam. Every unit of the Fleet was equipped with these and though the enemy possessed similar weapons their installations were generally of lesser power. Moreover, we had behind us a far greater military research organization, and with this initial advantage we could not

25 possibly lose.

The campaign proceeded according to plan until the Battle of the Five Suns. We won this, of course, but the opposition proved stronger than we had expected. It was realized that victory might be more difficult, and more delayed, than had first been imagined. A conference of supreme commanders was therefore called to discuss our

30 future strategy.

Part 2

Present for the first time at one of our war conferences was Professor-General Norden, the new Chief of the Research Staff, who had just been appointed to fill the gap left by the death of Malvar, our greatest scientist. Malvar's leadership had been responsible, more than any other single factor, for the efficiency and power of our weapons. His

35 loss was a very serious blow, but no one doubted the brilliance of his successor – though many of us disputed the wisdom of appointing a theoretical scientist to fill a post of such vital importance. But we had been overruled.

I can well remember the impression Norden made at that conference. The military advisers were worried, and as usual turned to the scientists for help. Would it be possible to improve our existing weapons, they asked, so that our present advantage could be increased still further?

Norden's reply was quite unexpected. Malvar had often been asked such a question – and he had always done what we requested.

"Frankly, gentlemen," said Norden, "I doubt it. Our existing weapons have practically reached finality. I don't wish to criticize my predecessor, or the excellent work done by the Research Staff in the last few generations, but do you realize that there has been no basic change in armaments for over a century? It is, I am afraid, the result of a tradition that has become conservative. For too long, the Research Staff has devoted itself to perfecting old weapons instead of developing new ones. It is fortunate for us that our opponents have been no wiser: we cannot assume that this will always be so."

Norden's words left an uncomfortable impression, as he had no doubt intended. He quickly pressed home the attack. "What we want are new weapons – weapons totally different from any that have been employed before. Such weapons can be made: it will take time, of course, but since assuming charge I have replaced some of the older scientists with young men and have directed research into several unexplored fields which show great promise. I believe, in fact, that a revolution in warfare may soon be upon us."

We were skeptical. There was a bombastic tone in Norden's voice that made us [1] of his claims. We did not know, then, that he never promised anything that he had not already almost perfected in the laboratory. *In the laboratory* – that was the operative phrase.

Norden proved his case less than a month later, when he demonstrated the Sphere of Annihilation, which produced complete disintegration of matter over a radius of several hundred meters. We were [2] by the power of the new weapon, and were quite prepared to overlook one fundamental defect – the fact that it was a sphere and hence destroyed its rather complicated generating equipment at the instant of formation. This meant, of course, that it could not be used on warships but only on guided missiles, and a great program was started to convert all homing torpedoes to carry the new weapon. For the time being all further offensives were [3].

We realize now that this was our first mistake. I still think that it was a natural one, for it seemed to us then that all our existing weapons had become [4] overnight, and we already regarded them as almost primitive survivals. What we did not appreciate was the [5] of the task we were attempting, and the length of time it would take to get the revolutionary super-weapon into battle. Nothing like this had happened for a hundred years and we had no previous experience to guide us.

Arthur C. Clarke, 2000

1 Answer the following questions based on **Part 1** of the text.

   a In the first paragraph, the word 'prison' indicates that the speaker is in captivity. Find two other phrases in the same paragraph to prove this.

   b What is the statement the speaker is making?

   c What is the purpose of this statement?

   d Where is the speaker?

   e List the weapons used by the speaker's Fleet at the beginning of the war.

   f What made the Fleet superior in military power at the beginning of the war according to the speaker?

2 The statements below are either true or false. Choose the correct response, and then justify it by quoting a relevant phrase from the text.

   a The speaker is forced to make his statement in the Court.

   b According to the speaker, the news circulated by the media about the defeat has been mostly false accusations.

   c This is the second time the speaker has submitted his application.

   d The enemy troops were fewer in number compared to the allies' troops.

   e The enemies had different weapons from those used by the Fleet.

   f The Fleet won the Battle of the Five Suns with ease.

> ### Grammar
>
> **Repetition** is used twice in the text. What is the purpose of repeating and italicizing the following phrases?
> - 'by the inferior science of our enemies' (lines 13–14)
> - 'In the laboratory' (line 61)

3 Find a word or phrase in the text that has a similar meaning to each of the following:

   a alleviation

   b rebut

   c slanders

   d provoke

   e assemble

   f supplied with

   g moved on

4 Explain what the speaker means or refers to by the following, in the context of **Part 2**.

   a 'his successor' (line 35)

   b 'But we had been overruled' (line 37)

   c 'Norden's reply was quite unexpected' (line 42)

   d 'It is fortunate for us that our opponents have been no wiser' (lines 49–50)

   e 'our first mistake' (line 71)

5 Some of the words have been removed from the text between lines 60 and 75. From the table on the right, choose the word which best fits each numbered gap **[1]**–**[5]**.

appalled	intoxicated	magnitude
missiles	obsolete	promoted
realizable	suspended	suspicious

The HL Written Assignment

The previous text is only an excerpt from a complete short story by Arthur C. Clarke. Before you plan for and write your assignment, you must:

- Read the remainder of the short story carefully. Search for the full text on the Internet.
- Discuss the main theme with your teacher and classmates.

You need to:

1. Summarize the main theme.

2. Focus on one aspect of the story or one idea presented and think of how you can expand it or explore it further.

3. Clearly state your aim(s) and note down the way in which you are going to achieve them.

a	Why am I writing?
b	What am I writing?
c	To whom am I writing?
d	Why have I chosen this text type?

4. Discuss ideas with your teacher.

5. Write your rationale (150 words).

6. Write your assignment (500–600 words).

Exam tip

HL Written Assignment
For the external written assignment, you will base your written assignment on one of the literary works you've read in class.

CAS

You are to organize a presentation conducted by a high ranking army officer in your local community to highlight the most technological advancements in weaponry and armaments.

TOK

- How might the language used in polls, questionnaires and other information-gathering devices of this sort influence the conclusions reached?

- If there is an influence, does it occur in natural science research?

- Does the extent of the influence relate to the degree of certainty attributed to the natural sciences and the human sciences respectively, or to the social status or value associated with each?

Think about influencing opinion in your school. Take a social issue in your school such as meals, uniforms, homework, pressure, academic tests or another debatable topic. How easily can you create a questionnaire which predicts the results you want to hear? What techniques would you use to make sure you get the results you want? What does this tell you about the accuracy of information-gathering in social sciences. Are there any methods you could use to make your tests more objective and unbiased?

Leisure

BEFORE YOU READ

→ What images come to your mind when you read about international festivals?

→ How important are festivals and fairs?

→ Describe a significant festival or fair held in your own culture.

International Youth Festivals

1 Read the flyer and answer the following questions.
   a What is the aim of the flyer?
   b Having examined the text, what do you believe to be the important details that should be provided when designing any festival flyer?
   c Mention four activities that Aberdeen's Homecoming Tartan Day includes.
   d What do 'Homecoming' and 'Beating Retreat' traditionally represent?

2 The statements below are either true or false. Choose the correct response, and then justify it by quoting a relevant phrase from the text.
   a Aberdeen's Homecoming Tartan Day activities target the youth.
   b Gordons are originally from Scotland.
   c The 'Gordon Highlanders' is a newfound name.
   d The Aberdeen International Youth Festival attracts local performers and artists.

3 For each of the following words from the text, choose the word from the table on the right which is closest in meaning.

   a dazzling (column 1)

   b diversity (column 1)

   c affiliations (column 2)

   d spans (column 2)

   e exotic (column 3)

associations	binds	extraordinary
variety	detachments	mysterious
astounding	relates	extends across

The Gordon Highlanders Regiment dates back to 1794

Developing writing skills

Refer to *USAID's Global Climate Change Program* brochure (p. 57), the *Energy Conservation Guide* pamphlet (p. 64 & 65) and the *Aberdeen's Homecoming Tartan Day* flyer (p. 80). Copy the diagram below and fill the circles with features of a **brochure**, a **pamphlet** and a **flyer**. Similarities between them should be written where the circles overlap. Think of the following:

- Communicative purposes
- Language
- Target audience
- Register
- Layout

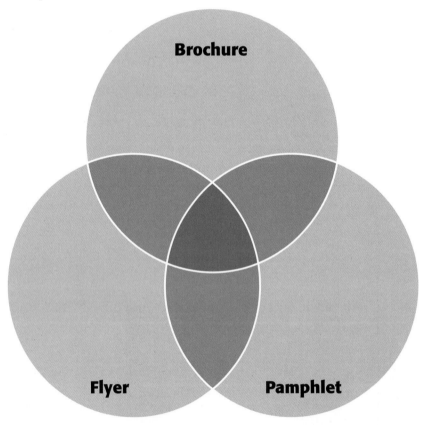

Before you start writing a brochure, pamphlet or flyer, ask yourself:

- What is your intended goal?
- Who is your audience?
- How will your audience respond to your message?
- What are your audience's needs?

CAS

Prepare for the activities that will take place during a multicultural festival at your school. Make sure the activities are targeted at 12–17 year-old students.

Remember

- Address your audience directly and clearly.
- Take readers straight to important information.
- Provide an eye-catching title.
- Use headings, sub-headings, bullets and numbers to highlight key information.
- Divide into manageable sections or paragraphs.
- Keep language simple and straightforward.
- Include contact information.

Book festivals

BOOKSGALORE.CO.UK

Book festivals bring out the brains in Britons

Turn off the TV, put [1] the papers, and take a tour of Britain's book festivals. We are a lot more cultured than you think.

Book festivals are exceptional events that prove something interesting [2] modern Britain: that it is a much more cultured place, with a far deeper hunger for
5   knowledge, than you would ever guess by watching television or, a lot of the time, reading the papers.

I've been [3] a bit of a festival tour this summer, performing at Hay, Ways with Words and most recently Edinburgh. The level of engagement you get [4] audiences is stunning.

10 In a way, the success of Edinburgh is the most impressive of all because it takes place as part of this city's famous festival season, in direct competition with the Fringe and other festivals. In fact the book festival site is just up the road from the Assembly Rooms on George Street where, for comparison, I saw Richard Herring do standup. He was funny, especially when he imagined being [5] a bike race
15 with his friend, but the contrast between the passive audience experience [6] the Assembly Rooms (laughing as if primed with electrodes, often before the joke) and the question-and-answer, talk-to-the-author electricity of the book festival was telling. There is arguably more real life and energy in the book festival than in other 'live' cultural forms – and this goes too, of course, for Hay, where a performance
20 by historian Niall Ferguson was one of the best and funniest one-man shows I have ever seen.

As serious entertainment, as provocation, as a chance to get [7] the skin of culture as it is made and ideas as they are formed, Britain's book festivals make a mockery of any belief we are getting dumber.

25 They raise the question: is it just the media and politicians who are dumb? [8] it seems Britain is full of people who want to talk about really interesting stuff.

Jonathan Jones, 2011

The Hay literary festival in Wales brings out the rain and the brains

1   The statements below are either true or false. Choose the correct response, and then justify it by quoting a relevant phrase from the text.

   a   The true cultural value of Britain is underestimated by the media.

   b   The blog writer attended the festival as an observer.

   c   The success of Edinburgh is due to its being this season's only event.

   d   According to the writer, live cultural forms are less 'lively' than book festivals.

   e   Britain's book festivals mock politicians and the media.

2   Some of the words have been removed from the text. From the table below, choose the word which best fits each numbered gap **[1]–[8]**.

at	under	on	down	about	to
with	into	from	in	for	above

Beyond the text...

➤ Conduct some quick research to find out the important international youth festivals held in different anglophone countries.

➤ Book festivals are believed to encourage children to read. To what degree do you think such festivals have succeeded in attaining this aim in the UK and Canada?

➤ In 2010, South Africa hosted the largest international youth festival in Pretoria. This was the first time in 65 years that this very significant conference was held in Southern Africa. Gather information about the activities included in this conference as well as participating countries. How much do you think such festivals help highlight issues pertinent to the hosting country?

➤ Certain festivals encourage understanding and appreciation for different cultures, while celebrating local heritage and cultural expressions. Reflect on this statement and search for at least two festivals in two different anglophone cultures that fulfill such a mission statement.

➤ Peruse the FSA International Heritage Festival website (www.fsafest.org) and choose one of the most appealing activities involved. Justify your choice.

The individual oral (HL/SL) 1

1   Investigate **one** of the following fairs or festivals in their relevant English-speaking countries.

- The London Book Fair
- Cape Town Jazz Festival
- Toronto International Film Festival
- Wallaby Creek Festival
- Austin Ice Cream Festival

2   Prepare your presentation, explaining the importance, main activities, location and time of your chosen fair or festival.

3   Present your information in class within 3–4 minutes.

4   Find a photograph to represent your chosen fair or festival.

The individual oral (HL/SL) 2

1   Describe what you see in the photograph below in no more than 1 minute.

2   Think of a suitable caption.

3   Discuss the importance of festivals like the one shown below and how such occasions form an opportunity for intercultural understanding.

Ludlow Food Festival, England

Writing activity

Choose one of the following and write 250–400 words.

1 A new festival is going to be launched under the umbrella of
'hand-in-hand for a better cultural understanding'. You are to
design a brochure which promotes the activities of this festival
and describes their benefits.

2 Ghandi once said: "No culture can live if it attempts to be
exclusive." Write a newspaper article in which you explain how
much festivals can contribute to nourishing roots of culture and
keeping them alive.

TOK

Can a study of other cultures be free of bias in the selection and interpretation of material?

● Do you think these tourist images give us an accurate picture of the UK today? Give reasons for your opinions.

Reflection point

● In Chapter 3, you have looked at climate change, energy
reserves, science and technology, and festivals. What has this
section taught you about how related the topics you have
explored are?
● What role do people have in alleviating the impact of global
warming and climate change? Would they be able to achieve
this in isolation from governments and media?
● What can humans do to avoid being totally controlled by
science and technology?
● How important are festivals and fairs in bringing people
together?
● What do you have to do to write a brochure, a pamphlet or
a flyer?

Literature

Studying literature in English B

How can you save the world, become immortal, rise from rags to riches and see yourself in a portrait, in the time it takes to turn a page? Reading fiction opens doors to times and places far away, or indeed closer to oneself. As the Language B guide states, reading literature will help English B **Higher level** students to 'broaden their vocabulary and to use language in a more creative manner, developing fluent reading skills, promoting interpretative and inferential skills, and contributing to intercultural understanding' (p. 21).

Literature transcends geographical boundaries. Reading literature in English can help you to reflect on your own cultures, as well as deepen your understanding and appreciation of anglophone societies.

At Higher level, we hope you will find enjoyment in reading and understanding literary works in English in some depth. You may also appreciate the sheer variety and power of expression. However, literary criticism as such is not required. At Higher level, you will come across literary texts in Paper 1, and your written assignment should be based on one of the two literary works you read in class.

Standard level students will also benefit from reading fiction in English, and you may find yourself reading contemporary prose, fan fiction, short stories, graphic novels, song lyrics or plot-driven detective stories, especially if your teacher gives your class an active role in selecting the texts.

> **TIP**
>
> When you study literary texts, keep the IB Learner Profile in mind. Can you see the qualities in the fictional characters you are studying? Would they make good IB students? Why? How does reading a literary work help you to develop these qualities?

Grandma makes meatballs

On Grandparents' Day at my school we had an international food fest. My teacher, Mrs Hodges, said it was a great
5 opportunity to encourage peace and understanding among the different cultures in our community.

My grandma cooked my favourite
10 food: meatballs.

But when we arrived at school Luca's grandma had cooked his favourite meatballs too, and so had Amber's granddad, and so
15 had Clara's grandma, and so had Kerem's grandma.

In fact, all the grandparents had cooked meatballs to share for lunch!

20 When Mrs Hodges found out she said, "Oh well then, who likes meatballs, class?" And we all put up our hands.

The cooking pots were all laid
25 out on the table ready for the adults to serve us and then the lids were lifted. That's when we noticed that [1] they all had meaty-looking balls inside, the
30 colours and smells were very different.

Luca's grandmother, who was standing beside her pot, [2] Mrs Hodges on the shoulder and said,
35 "Mrs Hodges, you must try my meatballs," as she scooped some onto a plate with a little spaghetti. "I make the best meatballs. It's a special Italian recipe. I use my
40 own homemade tomato sauce."

But before Mrs Hodges had finished eating them Amber's grandfather went up to Mrs Hodges nodding his head, saying,

45 "No, no, Mrs Hodges, you must try some of my meatballs." And he scooped some onto her plate with a little rice. "I make the best meatballs. It's a special Indian
50 recipe. It's vegetarian with mint and yoghurt."

But before Mrs Hodges had finished eating them, my grandmother went up to Mrs
55 Hodges and clicked her tongue saying, "No, no, Mrs Hodges, you must try some of my meatballs." And she scooped [3] onto her plate. "I make the best meatballs.
60 It's a special Greek recipe. I boil the meatballs first and then make an egg and lemon sauce."

But before Mrs Hodges had finished, Clara's grandmother
65 went up to Mrs Hodges and waved her hands saying, "No, no, Mrs Hodges, you must try some of my meatballs." And she scooped some onto her plate.
70 "We call them the Lion's Head and the shredded cabbage is the mane. I make the best meatballs. It's a special Chinese recipe."

Mrs Hodges was being jostled
75 around the table, tasting a little of the meatballs from each of the grandparents who were competing loudly with each other. She tried Turkish meatballs,
80 Swedish meatballs, Indonesian meatballs, Lebanese meatballs, Mexican meatballs, South African

meatballs; indeed, different versions of meatballs from all
85 around the world. But just when she thought she could not take one more bite, she noticed that though the children were happily tasting each other's meatballs,
90 the grandparents were looking angrily at one another. Some were glaring, or had turned away and many were refusing to talk.

I followed Mrs Hodges' alarmed
95 look around the room and knew just what to do, so I went up to her, "Excuse me Mrs Hodges," and whispered in her ear. Mrs Hodges addressed the assembly
100 while Kerem and I raced into Mrs Hodges' office to raid her Christmas stash.

"Well everybody, thank you so much for sharing your favourite
105 food, meatballs, with us today. It's fair to say that when it comes to cooking, and especially cooking meatballs, you all like to do it wonderfully differently. But as
110 Alexander has reminded me, there is one thing when it comes to food that we all have in common: We all love CHOCOLATE!" Everybody cheered and then
115 the grandparents chatted while Kerem and I handed around the chocolates.

Iona Massey
Special Prize in *Story for Children*, Commonwealth Short Story Competition, 2010

1 Based on its title, what do you expect from the text?

2 What text type do you think it is? Make a list of the conventions that are associated with this text type.

3 Whose voice do we hear? Who tells the story? What information is given about the narrator?

4 What reason is given for the 'international food fest' (line 2)? What does it suggest about the setting of the story?

5 What does the narrator discover upon arriving at the school?

6 What purpose does the action of putting up a hand serve in lines 22–23
 i to express disagreement
 ii to answer 'yes' or 'I' by raising a hand
 iii to insult someone by pointing
 iv to shake hands with each other

7 Who is going to serve the food? Who is going to eat the food?

8 Choose the word that best fits the gap labelled [1].
 A because
 B although
 C however
 D by
 E where

9 What did Luca's grandmother do to get the teacher's attention? Choose the word that best fits the gap labelled [2]. She…
 A topped
 B tipped
 C hopped
 D tapped

10 How is the dish cooked by Amber's grandfather different from Luca's grandmother's meatballs?

11 Who gets to taste the meatballs first?

12 What can clicking a tongue communicate in your culture? What do you think it means in this text (line 55)?

13 Choose the word that best fits the gap labelled [3].
 A none   D some
 B something   E less
 C other   F small

14 Find the words showing each grandparent's physical actions. What do they have in common? How are they different from each other? Which ones are commonly used in your culture?

15 When Mrs Hodges 'was being jostled' (line 74), what was done to her? She was…
 A pushed and shoved
 B politely encouraged
 C violently attacked
 D invited to skip and dance

16 What expression is used here to show that the teacher felt full after the food she had tasted?

17 Look at the text between the lines 85 and 94. What were the children doing? What were the adults doing? Why did Mrs Hodges look alarmed?

18 What does 'addressing the assembly' mean (line 99)?

19 Why did the narrator and Kerem go to Mrs Hodges' office? Find the word that reveals how fast they left.

20 Choose the expression which here means the same as 'when it comes to' (line 111).
 A without
 B upon arrival
 C the achievement of
 D undoubtedly
 E as regards
 F unlike
 G differing

21 Who is Alexander?

22 What effect does chocolate have in the story? Why does Mrs Hodges give everyone chocolate?

23 Did the text fulfil your expectations? Why?

24 Look at the list of conventions you made for question 2. Which ones apply to this text? If needed, amend your list.

25 This story won a Special Prize in the category of Story for Children in a short story competition. In your opinion, what makes it a good story for children? Can adults enjoy it, too?

The First Hello

The man from the telephone department got off the bus, and made his way to the
5 tea stall, wiping the sweat off his head, face, then slipping his hanky under his shirt to wipe his neck and
10 back. It was a year ago that the phone line had been installed,

six months later men from the public works department had come to put up the phone booth –
15 a neat box-like structure, with a glass window, and wooden ledges, yellow in colour. And days after that, a painter had taken an entire day to colour in broad, black brushstrokes, the words: STD Booth, local and STD* allowded.

20 No one could tell that the last word had been misspelled. Besides he had taken the entire day. After he had a cup of tea and a samosa, he had left, waving cheerfully. And now after a month, someone else was here again.

25 Everyone watched the man as he sat on the bench. No one said a word, and soon the sound of him slurping his tea filled the hot afternoon. A few leaves fell, heavy in the heat, and sometimes a car passed, on its way to the main city farther away.

30 When the man had finished, he made to pay but the tea shop owner who sat behind his steaming kettle and the washed upturned cups, waved him away.

"You are our guest here."

35 So the man took his hanky out again and wiped his face.

They crowded around him as he shut himself up in the phone booth. When the children pressed their nose against the glass, he shooed them away,
40 as he took out a shiny black instrument and placed it on the ledge. A sigh of satisfaction passed through everyone that soon changed to a rousing yell as they saw him dial a number, pressing a finger into the

ringed dialler of the phone and letting it go all the
45 way in a half-circle. A while later, they heard him say into the mouthpiece, "Hello."

"Hello," the children around the booth took up the cry, the teashop owner broke into a smile and the men waiting for a bus smiled and said hello
50 to each together. The sadhu who sat under the banyan tree nodded wisely. As the sound carried, more hellos were heard. The women winnowing grain giggled as they tried the word tentatively, the shepherds grazing their flocks called out to
55 their sheep, laughing as they used the word. The temple bells chimed last of all, and the echoes lingered long after the sound had dimmed. Only the cobbler kept quiet. He was a low caste man and was afraid of offending anyone by speaking
60 in English.

"It's a big occasion," said the headman, in an awed voice.

"It is," agreed those around him. The telephone man emerged and handed over a small chit of
65 paper to the headman. "This is the telephone number."

The headman looked at it reverently as if it were a mantra. The others around him read out the numbers slowly, digit-by-digit.

70 The telephone man was now too tired to notice the cheering around him. He knew he had to wait long before the bus to take him back arrived. As he sipped his second cup of tea, he remembered something else.

75 "Oh, you can't start using the phone now. The minister will come next month and inaugurate it."

No one said a word. No one was surprised. They had waited so long; a month more did not really matter.

Anuradha Kumar, India

Special Prize in *Science, Technology and Society*, Commonwealth Short Story competition, 2010

*STD = "subscriber trunk dialling"; long distance telephone calls can be made from STD booths.

1 Read the first two paragraphs. Choose the most appropriate response from the options below.
  a The beginning of the story introduces a man, who
    A is travelling to his work where he serves tea.
    B is asked to leave the bus because he is sweating too much.
    C knows how to deal with hot weather.
    D wishes he had a handkerchief.
  b In the story, fitting a working telephone booth
    A is a time-consuming process that has already taken 12 months.
    B is supervised by the managing director introduced at the beginning.
    C was something the telephone company failed to finish more than a year ago.
    D was an artistic challenge for a local painter.
  c A misspelled word on the booth
    A was a joke shared by the painter and the local people.
    B made the painter miss his tea break.
    C went unnoticed.
    D kept everyone occupied for an entire day.
  d When the man from the telephone department arrives
    A the hot afternoon is filled with quiet expectation.
    B there is a sudden rush of activity in the village.
    C he is greeted like an old friend.
    D he learns about the village while having a nice drink.

2 The following sentences are either true or false. Read the third paragraph, decide whether the sentences are true or false and justify it by quoting a relevant phrase from the text.
  a The man from the telephone department tries to pay for his tea.
  b The tea-shop owner offers an explanation for the free drink.
  c The local people leave the man alone while he is working.
  d When the man starts dialling, everyone keeps completely quiet.
  e The first attempt of a call from the booth is successful.

3 Read the fourth paragraph and answer the following questions:
  a What effect does the first telephone call have on the local people?
  b What sounds does the narrator mention? Compare paragraph 4 with paragraph 2. What has changed and why?
  c Which word or expression reveals that some local people felt a little shy and cautious saying the English word 'hello'?
  d With which words or expressions does the narrator describe the long-lasting effect of the temple bells?

4 Read the fifth paragraph and find the words or expressions in the paragraph which are similar in meaning to the following:
  a an important event
  b showing a feeling of admiration or being overwhelmed
  c with full respect
  d one number at a time.

5 From statements A to E, select the **two** that are true, according to the text.
  A The man from the telephone department has a physically demanding job.
  B The man from the telephone department shares the excitement the local people feel about their new telephone connection.
  C The local people will have to continue to wait for a working telephone booth.
  D Calls can be made only after someone from the government eventually opens the service.
  E The local people are disappointed with the day's events.

The Chase

"This one might be trouble."

    She heard one of them say this, only ten or so metres away in the darkness. Even over her fear, the sheer naked terror of being hunted, she felt a shiver of excitement, of something like triumph, when she realised they were talking about her. Yes, she thought, she would be trouble,

5 she already was trouble. And they were worried too; the hunters experienced their own fears during the chase. Well, at least one of them did. The man who'd spoken was Jasken; Veppers' principal bodyguard and chief of security. Jasken. Of course; who else?

    "You think so ... do you?" said a second man. That was Veppers himself. It felt as though something curdled inside her when she heard his deep, perfectly modulated voice, right now

10 attenuated to something just above a whisper. "But then ... they're all trouble." He sounded out of breath. "Can't you see ... anything with those?" He must be talking about Jasken's Enhancing Oculenses; a fabulously expensive piece of hardware like heavyduty sunglasses. They turned night to day, made heat visible and could see radio waves, allegedly. Jasken tended to wear them all the time, which she had always thought was just showing off, or betrayed some deep

15 insecurity. Wonderful though they might be, they had yet to deliver her into Veppers' exquisitely manicured hands.

    She was standing, flattened, against a flat scenery. In the gloom, a moment before she had spread herself against the enormous backdrop, she had been able to make out that it was just painted canvas with great sweeps of dark and light paint, but she had been too close to it to see

20 what it actually portrayed. She angled her head out a little and risked a quick look down and to the left, to where the two men were, standing on a gantry cantilevered out from the side of the fly tower's north wall. She glimpsed a pair of shadowy figures, one holding something that might have been a rifle. She couldn't be sure. Unlike Jasken, she had only her own eyes to see with.

    She brought her head back in again, quickly but smoothly, scared that she might be seen,

25 and tried to breathe deeply, evenly, silently. She twisted her neck this way and that, clenched and unclenched her fists, flexed her already aching legs. She was standing on a narrow wooden ledge at the bottom of the flat. It was slightly narrower than her shoes; she had to keep her feet splayed, toes pointing outwards in opposite directions, to stop herself from falling. Beneath, unseen in the darkness, the wide rear stage of the opera house was twenty metres further down. If she fell, there

30 were probably other cross-gantries or scenery towers in the way for her to hit on the way down.

    Above her, unseen in the gloom, was the rest of the fly tower and the gigantic carousel that sat over the rear of the opera house's stage and stored all the multifarious sets its elaborate productions required. She started to edge very slowly along the ledge, away from where the two men stood on the wall gantry. Her left heel still hurt where she'd dug out a tracer device, days earlier.

35   "Sulbazghi?" she heard Veppers say, voice low. He and Jasken had been talking quietly to each other; now they were probably using a radio or something similar. She didn't hear any answer from Dr. Sulbazghi; probably Jasken was wearing an earpiece. Maybe Veppers too, though he rarely carried a phone or any other comms gear.

    Veppers, Jasken and Dr. S. She wondered how many were chasing her as well as these

40 three. Veppers had guards to command, a whole retinue of servants, aides, helpers and other employees who might be pressed into service to help in a pursuit like this. The opera house's own security would help too, if called on; the place belonged to Veppers, after all. And no doubt Veppers' good friend, the city Chief of Police would lend any forces requested of him, in the highly unlikely event Veppers couldn't muster enough of his own. She kept on sliding her way

45 along the ledge.

Iain M. Banks, *Surface Detail,* 2010

1   Who says the first line? To what or whom does 'this one' refer?

2   The first paragraph mentions hunters. What or who are they trying to catch?

3   What feelings are mentioned in the first paragraph? Write the words you find in the text in a table like the one below, and tick the correct box to imply whether they have positive, neutral or negative connotations.

Word showing a feeling	Positive	Neutral	Negative

4   How does the narrator react to hearing Veppers' voice?

5   How do we know that the narrator knows Jasken and Veppers? Find the details in the text which reveal she is familiar with them.

6   What are the Oculenses used for? Why is Jasken wearing them now?

7   Where is the narrator? What is she trying to do?

8   Why are the narrator's legs aching?

9   Sketch a picture showing the location and position of the narrator and her pursuers. Compare your picture to your classmates' pictures. What similarities and differences are there? Why?

10   Why can't the narrator run?

11   Why does the narrator feel pain in her left heel?

12   Look at the last four paragraphs. For each of the words or phrases below, find a word or phrase in the text that has a similar meaning:
     a   relaxed, loosened
     b   wide apart
     c   varied
     d   complicated
     e   related
     f   asked for.

13   Why can't the narrator hear Dr. Sulbazghi's voice?

14   What technology are the characters using in the story?

15   Where and when do you think the story takes place? Why?

16   Why is the narrator not named in the text? How does this affect the reader's role and stance?

17   Whose side would you take – the hunters' or the narrator's? Why?

18   How do you think the story continues?

Not Yet, Jayette

This happened to me in LA once. Honestly. I was standing at a hamburger kiosk on Echo Park eating a chilé-dog. This guy in a dark green Lincoln pulls up at the kerb in front of me and leans out of the
5   window.

"Hey," he asks me, "do you know the way to San José?"

Well, that threw me, I had to admit it. In fact I almost told him. Then I got wise.

10   "Don't tell me," I say. "Let me guess. You're going back to find some peace of mind."

I only tell you this to give you some idea of what the city is like. It's full of jokers. And that guy, even though I'd figured him, still bad-mouthed me
15   before he drove away. That's the kind of place it is. I'm just telling you so's you know my day is for real.

Most mornings, early, I go down to the beach at Santa Monica to try and meet Christopher
20   Isherwood. A guy I know told me he likes to walk his dog down there before the beach freaks and the surfers show up. I haven't seen him yet but I've grown to like my mornings on the beach. The sea has that oily sheen to it, like an empty swimming
25   pool. The funny thing is, though, the Pacific Ocean nearly always looks cold. One morning someone was swinging on the bars, up and down, flinging himself about as if he was made of rubber. It was beautiful, and boy was he built. It's wonderful to
30   me what the human body can achieve if you treat it right. I like to keep in shape. I work out. So most days I hang around waiting to see if Christopher's going to show then I go jogging. I head south; down from the pier to Pacific Ocean Park. I've got
35   to know some of the bums that live around the beach, the junkies and derelicts.

"Hi Charlie," they shout when they see me jogging by.

There's a café in Venice where I eat breakfast.
40   A girl works there most mornings, thin, bottle-blonde, kind of tired-looking. I'm pretty sure she's on something heavy. So that doesn't make her anything special but she can't be more than eighteen. She knows my name, I don't know how,
45   I never told her. Anyway each morning when she brings me my coffee and doughnut she says, "Hi, there, Charlie. Lucked-out yet?"

I just smile and say, "Not yet, Jayette."

Jayette's the name she's got sewn across her top.
50   I'm not sure I like the way she speaks to me – I don't exactly know what she's referring to. But seeing how she knows my name I think it must be my career she's talking about. Because I used to be a star, well, a TV star anyway. Between the ages of
55   nine and eleven I earned twelve thousand dollars a week. Perhaps you remember the show, a TV soap opera called 'The Scrantons'. I was the little brother, Chuck. For two years I was a star. I got the whole treatment: my own trailer, chauffeured limousines,
60   private tutors. Trouble was my puberty came too early. Suddenly I was like a teenage gatecrasher at a kids' party. My voice went, I got zits all over my chin, fluff on my lip. It spoilt everything. Within a month the scenario for my contractual death was
65   drawn up. I think it was pneumonia, or maybe an accident with the thresher. I can't really remember, I don't like to look back on those final days.

Though I must confess it was fun meeting all the stars. The big ones: Jeanne Lamont, Eddy Cornelle,
70   Mary and Marvin Keen – you remember them. One of the most bizarre features of my life since I left the studio is that nowadays I never see stars anymore. Isn't that ridiculous? Someone like me who worked with them who practically lives in
75   Hollywood? Somehow I never get to see the stars any more. I just miss them.

"Oh, he left five minutes ago, bub," or "Oh, no, I think she's on location in Europe, she hasn't been here for weeks." The same old story.

80 I think that's what Jayette's referring to when she asks if I've lucked-out. She knows I'm still hanging in there, waiting. I mean, I've kept on my own agent. The way I see it is that once you've been in front of the cameras something's going to
85 keep driving you until you get back. I know it'll happen to me again one day, I just have this feeling inside.

After breakfast I jog back up the beach to where I left the car. One morning I got to thinking about
90 Jayette. What does she think when she sees me now and remembers me from the days of 'The Scrantons'? It seems to me that everybody in their life is at least two people. Once when you're a child and once when you're an adult.
95 It's the saddest thing. I don't just mean that you see things differently when you're a child – that's something else again – what's sad is that you can't seem to keep the personality. I know I'm not the same person any more as young Chuck Scranton
100 was, and I find that depressing. I could meet little Charlie on the beach today and say, "Look, there goes a sharp kid." And never recognize him if you see what I mean. It's a shame.

I don't like the jog back so much, as all the
105 people are coming out. Lying around, surfing, cruising, shooting up, tricking. Hell, the things I've seen on that sand, I could tell you a few stories. Sometimes I like to go down to El Segundo or Redondo beach just to feel normal.
110 I usually park the car on Santa Monica Palisades. I tidy up, change into my clothes and shave. I have a small battery-powered electric razor that I use. Then I have a beer, wander around, buy a newspaper. Mostly I then drive north to Malibu.
115 There's a place I know where you can get a fair view of a longish stretch of the beach. It's almost impossible to get down there in summer; they don't like strangers. So I pull off the highway and climb this small dune-hill. I have a pair of opera glasses
120 of my aunt's that I use to see better – my eyesight's not too hot. I spotted Rod Steiger one day, and Jane Fonda. I think but I can't be sure, the glasses tend to fuzz everything a bit over four hundred yards. Anyway I like the quiet on that dune, it's restful.
125 I have been down on to Malibu beach, but only in the winter season. The houses are all shut up but you can still get the feel of it. Some people were having a bar-b-q one day. It looked good. They had a fire going on a big porch that jutted out high over

130 the sand. They waved and shouted when I went past.

Lunch is bad. The worst part of the day for me because I have to go home. I live with my aunt. I call her my aunt though I'm not related to her
135 at all. She was my mother's companion. I believe that's the right word – until my mother stuffed her face with a gross of Seconal one afternoon in a motel at Corona del Mar. I was fifteen then and Vanessa – my 'aunt' – became some kind of legal
140 guardian to me and had control of all the money I'd made from 'The Scrantons'. Well, she bought an apartment in Beverly Glen because she liked the address. Man, was she swallowed by the realtor. They build these tiny apartment blocks on cliff-
145 faces of bug-name canyons just so you can say you live off Mulholland Drive or in Bel Air. It's a load. I'd rather live in Watts or on Imperial highway. I practically have to rope-up and wear crampons to get to my front door. And it's mine. I paid for it.
150 Maybe that's why Vanessa never leaves her bed. It's just too much effort getting in and out of the house. She just stays in bed all day and eats, watches TV and feeds her two dogs. I only go in there for lunch; it's my only 'family' ritual. I take a glass of
155 milk and a salad sandwich but she phones out for pizza and enchiladas and burgers – any kind she can smear over her face and down her front. She's really grown fat in the ten years since my mother bombed out. But she still sits up in bed with those
160 hairy yipping dogs under her armpits, and she's got her top and bottom false eyelashes, her hairpiece and purple lipstick on. I say nothing usually. For someone who never gets out she sure can talk a lot. She wears these tacky satin and lace peignoirs, show
165 half her chest. Her arms look like a couple of Indian clubs rolling around under the shimmer. It's unfair I suppose, but when I drive back into the foothills I like to think I'm going to have a luncheon date with . . . with someone like Grace Kelly – as was – or
170 maybe Alexis Smith. I don't know. I wouldn't mind a meal and a civilized conversation with some nice people like that. But lunch with Vanessa? Thanks for nothing, pal. God, you can keep it. She's a real klutz. I'm sure Grace and Alexis would never let
175 themselves get that way – you know, like Vanessa's always dropping tacos down her cleavage or smearing mustard on her chins.

I always get depressed after lunch. It figures, I hear you say. I go to my room and sometimes
180 I have a drink (I don't smoke, so dope's out). Other days I play my guitar or else work on my screenplay. It's called 'Walk. Don't Walk'. I get a lot

of good ideas after lunch for some reason. That's when I got the idea for my screenplay. It just came to me. I remembered how I'd been stuck one day at the corner of Arteria Boulevard and Normandie Avenue. There was a pile of traffic and the pedestrian signs were going berserk. 'Walk' would come on so I'd start across. Two seconds later 'Don't Walk' so I go back. Then on comes 'Walk' again. This went on for ten minutes: 'Walk. Don't Walk. Walk. Don't Walk.' I was practically out of my box. But what really stunned me was the way I just stayed there and obeyed the goddam machine for so long – I never even thought about going it alone. Then one afternoon after lunch it came to me that it was a neat image of life; just the right kind of metaphor for the whole can of worms. The final scene of this movie is going to be a slow crane shot away from this malfunctioning traffic sign going 'Walk. Don't Walk.' Then the camera pulls further up and away in a helicopter and you see that in fact the whole city is fouled up because of this one sign flashing. They don't know what to do; the programming's gone wrong. It's a great final scene. Only problem is I'm having some difficulty writing my way towards it. Still, it'll come, I guess.

In the late afternoon I go to work. I work at the Beverly Hills Hotel. Vanessa's brother-in-law got me the job. I park cars. I keep hoping I'm going to park the car of someone really important. Frank – that's Vanessa's brother-in-law – will say to me, "Give this one a shine-up, Charlie, it belongs to so-and-so, he produced this film," or "That guy's the money behind X's new movie," or "Look out, he's Senior Vice-President of Something incorporated." I say big deal. These guys hand me the keys – they all look like bank clerks. If that's the movies nowadays I'm not so sure I want back in.

Afternoons are quiet at the hotel so I catch up on my reading. I'm reading Camus at the moment but I think I've learnt all I can from him so I'm going on to Jung. I don't know too much about Jung but I'm told he was really into astrology which has always been a pet interest of mine. One thing I will say for quitting the movies when I did means that I didn't miss out on my education. I hear that some of these stars today are really dumb; you know, they've got their brains in the neck and points south.

After work I drive back down to the Santa Monica pier and think about what I'm going to do all night. The Santa Monica pier is a kind of special place for me: it's the last place I saw my wife and son. I got married at seventeen and was divorced by twenty-two, though we were apart for a couple of years before that. Her name was Harriet. It was okay for a while but I don't think she liked Vanessa. Anyway, get this. She left me for a guy who was the assistant manager in the credit collection department of a large mail order firm. I couldn't believe it when she told me. I said to her when she moved out that it had to be the world's most boring job and did she know what she was getting into? I mean, what sort of person do you have to be to take on that kind of work? The bad thing was she took my son Skiff with her. It's a dumb name I know, but at the time he was born all the kids were being called things like Sky and Saffron and Powie, and I was really sold on sailing. I hope he doesn't hold it against me.

The divorce was messy and she got custody, though I'll never understand why. She had left some clothes at the house and wanted them back so she suggested we meet at the end of the Santa Monica pier for some reason. I didn't mind, it was the impetuous side to her nature that first attracted me. I handed the clothes over. She was a bit tense. Skiff was running about; he didn't seem to know who I was. She was smoking a lot; those long thin menthol cigarettes. I really didn't say anything much at all, asked how she was, what school Skiff was going to. Then she just burst out, "Take a good look, Charlie, then don't come near us ever again!" Her exact words. Then they went away.

So I go down to the end of the pier most nights and look out at the ocean and count the planes going in to land at LA International and try to work things out. Just the other evening I wandered up the beach a way and this thin-faced man with short grey hair came up to me and said, "Jordan, is that you?" And when he saw he'd made a mistake he smiled a nice smile, apologized and walked off. It was only this morning that I thought it might have been Christopher Isherwood himself. The more I think about it the more convinced I become. What a perfect opportunity and I had to go and miss it. As I say; 'Walk. Don't Walk.' That's the bottom line.

I suppose I must have been preoccupied. The pier brings back all these memories like some private video-loop, and my head gets to feel like it's full of birds all flapping around trying to get out. And also things haven't been so good lately. On Friday Frank told me not to bother showing up at the hotel next week, I can't seem to make any headway with the screenplay and for the last three nights Vanessa's tried to climb into my bed.

Well, tonight I think I'll drive to this small bar I know on Sunset. Nothing too great, a little dark. They do a nice white wine with peach slices in it, and I hear tell that Bobby de Niro sometimes shows up for a drink.

William Boyd, *On the Yankee Station*, 1982

1   Where does the story take place?

2   When does the story take place? How do you know?

3   Who do you think Christopher Isherwood is, and why does the narrator want to meet him?

4   At the beginning of the story, what does the narrator say about himself? At what point does the reader find out the narrator's name?

5   How does the narrator describe the girl who works at the café in Venice? Look at the adjectives used and discuss their **connotations**: do they present her in a positive light? Why? Would all readers worldwide have the same opinion?

6   The narrator says, 'I'm pretty sure she is on something heavy. So that doesn't make her anything special but she can't be more than eighteen.' What does this suggest about the girl? What does this suggest about the narrator? What does this suggest about the setting of the story?

7   After the short dialogue with Jayette, the narrator describes his career. Does this change the way you see him? Why?

8   What interpretation of Jayette's question does the narrator offer?

9   How much interaction does the narrator have with other people? What conclusion can you draw?

10 What is the relationship between the narrator and Vanessa like? How does he describe her? What feelings are mentioned? What does he mean by saying 'She's a real klutz'?

11 Talking about his screenplay, what does the narrator see as a **metaphor** for his life?

12 Where does the narrator work in the afternoons? How does he feel about it?

13 Well into the story and after listing mundane events, the narrator reveals why Santa Monica is a special place for him. What happened there?

14 How did the narrator feel about the reasons his wife had for leaving him?

15 Why does the narrator go to Santa Monica pier?

16 'I suppose I must have been preoccupied' (line 278) is how the narrator explains why he misses an important opportunity. Find another phrase in the story suggesting that the narrator is unable to take an active role in his own life.

17 At the end of the story, what three factors does the narrator list as causing him problems? What do these factors foreshadow?

18 In what mood does the narrator conclude his story?

Appreciating literary features

1   Read the opening paragraph. How does the narrator create a connection between himself and the audience? What words or expressions show he wants to convince his audience?

2   Why is the first paragraph written in the past tense, but the rest of the story presented in the present tense?

3   The title of the story appears as the first line the narrator speaks in a dialogue with Jayette. Find the other lines which mark dialogue in the story. What conclusion can you make?

4   The story includes names of real actors and actresses but also fictitious names. How does this affect your reading of the story? What do you think the author is saying?

5   Why does the narrator mention meal times throughout the story?

6   Three women are introduced in the story. What do they mean to the narrator? What roles do they have in the narrator's life?

7   The saddest thing, according to the narrator, is that 'It seems to me that everybody in their life is at least two people.' How does Boyd's short story either defend or oppose this claim?

8   At Santa Monica pier, the narrator is mistaken for somebody called Jordan, probably by Christopher Isherwood. What does the author seem to suggest? Why does he recite the name of his screenplay in relation to possibly meeting Isherwood?

9   How does finding out about the real Christopher Isherwood affect your reading of the story? What effect does the **allusion** have on:
    a   how you see the narrator?
    b   how you understand Jayette's question "Lucked-out yet?"?
    c   how you interpret Boyd's short story?

10   Other allusions include Camus and Jung. How do these affect the reader?

Christopher Isherwood (1904–1986) was a British-born novelist and playwright who lived and worked in California.

At the age of 48, he met a teenager called Don Bachardy on the beach. The two men became inseparable, and eventually set up a hill-side home in Santa Monica. With many friends in Hollywood, the couple was well-known in Californian society.

For further discussion: Research information on Isherwood's novel *A Single Man* (1964) to see parallels in the texts.

AFTER YOU READ

1 What do you see as the most important points in the story? Why? Summarize the story
   a in fewer than 100 words.
   b in fewer than 10 statements (or bullet points).

2 Describe the narrator.
   a How does he spend his day? What objectives does he have and does he succeed in his pursuits? Why?
   b Imagine you are the agent who is helping him to find work as an actor on TV. Write an email to a casting director introducing your client. What roles do you think he would be best suited for?
   c Look up the following words in a dictionary and discuss their meaning and connotations. To what degree do they fit the narrator's description?

strong	obstinate	vivacious	bitter	talented	impetuous	warm
honest	broken	ambitious	withdrawn	disillusioned	normal	sad

3 Based on your interpretation, what does the author want to say with this short story?
   a Design a poster for the story.
   b Write out your take on the **theme** as a statement.

4 Revisit your thoughts about the title. Has the meaning changed? Why?

5 Did the story meet your expectations? Why?

Reflection point

- Which linguistic elements did you find difficult to understand?
  ▸ Make a list of new vocabulary and structures.
- What skills did you need to interpret the story?
  ▸ What is expected from the reader?
  ▸ Make a list of literary features.
- How does Boyd's story link with the core topics of communication and media, global issues and social relationships?
- Draw a mindmap to illustrate the links between the story and core topics.
- How does Boyd's story relate to the options you have studied: cultural diversity, customs and traditions, health, leisure, and science and technology?
- How did the story make you feel? Why?
- Can you identify with the author's life or situation?

Read the text titled *From Dark* carefully.
Use your active reading skills to:
→ predict both the content and the conventions of the text; reflect on your expectations.
→ reflect on your comprehension of the text.
→ reflect on your interpretation of the text.
→ keep an eye on new vocabulary and structures.
→ keep an eye on how the text works as a whole.
→ keep an eye on literary features.

From Dark

Already for two months the men had lived underground, unable to tell day from night, working and sleeping in darkness; [1] that when the cave-in occurred, preventing them from escape, nothing altered for them. What had been black and shadow remained as it had been, [2] did the heat, and the
5　smell of rock.

Nine men remained in a small chamber. They had water and food, and torchlight [3] the batteries ran out. Four of them had worked legally, before losing their jobs, along with 50,000 others. They spoke of their rescue [4] confidence and shared stories about their families, their children. But the
10　experienced ones, those who had mined the abandoned shafts previously, remained silent, knowing that many would have died in the collapse, and [5] those few who had escaped would not go for help in fear of arrest. The syndicate bosses, they knew, would do nothing. Fresh workers were easy enough to recruit.

15　Youngsters, 14, 15, 17, watched the two groups of men, trying to gauge what their own reactions should be. They had come down the mines during the school holidays, extending their vacations so that they could make money to take back to their families. Underground they suffered. Thoughts of soccer, of girls and of the sky stayed with them. They missed home-cooking and sweets.
20　Hawkers, sent by the bosses, sold them food at prices too frightening for them to say out loud. In the first week the boys watched with fascination as the men pulled out bankrolls of hundreds to buy a few beers. [6] soon, as their wages came and as the heat of the place entered muscle and bone, they [7] bought beer, unflinchingly. Working naked in the heat, slamming their picks into rock,
25　their bodies ached and changed. Muscles formed where none had been and they watched each others' frames spreading out, thickening. In the dark they had become men.

Karen Jennings, South Africa
Regional Winner for Africa
Commonwealth Short Story Competition, 2010

Based on your reading of the text, answer the questions below.

Vocabulary

1 Use your own words to explain or give synonyms for the following words from the text.
   a cave-in (line 2)
   b abandoned (line 10)
   c gauge (line 15)
   d Hawkers (line 20)
   e unflinchingly (line 24)
   f frames (line 26)

2 For each of the following, find a word or expression from the text that is similar in meaning.
   a not capable
   b not allowing
   c stayed
   d together with
   e being afraid of
   f stretching
   g great interest and curiosity
   h hitting very hard
   i become more solid

Structures

3 The text is missing some words. Choose from the list below to fill the gaps [1]–[7].
   A and   F so
   B but   G as
   C by   H too
   D that   I until
   E with   J then

4 To what or whom does 'they' refer in line 13 in the second paragraph?

5 To what or whom does 'their' refer in line 16 in the third paragraph?

Comprehension

6 Decide whether each of the following statements are true or false and justify your answers with a relevant quotation from the text.
   a The men had just started their work underground.
   b The strong lights were dimmed at night so the men could sleep better.
   c The miners had something to eat and drink.
   d Most of the men had had legal jobs.
   e All the men preferred to be silent after the cave-in.
   f The experienced men were afraid no one would come to help them.
   g The youngsters were working without pay.
   h The youngsters enjoyed working underground.
   i Food was sold at discount prices to teenage miners.
   j Physical work made the youngsters grow muscles.

Literary features

7 In the first paragraph, what senses are evoked in the description of the cave? How does this affect the reader?

8 How do you interpret the title? Why is it *From Dark* and not *In Dark* or *Into Dark*?

For the next three questions, choose the best option to complete the sentence.

9 By revealing the experienced men's thoughts, the narrator…
   a lightens the tone of the story.
   b increases the tension in the story.
   c attacks the class system and the arrogant new workers.
   d ridicules the naivety of the younger miners.

10 'The youngsters missing soccer, girls, the sky above, home-cooking and sweets…'
   a emphasizes the difference between them and the rest of the miners.
   b reveals how miserable life underground is and how miners dream of a normal life.
   c proves they are desperate to become men.
   d is in contrast with their adult-like behaviour.

11 In this story, growing up…
   a is a happy event encouraged by peer support.
   b is only achieved through suffering and mental sacrifice.
   c is a brutal competition where only the strongest survive.
   d can be a mysterious and involuntary result of a twist of fate.

Poems on the underground

1   Look at the structure of the poem below. What observations can you make?

2   What is repeated in the poem? What effect does the repetition have?

3   What images are created in the poem? Which senses are evoked?

4   In line 8, the drunk and the crazy 'Aspire to converse.' Why has the poet not said simply, 'Want to talk'?

5   What is meant by the poet perusing his poem among the adverts (lines 9–10)?

6   To what time and place does the poem take us? Why?

7   What does the poem say about
    a people?
    b people in small spaces?
    c people's behaviour towards one other?

8   What is the tone of the poem? Take turns to read the poem aloud. Change the tone and emphasize different details.

9   Imagine turning this poem into a song. What instruments would you use? What would the beat and the rhythm be like? Who would you choose as the vocalist?

10   Draw a comic based on the poem.

Poem on the Underground

Proud readers
Hide behind tall newspapers.
The young are all arms and legs
Knackered by youth.
Tourists sit bolt upright
Trusting in nothing.
Only the drunk and the crazy
Aspire to converse.
Only the poet
Peruses his poem among the adverts.
Only the elderly person
Observes the request that the seat be offered to an elderly person.

D. J. Enright (1920–2002)
New Poems on the Underground, 2006

Do you sometimes wonder who the strangers around you are?

This novel happens in London, England, on an underground train.
There are seven carriages on a Bakerloo Line train, each with 36 seats.

Car 1, seat 20: Mrs Joy Harvey

Outward appearance

Polished black woman. Huge coils of hair, like someone out of *Dynasty*. Burgundy business jacket, yellow sweater. She looks enraged and keeps pulling down on her sweater.

Inside information

Works in a one-stop shop for the Council. Today her mobile surgery will be held at the Wasteco Superstore in the Elephant and Castle. The surgery was set up to provide information about local events and the Council's activities. But people want services instead of information. Joy has become a one-stop advocate for the illiterate who have received a final Council Tax demand, the aged who aren't claiming benefit, the young men who can't get a council flat, people who can't get their garbage collected, etc.

What she is doing or thinking

She is looking at the obviously homeless man next to her. She deliberately sat next to him in case no one else would. She takes in his stained, rumpled trousers, the tiny woman's coat, the thin shirt, the shoes with white water marks. Poor man, look, he's shaved and washed. He's spent money to clean himself up and he probably could have used it for food. And look at people, wrinkling their noses at him. Aren't they horrible.

"Are you all right?" she asks. He looks around at her in misery. "Are you all right?" she asks again, touching her new purse.

"No, no," he pleads, holding up his hands. "I don't need anything."

Good, she thinks, that's good. Pride. She receives an energizing jolt of anger that will see her through another day. She pulls down again on her sweater.

Car 1, seat 21: Mr Justin Holmes

Outward appearance

Homeless person. Ill fitting, flimsy clothes. His coat is orange with black fur trim, and is too small for him. The shirt is thin summer cotton and is missing a button, showing his pale tummy. His hair is curious – it is disordered but layered.

Inside information

Freelance journalist posing as a homeless person. He has spent the last week in the concourse under Waterloo Bridge roundabout. Slept two nights in a cardboard box with an older longhair who made a pass at him but was easily deflected. Moved to a doorway in the Strand. Last night spent some of the money hidden in his shoe to shower in Waterloo Station. Went home. His flat was dark and locked. The porter came with spare keys. The locks had been changed.

Justin is now homeless for real. He will wash again at Waterloo and go to Lambeth North police station.

What he is doing or thinking

He remembers his girlfriend's face. "You can borrow my old coat, but don't expect me here when you get back," she told him. He has no ID, no keys, no plastic and only five pounds left. When has he ever been fingerprinted? How can you prove who you are?

The woman next to him is talking. He looks around. "Are you all right?" she asks, about to give him money. A terrible sense of fraudulence comes over him, and he pleads with her to put away the money, the sympathy.

He remembers his girlfriend's face, and understands. He wants to go home.

He thinks of his article.

Geoff Ryman, *253*
www.ryman-novel.com

The HL Written Assignment (1)

1 Start by reading the excerpt on page 103 from Geoff Ryman's novel *253* and answer these questions:

a What is the text about?

b What effect is created by presenting the text in three columns? How much freedom does the reader have in constructing the story?

c Is there a plot? How is this achieved? Are there any surprises?

d What does the text say about the individuals portrayed? What does it say about people's behaviour? What does it say about the society?

e How does the excerpt make you feel? Why?

2 Study the Language B HL Written Assignment assessment criteria carefully and keep them in mind throughout the writing process.

3 Now decide which text type you would like to use for your assignment. The completed assignment must be between 500 and 600 words, and you can choose from the following or decide on another text type:

- Article
- Interview
- Review
- Blog/Diary entry
- Introduction to debate, speech, talk, presentation
- Set of instructions, guidelines
- Brochure, leaflet, flyer, pamphlet, advertisement
- News report
- Written correspondence
- Essay
- Official report

For *253*, you could, for example, write:

a a series of letters between Joy Harvey and Justin Holmes after they have become friends or colleagues.

b a blog entry by Justin Holmes describing his week sleeping rough as a homeless person.

c a police report following an incident on the underground involving Joy Harvey and Justin Holmes.

d an interview with Joy Harvey or Justin Holmes after they started working together for a common cause.

e a speech given by Joy Harvey at a charity dinner organized by the Council.

4 Draft your **rationale**, which in 150 words introduces your assignment and explains the choices you have made. Remember:

a What is the focal point in your assignment? How is it linked to the excerpt and what is the relationship between them?

b What does your piece say about the excerpt? What features do you want to highlight?

c What does your piece have in common with the excerpt? How is it different? Why?

d Why did you choose your text type and audience?

5 Start writing your assignment. Keep an eye on your rationale and make sure you include all the features you mention.

6 Compare your assignment and the rationale. Do they work together? Make amendments where necessary.

7 Put your assignment aside. After a couple of days, read your assignment with fresh eyes and evaluate its effectiveness.
Revisit the assessment criteria and assess your work. In addition to proofreading, make any last-minute adjustments to your final copy.

The skills you have used in this exercise will become useful when you start working on your 'official' written assignment. Remember that your written assignment will be based on one of the two literary works studied in class.

Remember

You can also try drafting a rationale before deciding on a text type to see where your reading and interpretation naturally lead to.

Consider carefully whether the text type you have chosen allows you to illustrate best the features you mention in your rationale. Your creative piece and the rationale must support each other!

The HL Written Assignment (2)

1   Start by reading the poems on pages 106–109 and answer these questions:

   a   What are the poems about? What do they share? How are they different from each other? Why?

   b   Order the poems based on:
   - ease of language
   - their use of symbols and imagery
   - their structure or form
   - the tone of the poem on a scale, for example from light and good-humoured to dark and sombre
   - feeling(s) expressed in the poem
   - complexity of thought
   - how much you can identify with the thought presented in the poem: how is the common ground created?
   - your personal preference.

   c   What do the poems say about life under and above ground? What contrasts are made?

   d   What do the poems sound like? Read them aloud and listen to their different rhythms and pace. How does language achieve this?

   e   What role does the local setting play in the poems?

2   Study the Language B HL Written Assignment assessment criteria carefully and keep them in mind throughout the writing process.

3   Now decide which poem(s) you want to focus on. Then decide which text type to use for your piece of creative writing. The completed assignment must be between 500 and 600 words, and you can choose from the following or decide on another text type:
   - Article
   - Interview
   - Review
   - Blog/Diary entry
   - Introduction to debate, speech, talk, presentation
   - Set of instructions, guidelines
   - Brochure, leaflet, flyer, pamphlet, advertisement
   - News report
   - Written correspondence
   - Essay
   - Official report

   Based on these poems, you could, for example, write:

   a   an article on urban human relationships, to be published in a teen magazine

   b   an opening to a debate defending or opposing the argument 'Technology has not affected how humans behave'

   c   a series of entries in a blog titled 'Urban jungle'

   d   an essay titled, 'Hopes and dreams emerge from underground' to be posted at your school's website

   e   a humorous set of instructions for people who are attempting their first underground journey

   f   an interview with a character from one of the poems after they have visited the setting of another poem, to be published in an online creative writing journal

   g   a review of one or more poems, to be published in a literary supplement of your school magazine

   h   a speech to aspiring poets giving advice on writing poetry based on personal experiences.

4   Draft your **rationale**, which in 150 words introduces your assignment and explains the choices you have made.

   a   What is the focal point of your assignment? How is it linked to the excerpt and what is the relationship between them?

   b   What does your piece say about the excerpt? What features do you want to highlight?

   c   What does your piece have in common with the excerpt? How is it different? Why?

   d   Why did you choose your text type and audience?

5   Start writing your assignment. Keep an eye on your rationale and make sure you include all the features you mention.

6   Compare your assignment and the rationale. Do they work together? Make amendments where necessary.

7   Put your assignment aside. After a couple of days, read your assignment with fresh eyes and evaluate its effectiveness. Revisit the assessment criteria and assess your work. In addition to proofreading, make any last-minute adjustments to your final copy.

The skills you have used in this exercise will become useful when you start working on your 'official' Written Assignment. Remember that your Written Assignment will be based on one of the two literary works studied in class.

The Delhi Metro

The doors slid open
And I stepped in…
What a great relief it was
To be so far away
From the madding crowds,
The smoke and the chaotic traffic,
The rashly driven blueline buses,
The stray cattle on the roads…

The doors closed
And the train started gliding…
What a great relief it was
To be so far away
From the scorching heat,
The terribly long power cuts,
The little, gnawing worries,
The daily drudgery of existence…

I spotted a vacant seat
And I sat down…
What a great relief it was
To see
Everything so spotlessly clean;
Not a single scratch,
Not a single speck of dust,
Not a single perverted message
Scratched on the walls…

I relaxed
And I began to daydream…
What a great relief it was
To let
My thoughts wander
Like naughty, restless children
Swing up into the sky,
Ride on the clouds
Run on the green grass…

The train stopped
And I woke up with a start…
What a great shock it was
To find
I had reached my "stop."
On the opposite seat
Sat a newly-married couple
Still too engrossed with each other
Oblivious to everything else…

The doors slid open
And I stepped out…
What a rude contrast it was
To be back
Into the madding crowds,
The smoke and the chaotic traffic
The rashly-driven blueline buses
The stray cattle on the roads…

Jasbir Chatterjee

Subway Wind

Far down, down through the city's great, gaunt gut,
    The gray train rushing bears the weary wind;
In the packed cars the fans the crowd's breath cut,
    Leaving the sick and heavy air behind.
And pale-cheeked children seek the upper door
    To give their summer jackets to the breeze;
Their laugh is swallowed in the deafening roar
    Of captive wind that moans for fields and seas;
Seas cooling warm where native schooners drift
    Through sleepy waters, while gulls wheel and sweep,
Waiting for windy waves the keels to lift
    Lightly among the islands of the deep;
Islands of lofty palm trees blooming white
    That lend their perfume to the tropic sea,
Where fields lie idle in the dew drenched night,
    And the Trades float above them fresh and free.

Claude McKay

The Underground

There we were in the vaulted tunnel running,
You in your going-away coat speeding ahead
And me, me then like a fleet god gaining
Upon you before you turned to a reed
Or some new white flower japped with crimson
As the coat flapped wild and button after button
Sprang off and fell in a trail
Between the Underground and the Albert Hall.
Honeymooning, moonlighting, late for the Proms,
Our echoes die in that corridor and now
I come as Hansel came on the moonlit stones
Retracing the path back, lifting the buttons
To end up in a draughty lamplit station
After the trains have gone, the wet track
Bared and tensed as I am, all attention
For your step following and damned if I look back.

Seamus Heaney

On the Subway

The boy and I face each other.
His feet are huge, in black sneakers
laced with white in a complex pattern like a
a set of intentional scars. We are stuck on
opposite sides of the car, a couple of
molecules stuck in a rod of light
rapidly moving through darkness. He has the
casual cold look of a mugger,
alert under hooded lids. He is wearing
red, like the inside of the body
exposed. I am wearing dark fur, the
whole skin of an animal taken and
used. I look at his raw face,
he looks at my fur coat, and I didn't
know if I am in his power –
he could take my coat so easily, my
briefcase, my life –
or if he is in my power, the way I am
living off his life, eating the steak
he does not eat, as if I am taking
the food from his mouth. And he is black
and I am white, and without meaning or
trying to I must profit from his darkness,
the way he absorbs the murderous beams of the
nation's heart, as black cotton
absorbs the heat of the sun and holds it. There is
no way to know how easy this
white skin makes my life, this
life he could take so easily and
break across his knee like a stick the way
his own back is being broken, the
rob of his soul that at birth was dark and
fluid and rich as the heart of a seedling
ready to thrust up into any available light.

Sharon Olds

Underground Train

every day we
feed our tokens into the turnstile
slot machines for the chance
to hang like ornaments
suspended
from the hand-straps
of the meteor-rocket subway line

herded
into standing room only
we sway on our platform shoes
eye-ball to eye-ball
with the advertising poster
that extols the virtues of a
pink flamingo land
in acknowledgment
there lurks the green-eyed
monster alligator
underneath the sunflower seeds
that crackle under our feet

in the back of the car
young punks rattle the bones
a throw of dice
as a grizzled old man who sleeps
keeps time with his tapping bunny
slippers
twitches, moans and jerks
wakes up muttering
"it ain't vanilla!"
to stare red-rimmed into the past
thousand yards

we all for a moment blink
when dark flashes into the neon life
of a terminal station

Wordancer

Round and round the London Underground

Round and round the London Underground
Interrupted by the braking screeching sounds
Round and round the circle line

The London Underground
With its stops is an elongated list
Drunks battle in tunnels with open fists
Hidden somewhere is a network of CCTV Cameras
Recording your every move from afar
Watch out for the picker-pockets, I insist
They swindle even the most experienced tourist

Inside the trains, shine disoriented faces
Bodies usually squeezed into tight spaces
'Please stand clear of the door'
It is an advice not yet a law

Stations by station, trains pass by
Stuck in a tunnel, let out a sigh
Train timetables from my perception
Is regularity, and a common deception

Round and round the London Underground
Interrupted by the braking screeching sounds
Round and round the circle line

Bored, read the metro
It is free, when displayed on show
For those who know
Where to go
Plan your alternative routes
Prepare for train strikes and disputes
Check out the cancellation signs
May your journey be divine!

Sylvia Chidi

In a Subway Station

After a year I came again to the place;
The tireless lights and the reverberation,
The angry thunder of trains that burrow the ground,
The hunted, hurrying people were still the same –
But oh, another man beside me and not you!
Another voice and other eyes in mine!
And suddenly I turned and saw again
The gleaming curve of tracks, the bridge above –
They were burned deep into my heart before,
The night I watched them to avoid your eyes,
When you were saying, "Oh, look up at me!"
When you were saying, "Will you never love me?"
And when I answered with a lie. Oh then
You dropped your eyes. I felt your utter pain.
I would have died to say the truth to you.
After a year I came again to the place –
The hunted hurrying people were still the same...

Sara Teasdale

On the metro

On the metro, I have to ask a young woman to move the packages beside her to make room for me;
she's reading, her foot propped on the seat in front of her, and barely looks up as she pulls them to her.
I sit, take out my own book – Cioran, *The Temptation to Exist* – and notice her glancing up from hers
to take in the title of mine, and then, as Gombrowicz puts it, she "affirms herself physically," that is,
becomes present in a way she hadn't been before: though she hasn't moved, she's allowed herself
to come more sharply into focus, be more accessible to my sensual perception, so I can't help but remark
her strong figure and very tan skin – (how literally golden young women can look at the end of summer).
She leans back now, and as the train rocks and her arm brushes mine she doesn't pull it away;
she seems to be allowing our surfaces to unite: the fine hairs on both our forearms, sensitive, alive,
achingly alive, bring news of someone touched, someone sensed, and thus acknowledged, known.

I understand that in no way is she offering more than this, and in truth I have no desire for more,
but it's still enough for me to be taken by a surge, first of warmth then of something like its opposite:
a memory – a girl I'd mooned for from afar, across the table from me in the library in school now,
our feet I thought touching, touching even again, and then, with all I craved that touch to mean,
my having to realize it wasn't her flesh my flesh for that gleaming time had pressed, but a table leg.
The young woman today removes her arm now, stands, swaying against the lurch of the slowing train,
and crossing before me brushes my knee and does that thing again, asserts her bodily being again,
(Gombrowicz again), then quickly moves to the door of the car and descends, not once looking back,
(to my relief not looking back), and I allow myself the thought that though I must be to her again
as senseless as that table of my youth, as wooden, as unfeeling, perhaps there was a moment I was not.

C. K. Williams

TOK

落叶哀蝉曲
LI FU-JEN

刘彻
Wu-ti

罗 袂 兮 无 声，

玉 墀 兮 尘 生。

虚 房 冷 而 寂 寞，

落 叶 依 于 重 扃。

望 彼 美 之 女 兮，

安 得 感 余 心 之 未 宁！

This Chinese poem called *Li Fu-jen* was written by Wu-ti, sixth emperor of the Han dynasty (206 BC–220 AD) on the death of his mistress, Li Fu-jen. Unable to bear his grief, he sent for magicians from all parts of China, hoping that they would be able to put him into communication with her spirit.

Here are two English versions of the poem. They are quite different from one another.

Falling Leaves and the Sadness of the Cicada's Song

The sound of her silk skirt has stopped.

On the marble pavement dust grows.

Her empty room is cold and still.

Fallen leaves are piled against the doors.

Longing for that lovely lady

How can I bring my aching heart to rest?

Arthur Waley

To the Air: "The Fallen Leaves and the Plaintive Cicada"

There is not rustle of silken sleeves,

Dust gathers in the Jade Courtyard,

The empty houses are cold, still, without sound.

The leaves fall and lie upon the bars of doorway after doorway.

I long for the Most Beautiful One; how can I attain my desire?

Pain bursts my heart. There is no peace.

Amy Lowell

List the similarities you can find between the two translations.

Use the different TOK Ways of Knowing (language, sense perception, reason, and emotion) to analyse the two poems to see how the meaning of each is different. You may want to use a table like the one below. Although the translated poems are based on the same original text, do they convey the same messages? What does this suggest about translation?

Ways of knowing	Falling Leaves and the Sadness of the Cicada's Song	To the Air: "The Fallen Leaves and the Plaintive Cicada"
Logic How is the poem organized? What is its structure?		
Sense perception What sights, smells, sounds, and touch sensations can you find?		
Language What do you notice about the writer's choice of vocabulary and use of imagery? Which ambiguities and metaphors does the writer use?		
Emotion What feelings does the speaker have towards the woman?		

CAS

Does your school have a newspaper or a magazine, printed or online, which could publish your poems, short stories, or other creative writing pieces? You could also contribute towards the culture of reading and intercultural understanding at your school by sharing reading tips and reviews. Another idea would be to set up a literary club or a blog in which you could read and discuss classics or contemporary works in English. Finally, how about translating a literary text (e.g. a series of poems, song lyrics, a short story, an extract of a novel) which has affected you as a reader?

The individual oral (HL/ SL)

Imagine you are an English B teacher for a day. Your students will be taking their individual oral exams today, and your task is to come up with titles or captions which will help your students describe the photo below. Fill in a table like the one below with your titles or captions. Some examples are given in the table.

Option	Title or caption
Cultural diversity	Do actions speak louder than words?
Customs and traditions	And they lived happily ever after
Health	Did you hear the one about the princess and the frog?
Leisure	Similar interests bring people together
Science and technology	Alone at last! Hearing you loud and clear

What would you expect your students to know or say? Base your expectations on the Language B Individual Oral assessment criteria. Now choose your students and start examining!

Text booklet

Text A

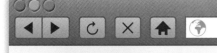

Clean Water Campaign 'I'm In'
2011 ESSAY CONTEST
District-wide Winner: $100 Cash!
County Winners: $25 Cash!
<u>Deadline: September 30, 2011</u>

www.cleanwatercampaign.com

www.mydropcounts.org

Sponsored by the Metropolitan North Georgia Water Planning District

Sixth, seventh, and eighth graders in Bartow, Cherokee, Clayton, Cobb, Coweta, DeKalb, Douglas, Fayette, Fulton, Forsyth, Gwinnett, Hall, Henry, Paulding, and Rockdale counties are invited to participate in the annual essay contest promoting better water quality and water conservation practices in the metro Atlanta area.

ESSAY TOPICS

Essays may be handwritten or typed. Students should write a **300 to 500**-word essay about how citizens can protect water quality in rivers and lakes and conserve water (at home, school or in the community). The essay must include why
5 **both** water quality protection and water conservation are important. Students must also explain how they would begin making a difference in their communities.

Essays **must** answer **one** of the following questions:

1. What are the most important messages concerning water
10 pollution and conservation? What would you want the public to do to prevent water pollution and promote conservation?

2. What kind of plan would you create to further the protection and conservation of our water resources at
15 home?

3. What would you want elected officials to do about water quality and conservation? What concerns would you want to communicate to them?

4. What would our lives be like with very little water or
20 very polluted water resources? What are the benefits of protecting the quality and quantity of our water supply?

5. What can *you* do in your community to protect and conserve Atlanta's water?

GUIDELINES

- Each school may only submit one essay per grade level to
25 the contest – please select the best essay(s) to represent your school.
- Each essay must be submitted with attached entry form.
- All essays must be received no later than **September 30, 2011**. Submit essays via:
30 Email: info@cleanwatercampaign.com
    or
    Mail: Clean Water Campaign
         Attn: Water Essay 2011 Contest
         40 Courtland Street, NE
35   Atlanta, GA 30303
    or
    Fax: 678-726-0775

AWARDS

[X] essays submitted will be acknowledged. One county
40 winner from **[9]** of the 15 counties will be selected to receive $25 and a certificate. The District-wide winner will be selected from the county winners to receive the grand prize – **[10]** engraved plaque and $100! Winners will be notified by October 7, 2011.

JUDGING
45
Essays will be judged on content, creativity, and organization. Essays should include discussion of both water quality and conservation. Essays without complete name and contact information will be disqualified.

For more information concerning the essay contest, please contact Charlene Njoroge at 404-463-3259 or cnjoroge@atlantaregional.com.

Text B

Foods of the Irish

Irish food is known for the quality and freshness of its ingredients. Most cooking is done without herbs or spices, except for salt and pepper. Foods are usually served without sauce or gravy. The staples of the Irish diet have traditionally been potatoes, grains (especially oats), and dairy products. Potatoes still appear at most Irish meals, with potato scones, similar to biscuits or muffins, a specialty in the north. The Irish have also been accomplished cheesemakers for centuries. Ireland makes about fifty types of homemade "farmhouse" cheeses, which are considered delicacies.

Soups of all types, seafood, and meats also play important roles in the Irish diet. Irish soups are thick, hearty, and filling, with potatoes, seafood, and various meats being common ingredients. Since their country is surrounded by water, the Irish enjoy many types of seafood, including salmon, scallops, lobster, mussels, and oysters. However, meat is eaten more frequently at Irish meals. The most common meats are beef, lamb, and pork.

Irish stew has been recognized as the national dish for at least two centuries. A poem from the early 1800s praised Irish stew for satisfying the hunger of anyone who ate it:

Then hurrah for an Irish Stew
That will stick to your belly like glue.

Bread is an important part of Irish culture. Fresh soda bread, a crusty brown bread made from whole-wheat flour and buttermilk, is another national dish of Ireland. Irish bakers don't stop with soda bread, however. They bake a wide variety of other hearty breads and cakes.

The most common everyday beverage in Ireland is tea. It is served with scones, probably the most popular snack in Ireland. Popular alcoholic beverages include whiskey, beer, stout and ale. Coffee mixed with whiskey and whipped cream is known throughout the world as "Irish coffee."

Meals bring the people together

The Irish value hospitality, and generous portions of food are common at home and in restaurants. A large breakfast was traditionally eaten in rural Ireland. Common breakfast foods included soda bread, pancakes, porridge, eggs, and various meat products. A full old-fashioned country breakfast might include fresh fruit juice, porridge, a "mixed grill" of breakfast meats and black pudding, scones, and soda bread with butter and preserves, tea, and coffee with hot milk.

Dinner, the main meal of the day, used to be eaten at lunchtime. A typical dish was "Dublin coddle," a bacon, sausage, potato, and onion soup. Today, however, many Irish people eat lighter meals in the morning and at midday. They have their main meal later in the day, **[18]** they come home from work or school. Lunch is **[19]** a bowl of hot soup that is served with freshly baked soda bread. **[20]**, many pubs still serve the traditional large midday dinner. "Supper" in Ireland means a late-night snack. A typical supper is a slice of bread with butter and a glass of milk.

www.foodbycountry.com

Text C

Proper etiquette of social networking

Etiquette is the type of broadly interpreted social science that can inspire an entire book worth of tips, understandings and precedents.
5 However, we only have time to provide the basics of social media etiquette in this feature. There are multiple disciplines of proper etiquette, including behavior
10 concerning social media websites and portable devices in the office, as well as how to generally "type" to people online. The main focus of this article is to share how one
15 goes about presenting himself or herself as a professional company.

Being a friend first, a company second

While there are various instances
20 of impoliteness on social media, the one golden rule everyone must abide by is that social media doesn't tolerate spam. If you spam a person's page
25 or post a comment advertising your services, you will probably find your comments deleted and your ID blocked as a friend forever. Social media is a walled
30 paradise away from the "hard sell" business world outside and the last thing anyone wants to see is an unsolicited advertisement.

How then do you go about
35 "advertising" without advertising? Usually by way of sharing helpful and objective information about your industry; posting about incentives, discounts or gifts to
40 your customers; company news, local shows, new directions, new campaigns; multimedia content;

sharing links to third party sites that fit in with your message and
45 are objective.

You can also modestly advertise by showing yourself to be an expert in your field, one who doesn't need to advertise or
50 beg for attention. You focus on establishing credibility and creating brand awareness – not on making promises or bragging about your accomplishments.

55 Social media interaction etiquette

When the time to make friends and spread goodwill through cyberspace comes, make sure
60 you approach your pages and their pages professionally and respectfully. This not only requires a positive and dignified manner of speaking, but also requires some
65 tact when it comes to talking with the community.

Make the effort to fill out your profile page completely, if for no other reason than to link people
70 back to your sales website. Explain the type of person you want to befriend on your profile so that there are no misunderstandings. It is similarly impolite to befriend
75 people randomly without any introduction or explanation as to who you are. While you can take a chance and "add" a person based on just his/her likable profile,
80 never start selling your business immediately after adding, because this will forever associate you as a spammer.

Make sure that all posts are
85 dignified, relevant and politically correct. Not only should you reflect honor and discretion in your posts, but you should also make sure that you are not forwarding
90 a profuse number of messages to your friends or sending out time-wasting posts.

Following these tips can help build your brand awareness over
95 time, and more importantly, build your brand trust amongst the community. What tips would you suggest?

Karriann Graf, 7 June 2011
www.karrianngraf.com/
proper-etiquette-of-social networking

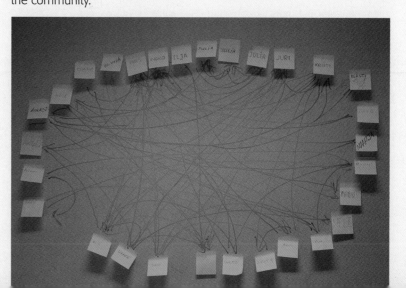

Text D

Blue Blood (2010)

Story – Okey Zubela Okoh
Screenplay – Okey Zubela Okoh, Onyinye Ukora
Director – Okey Zubela Okoh
Producer – Uche Nancy, Hyacinth Onwuka

Starring:

Ini Edo – Princess Oluchi
Tonto Dikeh – Nkem
Collette Nkem – Orji
Yemi Blaq – Onyema
Eve Esiri – Jessy
Mary Uranta – Peace
Nse Ikpi Etim – Chimamanda
Jibola Dabo – Chied Iekmefuna
Andy Ike – Ndidi Amaka
Chigozie Okoli – Guard 1

Okoye Emeka – Guard 2
Uchester Eluaka – Lecturer
Uju Aroh – Mama Onye
Junior Pope Odonwodo – Bayo
Escort Kamar – Joseph
Uche Ebere – Mama Chimamanda
Zainab Egwuonwu – Andy
Ed Nnasor – Elder
Micheal Godson – John
Gaddiel Onwudiwe – Chief Daniel

Themes Explored:
Royalty
Tradition vs Assimilation
Forgiveness

My rating – 40%

About Nollywood Forever

Nollywood Forever Movie Reviews offers down to earth, unbiased reviews of the latest African Movies (Nigerian and Ghanaian) on the market.

If you love film, are a Nollywood enthusiast and can't get enough of movies from Ghana and Nigeria or even if you are simply a casual viewer, then Nollywood Forever Movie Reviews is the site for you! You can read movie reviews before you buy, or come and visit after you have watched. Whether you loved the movie or hated it, let's discuss!

Ini Edo plays Princess Oluchi. She is thought of as a snob on campus because of her attitude, her royal attire and the guards that accompany her everywhere she goes. It is not until she makes friends with Nkem and realises that she too
5 is a princess but stays understated that Oluchi starts thinking that it is not a necessity to flaunt her status at every given opportunity.

At one stage she is so full of herself that when she finds a student sitting in "her seat" in the library, she slaps him after
10 he refuses to move. This student is called Onye, played by Yemi Blaq.

Onye has a history. He was left to bring up his young son after his ex-wife Chimamanda, played by Nse Ikpi-Etim, left him after an abusive relationship to begin a new life at
15 university. Their paths soon cross when he ends up studying at the same university as her. She supposedly hates him but does not want to see him with the Princess either.

Both Ini and Tonto look atrocious. Nse and Yemi look too old to be students. Even if they are both 20 years old, they most
20 certainly do not look it, so for me it defied realism. They both look at LEAST 30 years old! Nse kept on putting on a baby voice that was rather strange and annoying.

For supposed royal chicks, the accommodation we see Nkem and Princess Oluchi lodging in looks less than royal. It looks
25 like any accommodation that a regular student would lodge in.

For me, the royal story line was a bust and I didn't get why Tonto and Ini had to be made royal. Why not just make them from really rich or from influential families? The whole
30 concept of royalty as it was presented in the movie seemed somewhat dated in modern times.

Chief wants Chimamanda to marry and bear a son for him as his wife has had 4 daughters and his wife cannot have any more children. He is searching for an heir. In Nollywood, I
35 wonder why the women who receive proposals like this don't ever stand up for themselves and wonder what will happen to them if they bear a daughter instead of a son. Unreal! Why don't they ever think that they will get discarded just like the wife was? There also needs to be a point when a woman who
40 is blamed for producing a girl turns to the man and tells him, "OI! I only produce X Chromosomes and you produce X and Y; therefore, it is YOU that is to blame."

One ridiculous scene was when Princess Oluchi invites Nkem to a party. She pleads with her to go, her reason
45 being that she does not want to go alone. We then find out that Onye has been invited too and then we see all three of them sitting at the party together and most of the time they are off together, leaving Nkem to sit alone. What a cheek! At the party we see waaaaaaay too much dancing where
50 nothing at all is happening. Good editing is vital to keep the viewers' attention and having ten minutes of dancing with no dialogue and NOTHING happening is not a good move.

It wasn't brilliant but I would recommend watching the movie when you are bored, as it was **[37]** entertaining. We learn
55 **[38]** about Tradition vs Assimilation, forgiveness and giving second chances. Onye may have been a monster in his past, but we can see in his behaviour how he has made a **[39]** change and deserved to be forgiven for his past actions. I felt that there wasn't clear focus in the movie; it seemed a bit
60 **[40]** in the way that it was put together. Great cast but I feel they were a little wasted. The story and characters needed to be developed a bit more as they felt **[41]** .

http://nollywoodforever.com/blue-blood

Question and answer booklet

Text A: Clean water campaign

1 From statements A–H, select the three that are true according to the text. Write the appropriate letters in the boxes provided.

(3 marks)

A Text A is an advertisement for bottled water.

B *Text A is about an essay competition.*

C The competition offers money prizes to winners.

D It costs $25 to enter the contest.

E Everyone living in Metropolitan North Georgia can take part in the contest.

F Text A introduces a new writing competition that is organized for the first time.

G The competition is aimed at students in Atlanta.

H With the contest, the organizers hope to raise people's awareness of how water is used.

Example | B |

| □ |

| □ |

| □ |

The sentences below are either true or false. Tick ✓ the correct response then justify it with a relevant brief quotation from the text.

Both a tick ✓ and a quotation are required for one mark.

Example: One can enter the competition with an essay written by hand.

Justification: ......*Essays may be handwritten or typed*...............

	True	False
	✓	□

2 A student entering the competition may decide the length of his essay.

Justification: ....   □ □

3 A competing essay can discuss either quality of water or discuss the importance of conservation.

Justification: ....   □ □

4 In his essay, a student entering the competition must give details of what he could do to promote cleaner water.

Justification: ....   □ □

Find the words in the text which mean the following (lines 1–23).

Example: respond to   ....*answer*.................

5 put a stop to   ....

6 advance   ....

7 tell   ....

8 Choose the most appropriate response from the options below. Write the letter in the answer box provided.

When entering the contest,

☐

   A the student body must choose one essay to represent the school.

   B it is best to email all essays at once.

   C the school can send in one best preferred essay from each grade.

   D a supervising teacher must sign the entry form.

Which words go in the gaps between lines 39 and 44? Choose the words from the list and write them below.

         all   each   none

           an   every   the

Example: ....*all*..............

9   ....

10   ....

Text B: Foods of the Irish

Choose the correct answer from A, B, C, or D Write the letter in the box provided.

11   In Irish food, spices

   A   are favoured over herbs.

   B   are not needed.

   C   are avoided altogether.

   D   are used in moderation.

12   An Irish meal

   A   is usually based on potatoes, bread or other grains, and cheese.

   B   rarely has dairy products other than cheese.

   C   is too heavy on potatoes.

   D   is considered, world-wide, a rare delicacy.

13   In Ireland, seafood

   A   is difficult to find and considered a rarity for its high price.

   B   is readily available but is not a staple part of the diet.

   C   is used for dinner on a daily basis.

   D   is seen as something best used in light and delicate soups.

14   The early 19th century poem

   A   mocks the poor quality of the national dish.

   B   admires the appetite-suppressing qualities of the Irish stew.

   C   humorously describes the effects of eating the national dish.

   D   warns against trying the belly-busting stew.

Answer the following questions.

15   To what or whom does the word 'They' (line 47) refer?

   ....

16   According to the text, what drink do the Irish prefer most?

   ....

17   What explanation does the text give for large portion sizes of Irish meals?

   ....

Which words go in the gaps between lines 85 and 90? Choose the words from the list and write them below.

   often   never   simultaneously   again   when   however

18   ....

19   ....

20   ....

Text C: Proper etiquette of social networking

21   From statements A to F, select the 2 that are true according to text C. Write the appropriate letters in the boxes provided.

(2 marks)

A   The main purpose of Text C is to define the new concept of 'online etiquette'.

B   According to the author, non-academic people can never agree on correct etiquette.

C   According to the author, etiquette is too complex an idea to characterize in a brief article.

D   According to the author, someone who is familiar with proper etiquette knows how to conduct themselves in social media.

E   In Text C, the author wishes to offer tips on how to make a good impression in an online environment.

F   Text C is a cleverly disguised advertisement attempting to attract business.

The sentences below are either true or false. Tick ✓ the correct response then justify it with a relevant brief quotation from the text. Both a tick ✓ and a quotation are required for one mark.

True   False

22   Spamming is an accepted aspect of social media.

Justification: ....

23   The author compares social media to a safe haven, far removed from the harsh world of business.

Justification: ....

24   A good way to advertise on social media is to inform people about gifts.

Justification: ....

25   The author suggests that presenting oneself as a specialist or a particularly skilled person is a subtle way of advertising.

Justification: ....

Match the first part of the sentence with the appropriate ending on the right. Write the appropriate letter in the boxes provided.

Example:

Making friends online is easier, if one is able.... | B |

| A | to misunderstand the proper code of conduct online. |

25 The author thinks it shows bad manners... | |

| B | *to communicate respect towards others and act in a professional manner.* |

| C | to become identified as a source of unsolicited postings. |

26 Talking business soon after befriending someone may cause you... | |

| D | to collect as many likable friends as possible. |

| E | to search the web for random business opportunities. |

| F | to make friends with strangers without introducing oneself properly. |

Answer the following questions.

27 What negative effect does the author believe sending too many messages can have?

....

28 What words does the author use to show that she regards brand trust more valuable than brand awareness?

....

Text D: Blue Blood

Choose the correct answer from A, B, C, or D. Write the letter in the box provided.

29 What is the purpose of Text D?

    A It acts as part of an interactive forum aimed at professional film critics.

    B It is aimed at fans of the Nollywood enthusiast Okey Zubela Okoh.

    C It presents the author's subjective review of a Nollywood film.

    D It presents a view counteracting the promotion of a film by Okey Zubela Okoh.

30 The body of the text starts

    A by giving an overview of the plot.

    B by pointing out the weaknesses of the cast.

    C by forecasting a tragic romance between a naïve royal and a clever but poor student.

    D with a brief introduction to how the film was made.

31 The character Onye

    A is based on a real historical person.

    B has a mysterious past as a dangerous assassin.

    C has left his wife and their son to pursue an academic career.

    D is caught between two women in the film.

Fill in the chart below based on the information you find in the text.
Look for the words or phrases that reveal the author's view and indicate
whether they are positive or negative. Both answers are required for one
mark. An example is included.

Topic	The author's view	Is the author's comment positive or negative? P / N
Example: The outward appearance of Ini and Tonto	*atrocious*	N
32 The setting where the princesses live.		
33 How royals are portrayed in the film.		
34 How in films women marry men simply to produce heirs.		
35 Princess Oluchi ignores her girlfriend at a party.		
36 At the party, there is more dance than talk.		

Which words go in the gaps between lines 53 and 62? Choose the words from the list
and write them below.

| something | vague | somewhat | regular | neither |
| drastic | excellent | haphazard | organized | one-dimensional |

37 ....

38 ....

39 ....

40 ....

41 ....

Paper 2 (SL)

Complete **one** of the following tasks. Write 250 to 400 words.

1 **Cultural diversity**

A new restaurant called Albion Delights has opened in your hometown. It celebrates traditional British food over the centuries and promises to offer "an evening to remember". Based on a recent visit, write about your culinary adventure in your blog.

2 **Customs & traditions**

You recently visited an English-speaking country and paid attention to how teenagers were dressed. Write an article to be published in your school magazine on the fashion and trends you saw during your visit.

3 **Health**

Recent budget cuts are affecting health services at your school, and now the school nurse's office is to close down. Write a letter to your school's administration explaining why the school needs to have a resident nurse and trying to convince them that funding must be found.

4 **Leisure**

A local sports team has announced a competition for schools where the winning entry will receive a large donation. The competition calls for ideas to "improve students' physical well-being". Write a proposal in which you describe how the money would be used to promote students' sports activities at your school.

5 **Science & technology**

As a bet, your friends challenged you to spend a whole week without computers and mobile phones. It's the last day of that week and you are reporting back to your friends. Write your friends an email in which you reflect on your week without IT.

Further activities on the internal assessment

Individual oral

A

B

Option	Possible titles or captions
Cultural diversity	Dance is a link between people, connecting heaven and earth. Dance celebrates what makes us human. We carry the world in our bodies.
Customs & traditions	People have always danced to celebrate the crucial moments of life, and our bodies carry the memory of all the possible human experiences.
Health	When we dance, we naturally use the mechanics of our body and all our senses to express joy, sadness, the things we care about.
Leisure	We can dance alone, and we can dance together. We can share what makes us the same, what makes us different from each other.
Science & technology	For me dancing is a way of thinking. Through dance we can embody the most abstract ideas, and thus reveal what we cannot see, what we cannot name.

All titles and captions are quotes from the message given by Anne
Teresa De Keersmaeker on International Dance Day 2011.
They can be used with both photo A and photo B.

Source: www.iti-worldwide.org/danceday_2011.php

C

D

Option	Possible titles or captions
Cultural diversity	*The Oxford English Dictionary*: **brotherhood** mass noun • the relationship between brothers. • the feeling of kinship with and closeness to a group of people or all people.
Customs & traditions	*The Oxford English Dictionary*: **gang** noun • an organized group of criminals. • a group of young people involved in petty crime or violence. • (informal) a group of people, especially young people, who regularly associate together.
Health	*The Oxford English Dictionary*: **well-being** mass noun • the state of being comfortable, healthy, or happy.
Leisure	*The Oxford English Dictionary*: **recreation** mass noun • activity done for enjoyment when one is not working. Origin: late Middle English (also in the sense 'mental or spiritual consolation'): via Old French from Latin recreatio(n-), from recreare, 'create again, renew'.
Science & technology	*The Oxford English Dictionary*: **social** adjective • needing companionship and therefore best suited to living in communities: we are social beings as well as individuals. • relating to or designed for activities in which people meet each other for pleasure. • (of a bird) gregarious; breeding or nesting in colonies. • (of an insect) living together in organized communities, typically with different castes, as ants, bees, wasps, and termites do. • (of a mammal) living together in groups, typically in a hierarchical system with complex communication.

Match the suggestions of titles and captions below with photographs
E–H. Which option(s) is each linked to and how do they guide the
presentation?

- 'Nothing of me is original. I am the combined effort of everybody I've ever known.' (*Chuck Palahniuk*)

- 'Love looks not with the eyes but with the mind.' (*William Shakespeare*)

- 'Never fight an inanimate object.' (*P.J. O'Rourke*)

- 'I do not fear computers. I fear the lack of them.' (*Isaac Asimov*)

- 'My salad days, / When I was green in judgment.' (*William Shakespeare*)

- 'For a list of all the ways technology has failed to improve the quality of life, please press three.' (*Alice Kahn*)

- 'As I see it, every day you do one of two things: build health or produce disease in yourself.' (*Adelle Davis*)

- 'There's no point in being grown up if you can't be childish sometimes.' (*Doctor Who*)

- 'Sport has a unique capacity for making good things happen. It can in a very real sense change the shape of the world.' (*Geelong Advertises*, 14 July 2011)

- 'Fast food not only makes us fat, it brings us down. People who have healthier diets are less likely to become anxious and depressed.' (*Herald Sun*, 13 July 2011)

- 'The Death of the Book has Been Greatly Exaggerated' (*Technology Review*, published by MIT)

- 'Reading books is the only out-of-school activity for 16-year-olds that is linked to getting a managerial or professional job in later life, says an Oxford study.' (*ScienceDaily*, 9 May 2011)

- 'The concept of beauty may be different from place to place. In the West, many women risk skin cancer by sunbathing and visiting tanning salons in pursuit of an exotic, tanned look.' (*The Jakarta Post*, 15 July 2011)

- 'Peer support has been found to decrease isolation, reduce stress, increase the sharing of health information and provide role models' (*e! Science News*, 15 Feb 2011)

E

F

G

H

Interactive oral – Activity 1

Three interactive activities will be carried out in the classroom during the course and assessed by the teacher. One of these **must** be based on a listening activity.

Listening activity

1 Watch *The First World Problems Rap* available on **www.youtube.com**

   - What is the rap about? What is the subject matter?
   - What is the mood like?
   - What does the title mean?

2 Play the rap again, but this time close your eyes and focus on listening to the words.

   - Are you able to follow the language used? Why/Why not?
   - What is the language like? How familiar are you with the vocabulary and expressions used?
   - What is the rhythm like? Are you able to tap it?

3 Read the lyrics of the rap on the right.

   - How familiar are you with the ideas presented in the rap? Can you think of more examples of First World problems?
   - Can you identify with Zach? Why/Why not?
   - What emotions does the rap evoke in you?

4 Play the rap again, and look at the lyrics while listening. If you wish, you can mouth the words silently.

   - Can you identify words that rhyme?
   - How is the setting of a modern, Western world created?
   - Imagine going back 50 years in time and playing this rap to someone living in the past. How would they react to the language and the ideas presented?

5 Play the rap again, and join in by reading aloud the lyrics. Can you keep up with Zach? How about finally performing the rap without the backing video?

   - In your opinion, who is the best audience for this rap? Why?
   - Has your initial reaction to the rap changed? Why/Why not?
   - What does the title mean? Has your interpretation of it changed? Why?

The First World Problems Rap

by funnyz (aka Zach Katz)

People of the first world, yah!
We got these First World Problems
My fridge is so full I have to reach way back
And my sports car doesn't even have an audio jack
My laptop's battery is low but my charger is over there
I can never find the right lid for my Tupperware
I woke up at noon, do I eat breakfast or lunch?
I don't like organic milk and I don't have fruit punch
My neighbour put a password on their wi-fi
And the freezer makes the ice cream hard to scoop, why try?
My hot water ran out in the shower, which sucks cause I was only in there for half an hour
The other side of my pillow is not much cooler
There's no measure for inches or feet on this ruler (what' the heck's a decimeter!)
Something just beeped and I don't know what it was:
What is my Roomba, my Convection oven or just Google Buzz
There's some cereal left but not enough to make a bowl
I hate replacing batteries on my Wi remote control
People keep texting me when I'm playing Tiny Wings
My cleaning lady is vacuuming I can't hear a thing
I didn't read 'Shake Well' now I feel like I missed out
When I opened my birthday card no money fell out
I meant to turn on the light but it was the disposal
My Vespa's in the shop, now how can I be mobil
Net flicks is suggesting things I already seen
And my suit is too fancy for the washing machine
There's a pebble in my shoe, I have to stop and shake it
I have to add water to this cup cake mix and then bake it?
My pillow is too soft and I have too many sheets
And what the heck do I do with all these Starbucks receipts
My walk-in closet door is kind of hard to close
And my private school teacher calls my rap songs prose
My fridge doesn't have a touch screen; it's a first world issue
Killed a Spider with a dollar cause I didn't have a tissue.

Here are some classroom activities following the exploration of *The First World Problems Rap*.

1   A debate on one of the following topics:
  a   "Zach Katz's rap should be taken seriously."
  b   "An IB student who has taken part in the CAS programme cannot identify with the First World problems."
  c   "Adopting the IB Learner Profile is the best way to dismiss First World problems."

2   A class discussion evaluating the problems presented in the rap. Which ones do or do not apply to the students' circumstances and why?

3   An improvised interview where students play celebrities or fictional characters tormented by First World problems.

4   A role-play between a therapist and a patient suffering from First World problems. The aim is to look for solutions to the problems.

5   A localized pastiche, an imitation or an adaptation of the rap, i.e. adding local setting, details, objects, issues, names, and introduction.

6   A role play where the host of a popular Third World TV talk show meets a celebrity who complains about First World problems.

Further activities

Why not use *The First World Problems Rap* as a starting point for your written assignment? Look for more texts on the subject of 'First World problems', also known as 'white whine'.

Interactive oral – Activity 2

Reading activity

Read the four poems by Benjamin Zephaniah. Start by studying the poems individually, and then look at them as a collection.

- What is the poem about? What is the subject matter?

- What is the mood like in the poem? What feelings are expressed?

- Look at the language: How complex are the structures and vocabulary?

- What is the rhythm like? If it were a song or a piece of music, what would it sound like?

- What is the relationship between the title and the poem?

- What does the poem make you feel or understand? Why?

- Can you identify with the feelings and thoughts expressed? Why?

- What do the poems share? In what way are they different from one other?

- **(HL)** What literary devices are used in the poem?

Neighbours

I am the type you are supposed to fear
Black and foreign
Big and dreadlocks
An uneducated grass eater.

I talk in tongues
I chant at night
I appear anywhere,
I sleep with lions
And when the moon gets me
I am a Wailer.

I am moving in
Next door to you
So you can get to know me,
You will see my shadow
In the bathroom window,
My aromas will occupy

Your space,
Our ball will be in your court.
How will you feel?

You should feel good
You have been chosen.

I am the type you are supposed to love
Dark and mysterious
Tall and natural
Thinking, tea total.
I talk in schools
I sing on TV
I am in the papers,
I keep cool cats.

And when the sun is shining
I go Carnival.

The British (serves 60 million)

Take some Picts, Celts and Silures
And let them settle,
Then overrun them with Roman conquerors.

Remove the Romans after approximately 400 years
Add lots of Norman French to some
Angles, Saxons, Jutes and Vikings, then stir vigorously.

Mix some hot Chileans, cool Jamaicans, Dominicans,
Trinidadians and Bajans with some Ethiopians, Chinese,
Vietnamese and Sudanese.

Then take a blend of Somalians, Sri Lankans, Nigerians
And Pakistanis,
Combine with some Guyanese
And turn up the heat.

Sprinkle some fresh Indians, Malaysians, Bosnians,
Iraqis and Bangladeshis together with some
Afghans, Spanish, Turkish, Kurdish, Japanese

And Palestinians
Then add to the melting pot.

Leave the ingredients to simmer.

As they mix and blend allow their languages to flourish
Binding them together with English.

Allow time to be cool.

Add some unity, understanding, and respect for the future,
Serve with justice
And enjoy.

Note: All the ingredients are equally important. Treating one
ingredient better than another will leave a bitter unpleasant
taste.

Warning: An unequal spread of justice will damage the
people and cause pain. Give justice and equality to all.

We Refugees

I come from a musical place
Where they shoot me for my song
And my brother has been tortured
By my brother in my land.

I come from a beautiful place
Where they hate my shade of skin
They don't like the way I pray
And they ban free poetry.

I come from a beautiful place
Where girls cannot go to school
There you are told what to believe
And even young boys must grow beards.

I come from a great old forest
I think it is now a field
And the people I once knew
Are not there now.

We can all be refugees
Nobody is safe,
All it takes is a mad leader
Or no rain to bring forth food,
We can all be refugees
We can all be told to go,
We can be hated by someone
For being someone.

I come from a beautiful place
Where the valley floods each year
And each year the hurricane tells us
That we must keep moving on.

I come from an ancient place
All my family were born there
And I would like to go there
But I really want to live.

I come from a sunny, sandy place
Where tourists go to darken skin
And dealers like to sell guns there
I just can't tell you what's the price.

I am told I have no country now
I am told I am a lie
I am told that modern history books
May forget my name.

We can all be refugees
Sometimes it only takes a day,
Sometimes it only takes a handshake
Or a paper that is signed.
We all came from refugees
Nobody simply just appeared,
Nobody's here without a struggle,
And why should we live in fear
Of the weather or the troubles?
We all came here from somewhere.

Everybody is Doing It

In Hawaii they Hula
They Tango in Argentina
They Reggae in Jamaica
And they Rumba down in Cuba,
In Trinidad and Tobago
They do the Calypso
And in Spain the Spanish
They really do Flamenco.

In the Punjab they Bhangra
How they dance Kathak in India
Over in Guatemala
They dance the sweet Marimba,
Even foxes dance a lot
They invented the Fox Trot,
In Australia it's true
They dance to the Didgeridoo.

In Kenya they Benga
They Highlife in Ghana
They dance Ballet all over

And Rai dance in Algeria,
They Jali in Mali
In Brazil they Samba
And the girls do Belly Dancing
In the northern parts of Africa.

Everybody does the Disco
From Baghdad to San Francisco
Many folk with razzamataz
Cannot help dancing to Jazz,
They do the Jig in Ireland
And it is really true
They still Morris
dance in England
When they can find
time to."

Benjamin Zephaniah

Here are some classroom activities following the exploration of Benjamin Zephaniah's poems.

1   A debate on one of the following topics:
    a   "Benjamin Zephaniah's poems speak to a wide audience."
    b   "Benjamin Zephaniah's poems address global problems."
    c   "Benjamin Zephaniah must have been an IB student."

2   A class discussion on the problems and challenges presented in the poem(s). Which ones have students experienced? Which ones can students identify with?

3   A role-play interview with Benjamin Zephaniah following recent reports claiming that young people are increasingly less interested in politics.

4   Imagine that Benjamin Zephaniah will be visiting your home town, and a group of students are hoping he would visit the school. In pairs, students give a justified talk in front of the (imagined) school management team to either support or oppose the poet's visit.

5   Using examples from Benjamin Zephaniah's poetry, a series of presentations (individual or in pairs), on one of the following topics:
    a   subcultures
    b   what unites and separates people
    c   pride and prejudice.

6   Small group discussions on the role and interpretation of the last lines of Benjamin Zephaniah's poems.

> **TIP**
>
> Watch Benjamin Zephaniah reading his poetry on www.benjaminzephaniah.com and www.youtube.com. The poem called *Money* (www.youtube.com/watch?v=tAXpuW3yFJM) could be an interesting listening stimulus for interactive oral work.

Cultural diversity

BEFORE YOU READ

→ Singapore is a small multicultural island nation in SE Asia where English is the dominant language of government, business, and education. Find Singapore on a map and make some predictions about the nature and heritage of the population.

→ Historically, Singapore society has been created by waves of immigration. To what extent is this true of your own country or the society in which you live?

→ To what extent is your society a monocultural or a multicultural one?

→ In former times each culture left its mark on local Singapore architecture. Do the buildings in your home city have a distinctive look that makes them identifiable with specific cultures and periods in history?

→ Does it matter that the new buildings in the modern city are much less distinctive and more international in design?

Population diversity

Traditional cultures in Singapore

A SINGAPORE IS strategically located at the southern tip of the Malaysian peninsula. This has ensured its importance on South East Asian trade routes and, as the port and city developed in the 19th century, so did its multi-cultural population. The national culture of Singapore stems from the cultural diversity of this island state. It is a cosmopolitan society where Malay, Chinese, Indian, and European influences have all intertwined.

B Drawn by the lure of better prospects, the immigrants of the 19th century brought with them their own cultures, languages, customs, and festivals. Intermarriage and integration wove these diverse influences into the fabric of Singapore's multi-faceted society. A vibrant and diverse cultural heritage developed. By the end of the 19th century, Singapore became one of the most cosmopolitan cities in Asia. In those days the major ethnic groups in the city were the indigenous Malays, Chinese, Indians, Peranakans (Chinese-Malays), and Eurasians.

C Today, ethnic Chinese form 74.2% of a Singaporean population of about 5 million, with the country's original inhabitants, the Malays, totaling 13.4%. Singapore's Indians make up 9.2%, and Eurasians, Peranakans and others making up a combined 3.2%. Singapore is also home to many expatriates, with almost 20% of the population made up of non-resident workers from the Philippines, Indonesia and Bangladesh. The rest come from places as diverse as North America, Australia, Europe, Japan, Malaysia, South Korea, China and India.

D However, behind the facade of a modern industrialised city, ethnic enclaves are still evident. The areas for the different cultures were designated by colonial Singapore's British founder, Sir Stamford Raffles. Each still bears its own unique character. The old streets of Chinatown can still be seen; Muslim characteristics are still visible in Arab Street; and Little India along Serangoon Road still has its distinct ambience. Nevertheless you can find a mosque and a Hindu temple in Chinatown, Indian restaurants in Arab Street and Chinese gold shops in Little India. Furthermore, there are marks of the British colonial influence in the neo-classical buildings all around the city centre. However, lest we forget, Singapore is now a bustling 21st century city with high-rise buildings and landscape gardens all over the city centre.

Adapted from
www.singaporeexpate.com, 2011

1   Skim the text and match each of the focal ideas below to the relevant paragraph (marked A–D).
    a   Singapore's multicultural society is the result of history and geography.
    b   The diverse society in Singapore developed in the 19th century as a result of immigration.
    c   The ethnic make-up of modern Singapore.
    d   The diversity of architecture in Singapore reflects the complexity of the society.

2   Scan the text and choose the correct answer.

a   intertwined (line 16) suggests:
    A   changed
    B   blended together
    C   disappeared

b   lure (line 17) suggests:
    A   attraction
    B   anchor
    C   thread

c   wove (line 23) suggests:
    A   created
    B   united
    C   drew

d   fabric (line 24) suggests:
    A   a cloth
    B   cultivation
    C   a population

e   cosmopolitan (line 30) suggests:
    A   sophisticated
    B   civil
    C   multi-ethnic

f   indigenous (line 33) means:
    A   home-grown
    B   aboriginal
    C   original

g   totaling (line 42) means:
    A   consisting of
    B   containing
    C   constraining

h   expatriates (line 47) are:
    A   exiles
    B   overseas workers
    C   émigrés

i   diverse (line 52) means:
    A   separate
    B   assorted
    C   miscellaneous

j   facade (line 56) suggests:
    A   face
    B   appearance
    C   features

k   designated (line 61) means:
    A   selected
    B   ordered
    C   commanded

l   bears (line 64) suggests:
    A   uses
    B   impresses
    C   carries

m   ambience (line 71) means:
    A   impression
    B   air
    C   atmosphere

n   marks (line 77) means:
    A   sights
    B   remains
    C   characteristics

o   bustling (line 82) means:
    A   harried
    B   busy
    C   diligent

Definition

The exercise requires you to find a synonym – a word almost identical in meaning to the one in the text. The vocabulary used in this exercise is quite complex and some of the words you have to choose between are similar in meaning. You may be able to work out the meaning from the context. However, in order to complete this exercise you may need to use a dictionary or thesaurus to find the best synonym.

Remember

In some cases the word you need to replace may have a metaphorical meaning as well as a literal one!

3   Read the text and write down to whom or to what the following words or phrases refer.
    a   This (line 3)
    b   its (line 8)
    c   It (line 12)
    d   their (line 20)
    e   In those days (line 31)
    f   others (line 45)
    g   The rest (line 51)
    h   Each (line 63)

Developing writing skills: Feature article

Feature articles are found in magazines and the non-news sections of newspapers. They are not concerned with events that are in the news but instead can explore a range of issues, opinions, experiences, and ideas. Thus they can offer an opinion about current affairs, but they can also simply present a personal or humorous perspective on modern day life. Either way, article writers go beyond just giving the facts on the surface and add colour, descriptive detail, background, and personal comment.

Feature articles can inform, entertain, and persuade readers, or may simply satisfy the reader's curiosity about a particular topic. Professional articles may do all these things at the same time. A feature article should give a personal perspective on the subject. The best feature writers will have a point of view or angle that makes the article interesting and unique.

You need to establish the relationship between you as the writer and your readership, so always keep your reader in mind and remember to use appropriate vocabulary. However, if you are writing a formal article for a wide audience, then formal English is required. Look at the text *Traditional cultures in Singapore* on page 134. What techniques does the writer use to maintain a formal style of writing throughout the text?

If you are writing for a teenage readership, it can be appropriate to use fairly informal language, especially when reporting the speech of a young person. In such cases, it is acceptable to use contractions such as *doesn't, can't,* and *won't.* It might also be appropriate to use fairly informal vocabulary such as *cool, weird,* or *brilliant* to describe people and places.

Feature articles are often found in magazines

Remember

Writing a feature article for a specific audience

If you choose to write a magazine article, you must think about the audience. Feature articles should appeal to the particular audience that the magazine is targeting. For example, if a magazine is targeted at teenage girls, then the articles, advertising, and pictures within that magazine might reflect their interest in lifestyles, studying, fashion, health, and relationships.

One of the best ways to research magazine audiences is to look at sample issues. You can find them online, on the newsstands or in the library, receive copies from friends, or order back issues from publishers. Besides the articles themselves, make sure to look at any advertising. The advertisements can give you an idea of the age and interests of the people reading the magazine. Are they playful and colourful, or subtle and serious? The same approach is likely to be true of the articles in the magazine itself.

Individual oral activity (SL)

Look at the two photographs and captions. Which one would you choose to talk about? Here are some things to consider when making your choice.

- Can you easily identify the option and the aspect?
- Which photograph can you describe in more detail?
- Do you have the vocabulary to name the objects that seem significant for the scene in the picture?
- What can you say about the caption under the image? What feelings, ideas, or opinions does it evoke?

Tourist heaven in Singapore's Chinatown

Malay-Muslim, Chinese, and British influences

Writing activity

Choose one of the following topics and write a feature article in 250–400 words.

a An analysis and opinion on language issues in an English-speaking country.

b A profile of or an interview with a well-known celebrity or a character from a book. In the context of this section, the interview might centre around issues such as language, society, and identity.

c A local, national or international event, or celebration, such as a cultural festival.

d A human interest story about a strange or unusual event in an English-speaking country.

Interlinguistic influence

BEFORE YOU READ

Julia Sherstyuk is a Russian living in Singapore. In her blog, she frequently comments on her experiences in a society that appears very different to her own and to other places in the world where she has lived.

→ Before you read her blog, imagine you were living in another country and make a list of the aspects of society you might comment on. In what order of importance might you put the different topics? Why would you give certain aspects more importance than others?

→ The writer talks about the differences between Standard English and Singlish, the local dialect. Make a list of the different aspects of language the writer might talk about in her blog.

→ There are many different varieties of English throughout the world. Who decides what is good English or bad English? Are there differences between good and bad spoken and written English?

→ What is the difference between an accent and a dialect?

→ Think about your own culture and society. Are there many different accents and dialects? Which ones have high status or prestige and which do not? Why?

→ Do you use the same accent and dialect at all times or does your language change depending on the social context you find yourself in? Why is this?

Definition

Singlish vocabulary

makan – to eat

chope – to reserve something

cheem – difficult, complicated

ang mo – a white person

rojak – mixed, a mix of

liao – finished, the end

kiasu – afraid to lose face

Speakers of Singlish will usually end their sentences with a distinctive exclamation. The four most common are 'ah', 'lah', 'ley' and 'what'. For example:

"OK lah, bye bye."

"Don't like that lah."

"You are going there ah?"

"No parking lots here, what."

"The price is too high for me lah."

"And then how many rooms ah?"

"It is very troublesome ley."

"Don't be like that ley!"

"I'm not at home lah. That's why ah."

AN ESSENTIAL GUIDE TO SINGLISH

DO YOU speak ENGLISH?

Of course lah! SINGLISH also caaan

Illustrations by Miel

SINGLISH: Broken English or Badge of Identity?

An intelligent way of experiencing a new country and its people's mentality is learning the local language. In the case of Singapore, nothing could be truer.

5 **1** Two things struck me as incomprehensible when I first came to Singapore: its incessant humid heat and the local English, quirky enough to instil an inferiority complex in a linguist like me who had been painstakingly mastering
10 English as a second language. With Professor Higgins as a role model, I could differentiate a Manchester accent from that of a Dubliner's, and would never confuse the dynamic verbalisation of New Yorkers with the sluggish Dixie drawl.
15 But the language spoken in the Lion City remained a mystery to me for months.

2 Singlish is rooted in Singapore's short but tumultuous history. Immigrants of three major ethnicities – Malay, Chinese and Indian – came
20 to the island in the early 19th century to establish trade here. They all spoke different languages and dialects, turning Singapore into a Babylon of sorts. Over time, these tongues affected each other and, in a much stronger way,
25 the English language of the British colonisers. This resulted in Singlish, a colourful and unique Singaporean English that lives by the rules of Chinese grammar and is generously sprinkled with words from Hokkien, Malay and Indian
30 dialects. On top of that, the intonation has a sing-song quality to it drawn from indigenous Asian cultures.

3 As if it is not mind-boggling enough, Singlish is spoken at machine-gun speed with words
35 pronounced so abruptly that the most common and simplest of them become a challenge to Western ears. For instance, 'act', 'cast', 'stopped' or 'file' are chopped in Singlish to 'ac', 'cas', 'stop', and 'fi'. The dental fricative 'th' is more
40 often than not substituted with 't' or 'd', turning 'thighs' into 'ties', 'three' into 'tree' and 'that' into 'dat'.

4 In written form, Singlish is no less puzzling: complex phrases are avoided, verbs may be left
45 out, definite articles are generally ignored and indications of plurality, tenses and voices are optional. Have a look at an eye surgery ad which I personally have come across more than once in local media: "Advantage of Epi-LASIK: preserve
50 more cornea tissue; suitable for those involve in contact or aggressive sports." I assure you, those are not typos – this is Singlish at work.

5 Nearly all Singaporeans are bilingual, learning an Asian language or dialect with the family
55 and English at school. Many speak three or four languages. The influence of their mother tongue is evident in the way Singaporeans pronounce English words and the intonation they employ. If you are exposed to Singlish long enough,
60 you will be able to tell to which ethnic group a person who telephones you belongs. Chinese Singaporeans have the strongest accent. This was the reason why a Russian friend of mine, while taking driving classes in Singapore, asked for an
65 instructor of Malay origin.

6 The government admonishes its citizens for speaking Singlish and advises them to learn proper English to boost the city-state's image as a commercial and financial hub. Since 1980,
70 all school education has been taught in the English language which serves as the official language for business and administration among Singapore's four state languages.

7 Today, most of overseas-educated or simply
75 language-conscious Singaporeans are able to switch smoothly from Singlish to standard English, while less educated citizens stick to the grammatically and phonetically unconventional Singlish, which is a recipe for disaster for tourists
80 visiting Singapore, especially those whose mother tongue is not English.

8 While purists may bemoan the loss of Queen's English, those who see a broader picture admit that Singlish is the first building block of a
85 Singaporean cultural identity and a distinct legacy of the country's unique story. Fun, energetic, and extremely laconic, Singlish is spoken by all classes of Singaporean society.

Julia Sherstyuk

1 From the list below, choose an appropriate heading for paragraphs 1–8. There are more headings than you will need.

    A In print

    B The future of Singlish

    C A national badge

    D First impressions

    E Grammatical features

    F Local culture

    G Origins

    H Singapore accents

    I Singlish in the local media

    J Pronunciation

    K Language flexibility

    L The official view

2 Read the text carefully and answer the following questions.

    a From the perspective of a language expert, what was unusual about Singlish?

    b According to the writer why did Singlish develop?

    c How did Singlish develop?

    d What were the two features of spoken Singlish that the writer noticed?

    e In what ways is the grammar of written Singlish different to standard English?

    f What was unusual about the language of the local advertisement for eye surgery?

    g Why is there no single variety of Singlish?

    h Why does the Singapore government criticize the use of Singlish?

    i How do educated Singaporeans use Singlish?

    j What is the writer's overall view of Singlish?

3 Find synonyms for the following words and phrases that appear in the text.

    a incessant (line 6)

    b painstakingly (line 9)

    c verbalisation (line 13)

    d tumultuous (line 18)

    e indigenous (line 31)

    f bemoan (line 82)

    g laconic (line 87)

4 Paragraphs 1 and 2 contain the following cultural references. Look them up and explain their origins and significance in the text.

    a Professor Higgins

    b The Lion City

    c Dixie

    d Babylon

Whatever happened to the English language?

Individual oral activity: Analysing a photograph

When analysing the photograph, go from the general to the specific.

- The photograph will always exemplify or emphasize a point related to the options. Think about why the photograph was chosen and how it relates to an English B option, for example, cultural diversity. Ask yourself: "Why did the photographer take the picture?"

- Photos rarely have an existence of their own. They usually have a **context**. Think about where, when, and why the photograph was taken. Is the photograph part of a larger narrative? What had happened before the photograph? What might happen next?

- Describe the general details of the photograph such as people, animals, or objects and their position in relation to one another.

- It is also useful to think about the target audience. Who was the photograph taken for? What was the audience supposed to see, to think, and to feel? What evidence in the picture gives you these ideas?

- Next look at the picture and identify what it shows. Describe the general details. If appropriate, you can go into further details (colours, proportions, and their effect).

- After examining the picture for what it shows, look at it again and decide what message it conveys. Is it supposed to speak for or against an issue?

Singapore in the 21st century

Beyond the text...

Pidgins and Creoles

Pidgins are grammatically simplified forms of a language which include elements from local languages. **Creoles** are new languages which (may) have pidgin beginnings. That is, they start as pidgins but develop into full languages. A Creole has first language speakers and is a language in its own right. It can communicate complex ideas in a full range of social situations. Creoles have the same linguistic and intellectual range as other languages.

➤ You could research the spread of English Pidgins and Creoles throughout the world.

➤ How would you react if you were told that Modern English is a Creole developed from French, Norse, German, and other languages? Would you believe it? Can you prove that the statement is true?

➤ Take any text written in English and find out with the use of dictionaries the etymology of individual words.

BEFORE YOU READ

In the following text, Singapore writer Minfong Ho talks about her experiences as a multilingual language learner. She grew up in a Chinese-speaking household in Bangkok, Thailand. Only after starting school did she begin to learn English.

→ What advantages do you think multilinguals have over monolinguals?

→ What difficulties do multilinguals have? Do you think it likely that they confuse languages?

→ Do you ever confuse languages? When does this happen? Is it something that happens naturally or just when you are nervous or excited? Can you adjust easily from one language to another?

→ In the text, the writer associates her different languages with different cultures. Do you think this is a realistic way of looking at the world?

Multilingual identity

The voices of my earliest childhood speak to me in Chinese. My father, in his deep quiet monotone, would tell me wonderful bedtime stories in Cantonese that he made up, about giants and
5 turtles and emperors. My grandmother, my aunts, my amah[1] spoke in Cantonese, teasing or scolding me, or laughing and whispering among themselves, in an easy conspiracy. My mother's voice was cooler, more aloof, as she taught us
10 T'ang Dynasty poems in Mandarin, evoking through them images of an exquisite but remote China. With her own friends and relatives she would speak in rapid-fire Hunanese or sibilant Shanghaiese, as I eavesdropped to pick up the
15 latest gossip. As naturally and unquestioningly as I absorbed the basic feelings of love and anger, praise and blame that my family poured over me, so I also absorbed these four Chinese dialects. As my first language, Chinese is the
20 language with the deepest emotional resonance for me. Throughout my childhood, it was the only language that mattered. I heard it, spoke it, whispered it, screamed it, dreamed in it and cried in it. Even now, when I cry, I cry in Chinese.
25 Perhaps that's why I think of Chinese as the language of my heart.

If Chinese is the language of my heart, then Thai is the language of my hands, a functional language which connected me to the wide world
30 outside my family. Growing up on the outskirts of Bangkok in Thailand, I absorbed the simple Thai spoken by peddlers of fried bananas or pickled mangoes as they walked down our street with their baskets of fruit on their shoulder poles. It
35 was in Thai that I would ask for a ripe guava or rose-apple, mixed with sugar or salt or chili sauce. At the Sunday market at Sanam Luang, it was Thai that I bargained in, picking out a potted orchid or a caged rabbit. And within the gleaming
40 Emerald Buddha Temple, it was Thai that the saffron-robed monks chanted, their faces hidden behind the staff each held.

Our house was an airy wooden building on stilts over a "klong", or small pond. I could lie on
45 my stomach in our dining room, and push rice through the crack of the floorboards down to the fish below. We seeded the pond with tiny fish, and once a year the water from the "klong" would be drained, and we would be thigh-deep in mud next
50 to fisherman to net the fish wallowing in the mud. This busy beautiful world, of fruits and fish, of monks and marketwomen, swirled with the light, nuanced sounds of Thai, and I had only to reach out to touch it, connect with it. I taste and touch
55 in Thai, so that I think of Thai as the language of my hands.

English came only much later, when I started learning it in school, in about the third or fourth

---

1   Nurse or housekeeper (*Malay*).

grade. For a long time it remained a school language, separate from the Chinese or Thai of my immediate world. Learning English was a form of intellectual exercise, crammed with rules and regulations which were rigidly enforced by strict teachers. Thus I might know the difference between the present and past participle, yet be unable to jump-rope or play hopscotch in English. English was confined to the stark, alien world of textbooks and examinations, devoid of feelings or sense of taste and touch. No wonder then that English is for me a language of the head.

What happens when you have a different language for your heart, your hands, your head? When your head cannot express what your heart feels, or what your hands touch? Fragmentation. I felt a strange split, a kind of linguistic schizophrenia. In school, I was made to recite Wordsworth's poem on the daffodils, without ever having laid eyes on that flower. Yet I did not know the English names of the common flowers growing all around me. (Years later, I discovered that the little purple blossom that grew wild everywhere in Thailand was called, "Madagascar periwinkle," which made it sound impossibly exotic.) Or, conversely, Thai words for everyday things, once I translated them into English – like my favorite foods "pomelo" or "minced fish patty" – sounded odd and unfamiliar.

Growing up is hard enough to do, without having to feel that one's head can't communicate with one's heart or hands. In an effort to piece together the bits and pieces of my life, I tried to write – strictly for myself, and at first in an awkward jumble of Chinese, Thai, English. Gradually, because English – through all those years of formal education – has become the language that I am most adept in, I wrote more and more in English. Despite the frustrations involved, I kept on writing, because writing was becoming a way to integrate the different experiences and languages of my head, my hands and my heart.

It is ironic that the language that I've become most proficient in, is the one which means the least to me, evoking very little feeling or memories. I have no easy English words for them, these Chinese voices lodged in my heart, or the Thai things I touched with my hands. And when, through some tedious processing of translation in my head, the Chinese and Thai come out in English, the original experience becomes distorted.

Yes, it was frustrating for me to write in English. How do I, for instance, write convincing dialogue when my characters don't even speak English? How do I translate local idioms without making them sound quaint? How can I portray complex traditions? It wasn't easy. It doesn't help, either, that sometimes I am made to feel like a kind of cultural Frankenstein, when those who speak only English look upon my fluency in 'their' language as freakish, an interesting but somewhat grotesque mimicry of their own language which they had somehow bequeathed me.

It was in the depth of my first winter in America that I really started to write. As a freshman at Cornell University, when it was snowing and bleak outside, I used to go to the campus conservatory and just stand next to a potted banana tree growing inside. I missed the tropical sun, and the green leaves and naked brown babies splashing in the ponds. By standing near that banana tree I felt a little more connected with home. But one day some biology class must have chopped up my banana tree for an experiment, because only its spongy trunk was left. That afternoon, I went back to my dorm room and started writing what would become my first book, about a village girl in Thailand.

In a way, I still write for the same reason: to bring back what is gone, to relive what is lost, to make a mosaic out of fragments. And to feel – head, hands, and heart – whole again.

Minfong Ho

1   Scan the text to understand its general ideas. To help, look at the
    following table and find the appropriate answers in the text.
    Some of the answers need to be inferred.

	Chinese	Thai	English
In which social domains of the author's life was each language used?			
Who did Minfong Ho learn each language from?			
How did she learn this language?			
To which part of the body does the writer relate each language?			
What problems did she have with each language?			
What expressions might she use to describe her relationship with each language?			
What does the writer wish to convey by these expressions?			

2   Read the text carefully and answer the following questions.
    a   What happy memories does the writer have of her Chinese childhood?
    b   Why do you think she was able to understand four different varieties of
        Chinese?
    c   List the activities Minfong Ho remembers from her Thai childhood.
    d   Under what circumstances did she learn English?
    e   How did she feel towards the English language while she was at school?
    f   What does she mean by 'linguistic schizophrenia' (lines 75–76)?
    g   Describe Minfong Ho's first attempts to write imaginative prose.
    h   What does she mean by the phrase, 'sometimes I am made to feel like a
        kind of cultural Frankenstein' (lines 118–119)?
    i   Minfong Ho writes in English about characters from Thailand, Singapore
        and Cambodia. What special challenges does that represent?
    j   Why did the banana tree inspire her to write her first novel?

3   Find synonyms for the following words and phrases that appear in the text.
    a   in an easy conspiracy (line 8)   e   unquestioningly (line 15)
    b   aloof (line 9)   f   resonance (line 20)
    c   evoking (line 10)   g   wallowing (line 50)
    d   sibilant (line 13)   h   nuanced (line 53)

Developing writing skills

Another kind of feature article is the **profile**, in which you interview a
celebrity and find out about their personality, their life, their motives, and
ambitions.

●   Research the life and work of the writer Minfong Ho, or another
    multilingual personality, such as a sportsman or sportswoman, a film or TV
    star, or someone who has been in the news recently. Write about their past,
    their reasons for learning English, their problems, and their successes.

●   Alternatively take the idea of 'languages of the heart, hands and head' and
    write a profile of yourself for your school magazine, or a publication like
    IB World.

●   In groups, discuss the topic of living with different cultures. How does
    this affect people in your class? Make notes about the different ideas and
    opinions. Use the discussion to write a feature article for a teen magazine.

Beyond the text...

Fluency versus accuracy

When learning a language, we want to be able to communicate our ideas quickly and effectively without having to worry about every single word. In other words, we want to be fluent. At the same time we need to be accurate in our use of the language. Read this statement by an English B teacher in an international school.

"Some of my English B students can find language learning a very stressful activity, especially if they are very self-conscious about speaking English and 'getting it right'. Although they are keen to speak English with their peers outside class they become shy and inhibited when it comes to speaking in class – which is a very public activity. As a result some English B students can find it difficult to develop a totally positive self-concept. This can be because they cannot express themselves as fluently or unselfconsciously as they can in their mother tongue. This can be frustrating for them and can lead to a loss of self-esteem. Before a test at school or an oral examination, some students may develop a mental block. This can prevent them from remembering and communicating."

➤ Do you think this is an accurate description of your situation? To what extent can you identify with the teacher's students? What advice would you give the students?

TOK

Meta-learning: learning about learning

What differences were there between the ways Minfong Ho learned Chinese and Thai as first languages and the way she learned English? Think about the ways in which you learned your various languages. We can learn grammar intuitively, without conscious thought, or formally, by stating rules. What are the strengths and weaknesses of each approach?

Do you think the statement above is true for your first language (IB Language A) and English?

CAS

In cooperation with your teacher and CAS coordinator, design a survey to find out the number of languages spoken by students in your school. With permission, you could carry out the survey and publish the results in a report. Analyse your findings and make recommendations as to whether minority languages could be better catered for by the school community.

Social relationships

BEFORE YOU READ

→ Third Culture Kids are defined in the following article as 'Children who accompany their parents into another culture'. Do you think this definition applies to you, or your friends and classmates?

→ In what ways do you think that students who have lived abroad are different from those who have lived their lives in one country?

→ If you were living in a different culture, what do you think the most exciting parts of the experience would be? Which aspects of life abroad would be the most difficult to deal with?

→ It is sometimes said that 'Home is where the heart is'. Is it possible for home to be a foreign country?

→ What kinds of problems do you think Third Culture Kids might face when they return to their home country?

Cultural identity

Third Culture Kids

AS MORE cities and companies become increasingly international, there is a growing number of children that are creating their own sub-culture. Often referred to as TCKs (Third Culture Kids) or Global Nomads, these students have a tremendous impact on the global community. They are "raised in the margin of mosaic" and learn to balance worlds from within.

So who are these Third Culture Kids? They are not a new phenomenon. As one looks back over history, there is a realisation that certain groups of people have led highly mobile lives, a key factor in describing TCKs. They often relocate to new homes and/or countries. They are exposed to new cultures and to other people in the community who also move constantly.

Dr. Ruth Useem was the first person to coin the phrase Third Culture Kid. Dr. Useem's study of Americans living in India led her to define TCKs as "Children whose parents work abroad to live" (Useem, 1960). More recently, she redefined TCKs as "Children who accompany their parents into another culture" (Useem, 1970).

David C. Pollock and his co-author Ruth Van Reken, describe a TCK as "a person who has spent a significant part of his or her developmental years outside the parents' culture. The TCK builds relationships to all of the cultures, while not having full ownership of any. Although elements from each culture are assimilated into the TCK's life experience, the sense of belonging is in relationship to others of a similar background" (Pollock & Van Reken, 1999).

TCKs represent many countries and cultures. Their numbers extend into the hundreds of thousands and are increasing. Ease of travel and constant relocation of people through multinational companies and global business links contribute to this trend.

The question "Who am I?" is frequently asked by TCKs. They have accumulated a host of cultural identities, lived in many countries and have been introduced to a variety of global people. They are not the culture of their parents. TCKs position themselves by integrating a huge pool of values, norms, behaviours, beliefs, mannerisms and thoughts in order to identify self.

As you enter into the world of TCKs, one might suspect they are no different. But it is clear, after spending only a short time with them, that they bring a deep knowledge from within and a special ability to compare international and local issues. They are the future cross-culturalists and hopefully future politicians, diplomats, multi-nationals, government employees and educators. TCKs have a deep understanding of human rights.

They certainly encounter a different lifestyle compared to their mono-cultural peers but we can draw on their global and professional lives. So, whatever one chooses to label the international students as – TCKs, Global Nomads, Expatriates or Global Souls – we will reap unbelievable rewards and a true sense of satisfaction.

Lesley Lewis

1   Answer the following questions.

    a   What reason is given for the growing number of TCKs?

    b   Find two reasons why TCKs are different from other children.

    c   Dr Ruth Useem has given two definitions of TCKs. In what way is the second definition different from the first?

    d   According to researchers Pollock and Van Reken, with whom are TCKs likely to form friendships?

    e   According to the writer, what advantages do TCKs have in terms of knowledge of the world?

    f   Although it is not expressly stated, why are these children called Third Culture Kids? What are the three cultures to which they belong?

2   Find the word in the column on the right that could meaningfully replace each of the words on the left.

    a   sub-culture (line 5)

    b   phenomenon (line 15)

    c   relocate (line 20)

    d   exposed (line 21)

    e   assimilated (line 45)

    f   accumulated (line 62)

    g   position themselves (lines 67–68)

    h   integrating (line 68)

    i   cross-culturalists (lines 80–81)

    j   peers (line 88)

    1   combine

    2   find their place

    3   social nomads

    4   interpretation

    5   lost over time

    6   shown

    7   people of the same age

    8   absorbed

    9   including

    10   move home

    11   of the same period

    12   insignificant

    13   collected

    14   added to

    15   social trend

3   Scan the text to find whether the following sentences are true or false. Justify each answer with a relevant quotation from the text.

    a   Third Culture Kids belong to a new social trend.

    b   TCKs tend to live outside their own country while growing up.

    c   TCKs can have contact with several different cultures.

    d   Some TCKs have identity problems.

    e   Some TCKs tend to be very fixed in their views.

4   Write the meaning of the following phrases and then use them in sentences to describe Third Culture Kids.

    a   Global Nomad (line 7)

    b   raised in the margin of mosaic (lines 10–11)

    c   to coin the phrase (line 26)

    d   a host of cultural identities (lines 62–63)

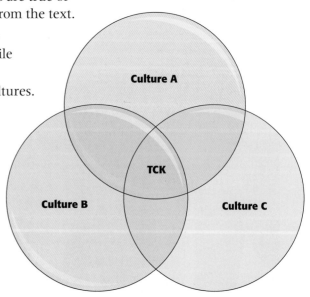

5 Draw a chart and sort the sentences numbered 1–30 below into three categories:

A Those that **describe advantages** for TCKs

B Those that **describe challenges** facing TCKs

C Those that **define and describe** TCKs

1 A crisis of identity – 'Who am I?'

2 A life filled with high mobility – TCKs know an airport better than most people.

3 They adapt quickly to unfamiliar countries and people.

4 They converse well with adults.

5 They are culturally astute, cross-culturally enriched, and less prejudiced.

6 They have difficulty with commitment to people, places, schools, or school systems as these constantly change.

7 They are educational achievers – a high percentage will attend university and obtain advanced degrees.

8 They establish relationships quickly – they cut through many of the initial levels of diffidence when forming relationships.

9 They are excellent observers of other people.

10 They feel different from others, which is difficult in forming peer relationships.

11 They live more in the present, more for the moment.

12 Loss of relationships, loss of community or school is equal to a loss of their world.

13 They make great culture bridges – they have multiple frames of reference.

14 They are more mature in their social skills.

15 They are more welcoming of newcomers into a community.

16 TCKs often become too observant and sensitive.

17 They are politically astute – TCKs tend to read the newspaper and watch the news more often than other children.

18 A feeling of powerlessness that they have no control over events and that these are often taken out of their hands anyway by the inevitability of the move.

19 They prefer to socialize with other TCKs as they enter adulthood and often become expatriates themselves.

20 A privileged lifestyle – their socio-economic lifestyle tends to be at a higher standard due to the advantages of relocations or the expatriate status offered by some companies (for example they have access to helpers, drivers, club memberships, and money).

21 They have problems with decision-making.

22 Rootlessness and restlessness can be a problem.

23 They speak more than one language – often they speak three or four. English may be one language they function in, but they can think and feel in several.

24 The elusive concept: 'Where is home?'

25 The frequent necessity of changing countries and homes.

26 The sense of belonging everywhere and nowhere.

27 They are great debaters. They are often aware of the background of political decisions and implications for the people concerned.

28 Travelling is a way of life – many holidays are taken outside the home country.

29 An uncertain cultural identity.

30 When returning to their 'passport' country, they are misunderstood by their fellow countrymen.

Developing writing skills: Set of instructions or guidelines

A set of instructions can give step-by-step guidance on how to do something. Sentences are usually chronologically ordered so the reader begins at the start of the process and finishes up at the end. As a result of following all the instructions, the reader is able to complete an action, for example putting together a piece of furniture from a kit (see Chapter 2, page 29). Such instructions are sometimes accompanied by visuals.

However, some instructions take the form of advice. These tend to be much less systematically ordered and are more personal in style and address.

Look again at the list of challenges facing Third Culture Kids on page 149. Write down the challenges you consider the greatest for TCKs. What advice would you give for each problem? Write up your answers in the form of a set of instructions to TCKs who are about to return to their passport countries for university regarding how to handle their return. The table below will help you to organize your ideas. Use the concepts and vocabulary items you have learned in this chapter.

Problem	Advice
The sense of belonging everywhere and nowhere.	

Once you have completed your notes put the sentences into a logical order. This can be done by grouping the ideas into subtopics each dealing with a different aspect of return. This new focus will give your readers coherent guidelines rather than a set of random points.

The personal response (HL)

Based on the following stimulus, give a personal response and justify it. Write a speech using 150 to 250 words.

> *"Some Third Culture Kids have nothing beyond their passports to connect them with their home country. TCKs lose and gain from the fact that they grow up outside their passport country."*

Before you start writing, ask yourself the following questions.

- What is your immediate reaction to the statement?
- What will be the thesis you will prove?
- Does this thesis require a one-sided or a balanced answer?
- Who will be the audience you will be addressing?
- What points will you make and what factual evidence can you find to support each point?
- What connective vocabulary will you use to make sure that your ideas flow?
- Given your audience, how will you conclude?

> **Exam tip**
>
> **HL P2 Section B**
> In the external examination you may wish to write a mini-essay if it suits your purpose.

Interactive oral activity: Debate

President Barack Obama could be described as the world's most powerful TCK. Is it true to say that the advantages of growing up in different cultures and coming from different heritages are far greater than the disadvantages? Debate this issue.

Barack Obama

Remember

- Preparation is necessary for such a discussion.
- Choose someone to 'chair' the discussion.
- Have two teams each speaking for opposing sides of the debate.
- Each team will need to plan together how to structure the discussion.
- Decide how to begin and wrap up the discussion.
- Ensure that everyone gets a chance to speak.
- Give each person a point to argue.
- Allow enough time to have an open debate once everyone has made their prepared point.
- Decide how to prevent one person from dominating the discussion.

Beyond the text...

Colors

I grew up in a Yellow country
But my parents are Blue.
I'm Blue.
Or at least, that is what they told me.
But I play with the Yellows.
I went to school with the Yellows.
I spoke the Yellow language.
I even dressed and appeared to be Yellow.
Then I moved to the Blue land.
Now I go to school with the Blues.
I speak the Blue language.
I even dress and look Blue.
But deep down, inside me, something's Yellow.
I love the Blue country.
But my ways are tinted with Yellow.
When I am in the Blue land,
I want to be Yellow.
When I am in the Yellow land,
I want to be Blue.
Why can't I be both?
A place where I can be me.
A place where I can be green.
I just want to be green.

Whitni Thomas (1991)

In this poem, Whitni Thomas describes her sense of belonging to three different cultures. She uses a number of **metaphors** to describe how it feels to be a Third Culture Kid. Metaphors work by creating pictures which help to understand an idea.

In the poem we can see three colours used as metaphors for identity: blue, yellow, and green.

Which culture does each colour stand for?

Explain the meaning of these phrases:

➤ I'm Blue. Or at least, that is what they told me.

➤ I even dressed and appeared to be Yellow.

➤ Now I go to school with the Blues.

➤ But deep down, inside me, something's Yellow.

➤ But my ways are tinted with Yellow.

➤ I just want to be green.

Do you think that the writer can be ever become truly green?

BEFORE YOU READ

In the following text, Ugandan writer Emma Makeri offers advice to parents in the process of moving abroad and who want to ensure that their children remain connected with their own culture.

→ Can you predict what advice she might give to maintain language and cultural heritage? As the world becomes more globalized, is there any point in retaining traditional customs and ideas?

→ Can you remember going abroad for the first time? What did you notice about the country you were in and the behaviour of its people? Were you drawn towards the differences or the similarities between your own country and the one you found yourself in?

→ Have you spent significant periods of your life in a culture other than your own? How do you feel towards the different cultures in which you live? To what extent do you feel accepted and to what extent do you remain an outsider?

"Help children maintain their culture in foreign environments"

UNLESS parents act as custodians of culture, children will get irreversibly engulfed in foreign norms, *writes Emma Makeri*.

In this era, we are witnessing an aspect of [a] which has increased the movement of people from country to country
5 for business, education, desire for a better life and escape from conflicts or natural disasters. Whatever the reason, living in a foreign country affects one's cultural roots, especially the younger generation.

This international [b] has led to the evolution of third culture
10 children. A third culture child is one who has spent a significant period of time in one or more cultures other than their own, thus [c] elements of those cultures and their own into a third culture. It's vital that parents and educators support children to retain their native cultures despite the differing cultural forces
15 around them.

The first step to instilling culture in a child's lifestyle is emphasising the [d] language. Parents should make children love their mother tongue through ways that motivate and encourage its learning. This can be achieved gradually by speaking to your
20 children in your mother tongue while at home and leaving the second language to the outside world. These efforts could be [e] by devoting time each day to reading and writing in your mother tongue with children until they can do it independently.

Since folklore has been a handy way of passing on culture
25 in Africa for ages, adopting it would be wise. In Nigeria, they say, "When an elder dies, a library is lost forever." This proverb was based on the notion that the older one grew, the more experienced they became in life matters. Elders used to [f] their wisdom by telling stories and quoting proverbs. Trying to tell
30 your children old tribal stories or making them appreciate the wisdom in African proverbs could go a long way in making the whole idea interesting to them. Tell stories and discuss interesting topics such as your childhood; children love to hear your home country culture, because this will develop both their oral and
35 vocabulary skills.

If you aren't so well equipped with folklore and cultural facts, having children [g] to books and multimedia in your home language can help. To spice up things even more, you could initiate a reward system and make learning a mother language
40 and other culture aspects competitive among children. Music in their native language can do magic.

However, a parent who takes the [h] to expose a child to their culture should be exposed too. It is quite uncomfortable to pressure one's child to learn their native culture when one isn't
45 exposed. The Liberians say, "A traveller with empty pockets can whistle in a robber's face," meaning that a free conscience brings comfort.

The Cameroonians say that; "It's no use carrying an umbrella if your shoes are leaking." This literally means that partial efforts
50 are always disappointing. In the same vein, telling your children to learn their culture without communicating your expectations and their [i] might cause disappointing results.

Relatives and other cultural setups can offer you support. You could for example organise visits to their country of origin, take
55 them to cultural events, museums or attend celebrations with families from the same cultural community.

The Sudanese say, "It is not with saying 'honey' that sweetness will come into the mouth." [j] a native culture in a child living in a foreign country does not happen spontaneously. Instead, it is
60 an [k] that requires commitment and determination, especially from the family.

While it's a good endeavour to retain native cultures, children in international cultural environments should not be limited to particular cultures. As long as they appreciate their native
65 cultures, they should be encouraged to become exposed and sensitive to other global cultures because this understanding will be beneficial in their future social, business and political interactions. They can therefore greatly [l] from bilingual education, where they get to master a different language.

Emma Makeri *The Ugandan Daily Monitor, 2011*

1   Some of the words have been removed from the text. From the table below, choose the word which best fits each gap marked **[a]–[l]**.

achievement	exposure
acquire	globalization
benefit	indigenous
disappointing	initiative
display	integrating
education	necessity
enhanced	particular
exposed	supposedly

2   Copy and complete the following table by indicating to whom or to what the word or phrase refers.

Word or phrase	Refers to
'those cultures' (line 12)	
'its' (line 19)	
'they' (line 28)	
'one' (line 44)	
'In the same vein' (line 50)	
'their' (line 54)	
'this understanding' (line 66)	

3   List the eight pieces of advice the writer offers to parents. With a partner, decide which pieces of advice are most practical and which ones seem less so.

4   In the text, the writer mentions four proverbs from different African countries. They are given below. Give the meaning of each in your own words.

   a   When an elder dies, a library is lost forever.

   b   A traveller with empty pockets can whistle in a robber's face.

   c   It's no use carrying an umbrella if your shoes are leaking.

   d   It is not with saying "honey" that sweetness will come into the mouth.

Beyond the text...

Proverbs

➤ Proverbs often offer advice or instruct us to behave in a certain way. As a piece of research, collect as many proverbs as you can and categorize them using headings such as Love, Money, Work, Morality, Relationships, Time, etc. Once you have collected a number of them, ask yourself whether these proverbs offer good or bad advice. Do any pairs of proverbs seem to offer contradictory advice?

➤ Find out whether you have the equivalent proverbs in your own language or culture. Are you able to translate them into English?

The personal response

Based on the following stimulus, give a personal response and justify it. Using 150 to 250 words, you could for example write a letter to the editor of the newspaper *The Ugandan Daily Monitor*. You can agree, disagree, or partially agree with the statement.

> *"This international exposure has led to the evolvement of third culture children. A third culture child is one who has spent a significant period of time in one or more cultures other than those of their parents, thus integrating elements of those cultures and their own into a third culture. It's vital that parents and educators support children to retain their native cultures despite the differing cultural forces around them."*

Before you start writing, ask yourself the following questions.

- What will be the main point of your letter?
- Does your response require a one-sided or a balanced answer?
- What factual evidence can you find to support each point?
- If you have no statistical evidence, can you use arguments based on personal experience?
- What connective vocabulary will you use to make sure that your ideas flow?
- How will you conclude?

Developing writing skills: Advice column

1   Based on your own reading about the issue of emigration, immigration, and cultural identity, write a set of instructions in the form of an advice column for parents soon to go abroad with younger children aged around 10 or 12 years old. Would your advice be similar to Emma Makeri's, or very different? Your instructions could include headings such as:

- Preparing to leave
- When you first arrive
- Maintaining your ties with home
- Preparing for the return
- Coping with the return

Your article might appear in a travel magazine or the leisure section of a Sunday newspaper.

2   When you have finished, try re-writing the advice for the children themselves. What changes would you make in order to address a much younger audience? Think about changes to content, vocabulary, formality, and tone.

Exam tip

The personal response
- A letter to the editor should always be written in formal language. It should express a clear opinion either in support or in opposition to the original article.
- Use a separate paragraph for each point.
- Such letters normally start with 'Dear Sir,' and end with a formal salutation.

Interactive oral activity

In groups, develop a role play for a family moving abroad for the first time. You can assign different roles and positions to the different characters. For example, one parent could be enthusiastic about the benefits abroad; the other concerned about the preservation of ties with home, culture, education, and language. One child could be very curious about a future in another country and education system; the other unenthusiastic and looking for objections.

Semi-scripted role plays

In a semi-scripted role play, the characters are assigned a role, for example 'enthusiastic sibling', and asked to think about the character's attitude to moving to another country. The person with this role should write down notes about the character's attitudes and outline the questions they would want to ask in the course of the role play. The actors must ask all the questions and make all the points they have written in their notes before the end of the role play.

Remember

In a role play one major aim is fluency. The purpose is to allow you to develop your confidence in communicating in English. In a semi-scripted role play you have the opportunity to communicate freely and naturally, without worrying about the small grammatical errors you may make.

Language & cultural identity

Feroz Salam spent most of his childhood shuttling between the Middle East and India, until an almost unhealthy addiction to computers drew him to university in London. When he's not busy

5 trying to unravel the mysteries of Computer Science, he's busy staring at a screen trying to meet an editor's deadline.

I don't understand the words

[a]

Walking past shisha bars in Knightsbridge,

10 London, the rasping Arabic instantly transports me to my childhood in Saudi Arabia. The clattering syllables of Hindi and Urdu outside curry houses in North London remind me of high school in India. And although I grew up in those countries,

15 and although I am Indian, I don't understand the words being said.

[b]

The only language I speak fluently is English, with the next best being rather mediocre French. It wasn't until I moved to England a few years ago

20 that I realized how much my identity was tied to the language I spoke. After years of living in places where I didn't speak the native tongue, I finally realized what it was like to feel 'at home' in a country.

[c]

25 Though I grew up in Saudi Arabia and India, I was raised speaking English. My parents, having been brought up in different states within India, spoke English around the house because it was their only shared language. Pre-school and elementary

30 school in Saudi Arabia were filled with the rich selection of English-speaking expatriates that the Middle East has to offer. It wasn't until later in life when I realized this monolingualism wasn't ordinary.

[d]

35 It all really hit home when I moved to India for high school. India is painfully multilingual – in urban areas most people speak at least two languages, while in rural areas you can drive for a day and pass through half a dozen different

40 linguistic zones. For the first time, I was immersed in life as an Indian, and not as an expatriate. Nothing can make you stand out more than a complete inability to speak a single Indian language in a country where most people speak

45 at least two.

[e]

I studied at an international school with friends much like myself, and despite trying my best, the most I could achieve in five years was broken Kannada, and Hindi remains a closed book. While

50 language wasn't much of a problem around my friends and family, who all spoke fluent English, many fundamental parts of Indian life remained a mystery. Supermarkets were fine, local grocers were a complete puzzle. Taxis were manageable

55 but the bus network was incomprehensible.

[f]

My extended Indian family's reaction to my monolingualism was an almost distressing medley of amusement, incredulity and borderline contempt. As I grew up, the question 'Do you
60 speak Kannada yet?' began to punctuate our family visits with wearying regularity. And even though I could see that my relatives wanted to know about my life – and I wanted to know about theirs – there is very little I can express beyond a smile and
65 a nod of the head.

[g]

India's enormous variety of languages and cultures give it a vibrancy that I have yet to experience in any other country. Yet for someone who speaks none of them fluently, I know I'm
70 missing out on a fundamental part of being an Indian. To be fair, I never noticed any of this at the time. Like most expats, there are some things we are just resigned to not doing in the country that we live in.

[h]

75 It was only when I arrived in London that I realized what I was missing. For once, I knew how to speak, fluently, the language of the majority. I can finally argue with people in a language we both understand instead of in three languages
80 neither of us speak fluently. I no longer needed a helping hand to deal with paperwork, and I don't

need a local guide to find my way around town. I was part of the mainstream. The entire country could speak my language.

[i]

85 Making friends has been an entirely new and exciting experience. As an expat kid you are raised in the company of other expat kids, even if it's just because only they speak your language. Yes, we're used to many different cultures and
90 backgrounds, but all of this is usually very much steeped in expat culture. My school in Saudi Arabia didn't have a single Saudi student, and my exposure to Arabic outside of school was minimal thanks to the virtually exclusive lives
95 expats and Saudis lead. When I landed in London, my friends no longer had to come from the same background as I did, and the variety has been a breath of fresh air.

[j]

I definitely wouldn't say I was English, but I have
100 discovered a strong feeling of 'home' here in London. It lies in the simplicity of being able to chat with the postman in the morning, or strike up a conversation with the lady behind the till at the supermarket. It might not sound like life-
105 changing stuff, but I finally know what it feels like to be 'at home'.

Feroz Salam

Can this be home to a global wanderer?

Cochin, India

1   From the list below, choose an appropriate heading for each of the paragraphs marked **[a]–[j]** in the text. There are more headings than you need.

- Independent
- Making progress
- Limits of learned languages
- Next year
- At home and an outsider
- My language ability
- Childhood memories
- Where I belong
- Picking up Hindi
- Multilingual communities
- Monolingual
- Unable to communicate
- Early days
- Saudi Arabia
- A fresh start

2   Answer the following questions.
   a   Why doesn't the writer understand either Hindi or Urdu?
   b   Which word between lines 9 and 19 is closest in meaning to 'below average'?
   c   What does the writer mean by 'this monolingualism wasn't ordinary?' (lines 33–34)
   d   How did the writer's family react when he admitted not speaking the local language?
   e   What is the meaning of 'vibrancy' in relation to Indian culture?
   f   What does 'this' refer to in the phrase 'I never noticed any of this' (line 71)?
   g   The writer says 'It was only when I arrived in London that I realized what I was missing' (lines 75–76). What does 'what' refer to?
   h   Why did the writer never learn Arabic?
   i   Why does London feel like home to an Indian national brought up in Saudi Arabia?
   j   Compared to the shops in India mentioned in the text, why does the supermarket in London feel different to the writer?

3   Explain the following phrases that appear in the text.
   a   clattering syllables (lines 11–12)
   b   It all really hit home (line 35)
   c   Hindi remains a closed book (line 49)
   d   distressing medley (lines 57–58)
   e   borderline contempt (lines 58–59)
   f   wearying regularity (line 61)
   g   steeped in expat culture (line 91)
   h   a breath of fresh air (line 98)

4   Re-read the text carefully. What have been the advantages and disadvantages for Feroz Salam in going to international schools and becoming a TCK? Use a table like the one below.

	Disadvantages	Advantages
Languages		
Family		
Being Indian		
Living in Saudi Arabia		
Being an English speaker		
Having a sense of home		
Living in London		
Other		

Interactive oral activity

Imagine a television programme about globalization and its effects on children. Organize a panel discussion in which members of your class play the roles of experts discussing the issue of Third Culture Kids.

Pick a question, such as 'TCKs: Global Nomads or Cultural Frankensteins?'

Your panel could include the following:

- an expert on TCKs, such as the writer of the text on page 152
- an international school counsellor
- a parent of TCKs
- a TCK currently studying for the IB Diploma and who has had very positive experiences
- a TCK currently studying for the IB Diploma and who has had much less positive experiences
- an adult TCK, such as Feroz Salam.

Each role player makes notes on their character. A moderator introduces the programme, asks a series of questions and moderates prepared questions from the rest of the class who can act as audience. Finally, the moderator should bring the discussion to a close.

The SL Written Assignment

For this component you first have to read three interrelated texts linked to the core, such as articles, blogs, and interviews. Your teacher will select the texts. The length of each source must be 300–400 words.

Re-read the texts on pages 147, 152 and 156. All of them relate to the subject of Third Culture Kids. For your SL written assignment, you may wish to examine this issue or one of these related themes:

- Educational systems
- Language and cultural identity, or self-identity
- Relationships
- Social behaviours and stances

Once you have chosen your subject matter, decide on a specific text type to write. Before you start planning and writing in detail, discuss your ideas with your teacher. You may wish to use the table below to review the aims of your written assignment and to plan a rationale.

Decide on…	
Topic	
Theme	
Text type	
Purpose	Describe / Explain / Inform / Instruct / Narrate / Persuade
Audience	
Structure	Introduction / Body / Conclusion
Language	Vocabulary / Tone of voice / Formality

The personal response (HL)

Based on the stimulus below, give a personal response and justify it. Choose any text type you have studied in class. Write 150–250 words.

> *"It would be typical for a Third Culture Kid to say that he is a citizen of a country, but with nothing beyond his passport to define that identification for him. Such children usually find it difficult to answer the question, "Where are you from?" Compared to their peers who have lived their entire lives in a single culture, TCKs have a globalized culture."*
>
> (Wikipedia)

Developing writing skills: Instructions

Organizing a discussion group

Is there an issue that you have a real burning desire to discuss at school? Create a discussion group with a view to forming a plan of action. This will take time, organization, and creativity. If it is well-planned, a discussion group can be an incredibly valuable experience.

Here are some key elements that are essential to the planning of a successful discussion group:

Agenda
Attendees
Date, time, and location
Visual aids
Discussions and activities
Follow-up plan
Seating arrangements
Purpose and goals

Exam tip

A quick check list!
Make sure that you have:
- an introduction
- a thesis to prove
- a paragraph format
- topic sentences for each paragraph
- use of examples
- explanation of how examples relate to the topic sentences
- well-connected paragraphs
- a logical conclusion.

Writing instructions

Practical instructions should give your readers a roadmap to follow and should explain each step carefully. The body of such instructions should be organized chronologically, so that readers can understand the whole process from beginning to end. It may help you to plan your work by sketching a flowchart to make sure that you have all the steps in the right order.

In many schools setting up a club, an activity, or discussion group can be a complicated process involving permissions and paperwork. Find out how it is done and write a clear set of instructions to set up a successful discussion group at your school for students who may want to discuss issues of identity and culture.

Remember

A lot of people don't like reading instructions so…

* explain each step of the operation
* limit the amount of information in each step
* always phrase your instructions clearly
* use bullet points or numbers.

CAS

In order to help students new to your school and new to your country, create a set of helpful guidelines so that they can settle in to the school. Your guidelines should set out some of the major issues facing such students and offer advice as to how they can cope and how they can find help.

Beyond the text...

It's Not Easy Being Green

It's not that easy being green;
Having to spend each day the color of the leaves.
When I think it could be nicer being red, or yellow or gold…
or something much more colorful like that.

It's not easy being green.
It seems you blend in with so many other ord'nary things.
And people tend to pass you over 'cause you're
not standing out like flashy sparkles in the water
or stars in the sky.

But green's the color of Spring.
And green can be cool and friendly-like.
And green can be big like an ocean, or important
like a mountain, or tall like a tree.

When green is all there is to be
It could make you wonder why, but why wonder why?
Wonder, I am green and it'll do fine, it's beautiful!
And I think it's what I want to be.

The Sesame Street Book and Record (c)1970 Jonico Music, Inc.
Sung by the character **Kermit the Frog**

How relevant to the topic of Third Culture Kids is Kermit's song? Is it just TCKs who have difficulty finding a place in modern society or are we all restricted by the constraints of society around us? How difficult is it to be an individual at school and outside it?

Education & minorities

In the following text, Maxine Hong Kingston describes her first year of learning English in an American elementary school. Coming from a Cantonese–Chinese speaking household, she knew no English.

→ What difficulties would you imagine she had? Are they all related to language or also to culture and behaviour?

→ When we say we have difficulty understanding someone who speaks another language, is it just the words we fail to understand or do we really fail to understand the person's culture too?

→ Discuss whether our languages are simply codes of communication or whether they are wrapped up with patterns of behaviour, such as:
- ways of showing respect
- politeness
- avoidance of taboo
- cultural beliefs, including religion
- superstitions and good luck totems
- gender roles.

Memories of a Chinese–American childhood

My silence was thickest – total – during the three years that I covered my school paintings with black paint. I painted layers of black over houses and flowers and suns, and when I
5 drew on the blackboard, I put a layer of chalk on top. I was making a stage curtain, and it was the moment before the curtain parted or rose. The teachers called my parents to school, and I saw they had been saving my pictures,
10 curling and cracking, all alike and black. The teachers pointed to the pictures and looked serious, talked seriously too, but my parents did not understand English. ("The parents and teachers of criminals were executed"
15 said my father.) My parents took the pictures home. I spread them out (so black and full of possibilities) and pretended the curtains were swinging open, flying up, one after another, sunlight underneath, mighty operas.
20   During the first silent year I spoke to no one at school, did not ask before going to the lavatory, and flunked kindergarten. My sister also said nothing for three years, silent in the playground and silent at lunch. There were
25 other quiet Chinese girls not of our family, but most of them got over it sooner than we did. I enjoyed the silence. At first it did not occur to me I was supposed to talk or to pass kindergarten. I talked at home and to one

30 or two of the Chinese kids in class. I made motions and even made some jokes. I drank out of a toy saucer when the water spilled out of the cup, and everybody laughed, pointing at me. So I did it some more. I didn't know that
35 Americans don't drink out of saucers.

It was when I found out I had to talk that school became a misery, that the silence became a misery. I did not speak and felt bad each time that I did not speak. I read aloud
40 in first grade, though, and heard the barest whisper with little squeaks come out of my throat. "Louder," said the teacher, who scared the voice away again. The other Chinese girls did not talk either, so I knew the silence had
45 to do with being a Chinese girl.

Reading out loud was easier than speaking because we did not have to make up what to say, but I stopped often, and the teacher would think I'd gone quiet again. I could
50 not understand 'I'. The Chinese 'I' has seven strokes, intricacies. How could the American 'I', assuredly wearing a hat like the Chinese, have only three strokes, the middle so straight? Was it out of politeness that this
55 writer left off strokes the way a Chinese has to write her own name small and crooked? No, it was not politeness; 'I' is a cap-ital and 'you' is a lower-case. I stared at that middle

line and waited so long for its black centre to
60 resolve into tight strokes and dots that I forgot to pronounce it. The other troublesome word was 'here', no strong consonant to hang on to, and so flat, when 'here' is two mountainous ideographs. The teacher, who had already told
65 me every day how to read 'I' and 'here', put me in the low corner under the stairs again, where the noisy boys usually sat.

When my second grade class did a play, the whole class went to the auditorium except
70 the Chinese girls. The teacher, lovely and Hawaiian, should have understood about us, but instead left us behind in the classroom. Our voices were too soft or nonexistent, and our parents never signed the permission
75 slips anyway. They never signed anything unnecessary. We opened the door a crack and peeked out, but closed it again quickly. One of us (not me) won every spelling bee, though.

I remember telling the Hawaiian teacher,
80 "We Chinese can't sing 'Land where our fathers died'." She argued with me about politics, while I meant because of curses. But how can I have that memory when I couldn't talk? My mother says that we, like the ghosts,
85 have no memories.

Maxine Hong Kingston

1   Answer the following questions.
   a   Estimate the young Maxine's age during her silent period. What
       evidence do you have for your answer?
   b   Why do you think this silent period lasted so long?
   c   Why were these black pictures so important to the girl?
   d   How could a small child 'flunk' kindergarten? What does the writer
       mean here?
   e   How do we know Maxine was not as silent at home as at school?
   f   What caused Maxine to pause so frequently during reading out loud?
   g   What was confusing for a reader of Chinese about the English words
       'you' and 'I'?
   h   How do we know that Maxine had already learned to read in Chinese
       at this time?
   i   After reading aloud, why was the girl put 'in the low corner under the
       stairs again'?
   j   Why were the Chinese girls left behind during the school play?

2   Suggest explanations for the following phrases taken from the text.
   a   In view of the girl's silence, explain these metaphors:
       ● 'I was making a stage curtain' (line 6)
       ● 'it was the moment before the curtain parted or rose' (lines 7–8)
   b   Explain the meaning of 'most of them got over it sooner than we did'
       (lines 26–27).
   c   What is suggested by the phrase 'had to' in, 'It was when I found out I
       had to talk that school became a misery' (lines 36–37)?
   d   What is meant by the phrase 'the teacher … scared the voice away'
       (line 42–43)?
   e   How do you interpret the phrase 'I knew the silence had to do with
       being a Chinese girl' (lines 44–45)?
   f   What is this phrase describing: 'I stared at that middle line and waited so
       long for its black centre to resolve into tight strokes and dots' (lines 58–60)?
   g   How can 'here' be 'flat' (line 63)?
   h   What is the significance of the phrase 'The teacher, lovely and
       Hawaiian, should have understood about us' (lines 70–71)?

3   Maxine's earliest days at school were full of cultural misunderstandings.
    Re-read the text and copy and complete the table below. You will need to
    infer many of the answers from the context of the passage.

Maxine's action	Her American teachers' interpretation of her action	Maxine's real reason for her action
Painting black over her pictures		
Not speaking or asking to go to the toilet		
Drinking out of a saucer		
Finding it hard to write the word 'I' in English		
Finding it hard to say the word 'here' in English		
Not taking part in the school play		
Not wanting to sing, Land where our fathers died'		

4   Based on your completed table in question 3 and your reading of the text,
    what are your impressions of:
   a   Maxine?
   b   her teachers?

Interactive oral activity

Your school has to take in 20 new students one year before the start of the IB Programme. Using your own experiences of learning English, come up with a plan to help the students integrate into classes and prepare for the IB Diploma in 12 months' time.

Work in small groups and present your plans to your classmates.

Developing writing skills

How successful is Maxine Hong Kingston at conveying the difficulties of learning English? Reflect on how you have learned English. Can you remember having difficulties with understanding, speaking, reading, and writing? Like Maxine, did you have problems because of interlinguistic interference, where your first language seems to be so different that some equivalent aspect of English made little sense?

Here are some of the issues mentioned in the text:

- Understanding the sounds of English
- Finding the self-confidence to speak
- Understanding the spelling and writing system

Add to the list and give examples of your own. Use these reflections to write a personal account of your struggles (and ultimate success) in the form of a blog entry in English.

> **Remember**
>
> Look at Feroz Salam's text on page 156 again. Can you see how the writer has structured his ideas in a certain order to make sure he communicates effectively? Remember this in your own writing.
>
> You might also like to borrow some descriptive techniques from Maxine Hong Kingston's text. She is renowned as a writer for her use of sense perception, in order to give the reader a clear picture of the scene she is describing.

The personal response (HL)

Based on the stimulus below, give a personal response and justify it. Choose any text type you have studied in class. Write 150–250 words.

> *"We are unaware that we are communicating in many different ways even when we are not speaking [...] We are rarely taught about this non-verbal form of communication in school [...] We informally learn how to use gestures, glances, slight changes in tone of voice, [...] to alter or emphasize what we say and do [...] We learn these culture-bound techniques largely by observing others and imitating them."*

1   What is the main point of the quote? Can you agree with the statement or would you prefer to challenge it? One way of tackling the personal response is to look at each part of the statement and address it. For each stage, you must provide evidence as to whether:

   a   we use gestures and other non-verbal forms to communicate, or not

   b   non-verbal communication is taught at school, or not

   c   we learn non-verbal, culture-bound communication by imitating others.

2   Can you find evidence in the text for the use of non-verbal communication which is learned at home rather than at school?

165

TOK

What do we mean by home? Whose view of home?
As seen in the texts, many Third Culture Kids and many bilinguals find it hard to relate to a single concept of home.

Explore the issue from the angles of different ways of knowing.

Language
Do you have the same image for the word 'home' in your Language A and your Language B? What are the similarities and what are the differences in the two words? Why do these differences occur? Which is your language of home?

Emotion
Which place do you feel emotionally most attached to: a building, a specific place, a community, a region, or a country?

Logic
Calculate in which places you have lived longest. Put them in rank order of time spent in each place. Logically, the place where you have spent most time is home. Is this true?

Perception
Think about the colours, sights, smells, and tastes of the places you have lived in. Which ones define the concept of home for you?

Using the different ways of knowing is it possible to define what you mean by home?

Whose idea of home is this?

Beyond the text...

Cultural context

➤ Maxine Hong Kingston is describing the Chinese immigrant experience of the US in the 1940s and 1950s. In the text on page 162, the writer makes three comments about her parents. First, the father says to Maxine, "The parents and teachers of criminals were executed." The writer notes that her parents 'never signed anything unnecessary'. Finally, Maxine reflects, 'But how can I have that memory when I couldn't talk? My mother says that we, like the ghosts, have no memories.'

To readers, these phrases seem obscure and mysterious. They seem to make little sense to a reader unfamiliar with these people's lives. This is because we do not understand the context of the words which can be best understood by reading about the history of China and the US during the above-mentioned times.

➤ Investigate immigration to anglophone countries and see how specific groups have coped with the difficulties of new cultures, new languages, poor employment prospects, and very difficult economic circumstances. Examine both their difficulties and their triumphs. This research might make a possible topic for an extended essay.

Global issues

BEFORE YOU READ

→ What is a stereotype? In what ways are stereotypes harmful? In what ways do they prevent us from learning about people from different cultures and backgrounds?

→ *Scrap the teen stereotypes* discusses the attitudes of adults towards teenagers and attempts to dispel some of the myths about teenagers. Make a list of the negative values some adults might have towards them. Do you think these ideas are in any way justifiable?

→ To what extent do the media create stereotypes? Can you think of some TV shows, films, advertisements, and Internet content that deliberately destroy negative stereotypical views of teenagers?

→ In the following interview, Dr. Bibby argues that Canadian youth are far more virtuous than they are given credit for. What personal qualities might they possess?

Is this a stereotypical view of teenagers?

Prejudice

SCRAP THE TEEN STEREOTYPES

When Kurt Cobain unleashed 'Smells like Teen Spirit' in 1991, the Nirvana song became a gritty anthem for a generation of disaffected youth. But the late grunge demigod might have been less inspired by a whiff of today's teens. In the Facebook age, where's the alienation? Teenagers are now a surprisingly virtuous lot, according to sociologist Reginald Bibby, author of 'The Emerging Millennials: How Canada's Newest Generation Is Responding to Change and Choice'. In his 2008 survey of 5,500 youth, Dr. Bibby found that Canadian teens place supreme importance on values such as honesty and caring for others. They actually like hanging out with their parents. And they're less likely to smoke, drink, do drugs and have sex than any group since he began tracking adolescent behaviour in 1984. Dr. Bibby spoke to The Globe and Mail about how today's parents are raising great kids – and why people get upset by his good news.

[1]

There are significant decreases in the percentage of kids who say they have a close friend who has experienced severe depression, bullying at school, drug and alcohol problems, gang violence, sexual abuse, or a suicide attempt. That's the biggest thing that surprised me overall.

[2]

Invariably, if I say things are looking pretty good for teens relative to the past, people get mad. We just have this assumption that this generation can't possibly turn out as well as previous generations.

[3]

I don't want to sound naive here but my sense is that post-boomers have recognized the importance of balancing career and family. They're focusing on building good relationships with their kids. And they're no longer using the old cliché about quality versus quantity time.

[4]

No, I think it is overplayed. What teens are saying in the survey is that friends are very important in terms of giving them sheer joy but when it comes to areas of influence, Mom and Dad are right up there. Parents are being shown more respect than they realize.

[5]

We have such tremendous resources, from governments as well as the corporate community, designed to elevate the lives of young people. If there's a violent incident at virtually any school in the country, for example, the next thing we hear is that grief counselors are being brought in. So it's no wonder we're seeing improvements in all these areas.

[6]

I try to tell social workers, give yourselves a cheer. Some people think they're going to get the pink slip here, but obviously there are other areas where kids need help. Maybe it's time to focus on teen gambling, for example.

[7]

One of the reasons kids aren't drinking as much on a Friday night is, frankly, they have other things they can do – they've got Facebook, YouTube, video games. Vice has to compete with all these entertainment options.

[8]

I don't think we can when they're teenagers. They're using technology for social and entertainment functions. They've got all this artillery to understand what's going on in the world but the percentage that say they follow the news has actually dropped off in the last decade. What's intriguing will be to see how they'll make use of technology when they get into their 20s and beyond.

[9]

No. In the course of doing all this research, I can't say I've been reading much in terms of parenting guides.

Adriana Barton

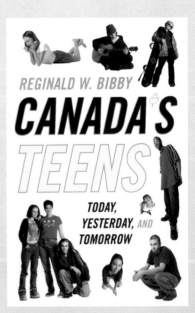

1   The interview questions have been removed from the text. Match the questions below with the gaps numbered **[1]–[9]** in the text. There are more than you need.

   A   About 99 per cent of teens watch TV and use computers daily, yet only 17 per cent keep up with the news. How can we get teens to become global thinkers?

   B   According to your research, today's adolescents have stronger ties to their parents than any teen cohort in the past 30 years. Are today's parents trying to be their kids' best friends?

   C   After analysing teenagers' replies to your 200-question survey, what surprised you most?

   D   As the father of three sons in their early 40s and a six-year-old girl, can you recommend any parenting books?

   E   Experts such as Gordon Neufeld, author of *Hold On to Your Kids,* claim that today's children are increasingly peer-oriented. Is this something we should worry about?

   F   How has the Internet influenced teen habits?

   G   In your experience, what do you think are the greatest pressures on teenagers today?

   H   Should we expect big cuts to social programs if politicians read your survey results?

   I   What are some of the most common stereotypical views of teenagers?

   J   What advice can you offer concerned parents of teenagers?

   K   Your book paints a rosy picture of today's youth but it's been met with considerable scepticism. Why?

   L   Your study found that teens are less likely to smoke, drink, or take drugs than they were eight years ago. Why?

2   Give a meaning for each of the following words or phrases as they appear in the text.

   a   unleashed (line 1)   **d**   grunge demigod (line 5)
   b   gritty anthem (line 3)   **e**   whiff (line 6)
   c   disaffected (line 4)   **f**   virtuous lot (line 9)

3   Answer the following questions.
   a   List five improvements to teenage behaviour over the last decade.
   b   To what does 'That's' relate in line 34?
   c   Why do certain people criticize Dr. Bibby for his optimism about teenagers?
   d   According to the text which three factors have contributed to a change in teenage behaviour in Canada?
   e   In what ways does he feel parents have contributed to the change?
   f   How does Dr. Bibby evaluate the role of friendship?
   g   In what ways has the partnership between government and business contributed to teenagers' welfare?
   h   According to Dr. Bibby, what new threats face teenagers?
   i   How has new technology changed teenage behaviour patterns?
   j   According to Dr Bibby, how have young people's attitudes changed to current affairs?
   k   Explain the meaning of the phrase 'they've got all this artillery' (line 89).
   l   What can we not predict about the present generation of teenagers?

4   Identify and explain the following cultural references mentioned in the text:
   a   post-boomers (line 44)
   b   quality versus quantity time (lines 50–51)
   c   get the pink slip (lines 73-74)

Interactive oral activity

- In groups, summarize all the findings of Dr Bibby's survey on teenage behaviour. Compile a list of both the causes and effects of behavioural patterns in the last decade.
- Make a list of 10–20 adjectival phrases to describe the Canadian teenagers investigated and surveyed.
- How does this list compare with stereotypical and often critical views on teenagers? Make a second list of negative attributes of teenagers. Use these notes to compare teenagers in your own society.
- Do you think teenagers in your country would agree with the conclusions reached about Canadian ones?

Conducting an interview

In your introduction, you should establish a rapport with the interviewee:

"Thanks for talking to our magazine."

You should also introduce the interviewee:

"Shahid Maqbool, you are known as the pioneer of the village mobile phone in Tanzania. Where did the idea come from?"

If you want your interview to cover personal issues, you might want to ask about less sensitive topics first and then move to specifics. For example, first ask about some facts ("Is it true that..?"). With this approach, respondents can feel more comfortable before warming up to more personal or sensitive matters. Your last question could allow the respondent to provide information about future plans:

"So what do you see as the next stage?"

The interview could be concluded by thanking the respondent.

Remember

To avoid yes/no it is a useful technique to ask 'open' questions such as:

"What can you tell our readers about...?" "How would you describe..."

Developing writing skills

Look at the text on page 168. What are the features of the interview?

Imagine a journalist interviewing your future self in 10–15 years' time. What will you have to say about yourself?

How do you see yourself in the future? Where will you be, in your home country or another? What job will you be doing? Will you be working for a huge corporation or a small or medium-sized company or organization? Or will you be your own boss? What will you have achieved? What about your personal life, family, friendships and relationships?

- Write the interview.
- Write an article based on your interview to be published in a local magazine.

The personal response (HL)

Based on the stimulus below, give a personal response and justify it. Choose any text type. Write 150–250 words.

> *"My teenage years were exactly what they were supposed to be. Everybody has their own path. It's laid out for you. It's just up to you to walk it."*
>
> **Justin Timberlake**

Beyond the text...

➤ Examine your local press and media and collect news reports and magazine features about teenagers in anglophone countries. What are the main characteristics of teenagers in these countries? How do they compare to teenagers in your own culture? Look at these images of Third Culture kids. How do they compare to images of young men and women in your local teenage magazines? What are the similarities and differences?

BEFORE YOU READ

→ What is a stand-up comic? How is this kind of performance different to acting? What special qualities must you have in order, like Shazia, to be successful on stage?

→ What difficulties do you think Shazia might have faced in developing her career?

→ What sorts of discrimination do you think she might have encountered in her professional career? How do you think she would have coped? What kind of strategies do you think she might have used?

→ In her stand-up comedy act Shazia plays on the stereotype of a British Muslim Asian woman. What might the characteristics of this stereotype be and how do you think she breaks these prejudices?

→ It is said that parents always want the best for their children. Is it right that children fulfill the dreams and ambitions of their parents? Is it right to pursue dreams and ambitions that do not conform to your parents' wishes?

The courage to change

Award-winning columnist Shazia Mirza on the trials and tribulations of entering the bear pit of comedy

Birmingham born Shazia Mirza is the UK's most prolific and, as yet, only female Muslim stand-up 5 **comedian. She started her professional stand-up career in September 2000. Prior to that she studied Biochemistry at university.** 10 **She eventually became a science teacher at a comprehensive school in London's East End but gave up her teaching in order** 15 **to become a comedian full time. Shazia has got her own radio show in London on ClubAsia AM. After appearing on** 20 **BBC1's** *Have I Got News for You***, she became a regular commentator on BBC Radio Five Live. Shazia has also landed her first** 25 **publishing deal and is currently writing a book.**

I am a stand-up comedian. Sometimes people ask me, "What is your real job?"
30 This is my real job. I am not a part time brain surgeon, lawyer, or veterinarian who fits in a few jokes in the evenings. This is it, I'm a clown.
35 My parents' plans for my life did not include comedy. They had it all planned out. Science A-levels, Oxbridge, Medicine, marriage to the Prime
40 Minister, children, mansion, so meticulously planned they would have even set a date for a heart attack and then death.

I always wanted to perform.
45 I remember my Aunt Vicious – (we used to call her that, because if anyone of us came out with a wrong answer, a wooden stick wouldn't be far
50 away) asking me what I wanted to be when I grew up? "I want to be on stage," I replied. I was seven. "You can't do that," she shouted.
55 I couldn't understand her reaction; I only wanted to be a comedian – not work at Spearmint Rhino.
Nothing is insuperable. I met
60 Boy George at a party when I was 21. He asked me what I did, at the time I was a student but I told him I really wanted to be on stage. He said "If you
65 want something badly enough you can have it, you'll have to suffer, but you can definitely have it." I used to spend every night in bed thinking "How can
70 I achieve my dreams?" I was prepared to do anything.
None of the people I admire have been exempt from the challenges and stereotypes
75 thrust upon us by family or society: Nelson Mandela, Richard Pryor, Joan Rivers, Kelly Holmes and Gandhi. I admire them all. People who
80 inspire don't set out to inspire, their inspiration is a by-product of their achievement. They consequently plant the seed of ambition into others and provide
85 us with the fuel of hope, without which there is no progress.

I always wanted to be a comedian but I never thought it would be possible. My parents
90 would never allow me, the comedy world would never understand and accept me, I would never make a living, and what if I failed? But I believed
95 in myself.
Self-belief is the revenge on all doubters.
In comedy I have struggled against people who wish me
100 badly, I have been bullied, I have experienced racism and sexism, I have had tomatoes in my face, I have been sad and lonely, unsupported, I
105 have cried many times and wondered what the heck I am doing.
The comedy world can be a bear pit. I am an outsider in
110 a world of outsiders, but I am motivated by ambition, and the desire to do something with my life, something that I love, but as an Asian woman I know
115 there is a price to pay.
Asian women feel the need to fulfil a role. Modern stereotypes are promoted and re-enforced from childhood and
120 we can be easily pigeon-holed into the way others think of us, but I'm sure the make-up of all mankind involves having some expectations. Asian culture is
125 success-driven. My mum always says, "I don't care what you do, just be the best at it."
It takes audacity and courage to make a change but the self-
130 confidence one builds from achieving difficult things and accomplishing goals is the best achievement of all.

Shazia Mirza

1   Re-read the text to find whether the following ideas are true or
    false. Justify each answer with evidence from the passage.
    a   Shazia's parents always fully supported her ambition to be a
        comic.
    b   Shazia's Aunt Vicious never understood her.
    c   Shazia's desire to become a comic first developed when she was
        a university student.
    d   Shazia always believed that she would become a comic.
    e   Her audiences have always been really supportive.
    f   Shazia's relaionship with her parents is now very good.

2   Answer the following questions.
    a   What were Shazia's parents' hopes and expectations for her?
    b   What do you think was stereotypical about her parents' choice
        of career for her?
    c   What was Aunt Vicious' reaction to her niece's career choice?
    d   What advice did Boy George give to Shazia?
    e   From what kinds of people did she face hostility in the first few
        years of her career as a comic?
    f   What personal quality gave Shazia the will to succeed despite
        the obstacles she faced?
    g   What specific problems has she faced as a female Muslim
        British Asian comic?
    h   What does she consider to be her most important achievement
        in her professional and personal life?

3   To what do these words and phrases refer in the text?
    a   'This is it ' (line 33)
    b   'it' (line 37)
    c   'that' (line 53)
    d   'there is a price to pay' (line 115)
    e   'it' (line 127)

4   Choose the correct answer from A, B, or C to replace each word or
    phrase below.
    a   meticulously (line 41)   e   bear pit (line 109)
        A   in great detail   A   difficult challenge
        B   calculatingly   B   a nasty fight
        C   approximately   C   an ugly scene
    b   insuperable (line 59)   f   promoted (line 118)
        A   undefeated   A   encouraged
        B   easy   B   developed
        C   impossible   C   given a better position
    c   be exempt (line 73)   g   pigeon-holed (line 120)
        A   ignore   A   sorted
        B   excused   B   categorized
        C   free   C   stereotyped
    d   by-product (line 81)   h   audacity (line 128)
        A   consequence   A   boldness
        B   side effect   B   cheekiness
        C   derivative   C   overconfidence

Interactive oral activity: Role play

Imagine that you have chosen an unusual undergraduate degree or career and have to confront your parents about your plans for the future.

- In groups, create a role play in which the parents want the child to succeed, but on their terms. The teenager concerned has totally different ideas about his or her future. You might know of friends or relatives who have had to deal with such issues.

Create four roles:

A the student
B a supportive brother or sister
C a parent who has very fixed ideas
D a parent who is more sympathetic.

- The aim of the role play is to demonstrate the initial problem, show different sides of the argument and find a compromise acceptable to all parties.

Here is a table to assess your own performance in the interactive oral. In order to make a realistic judgment, compare your scores with those given by your teacher.

Criterion A: Productive skills

	0	1	2	3	4	5
Language Command						
Production						
Intonation						

Criterion B: Interactive and receptive skills

	0	1	2	3	4	5
Ideas understood						
Intonation						
Ideas presented						

Developing writing skills

In the text on page 173, Shazia writes:

'In comedy I have struggled against people who wish me badly, I have been bullied, I have experienced racism and sexism, I have had tomatoes in my face, I have been sad and lonely, unsupported, I have cried many times and wondered what the heck I am doing.'

- Pick a personality you admire and who has suffered discrimination, yet has managed to overcome such obstacles. The person chosen could be historical or contemporary but their story should be one of courage in the face of discrimination. If necessary you can undertake further study on the person.
- If you had the opportunity to interview this hero, what questions would you like to put to him or her? Order your questions (straightforward ones first and more personal ones later). Imagine the responses and note them. Use your jottings to write your imaginary interview with that person.
- Now write an article based on this interview to be published in your school's newspaper.

> **Exam tip**
>
> **Structuring an interview**
> - Have you explained the background and the reason behind the interview in your introduction?
> - Have you created a series of clear questions which lead the reader into an understanding of the personality of the interviewee?
> - Is there a clear wrap-up or conclusion at the end of the interview?

The personal response (HL)

Based on the stimulus below, give a personal response and justify it. Choose a text type you have studied in class. Write 150–250 words.

> *"Asian women feel the need to fulfil a role. Modern stereotypes are promoted and re-enforced from childhood and we can be easily pigeon-holed into the way others think of us."*
> **Shazia Mirza**

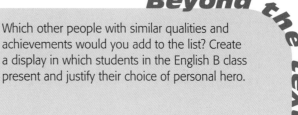

➤ In the text, Shazia mentions that the following people are among her list of personal heroes and heroines: Nelson Mandela, Richard Pryor, Joan Rivers, Kelly Holmes and Gandhi. Research each name and find out what qualities and achievements bind this group together.

➤ Which other people with similar qualities and achievements would you add to the list? Create a display in which students in the English B class present and justify their choice of personal hero.

Beyond the text...

Racism

BEFORE YOU READ

→ What is the difference between prejudice and discrimination?
→ How do concepts like racism, ageism, and sexism relate to prejudice and discrimination?
→ In the following text, a former Liverpool and England footballer talks about the racism he encountered on the football terraces in England and the measures he took both as a player and later as an administrator. What do you think he would have done to counter racist behaviour?

3 | News

Ignoring the Bananas

How John Barnes tackled racism in English football

FOR MANY black players plying their trade all over the globe the infamous monkey chant or throwing bananas on the pitch is the ultimate insult. It is a gesture that attempts to denote the individual as being less than human, unintelligent primates scampering around the park simply for the sake of **[a]** and amusement. Though it's less prominent in football these days, the phenomenon still remains **[b]** far and wide across the planet, like an incurable disease.

Understandably, those who continue to be touched by the curse have **[c]** their frustration in various ways. Two years ago, an **[d]** Samuel Eto'o attempted to leave the pitch after fans of Spanish team Real Zaragoza performed monkey chants and threw peanuts on the pitch whenever the Cameroonian international touched the ball. Now in his fourth season at Barcelona, the talented striker still refuses to take his children to watch him play.

It is a similar situation for teammate Idriss Carlos Kameni, who plays for Espanyol. In Germany, Gerard Asamoah, the first black player to play for that country, threatened to quit national duty soon after the World Cup if chanting around the German league did not **[e]**.

The list goes on, but none of these players can claim to have faced the level of intolerance **[f]** to one man in the 1980s in England.

In a time when **[g]** was rampant, Jamaica-born John Barnes looked the monster of discrimination dead in the eye and never seemed to **[h]**.

"It happened and it really meant nothing to me; it was like water off a duck's back," said the former Liverpool great.

"You see, I consider racists to be ignorant people so they did not affect me at all," Barnes remarked simply.

[1]

Born in Kingston on November 11, 1963, the son of well-respected army man Colonel Ken Barnes and his wife, Jean, a television presenter, young John showcased his talent within the confines of the Jamaica Defence Force (JDF) headquarters at UP Park Camp before playing in the Colts schoolboy competition for North Street high school St George's.

Moving to England at the age of 13, Barnes then playing for non-league team Sudbury Court, was spotted by Watford and signed in July 1981. He was on his way to the big time, but the experiences Barnes was to face at his new club, which gained promotion to the top flight in the 1981–82 season would be unlike any he had faced before at small-time Sudbury Court – a world away in Jamaica.

"Racism was rife. You had bananas coming on the field, you had monkey chants, you had all sorts of obscenities being shouted at you," Barnes, who was in the island recently for the Digicel Football Clinics, recalled.

"It was an accepted part of football the authorities never did anything, the referees never did anything ... what could the players do?" he said.

"Now the authorities get involved, they eject people from the ground and fine football clubs but back then it was the normal way of football in England," he said.

[2]

Six years and 65 goals later, Barnes secured a move to powerhouse team Liverpool but on his debut he was warned that it would be more of the same.

However, just as he had done before, the winger was cool and even casual in his approach. In a famous picture seen all over the world, the player, clad in the famous red of his Merseyside team, is seeing back heeling away a banana, as if he hadn't even given the symbol of degradation a second thought.

"I don't remember doing that. I mean the picture is there but bananas back then were common," Barnes said of the shot.

"The reason it all came to the fore is because I was playing for a high-profile club like Liverpool. For six years before, that happened every week, but because it was a small club it wasn't highlighted." he said.

"In terms of me being angry and wanting to fight people in the stands though, it never happened, I consider those people to be ignorant, so how could they affect any part of life or any part of my demeanour?

"You have to do what makes you comfortable with yourself. We all react differently to every situation," he said.

In June 1984, Barnes, already an established names for Liverpool, would score possibly one of his best ever goals, (albeit according to him not his favourite goal) in an England jersey against Brazil. At the Est-dio do Maracan, picking up the ball on the left wing, Barnes strolled past several defenders before rounding the 'keeper and stroking the ball into the back of the net.

A sensational goal but not even that failed to free the player from the spectre of racial abuse, on the plane ride back members of the National Front, a right wing group, which had gone to the game claiming to support England said the game had finished 1–0 because Barnes's goal didn't count. The group had opposed Barnes' selection to play for England based on the fact that he was black.

Barnes went on to score 12 goals in 79 appearances for England.

[3]

Now an ambassador of the game, Barnes, an inductee in 2005 into the English Football Hall of Fame, works at fighting racism in the sport through the Kick It Out Campaign, which has attempted to eradicate racism from the sport. While positive that racism still exists in the game, Barnes is confident that players are a lot better off in England than they were 20 years ago.

"As long as there's racism in society there will be racism in all walks of society, you just don't hear it anymore," Barnes said.

"Racism still exists in life ... football fans are told that any racist chanting and you're kicked out of the ground, so you keep your mouth shut and then you're racist the other six days of the week.

"However it doesn't exist in terms of black footballers not being given the opportunities as they were in the '70s or '80s.

"Then if you were a black goalkeeper or black centre back or midfielder, you never made it because you were told as a black man you're fast so you don't have to think too much.

[4]

"You weren't put in any positions of responsibility, so you were a winger or a centre forward. Back then all black players were wingers or centre forwards.

"Now, if you look at Arsenal they have had 10 black players on the field at once and England have had a black goalkeeper so there is no discrimination against you from a positional standpoint and you don't hear it in the grounds anymore," he said. However, this does not mean that the former Liverpool man is quick to give the English game a pat on the back. In fact, he has found it to be even a bit hypocritical in its approach to other European countries still plagued by racism.

"When England has had a black community since 1950, how come until 1980 we were still going through it – racism? You have black people in your country and know the ramifications of the black-and-white issue," he said.

"When I was playing in the '80s we still got it (racist taunts). So how can we then come down hard on Macedonia and Estonia? They don't have black communities to deal with.

"Racist chanting is completely wrong but they do not go through every day dealing with a black and a white situation."

"Football has to come down hard on it but England should have sorted out this issue a long time ago and now it is ready to come down hard on everybody else," he said.

Kwesi Mugisa, 2008
Jamaica Gleaner

1   Skim through the text and choose the correct heading from the list below for each gap numbered **[1]–[4]**.

   a   A flying start

   b   Winger or centre forward

   c   Move to Liverpool

   d   First encounters

   e   Fighting the beast

   f   Army man

2   Which words go in the gaps **[a]–[h]** between lines 1 and 44? Choose the words from the table below. There are more than you need.

anger	gimmickry	speckled	aggravated
bigotry	unruly	subside	isolated
dished out	flinched	vented	ruined

3   Read the text again and decide whether the sentences below are true or false. Justify your answer with a brief quotation from the text.

   a   Football spectators throw bananas to show their appreciation of a player.

   b   Racism is a thing of the past at football matches.

   c   Some black and African players in Europe still face racism today.

   d   While playing at Liverpool, John Barnes was upset by ignorant racists.

   e   In English football in the 1980s, there was a strong anti-racist movement.

   f   At Liverpool, Barnes deliberately kicked bananas off the pitch.

   g   Even racist supporters celebrated Barnes's goal against Brazil.

   h   Barnes went on to collaborate with anti-racist organizations.

   i   Even successful black players were stereotyped by their clubs.

   j   Barnes thinks the UK is free of racism these days.

4   What does each of the following refer to in the text?

   a   'the island' (lines 80–81)

   b   'It' (line 83)

   c   'that' (line 109)

   d   'it all' (line 113)

   e   'it' (line 117)

5   Suggest synonyms for the following words.

   a   showcased (line 57)

   b   confines (line 58)

   c   rife (line 76)

   d   powerhouse (line 95)

   e   demeanour (line 126)

6   The journalist uses figurative language in several places in the
    text. What meaning is suggested by each of these phrases in the
    context of the text?

    a   'plying their trade' (lines 1–2)

    b   'look (something) dead in the eye' (lines 43–44)

    c   'like water off a duck's back' (lines 46–47)

    d   'the top flight' (lines 71–72)

    e   'not give (something) a second thought' (lines 106–108)

    f   '(something) came to the fore' (lines 113–114)

    g   'free (someone) from the spectre of' (lines 144–145)

7   According to your reading of the text, is John Barnes convinced
    racism has been completely eradicated?

Interactive oral activity

From line 158 onwards of the text, John Barnes discusses the
changes to UK society and the professional roles of black footballers
since the 1990s. After reading this part of the text, you can use a
table like the one below to focus your ideas.

	Which aspects of life have remained unchanged?	Which aspects have improved?
For black footballers		
In UK society in general		

- Many organizations exist throughout the English-speaking
  world to tackle racist discrimination in all its forms. You can
  find a list of some of them at **http://en.wikipedia.org/
  wiki/Category:Anti-racist_organizations**, including the
  organization supported by John Barnes, *Kick It Out.*

- In groups, research one of these anti-discriminatory bodies
  and look at the organization's origins, aims and methods of
  communicating its message. Present your findings to your
  classmates. Follow this up with a general discussion about how
  schools and sports bodies in your own society might further
  contribute to 'kicking out' racism.

Developing writing skills

In your hometown, local musicians perform a 'Say No To Racism' concert. Write a newspaper report for a local newspaper about the event. Mention the reasons for the concert and describe the performances of the arts. You could also include quotes from the organizers, musicians, and members of the audience. Evaluate the concert's success as an event and to mention any further plans the organizers might have.

Exam tip

The structure of a news report
A news report will consist of the following items:
- Headline
- Standfirst (Subheading)
- Byline
- Lead paragraph
- Explanatory paragraphs
- Supporting paragraphs
- Concluding paragraph
- Coda (paragraph giving wider context – optional)

TOK

How does the following poem illustrate the link between a language and its cultural values?

White Comedy
I waz whitemailed
By a white witch,
Wid white magic
An white lies,
Branded by a white sheep
I slaved as a whitesmith
Near a white spot
Where I suffered whitewater fever.
Whitelisted as a whiteleg
I waz in de white book
As a master of white art,
It waz like white death.
People called me white jack
Some hailed me as a white wog,
So I joined de white watch
Trained as a white guard
Lived off the white economy.
Caught and beaten by de whiteshirts
I waz condemned to a white mass,
Don't worry,
I shall be writing to de Black House.

Benjamin Zephaniah

Remember

Text type: Newspaper reports

Newspaper reports require a different style of writing from what is used when writing a news story. When writing a newspaper report, the most important information comes first, the least important information last.

Newspaper reports are written in this manner because people might not read an entire newspaper report all the way through, so writers put the most important information at the beginning. The 'lead' of a news story tells the readership what details they will find further on in the report.

Why write a news report like this? Because it's news!

To be newsworthy the events must have just taken place. Such a report is going to be dramatic and the journalist is telling the readership something completely new. (This is as opposed to a feature article, which may be more analytical because the writer has had more time to reflect on the events.)

The SL Written Assignment

Re-read the following texts: *Scrap the teen stereotypes* (p. 168), *The courage to change* (p. 173) and *Ignoring the Bananas* (p. 176). All of them relate to the subject issues of prejudice, discrimination, or racism and efforts that individuals have made to counter or overcome such negative stereotyping. For your written assignment, examine these issues or a related theme such as:

- the founding of a group set up to counter a specific form of prejudice
- a specific incident and how it was dealt with by the authorities
- an anti-racist celebration, such as a concert, drama production or sports event.

Once you have chosen your subject matter, decide on a specific text type you wish to write. The text types you have explored in this chapter include an interview, a blog, and a feature article. In addition we have examined the newspaper article. You may wish to imitate the style and features of one of these text types.

As always, discuss your ideas with your teacher before detailed planning. In addition, you may wish to use the chart which appears earlier in this chapter to help you plan your work. Write the first draft of your rationale and review your written assignment before writing a final draft.

> ### TIP
>
> You must write between 400 and 500 words for the Written Assignment and include a rationale of 100 words.

The personal response (HL)

Based on the stimulus below, give a personal response and justify it. Choose any text type you have studied in class.
Write 150–250 words.

"Racism is man's gravest threat to man – the maximum of hatred for a minimum of reason."

Abraham J. Heschel

Prejudice, discrimination, & racism

The following text describes an incident of bullying in a junior high school in Hawaii.

→ How is bullying related to discrimination and prejudice? Why do some students threaten and even carry out acts of physical intimidation, as is the case in this text? What does this say about the character of the bully?

→ Another form of bullying is psychological bullying. Students are excluded from peer groups and shunned. Why are such acts carried out? Can, and should, schools intervene? What policies should a school have in place to prevent this kind of behaviour?

→ In the text, some of the characters speak in Hawaiian Pidgin. Do you think people are discriminated against because of the way they speak? For what other reasons are individuals and groups discriminated against? What can be done to prevent such discrimination?

This text is an extract from the novel *Wild Meat and the Bullyburgers* by the Japanese Hawaiian writer Lois-Ann Yamanaka. Bullied and abused herself, the teenage narrator Lovey becomes involved in picking on someone even more vulnerable than herself.

In our homeroom is Pillis. But Pillis is not her name. Her name is Phyllis. She's the one who pronounces it Pillis. Pillis Pilmoca the Pilipina. She doesn't look like the midgets I saw on *The*
5 *Wizard of Oz*. To me, she looks like a regular-looking person except in small portions. Her legs dangle off her chair.

Sometimes I wonder what size clothes Pillis buys. She has this nice sweater with pearl
10 buttons and a chain with hearts across the neckline. Pillis wears it like a cape. If I wear a girl's size 12, I figure she must be a girl's size 6. So small. Sometimes I wish I could have a sweater with a chain like hers.
15 I hate math, especially fractions. I cannot reduce them, and today I cannot reduce 8/14. And no one in the dumbest math class helps me.

Us dumb ones from Mr. Harvey's class go with Miss Mona Saiki for math. And we all like
20 Miss Saiki, except that when math time comes, all the dum-dums have to stand up to leave, while all the smart ones stare and snicker.

If Jerry were in this class, he'd give me the answers real fast. Jerry or Melvin. But I'm in
25 this class with other dum-dums and they laugh at me instead like I'm very stupid, stupider than them for not knowing how to reduce a stupid fraction.

"You real stoopid for one fricken Jap," says
30 Thomas Lorenzo. "But you ack real smut when you stay wit' all the odda Japs, eh, girl?"

"Yeah," says Wilma Kahale. "I thought all Japs sappose for be smut. But you cannot even reduce one stupid fraction, eh, you, Jap Crap.
35 Stupid, thass why, you Rice Eye, good-for-nuttin' Pearl Harba bomba."

I feel so small. I want to die. I want to die, it feels like a small little fist inside, twisting.

"What," says Wilma. "What you looking at,
40 hah, Jap? Watch how you make them Jap eyes at me. Like me buss' yo face?"

"Yeah, Wilma. Beef um recess time," Thomas Lorenzo whispers to her.

Die before recess. I put my knees on my
45 chair and draw my body into the desk. I put my head down. I see Pillis from the corner of my eye, thinking very hard.

She puts the eraser part of her pencil in her nose and twirls it around slowly as she thinks.
50 She scratches her head with her short wrinkled finger and writes her answer quickly on her paper. Then she puts the eraser up her nostril again.

"Jap. Jap Crap. Rice Eye. Stupid shit. I catch
55 you recess time, you wait."

They keep talking, so I yell very suddenly, "Ooooh, Pillis, digging your nose with your eraser. Ooooh, Pillis, eraser digger." Thomas, Wilma, and the whole class look at Pillis, so stunnned that she leaves the pencil eraser stuck in her nose. Her eyes open wide and buglike.

"Midget digging for small nuggets?" "Ho, Pillis, stretching your mina-chure nostrils?" "Midget eraser digging for gold?"

I see Pillis get small, smaller than a girl's size 6, smaller and smaller until she looks like a white-sweatered ball. She shoulder-shakes at her desk and sniffles to Miss Saiki, "I hate them. They make me like die." All of Pillis' pencils and erasers fall to the ground.

Miss Saiki waits. No one helps Pillis. Everyone continues laughing and calling her Eraser Digger. Miss Saiki, says, "You are all so appalling. You are dis-gusting." She comes over quickly to Pillis and places her hand on Pillis' back, rubs gently. "Don't say things like that, Phyllis. Everything's gonna be o-kay." Then Miss Mona Saiki tells the rest of us, "Back to work. Now."

Pillis doesn't look at me. She doesn't look at anyone. She smooths her wet binder paper with both tiny hands. Jerry likes Pillis. So do I, actually. Her big gummy laugh and her short legs that try to kick us when we tease her. She waves to us when the school bus drops her off outside their cane field and her tiny body getting tinier and tinier up the dirt road. She walks eight-tenths of a mile to her house next to the sugar mill.

I don't know what to say. Jerry would know. But I don't tell him.

That night, I struggle with my math problems on the linoleum table. My mother asks if I need my father's help. I tell her no, I'm just reducing fractions. The light above the table slides across the binder paper.

I think about Pillis. I put my pencil eraser tip in my nose. What a wonderful feeling, especially when you twirl it and you have to think. I do this to the other nostril too.

My mother tells me to knock it off. To get a Kleenex instead. I wonder if Thomas Lorenzo and Wilma Kahale are at home trying Pillis' eraser digger too.

I don't know what I'll say to Pillis tomorrow. I don't know if she will ever wave at me from outside the school bus again. But I know now how she feels. It is something I have always known.

1　Answer the following questions.
　　a　Why does Lovey hate her maths class so much?
　　b　How does she evaluate herself as a student?
　　c　What is the attitude of the other kids in the maths class towards Lovey?
　　d　How do you think the other students feel about being in Miss Saiki's maths class?
　　e　The other students swear at Lovey by making racist comments. Why do they pick on her?
　　f　Why does Lovey make fun of Phyllis?
　　g　What is Phyllis's reaction to this attention?
　　h　Why do you think the class is so cruel towards Phyllis and Lovey?
　　i　Does the teacher, Miss Saiki, deal with the situation well?
　　j　How could she improve the situation and atmosphere in her class?
　　k　How does Lovey feel about her treatment of Phyllis?
　　l　In the closing lines Lovey says, 'But I know now how she feels. It is something I have always known.' What does she mean by 'it'?

2　In the text, the students use Hawaiian Pidgin. Suggest alternatives for the following phrases in the context in which they appear in the text.
　　a　'you ack real smut' (line 30)
　　b　'What you looking at, hah?' (lines 39–40)
　　c　'Like me buss yo face?' (line 41)
　　d　'Beef um' (line 42)
　　e　'They make me like die' (line 69)

Why does the writer use Pidgin? What difference does the use of Hawaiian Pidgin make to the story?

3　Identify and explain the following cultural references:
　　a　'The Wizard of Oz' (lines 4–5)　　c　'a girl's size 12' (USA) (lines 11–12)
　　b　'a girl's size 6' (USA) (lines 12–13)　　d　'Pearl Harbor' (line 36)

4　Read the passage again and use a table like the one below to note information about the two main characters in the passage.

LOVEY	Observation 1	Interpretation 1	Observation 2	Interpretation 2
Her appearance and possessions	She wears size 12 clothes.	Suggests she is overweight.	She wants a sweater like Phyllis?	She might not have nice clothes.
Her voice and speech				
Her behaviour				
Reactions of others to her				
Her home and background				
Her thoughts and emotions				
PHYLLIS	Observation 1	Interpretation 1	Observation 2	Interpretation 2
Her appearance and possessions				
Her voice and speech				
Her behaviour				
Reactions of others to her				
Her home and background				
Her thoughts and emotions				

Interactive oral activity: Hot seating

What is hot seating?

This is a technique borrowed from drama. In hot seating you take on the role of a character from a story, and the rest of the class asks you questions. The characters have to answer the questions 'in character' and in as much detail as possible. It should be stressed that hot seating or role play does not involve acting skills, just enough imagination to put yourself in another person's shoes.

Why do hot seating?

We can develop an excellent understanding of characters from literature, especially about their motives, behaviour, and feelings by hot seating. It allows us to imagine what it is like to see things from another person's perspective.

Resources and preparation required

Put out chairs in front of the class group, one for each person in the exercise: Lovey, Phyllis, Miss Saiki, Wilma, and Thomas. The members of the class who are characters have time to think about what kind of questions will be asked and think of some answers which are consistent with their knowledge of the characters. In the meantime, working in pairs, the rest of the class should come up with a series of questions. When everyone has prepared sufficiently the members of the group ask their questions. There does not have to be a specific order. You can continue for a set time. At the end, discuss what you have found out about each of the characters and the subject of discrimination.

The HL Written Assignment

Look at the notes you have created for question 4 on page 184. You could use them to write a diary entry based on the observations of one of the characters, for example, Lovey and Phyllis regarding the discrimination, prejudice, and racism that they encounter. Alternatively you could take the role of Miss Mona Saiki, the maths teacher.

Remember

Text type: Diary entry

A diary entry is a very personal reflection on what you did/saw/felt on a particular occasion. These entries could be a straightforward account of the events of a day. However, many people keep diaries as a method of examining their lives. Consequently, a good diary entry is likely to emphasize your thoughts, feelings, and comments about the events of the day.

Diary writing is spontaneous, and therefore the language and the ideas should sound instinctive and unplanned. Nevertheless, you can still use the basic rules of paragraphing with each paragraph having a topic sentence and a clear focus. This structure can help you to understand your own emotions and reactions.

Some diary writers like to write to the diary as if it were a good friend. This technique is called direct address; it allows you to talk to your diary as 'you'.

Grammar

Diary writers are not always certain about their ideas and often have to clarify their ideas to themselves, so it is useful to begin some sentences with phrases like:

| I wonder | I suppose | I think | I reckon |
| I imagine | I hope | I doubt | |

You may also want to use verbs in the conditional tenses:

- I wonder what will happen if I go. (Future)
- I wonder what would happen if I went. (Theoretical situation in the present)
- I wonder what would have happened if I had gone. (Theoretical situation in the past)

TIP

For the HL Written Assignment you must write between 500 and 600 words. You must also include a rationale of up to 150 words.

The personal response

Based on the stimulus below, give a personal response and justify it. Choose any text type you have studied in class. Write 150–250 words.

> *"If I could, I'd like to introduce a drug that everyone who was a bully had to take to stop them bullying other people. I'd put such a drug in the water now."*
>
> **Jo Brand,** *comedian*

Beyond the text...

➤ Racist and sexist behaviour are two types of bullying. Design a leaflet to oppose bullying. Your leaflet should be informative and persuasive. It needs to be written in an easy-to-read format, so check the words you use and the design of your leaflet. As an extension to this topic you may wish to look at the following web site: www.antibullying.net

➤ Using the resources you have been given in class and other available information, produce an information booklet for younger students to create an effective anti-bullying campaign for your school. You may wish to use the following headings or create captions of your own.

- What is bullying?
- Why does it occur?
- What should you do if you are being bullied?
- What not to do
- Where can you find help?
- What should you do if you see an act of bullying?
- What can bullies do to find help?

Reflection point

- In this chapter, you have read about diversity, Third Culture Kids, multilingualism and how it affects self-identity, what it means to be socially acceptable, and some issues related to prejudice, racism and discrimination. How related are all those topics?
- How do languages affect our culture and identity?
- How important is it to be socially acceptable? What should a migrant do to gain social acceptance? Does this necessarily mean letting go of one's own cultural behaviours?
- How is language used to convey meaning? What do you have to do to write an article, an interview, a set of instructions or a news report?
- What do you have to do when you analyse a photograph?

Exam tip

For the personal response there is no right answer. You will be assessed on your ability to take a systematic approach to the stimulus. Do you agree, partially agree, or disagree with Jo Brand's statement? To score well you must be able to supply a logical, reasoned, and coherent response. You must make a series of points and support your ideas with evidence and state a valid conclusion.

CAS

When students are going through a serious personal crisis, such as the divorce of parents, or are facing a problem in school such as bullying, they may well need professional help and counselling. The majority of schools provide such services. In addition to counselling, many schools offer peer mentoring, whereby older and more experienced students provide a sympathetic ear to new and younger students. Peer mentors are frequently employed to offer guidance to newcomers in settling in and coping with new routines and lifestyles. They may also help with school work and study skills, as well as helping students to cope with peer pressure.

You may have been a peer mentor or you could research what systems are in place for peer mentoring in your school. Based on your findings, design a recruitment poster to attract IB Diploma students to a school peer mentoring scheme.

Customs & traditions

BEFORE YOU READ

→ How much do you think tattoos reflect cultural values and beliefs?
→ Should tattoos and piercings be prohibited in work places?
→ How would discrimination against tattooed and pierced individuals be minimized?
→ How do people in your own country react to tattooed individuals?
→ In your opinion, are tattoos and piercings considered part of the cultural tradition of a country?

Tattooing: A tradition

The Cultural Significance of Tattoos

FOR many people, tattoos are marks of machismo - a form of expression for sailors, bikers and convicts with little significance
5 outside of those subcultures. **[a] Furthermore / On the contrary / Although / On the other hand,** tattoos are often symbolic of rich cultural histories.

10 In many cases, tattoos are a way to place protective or therapeutic symbols permanently on the body. Polynesian cultures have developed elaborate geometric
15 tattoos over thousands of years. After British explorer James Cook's expedition to Tahiti in 1769, the marks became fashionable in Europe. **[b] Because of / So /
20 For / As a result,** European men in dangerous professions, in particular sailors and coal miners, have tattooed anchors or miner's lamps on their forearms for
25 protection **[c] by / for / until / since** the late 18th century. The tradition of tattooing a loved one's name also developed during this time.

30 In other cultures, tattoos mark people as part of specific social, political or religious groups. In the Maori culture of New Zealand, the head is considered the most
35 important part of the body. The face is embellished with elaborate tattoos, which serve as marks of high status. Each tattoo design is unique to the individual **[d] due
40 to / yet / as / but** it conveys specific information about that person's social status, ancestry and skills. Men are given tattoos at various stages in their lives, and
45 the decorations are designed to enhance their features and make them more attractive to potential wives. **[e] Although / Hence / In spite of / As a result**
50 Maori women are also tattooed on their faces, the markings are concentrated around the mouth. The Maori believe tattoos around the mouth and chin prevent the
55 skin becoming wrinkled and keep them young.

[f] Differently / On the other hand / Similarly / What's more, there are countless
60 meanings behind traditional Native American tattoos, but most tattoos were a symbol of a warrior's status within a tribe. It was also common for a tribe
65 to give tattoos to those who had proficiency in using the symbol that was tattooed upon their body. **[g] As a result / Still / For example / Such,** warriors
70 often had tattoos of weaponry, while women were given tattoos of various labor tools. Although Europeans have had the names of loved ones tattooed onto
75 their skin for centuries, Native Americans generally wore their own names.

Various groups throughout Africa employ tattoos as cultural
80 symbols. Berber tribes in Algeria, Tunisia and Libya tattoo fine dots on the faces of women after they give birth to a male heir. Women **[h] also / yet / still / hence**
85 tattoo their faces, hands, and ankles with symbols marking their ethnic identity. In Egypt, members of the Christian Copts sect bear small crosses on their
90 inner forearms. The elaborate facial tattoos of Wodaabe, nomadic herders and traders in western Africa, carry various meanings. Wodaabe women dot
95 their temples, cheeks and lips with geometric tattoos to ward off evil spirits. Men and women use black henna as a temporary tattoo covering entire hands,
100 forearm, feet and shins during weddings, baptism, and special holidays.

At times, tattoos are a form of artistic expression. Modern
105 Japanese tattoos are considered fully realized works of art. The highly skilled tattooists of Samoa consider tattooing both a craft and a spiritual awakening. They
110 create their art with the same tools as were used prior to the invention of modern tattooing equipment. This process is seen as a spiritual journey, a strongly
115 psychological experience that will change their lives forever.

In North America, the cultural status of tattooing has steadily evolved over the past thirty
120 years, from a rebellious, anti-social activity in the 1960s to a mainstream means of asserting one's identity in the 1990s. **[i] Due to / In spite of /
125 Although / Because** tattooing is simply a trendy fashion statement for many, others choose tattooing as a way of honoring their cultural, ethnic or religious heritage.
130 Tattoos often represent both fashion and cultural significance, as in the increasing popularity of Americanized geometric tribal tattoos.

Deon Melchior, 2012

1   For each of the gaps marked **[a]–[i]** in the text, choose one word or phrase
    from the options provided that renders the sentence meaningful.

2   Copy and complete the following table using information from the text:

Target Culture/Group	Tattoo Design	Significance
European sailors and miners		
	Facial tattoos	High status
Maori women	Tattoos around the mouth	
	Dotted temples/cheeks/ lips	

3   Answer the following questions.
    a   What is the widespread notion about tattoos given in the first paragraph?
    b   What is the opposing point the writer presents?
    c   What does the uniqueness of Maori tattoo designs reveal?
    d   Find a word between lines 30 and 56 which means 'prospective'.
    e   Why were Native American women given tattoos of labour tools?
    f   How has the cultural status of tattoos changed in North America?
    g   One aspect that tattoos may reflect is an individual's 'social status'.
        Mention FOUR other aspects that such designs mirror.

4   Choose the correct answer from A, B, C, or D.
    a   elaborate (line 14) means:
        A   enigmatic
        B   pertinent
        C   intricate
        D   scriptable
    b   nomadic (line 92) means:
        A   settled
        B   wandering
        C   primitive
        D   ancient
    c   ward off (lines 96–97) is closest in meaning to:
        A   prevent
        B   desert
        C   isolate
        D   attract

5   Copy and complete the following table by indicating to whom or to what
    the word indicated refers.

In the phrase...	the word/s...	refer/s to...
...miner's lamps on their forearms... (lines 23–24)	'their'	
...developed during this time. (lines 28–29)	'this time'	
...and make them more attractive... (lines 46–47)	'them'	
...becoming wrinkled and keep them young. (lines 55–56)	'them'	
...tattooed onto their skin... (lines 74–75)	'their'	
They create their art with the same tools... (lines 109–111)	'They'	

The purpose of the following exercise is to practise linking words in context and to examine how a letter of complaint is structured. When writing a letter of complaint, think about the following:

- Paragraph outline
- Tone
- Register
- Expressions used

1 Read the following letter and fill in the spaces marked **[a]**–**[l]** with the correct word or phrase from the box below.

because	despite	furthermore	but
therefore	although	during	when
in fact	as well as	in particular	due to
despite the fact that	to start with	not only… but also	otherwise

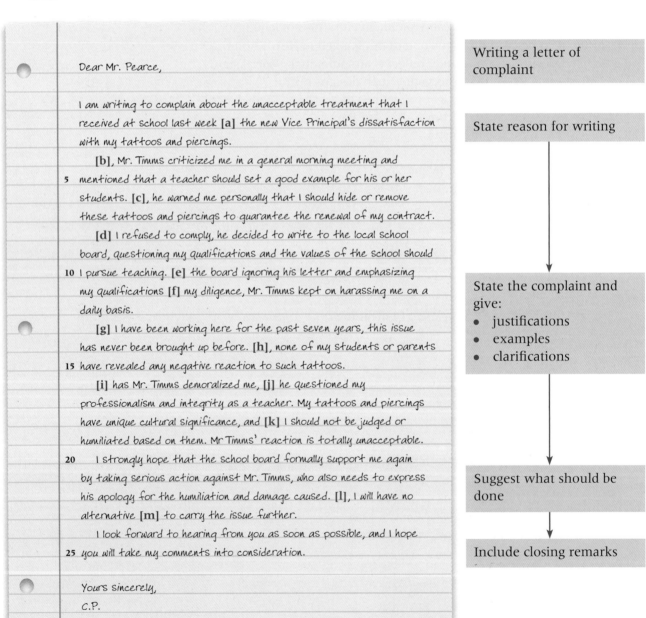

Grammar

Linking words glue parts of the text together and help others follow your ideas. They are used to:
- join words and phrases
- connect sentences
- link paragraphs
- develop ideas methodically
- provide coherence and cohesion.

Dear Mr. Pearce,

I am writing to complain about the unacceptable treatment that I received at school last week **[a]** the new Vice Principal's dissatisfaction with my tattoos and piercings.

[b], Mr. Timms criticized me in a general morning meeting and
5 mentioned that a teacher should set a good example for his or her students. **[c]**, he warned me personally that I should hide or remove these tattoos and piercings to guarantee the renewal of my contract.

[d] I refused to comply, he decided to write to the local school board, questioning my qualifications and the values of the school should
10 I pursue teaching. **[e]** the board ignoring his letter and emphasizing my qualifications **[f]** my diligence, Mr. Timms kept on harassing me on a daily basis.

[g] I have been working here for the past seven years, this issue has never been brought up before. **[h]**, none of my students or parents
15 have revealed any negative reaction to such tattoos.

[i] has Mr. Timms demoralized me, **[j]** he questioned my professionalism and integrity as a teacher. My tattoos and piercings have unique cultural significance, and **[k]** I should not be judged or humiliated based on them. Mr Timms' reaction is totally unacceptable.
20 I strongly hope that the school board formally support me again by taking serious action against Mr. Timms, who also needs to express his apology for the humiliation and damage caused. **[l]**, I will have no alternative **[m]** to carry the issue further.

I look forward to hearing from you as soon as possible, and I hope
25 you will take my comments into consideration.

Yours sincerely,
C.P.

Writing a letter of complaint

State reason for writing

State the complaint and give:
- justifications
- examples
- clarifications

Suggest what should be done

Include closing remarks

Developing writing skills

> 'A dash is a mark of separation stronger than a comma, less formal than a colon, and more relaxed than parentheses.'
>
> ***The Elements of Style***, fourth edition, by William Strunk Jr. and E. B. White, page 9

- **Look again at the text on page 188. Why is a dash used after the word 'machismo' in line 2?**
- Search for examples and discuss the usage of each of the following in writing:

There are four things a successful teacher should have: patience, passion, organization and knowledge.

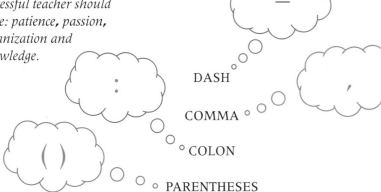

DASH

COMMA

COLON

PARENTHESES

The only thing his mom could do – if she could do anything at all – was to wait for Tom to come back.

My sister, who lives in New York, has bought a new car.

Leonardo da Vinci (1452–1519) was an Italian Renaissance painter, sculptor, and architect.

Writing activity

You are participating in a debate on the motion:

'Tattoos go beyond art and fashion; they reflect deep-rooted cultural and ethnic heritage.'

Write the text of your opening speech using 250–400 words. You need to include examples of the punctuation marks highlighted in the previous exercise.

The individual oral (HL/SL)

- In groups of three, describe the photograph.
- Reflect on the caption, and then discuss your reflections.
- Find out more about a subculture or culture to whom tattoos are significant. Remember to focus on English-speaking countries.
- Discuss your findings with other members in your group. Remember to comment on how tattoos reflect the following in your chosen culture or subculture.
  - ▶ Religion
  - ▶ Ethnicity
  - ▶ Art or fashion
  - ▶ Social status
  - ▶ Culture

Remember

- Organize your ideas.
- Provide supporting details.
- Use linking words.
- Refer to speech writing guidelines.

Tattoos: a fashion statement or a cultural tradition?

Workplace dress codes & tattooing

Tattoos and piercings cause discrimation in the workplace

THE MEDIA, fashion industry, and Hollywood **[a] have / has / is / are** played a major role in manipulating society to believe in what is acceptable or not. What to wear, what not to wear. If red is in season for the fashion world, it **[b] will clutter / would clutter / would have cluttered / will not clutter** the shelves of most department stores, minimizing the color choices. For those of us not wanting any of the colors the season brings, we have to search elsewhere, making our lives more difficult. Why make it hard?

A few of us still hold **[c] in / on / on to / to** our unique style and individuality, then there are the followers...when the next rave is to be rail thin, people will purge unwanted food to get into that size zero. If a celebrity sports a tattoo, then it becomes the latest fad and everyone wants one. Our western culture has turned into a **[d] clan / herd / school / flock** of zombies just waiting for someone else to decide our fate, forgetting we do have a mind and style of our own, but fearful of just being ourselves because of society's judgment that can prevent us from getting that certain career or promotion.

Society has labeled tattooed and pierced individuals as misfits, lazy, uneducated, and ungodly. What makes a piercing on the face/body any different than piercing through the ear lobes? Who makes this decision? Again, society has told us that it's okay to have our ear lobes pierced, **[e] so / but / for / thus** to pierce anywhere else on the body is unthinkable.

We have to remember that people with tattoos and piercings are also HUMAN, just as intelligent (or not) as you and I. Some have good intentions and some don't. The only difference is how they choose to express themselves. I call it unique and experimental. These body modifications are accepted in other parts of the world and have been around for many centuries. In some Indian tribes, a man or woman with tattoos **[f] are / is / is being / are being** believed to possess maturity and strength. If they didn't have it, then they **[g] weren't / aren't / wasn't / isn't** as strong or considered wise.

Today, tattoos have become more of an art form than anything, but some still get them **[h] despite / since / due to, / as** their culture or religion. If a woman with tattoos on her face **[i] will step / steps / stepped / has stepped** into a room for a job interview and was rejected because of her tattoos, that would be deemed as discrimination. Her interviewer wouldn't know if it's cultural or religious. Either way, employers should never ask what someone's religion, age, or sexual orientation is. It's just as true with people who have tattoos and or body piercings. It could very well be that it's just part of their culture. It's not for us to judge and use it against them.

Everyone should have the same equal opportunities. Discrimination keeps us shallow, and closed-minded, with an inability to see the person for who they are because we are distracted **[j] from / with / by / off** an appearance we are not familiar with. We are to look at a person's heart, mind, and soul before having any opinions.

As far as employers go, they need to focus on the resumé or how the employee is holding up at his/her new position. The company I work for caused a little bit of conversation when the dress code was explained in detail. No scuffs on shoes, no hair accessories, acceptable make-up/nail polish, limited jewelry, hide tattoos, appropriate nail length, etc. I work for the apartment industry and I've always had positive responses when people saw my tattoos, **[k] and / for / as / but** I guess the company is fearful of losing clients because of our appearance, whether it were my tattoo or someone's unacceptable nails.

In a perfect world, companies would hire employees based on education, experience, work ethic, cleanliness, characteristics, and reputation. In a perfect world, people will see through someone's physical appearance directly to their heart. **[l] In fact / Fortunately / Unfortunately / Therefore,** our world is not perfect. People will always be judged on their appearance, regardless of who they are **[m] from / in / on / by** the inside.

Companies will continue to reject many people who are highly qualified based on their looks, tattoos/piercings. Maybe this will change sometime soon, but for now, keep in mind that appearances are deceiving, so no one has the right to make the call as to who is a good or bad individual. That has to be proven in time.

Z. Dewara, 2007

1 For each of the gaps labelled **[a]–[m]** in the
   text, choose a word or phrase from the options
   provided that renders the sentence meaningful.
   Be prepared to justify your choices.

2 From statements **A** to **I**, select the four that are
   true according to the text.

   A Fashion helps us choose the colours that best
         suit us.

   B According to the writer, Westerners have
         unique styles but are indecisive.

   C Body modifications restrict job opportunities.

   D Individuals with tattoos and piercings are not
         as intelligent as others.

   E According to the article, people are judged by
         the society despite their unique abilities.

   F The writer has always been criticized for her
         tattoos.

   G The writer is aware that a change of attitude
         requires time.

   H Body modifications result from the constant
         judgements made by society.

   I Tattoos and piercings divert employers from
         their employees' qualifications.

Maori tattoos

3 Answer the following questions.

   a What is the thesis statement stated in the article?

   b What is the comparison presented in 'when the next rave is
         to be rail thin, people will purge unwanted food to get into
         that size zero' (lines 20–23)? What does the wtiter imply?

   c How are tattooed and pierced people stereotyped as
         mentioned between lines 35–45? How does the writer refute
         this notion?

   d What are the two supporting details between lines 64 and 83
         that the writer presents to prove discrimination in the work
         place is unacceptable?

   e What purpose does capitalizing the word 'HUMAN' (line 48)
         serve?

   f Why are parentheses used in '(or not)' in line 49?

   g What do the following words mean?
         ● 'fad' (line 24)
         ● 'misfits' (line 36)

Writing activity: Letters

Split into two groups.

Group 1

After reading the article, you decide to write a letter to the editor in which you agree or disagree with Z. Dewara's viewpoint about tattoos and piercings in the work place. Write 250–400 words.

Remember

Letter to the Editor

- Uses formal register and style.
- Written to express a point of view, list arguments supporting this opinion and reject those against it.
- May end by restating the writer's opinion or by offering suggestions for action.
- Such letters are similar to opinion essays, but in the format of a letter.

How to write?

1 Start by stating purpose. Refer to article, issue date, writer, and title of article. State the issue or topic and whether you approve or disapprove.
2 Support your argument. Give examples, clarifications, and details.
3 Refute any counter-arguments.
4 Provide suggestions or solutions to solve/handle the problem or topic.
5 Include closing remarks.

Group 2

After reading the article, you decide to write a letter to Z. Dewara in which you agree or disagree with her views about tattoos and piercings in the work place. Write 250–400 words.

Remember

Letter giving an opinion

- Use a semi-formal to formal register.
- Decide what your stand is (approve or disapprove of Dewara's opinion).
- Provide justifications and supporting details.
- Tone should be respectful and friendly even if you disagree with Dewara.

How to write?

1 Start with opening greetings.
2 State purpose, refer to article, title, newspaper issue, date, etc.
3 State opinion.
4 Support your argument.
5 Refute Dewara's argument (if needed).
6 Include closing remarks.

Exam tip

Remember that you also need to familiarize yourself with the following types in preparation for the external exam:

- Letters of apology
- Letters of request
- Letters of application
- Letters asking for advice
- Letters giving advice

You may wish to consult the following e-learning sources:

- www.letterwritingguide.com
- www.usingenglish.com/resources/letter-writing.php
- www.nald.ca/library/learning/academic/english/writing/letters/module9.pdf
- www.goodletterwriting.co.uk
- http://owl.english.purdue.edu

Developing writing skills

Use the address information below to produce a rough layout for a **formal**, an **informal**, and a **semi-formal** letter.

The Blue Star Hotel
Pearceway,
London,
GL19 2LL,
United Kingdom

General Manager
Mr. Stephen Dane

You may find it useful to arrange your ideas into 4 boxes with the following headings:

FORMAL – you know the recipient	FORMAL – you do not know the recipient

INFORMAL	SEMI-FORMAL

TOK

- To what extent does membership of a cultural group affect how we come to gain knowledge about other groups?
- Some groups who use tattoos extensively can seem very alien to social groups who do not use them. How can we understand such cultures? To what extent is it possible to understand different cultures if we are outside them? Or can we only understand cultures that we belong to?
- What are the differences between knowing a culture, knowing about a culture and knowing a person from that culture?

→ Are there any general dress codes in workplaces where you live? Do you think dress codes are effective?
→ In which other walks of life are dress codes important?
→ What are the dress codes of young people in your countries?
→ What do dress codes tell us about a culture?
→ What prohibitions are there on certain dress codes in your country? Why do these prohibitions exist?

Customs & dress codes in the workplace

Are dress codes in the workplace important?

[1]

It's a very interesting question. If you sit to discuss about dress codes you might end up in a debate. Creating a dress code for a workplace can be a tricky thing. Fashion is the word of the day and in such an atmosphere dress codes can certainly be a [a]!

[2]

It's very important to maintain dress codes in an office. Young boys and girls often dress shabbily without bothering what the world has to say. A [b] dress code can keep them under control and maintain a decent image in public.

If no dress codes are maintained in a workplace, then anyone will wear anything of his/her choice. This will distract other employees and have a [c] impact on their performance. If a colleague proves to be a distraction, the other employees will have a hard time concentrating on their work. Dress codes have to be reasonable, depending on the type of work.

[3]

It's very important that employees sign in neat for work. They might [d] casual or formal business attire, but this is something that will vary greatly from setting to setting.

Some things that are completely [e] dress codes are:
- clothing which has [f] or foul language
- tank tops, muscle shirts or halter tops
- wearing [g] jeans and tops
- hats or caps
- wearing sweatpants or [h] suits

[4]

Dress codes have to be reasonable depending on the type of work. At the time of developing a dress code the employer should [i] that they are:
- job related
- not treating one sex less favorably than the other
- not treating one race less favorably than the other

It's very important that the employer [j] these dress codes to the employees to follow.

www.fashiontrend.biz, 2009

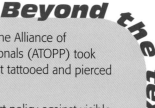

1 Read the text and choose an appropriate heading from the list
below for each of the paragraphs numbered **[1]–[4]**.

A What are dress codes?

B Are dress codes important?

C What things should employees avoid?

D Why are dress codes debatable?

E What things should employers keep
in mind when deciding a dress code?

F Dress codes for women

G Why are dress codes implemented?

H What to communicate?

I Dress codes for employees

2 Which words go in the gaps **[a]–[j]** in the text? Choose the
correct word or phrase for each gap from the list below.

abusive	helping hand	ensure
against	in favour of	give in
communicate	opt for	hard evidence
communication	to start with	sweaty
compulsory	severe	torn
enforce	sweat	minor

Beyond the text...

➤ Are policies against tattoos in the workplace examples
of gender discrimination? Do some research and find
out some statistics to support your findings. Make sure
you investigate at least two anglophone cultures.

➤ Find more details about the Maori culture and
history in New Zealand. You need to investigate two
important Maori tattoos that are different from the
ones you have read about in the text on page 188.
Use photographs to illustrate the significance of each
symbol.

➤ Investigate the actions that the Alliance of
Tattooed or Pierced Professionals (ATOPP) took
to fight discrimination against tattooed and pierced
professionals in the US.

➤ Some employers have a strict policy against visible
tattoos or body piercings. Is there a strong legal basis
to support the policy of such corporations? Investigate
this issue in the US and Canada.

➤ Peruse some sources to find a relationship between
dress codes and success in the work place.
Remember to focus on anglophone cultures.

The individual oral (HL/SL)

1 Describe the photograph, reflecting on an
anglophone culture.

2 In pairs, produce a suitable caption that links
the photograph with the topic of dress codes and
tattoos.

3 Prepare a 5-minute presentation and deliver it to
your classmates.

Are dress codes in the workplace necessary?

The paragraphs below are taken from a blog entry on dress codes in the workplace. Put the paragraphs in order to produce the complete blog entry, starting with paragraph D.

A Dress codes in business are really powerful if they mirror the company brand. If designed properly, a dress code can effectively communicate company values to customers and allow expressions of individuality by employees. In other words a dress code helps employees understand not only how a company wants them to dress, but also why.

B One alternative that companies have used is introducing a uniform. In some industries a uniform is totally sensible – a fire fighter wouldn't stand much chance in shorts and flip-flops – but in others, such as high street banks, why are they necessary? Wouldn't a clear statement on what is permissible be OK? The reason I prefer dress codes to uniforms (apart from the fact that uniforms never seem to fit anyone because they are designed for a mythical male or female figure) is that uniforms suppress individuality – and the person's individuality is one of the reasons they were employed in the first place.

C The key to an effective dress code is always to be as permissive as possible: 'Choose from the following…' rather than prescriptive 'You shall not wear…' The whole point is to make it easier for people in an organization to wear things in which they feel comfortable but at the same time reflect the company brand.

D Last week the newspapers were covering the story of a young woman relegated to the stockroom of the Abercrombie & Fitch flagship store in Saville Row because the 'look' of her prosthetic arm did not fit the company's public image (*The Guardian*, 24 June 2009). Many of the reporters went on to describe the content of the A & F 'Look Policy' as requiring a 'clean, natural appearance' with the colour of any nail varnish and visible tattoos at the discretion of the store manager!

E I know from a number of clients I have worked with, a lack of clear guidance and understanding about what to wear for work can lead to frustration and anxiety – and descriptions such as 'business smart' or 'smart/casual' mean nothing without a clear definition.

F So are dress codes in the work place really necessary? I believe they are. What I do not believe in is using them as a means of suppressing individuality or as a means of discrimination.

G But is the A & F story about the company dress code, or is it about whether they use their dress code as a means of taking off the shop floor a disabled employee? Is it about her look, or the look of her clothes?

Developing writing skills

'Conditional Sentences are also known as conditional clauses or 'if' clauses. They are used to express that an action can only take place if a certain condition is fulfilled.'

Adapted from ***English Grammar online***

Work in pairs to provide examples of conditional sentences used in the following situations. You can refer to the texts you have read where appropriate.

a It is possible and also *very likely* that the condition will be fulfilled.

b It is possible but *very unlikely*, that the condition will be fulfilled.

c It is *impossible* that the condition will be fulfilled because it is in the past.

> **TIP**
>
> Before you attempt the exercise, you may wish to learn more about conditional sentences, their formation, and their uses. The following websites may help you:
> - www.englishpage.com
> - www.esl.about.com
> - www.learnenglish.org.uk

Listen to each of the following songs:

'If today was your last day' by Nickleback

'What if' by Coldplay

'If I were a boy' by Beyonce

- Which of the three types of conditional sentences can you find in each song?
- Why is the word 'was' used in Coldplay's and Nickleback's songs, while 'were' is used in Beyonce's? What conclusions can you draw about the second type of conditional sentences?
- Would there be any difference in meaning if another type of conditional sentence were used in any of the three songs? Justify your answer.

Developing writing skills: Proposal

Imagine that you are to propose to your school principal a dress code to be used by all teachers. Write your proposal in 250–400 words.

1 The texts you have read can be of help.

2 Upon completing the proposal, refer to the Language B Guide (for first examination in 2013) and use the Assessment Criteria for P2 SL (pages 35–37) and P2 HL Section A (pages 44–45) to mark another student's proposal.

3 You need to justify the marks awarded.

CAS

Choose three corporations in your own town or area and investigate the purpose or effectiveness of any dress codes they have in place. You need to meet a senior manager in each corporation in order to familiarize yourself with the nature of work and the atmosphere.

A proposal is:

- formal
- informative
- impersonal
- written to provide suggestions or plans
- precise
- developed using headings and sub-headings
- written to gain approval or to persuade the recipient to take action

a State the aim of the proposal in the introduction.

b Clarify each of the aspects, suggestions, or points under a separate heading or sub-heading.

c Conclude with a general comment, opinion, or assessment.

Before you start, ask yourself again:

- to WHOM am I writing?
- WHAT am I writing?
- WHY am I writing?

Communication & media

→ Do you think video games and cartoons may result in violent behaviour?
→ Are some video games prohibited in your own country? If so, why?
→ Should parents control what their children watch?
→ In your opinion, what message does the picture below convey?
→ Does violence in video games serve any useful purpose?
→ At what age do you think children learn to distinguish between events on TV and real life? Are all children able to distinguish between violence on TV or films and real life?
→ Is it actually true to say that we live in a more violent age than previous generations?
→ The next text deals with whether video games trigger violence in the real world. Predict what arguments there will be in favour of and against this data.

Media & violence

Interview with Dr. Craig Anderson on

Video Game Violence

Dr. Craig Anderson, a leader in the research on the effects of exposure to violent video games on aggressive behavior, was invited to speak at Nebraska Wesleyan University. A group of Nebraska Wesleyan University students interviewed Dr. Anderson. We explored his interest and experiences in this research area.

Since 1997, Nebraska Wesleyan University (NE) has held an endowed lecture to honor the 40-year career of Dr. Clifford Fawl. The FAWL Lecture Series brings distinguished psychologists to the Wesleyan campus to present their research and interact with undergraduate psychology students. On March 22, 2007, we welcomed Dr. Craig Anderson as the FAWL lecturer to speak on Violent Video Games: Theory, Research, and Public Policy. Dr. Craig Anderson received his bachelors degree at Butler University (IN) in 1976. He earned a masters degree (1978) and PhD (1980) in psychology from Stanford University (CA). He is currently a distinguished professor of psychology at Iowa State University and is widely regarded as the leader in research on the effects of violent video games and other forms of media violence. He has published widely on depression, loneliness, and shyness; attribution processes; social judgment; and human aggression. He has earned recognition as the second most highly cited scholar in social psychology textbooks. He has testified before the U.S. Senate Committee on Commerce, Science and Transportation's hearing on "The Impact of Interactive Violence on Children" and has served on the Media Violence Expert Panel for the Surgeon General. Dr. Anderson started his visit by discussing the importance of good methodology to a research methods class. He was then interviewed by a small group of Wesleyan students concerning his work on violence and video games.

STUDENT: [1]

ANDERSON: It originally had to do with working on the General Aggression Model and learning about the media violence literature. There were literally hundreds of studies, but there were still gaps and unanswered questions. I had some students looking for research topics that were interesting and publishable, and then they identified gaps in the research. That was the initial reason. Later they basically extended the research using video games to test some aspects of the General Aggression Model. Next, my research team looked at priming issues, which prior to our work, had never been used in the context of media violence effects. After talking to some colleagues in cognitive psychology and debating about which method to use, we thought of using some cognitive measures such as a modified Stroop test but we chose a reading reaction time task.

STUDENT: Looking back on many of your articles, we noticed you first did a study on video games in 1987 and another in 1995, but the majority of your studies have been since 1999. **[2]**

ANDERSON: No, it had to do with an internal grant I received about 1996. It funded three graduate students and enabled us to start doing research on the effects of violent video games. I had been writing grant proposals on the topic for some time, but this was the first time I had the opportunity to do some of those studies. Then, Columbine came along.

STUDENT: [3]

ANDERSON: No, although I was asked to testify in the U.S. Senate hearing about violent video games some time after the shooting.

STUDENT: [4]

ANDERSON: Many researchers in the field of media violence think that people who are high on what you would call trait aggression (especially children and adolescents) are going to be more influenced by exposure to media violence than people who are low on trait aggression. In other words, many scholars believe that highly aggressive people are more susceptible to the harmful effects of media violence than are nonaggressive people. However, I think that the research evidence over the years doesn't bear that out, yet. Some studies show this heightened susceptibility of highly aggressive people, but some studies show the opposite including one of my studies (Anderson, 1997). That study found that people who are lowest on trait aggression showed the biggest effect of a violent movie manipulation. Those data yielded a significant interaction between measures of trait aggression and measures of media violence exposure. The nonaggressive people who watched a violent movie clip displayed more aggressive thoughts than nonaggressive people who saw the nonviolent clip, but highly aggressive people were relatively unaffected by the movie clip manipulation. Other researchers have found the opposite type of interaction. For example, in some studies those who those who score high on trait aggressiveness and have been exposed to a lot of violent media are the ones who are most likely to have, at some time in their lives, been arrested for assault. Well, is that because the media violence effect only operates on high trait-aggressive people? Perhaps low trait-aggressive people are equally affected, but because their general level of aggression is low,

media violence can't increase their willingness to aggress enough to rise to the level of assaulting someone.

STUDENT: **[5]**

150 *ANDERSON*: Well, very often, it's a convenience sample. However, the present grant research that my colleagues/students and I have been doing allows us to pay participants. So we

155 are able to pay kids to play video games, which they think is great (laughter). Some try to come in two or three times, and we have to tell them they cannot. In these situations, we have to select

160 samples to fit the particular research question or issue.

STUDENT: In your experimental research, how do you differentiate between the participants who regularly

165 play video games and those who have little to no experience?

ANDERSON: We usually give the participants questionnaires that tell us how much the individuals have

170 played and what kinds of games they play. Prior experience with video games can then figure into the data analysis. We seldom find any kind of difference in our experimental studies

175 between those participants with a lot of experience and those without. The one difference we do find is that participants with a lot of gaming experience really like being in the violent video game

180 condition. Typically, we do not find much of a statistically reliable effect of gaming experience on aggressive thought processes and behavior.

STUDENT: **[6]** If so, what impact do

185 you think it will have?

ANDERSON: Our research has probably had a bigger impact in countries other than the United States. Almost every other modern country has legal

190 restrictions on violent media including video games. Many of them ban some of the games outright and most have age-based restrictions. Certainly the research that my students and I have

195 done over the years has been used by child advocacy groups and others in these countries to make sure that these ratings are enforced. The research certainly has increased the awareness of

200 the issue in the United States. However, there are no U.S. laws regarding violent video games. I have never said publicly

whether I support a legislative solution, because my political opinion is not

205 relevant to what I regard as my scientific expertise. Even in the court cases with which I have been involved, I say upfront that I will not comment on what I think about the law under judicial review. I will

210 talk about what the science says or what it cannot say. The work and interviews that we've done concerning violence in video games is used to get the word out to parents about the effect of violent

215 video games. Our research has had a big impact on parents, but not as big as it needs to be. There are still people teaching their 2- or 3-year-olds how to shoot a gun in these video games.

220 **STUDENT:** **[7]** How do you counter those arguments?

ANDERSON: One of the best arguments, until recently, is that there are no longitudinal studies, but we

225 have now published one (Anderson, Gentile, & Buckley, 2007). Previously in my various talks, I had described the lack of longitudinal data on the effects of video games. The paucity of

230 these studies was due to the lack of government support for longitudinal research. The support for the longitudinal study I just mentioned came from non-governmental sources.

235 More recently, we finally got the funding needed to perform a larger, longer-term longitudinal study after being turned down six or seven times. There really aren't any long-term longitudinal

240 studies, such as when you follow the group of individuals and see where these participants end up after several years. Some participants may end up in jail, juvenile detention facilities, or

245 kicked out of school, which makes this an important field of interest. A response to this criticism about the lack of longitudinal studies on violent video games is that such studies

250 have already been done pertaining to television violence, which is the same phenomenon, but some individuals fail to see the similarities between violence on television and violence

255 in video games. People used this lack of a longitudinal study, focusing on violent video games, as a criticism for the evidence found between increased aggression and exposure to violent

260 video games. Of course, they can no longer do this.

STUDENT: Do you have any plans for the future implementation of your research? How should your research

265 be applied to schools, home, everyday life, etc.?

ANDERSON: We haven't been thinking much about intervention studies, mainly because I don't do intervention

270 studies. There is a group at Iowa State University that does intervention studies, but most of their work focuses on drug use and intervention to reduce kids' use of alcohol, tobacco,

275 and various illegal substances. There have been some TV/video game interventions done in school systems, but intervention as a whole is done by another group of researchers.

280 **STUDENT:** **[8]**

ANDERSON: There are two related issues that are going to be big soon. One is the identification of video game addiction or Internet addiction,

285 including text messaging, as a true addiction in need of clinical intervention for deficit disorder, especially in very young children who see a lot of TV.

*Authors' note: We would like to thank
290 Dr. Anderson for visiting with Nebraska Wesleyan students and faculty, and presenting his research regarding violence and video games. We would also like to give a special thanks to
295 Dr. Marilyn Petro, Dr. Michael Tagler, Allyson Bell, and Amanda Holmgren for their assistance with the process of this interview.*

Sarah Howe, Jennifer Stigge, and Brooke Sixta
Nebraska Wesleyan University

1 Some of the interview questions have been removed from the text. Match the questions below with the gaps numbered **[1]–[8]** in the text.
   a Where do you think video game research will go from here?
   b What were some of the obstacles faced upon conducting your research?
   c From where do you recruit your participants?
   d Were you asked to help with any of the Columbine research?
   e What is the difference between high trait-aggressive and low trait-aggressive people?
   f Do you feel that your research has or will have an impact on the video game industry?
   g Did this more recent increase in research on the effects of video games have anything to do with Columbine and other school shootings?
   h Do you pay your participants, and how?
   i What are some of the stronger arguments against your research?
   j What group of people do you think are the most susceptible to the effects of violent video games, and why?
   k What was your motivation for starting research on media violence and video games?

2 Decide whether each of the statements below is true or false and then justify your choice by quoting a relevant phrase from the text.
   a Dr. Anderson volunteered to participate in the FAWL Lecture Series.
   b Dr. Anderson is not the first eminent FAWL lecturer visiting Wesleyan University.
   c Dr. Anderson is currently employed by the Nebraska Wesleyan University.
   d As a reward, participants can play video games whenever they want.
   e Legal restirctions on violent video games are lacking in the US.
   f Dr. Anderson's political views are fundamental to supporting his testimony.
   g According to Dr. Anderson, the researches conducted have had the desired influence on parents.

3 Answer the following questions.
   a What was the title of Dr. Anderson's lecture at Wesleyan University?
   b Who was Dr Anderson's target audience?
   c In addition to violent video game effects, what other topics has Dr. Anderson researched and written about? Mention **four**.
   d Apart from publications, mention **three** distinguished achievements for Dr. Anderson.
   e What effect has Dr. Anderson's research had on modern countries?
   f Find a sentence between lines 99 and 118 which shows that there is no hard evidence to support researchers' belief that people of high trait aggression are more easily affected by media violence.
   g What two areas are covered in the questionnaire given to participants prior to the experimental research?
   h What is meant by 'longitudinal studies' referred to in line 224?
   i What are the long-term effects of violence exposure on participants?
   j 'Of course, they can no longer do this.' (lines 260-261)
      Who or what do 'they' and 'this' refer to? In context, why does Dr. Anderson believe '…they can longer do this'?
   k Who conducts intervention studies? What do these studies focus on? Mention **three** things.
   l According to Dr. Anderson, what is the new addiction that requires action?
   m What can cause attention deficit disorder?

4 Indicate to whom or what the following words or phrases refer.
   a 'this research area' (lines 10-11)
   b 'their' (line 18)
   c 'initial reason' (line 63)
   d 'the shooting' (line 97)
   e 'this heightened susceptibility' (lines 114-115)

5 Give a meaning for each of the following words or phrases as they appear in the text.
   a exposure (line 3)
   b prior to (line 68)
   c susceptible to (line 109)
   d yielded (line 122)
   e outright (line 192)

6 Choose the correct answer from A, B, C, or D.
   a upfront (line 207) means:
      A frankly
      B in a pre-meditated manner
      C impudently
      D instantly

   b paucity (line 229) means:
      A failure
      B shortcoming
      C strength
      D rarity

Developing writing skills:
Letter or email giving advice

You are Dr. Craig Anderson, and you have received an email from a parent who is worried about his or her child being addicted to violent video games. Write a reply email in which you advise the parent on how to deal with this issue and provide practical solutions and recommendations. Write 250–400 words.

1 Start by stating purpose for writing. Refer to the original request made: e-mail, letter, etc.

2 Give advice. Be precise and to the point.

3 Provide clarifications, justifications and details.

4 Include closing remarks.

A letter giving advice:
- can be formal or informal in style
- is written to give some advice upon someone's request
- should give solutions
- may include opinions and reference to personal experience.

Here are some phrases commonly used to give advice:
- If I were you, I would…
- You ought to…
- You should…
- You'd rather…
- Why don't you…?
- What about…?
- Make sure you…

Exam tip

When asked to write an informal email, avoid using chatty language and do not focus on authenticity at the expense of organization and methodical development of ideas.

From: ....
To: ....
Date: ....
Subject: ....

An email giving advice
This email is quite similar to a letter, the features of which are given in the box on the left. Instead of the letter layout explained earlier in this section, an email will use the format shown above to begin.

Censorship

Cartoon violence 'makes children more aggressive'

HIGH LEVELS of violence in cartoons such as Scooby-Doo can make children more aggressive, researchers claimed. They found that animated shows aimed at youngsters often have more brutality than programmes broadcast for general audiences. And they said [1] just as much as they would with screen actors. The study also found that [2] such as rumour-spreading, gossiping and eye-rolling.

The U.S. psychologists quizzed 95 girls aged 10 and 11 about their favourite TV shows, rating them for violent content and verbal and indirect aggression. The shows included 'Lost', 'Buffy the Vampire Slayer', 'American Idol', 'Scooby-Doo' and 'Pokemon'.

The researchers found that output aimed at children as young as seven, which included a number of cartoons, had the highest levels of violence. [3] compared with just five in shows aimed at general audience and nine in programmes deemed unsuitable for under-14s.

'Results indicated that [4] than in programmes for general audiences,' the study said.

It added that the TV industry distinguished between animated violence and non-animated violence and appeared to rate the former as less harmful. 'There is ample evidence that animated, sanitised and fantasy violence has an effect on children,' the study's authors said.

'Research on the effects of violent video games, which are all animated, indicates that [5] that violent TV shows have demonstrated.

'[a], even cartoonish children's games increase aggression. Labelling certain types of media violence as "fantasy" violence is [b] and may actually serve to increase children's access to harmful violent content by [c] parental concern.'

Too violent? Children's favourite Pokemon

The study, by academics at Iowa State University and published in the Journal of Applied Developmental Psychology, [d] found that children copied at school the verbal aggression they [e] on TV.

It said: 'In addition, the effects of televised physical aggression were [f], such that exposure to televised physical aggression was associated with a variety of negative behaviours in girls.' This [g] behaviour included verbal and physical aggression and [h] others from friendship groups.

Co-author Jennifer Linder said: 'There is ample evidence that physical aggression on TV is associated with increases in aggressive behaviour, [i] there was little until this study that has shown a link between televised aggression and resulting aggression [j] children.'

Professor Douglas Gentile, who led the study, said content ratings on TV programmes should provide detailed information [k] the aggression shown. The U.S. introduced a ratings system in the mid-1990s but the idea has not been [l] in Britain.

Laura Clark

Cartoons aimed at children, such as Scooby Doo, contain more brutality than programmes meant for general audiences, a study has found.

1   Some of the sentences have been removed from the text. From the list below, choose the sentence which best suits each of the gaps numbered **[1]–[5]**.

    A they recorded 26 acts of aggression an hour

    B they have the same effects on children's aggressive thoughts, feelings and behaviours

    C brutality had an impact on the audience

    D children copied and identified with fantasy characters

    E researchers conducted the experiment with different age groups

    F there are higher levels of physical aggression in children's programmes

    G parental control needs to be more effective

    H youngsters tended to mimic the negative behaviour they saw on TV

    I children ignored fantasy characters

    J researchers held parents responsible for children's aggression

2   What does each of the following refer to in the text?

    a 'They' (line 4)

    b 'the former' (line 37)

    c 'the idea' (line 86)

3   Which words go in the gaps **[a]–[l]** in the text? Choose the words from the table below.

also	between	for	misleading
among	but	had seen	on
and	cast off	have seen	picked up
anti-social	excluding	in fact	reducing
apparent	extensive	intensifying	thus

Developing writing skills: Letter of complaint

You have recently noticed that your younger brother or sister spends a lot of time watching cartoons that include plenty of violent and brutal scenes. As a concerned sibling, you decide to write a letter of complaint to the director of a local TV station which broadcasts such cartoons. Write 250–400 words.

Letter of complaint

- Use formal register and style.
- Explain your complaint at the beginning of the letter.
- Justify your complaint and provide examples.
- Provide solutions, recommendations, or suggestions.
- Do not sound patronising. Regardless of the weight of your complaint, your tone needs to remain respectful and friendly to an extent. Avoid using offensive language.
- Be concise and precise.
- It is recommended that you know the name of the recipient to enable better interaction and engagement.

Media vs. violence

Video games don't cause children to be violent

Proposals like this are a solution in search of a problem!

The Supreme Court recently decided to review a California law that would regulate the sale and rental of computer and video games to minors. We can all agree that parents are the best arbiters of determining what is right for their children. The issue at hand **[a]** is how best to support those parents. We believe that with parental controls, ratings awareness and retailer support, proposals
5 like this are a solution in search of a problem. **[b]**, there are numerous legal reasons why 12 courts have already rejected proposals similar to this one, and we believe there are sound constitutional reasons why we hope the Supreme Court will concur.

A few facts to consider: The average video game player is 35 years old and has been playing for 12 years. Forty percent of gamers are women, and one out of every four gamers is over age 50.
10 Video games are a mass medium form of entertainment that are enjoyed today in a majority of homes by players of all ages.

The myth that video games cause violent behavior is undermined by scientific research and common sense. **[c]** FBI statistics, youth violence has declined in recent years as computer and video game popularity soared. We do not claim that the increased popularity of games caused
15 the decline, **[d]** the evidence makes a mockery of the suggestion that video games cause violent behavior. **[e]**, as the U.S. Ninth Circuit Court of Appeals declared: "The state has not produced substantial evidence that … violent video games cause psychological or neurological harm to minors."

[f], addressing critics' claims that games are somehow different than other forms of art, the Hon.
20 Robin Cauthron of the United States District Court for the Western District of Oklahoma wrote in a permanent injunction against that state's attempt to regulate the sale of games to minors that, "the presence of increased viewer control and interactivity does not remove these games from the release of the First Amendment protection."

The industry **[g]** has an independent rating system, similar to the movie rating system, that
25 informs and empowers parents. Watchdog groups and government agencies, like the Federal Trade Commission, praise it as a system that works. A 2009 study by the FTC found that 87 percent of parents were satisfied with the computer and video game ratings. Last year, the FTC said the computer and video game industry "outpaces" other entertainment industries in restricting marketing of mature-rated products to children, clearly and prominently displaying
30 rating information and restricting children's access to mature-rated products.

Retailers are supportive of the ratings system and are playing a critical role in keeping mature-themed video games out of the wrong hands. Virtually all major U.S. retailers are working to help parents keep control of the games children play by enforcing age restrictions.

Parental controls are also built into all current-generation game consoles, enabling parents to
35 block video games they do not want their children to play. This ensures that parents' standards are enforced, **[h]** they are not at home.

As a medium, computer and video games are entitled to the same protections as the best of literature, music, movies, and art. **[i]**, Americans' rights to speech and expression are sacred and inviolate - and millions across the political spectrum agree with us.

Michael D. Gallagher
Michael D. Gallagher is the president and CEO of the Entertainment Software Association

1 Which one of the following is correct?
   The writer of the article

   A supports the California law being reviewed.

   B blames US retailers for the ineffective rating systems enforced.

   C hopes the new proposal will not be approved.

   D predicts parents will have a bigger role in controlling mature-themed video games.

2 From statements A to I below, select the four that are true according to the text.

   A According to the text, 60% of gamers are men.

   B The Supreme Court is the 12th court to reject the proposal of video games rental and sale to minors.

   C Video games are the most popular medium of entertainment nowadays.

   D Brutal crimes have escalated in number as a result of violent video games.

   E Less than 15% of parents are dissatisfied with computer and video games ratings.

   F Video games rating systems have proved to be effective.

   G Video games are similar in rights and protection to other media.

   H Parents need to be physically present to observe the content of video games.

   I Parents can control the mature-themed video games their children play.

3 Which words go in the gaps **[a]–[i]** in the text? Choose from the table below.

according to	despite	indeed	though
also	even when	in fact	thus
but	if	in the end	with regard to
	in addition	on the other hand	

4 Answer the following questions.

   a Name two parties that speak positively of the rating system pertinent to video games.

   b Find a sentence between lines 8 and 18 which proves that no adequate data is available to support the claim that violent video games cause adverse effects.

   c Find a phrase between lines 19 and 26 that is closest in meaning to 'lasting order'.

   d What does the writer mean by the sentence *'Proposals like this are a solution in search of a problem!'* (subtitle)?

5 For each of the words below, choose a word from the box that could meaningfully replace it.

a 'arbiters' (line 2)

b 'sound' (line 6)

c 'concur' (line 7)

d 'undermined' (line 12)

e 'outpaces' (line 28)

f 'prominently' (line 29)

g 'enforced' (line 36)

aggravated	imposed
anticipated	placed
authorities	performers
consent	surpasses
conspicuously	valid
discard	vigorously
famously	weakened

Beyond the text…

➤ The Entertainment Software Rating Board (ESRB) created and implemented age-based and content-based rating categories for computer and video games. Investigate how effective these ratings have been in helping parents monitor mature-themed videos and make computer and video game industries accountable for responsible marketing practices in US.

➤ Some recent studies have revealed that the percentage of female gamers has significantly increased. Examine this issue in two anglophone countries. Are there any differences between female gamers' behaviours and male ones?

➤ Find out if there are any laws regulating the sale and rental of computer and video games to minors in two anglophone countries other than the US. Have such censorship laws been effectively implemented in the countries you have investigated?

➤ Find studies pertinent to violent cartoons in New Zealand, UK, and South Africa. Examine the studies: are any cartoons banned or censored? Are there any cartoons that are believed by parents to be harmful to minors? Do you believe such programmes should be censored?

The personal response

Based on the following stimulus, give a personal response and justify it, using 150–250 words. Choose any text type you have studied so far.

"We are worried about violence being marketed to children as fun and entertaining… Our list is a little different this year because it highlights the 'brands' that are marketed to children through a combination of toys, video games, DVDs and other times."

Daphne White

Remember

- Decide what your stand is. (Do you agree? Disagree? Agree to some extent? etc.)
- Find justification through details and examples to support your stand.
- Organize your ideas.

💬 Interactive oral activity

As a class, split into three groups. Each group will look at one of the
following photographs.

A

B

C

Group 1 (using photograph A)
Impromptu presentation

- Provide a suitable caption
  linked to communication and
  media.
- In 15 minutes, prepare your
  presentation. Reflect on
  anglophone cultures.
- Present your ideas and
  argument in class in 3–4
  minutes.
- Answer questions asked by
  groups 2 and 3.

Group 2 (using photograph B)
Prepared activity

- Provide a suitable caption
  linked to communication and
  media.
- In 15 minutes, prepare your
  presentation. Reflect on
  anglophone cultures.
- **At home**, conduct further
  research to provide examples
  and statistics.
- Present your ideas and
  argument in class in 3–4
  minutes.
- Answer questions asked by
  groups 1 and 3.

Group 3 (using photograph C)
Recorded presentation

- Provide a suitable caption
  linked to communication and
  media.
- In 15 minutes, prepare your
  presentation.
- **At home,** research further,
  and in groups record your
  presentation.
- Groups 1 and 2 listen to the
  presentation and ask follow-
  up questions.

Each group's presentation can be assessed by the audience who need to award a mark using the
Interactive Oral Activity Assessment Criteria (Language B Guide: SL pp. 57–58 & HL pp. 64–65). The
marks awarded must be approved by all group members and justified.

Photograph A: James Cauty & Son, "Splatter" Cartoon Art Gift Shop Window featuring Operation Vigilant Justice, 2008

The SL Written Assignment

Based on the three texts you have read under the topic of communication and media in this section, produce a written assignment task in 300–400 words.

1 Re-read the texts and identify similarities and differences between them.

2 Which sub-topic are you going to explore further:
- Adverse effects of video games?
- Media violence resulting in brutality among minors?
- Myths about violent video games and TV shows?

3 What text type will you use? For example,
- letter
- diary entry
- blog entry
- article

4 Who is your audience? For example,
- the general public
- parents
- Supreme Court

5 Write your rationale (100 words).
- What is your assignment?
- What is your aim?
- How are you going to achieve your aim?

6 Write your assignment in 300–400 words.

CAS

Contact one or two psychologists in your own town or area to collect data and statistics about the effect of video games and violent cartoons on teenagers. Present your findings at one of your school's parent-teacher (PTA) meetings.

TOK

- Begin by reading the following chart about the arguments for and against censorship. Add additional arguments to both sides of the debate.
- How do you decide what should be censored?
- Are your arguments based on language, reason, sense perception, or emotion, or on a combination of different ways of knowing? Are the arguments for and against censorship true for all cultures at all times?
- What does the answer to this question suggest?

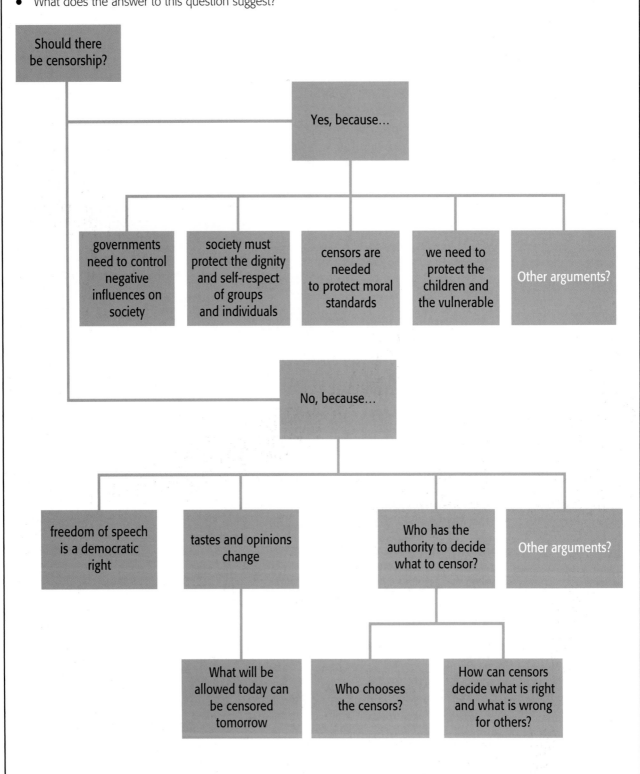

Social relationships

→ Do you believe that homeschooling weakens socialization skills?

→ What is homeschooling and why do you think some parents might choose it as a method to educate thair children?

→ Are there any homeschooling programmes in your own country? If so, what do you think their advantages and drawbacks are?

→ Would it be practical to take the IB Diploma as a homeschooled course?

→ Under what circumstances would you like to be homeschooled? Explain these scenarios.

→ What are some of the stereotypical gender roles existing in your culture?

→ How, in your opinion, can stereotypes be broken?

→ Do you think traumatic incidents, such as wars, leave an everlasting impact on human relationships? How? Why?

Stereotypes & gender roles

What are gender roles and stereotypes?

Keep Safe Stay Cool defines Gender Roles and Stereotypes as attitudes about how females and males should act and think.

Most of us grow up assuming that gender roles
5 and stereotypes are natural ways of being or behaving, **[a] but / and / so / still** we generally don't question them. From the day we are born we receive messages about male and female gender roles. We learn about them **[b] of / by /**
10 **from / through** a number of ways.

A good example of stereotyping gender roles is to think about how babies are colour coded, girls in pink and boys in blue for example. The kinds of toys that little girls receive
15 give messages about feminine traits, such as dolls, dress-ups and fairies. The kinds of toys that little boys receive give messages about masculinity; for example, cars, trucks and building blocks.

20 Messages about gender roles and stereotypes can come from many sources, such as the media, TV, magazines, war, books, marketing, sports, radio, fashion, commercial advertising, internet, fairytales and toys. Culture is a contributing
25 factor **[c] for / to / of / towards** giving rules about social norms and behaviour. Society is another factor **[d] as / though / due to / which** society validates gender roles and stereotypes, encouraging us to "fit in" to the dominant
30 culture.

Gender roles and stereotypes have a history steeped in tradition through religious, political, legal and economic systems. For example, it wasn't **[e] since / until / by / till** the war
35 brought about a shortage in male workers that women were encouraged to step outside the traditional housewife role to work.

Gender roles and stereotypes can place restrictions on our human rights. If you think
40 of a fundamental right, such as the right to employment, or to earn money, the traditional stereotype of women as housewives has placed restrictions and expectations on what a woman is socially and economically capable of doing.

Gender roles, stereotypes, and relationships

45 Statistics show that 95% of domestic violence involves a male perpetrator and a female victim. The other 5% includes same-sex relationships or a female perpetrator **[f] to / of / out / or** a male victim.

50 Gender roles and stereotypes can cause problems in relationships as they set **[g] up / out / from / off** inequality between males and females. Boys are not born to be violent, or have unhealthy attitudes towards girls. These
55 attitudes and behaviours are learned through stereotypes of what society thinks it means to act and behave like a man.

Inequality between a male and female in a relationship can be problematic **[h] unless /**
60 **even when / if / while** gender roles and stereotypes are present. If a couple in a relationship have bought into gender roles and stereotypes, they may not have the skills to create a fair and equitable relationship.
65 He might act controlling. She might behave passively, always putting his wishes first. This relationship has a basis for an unequal balance of power.

We all have a choice about how we act and
70 behave. We can behave like the stereotypes and act out gender roles in relationships, which can lead to unhappiness and possibly violence. **[i] In the end / What's more / On the other hand / In fact**, we can challenge them to have
75 healthier and meaningful relationships based on equality and respect.

www.keepsafestaycool.com.au, 2008

1   For each of the gaps marked **[a]-[i]** in the text, choose one word or phrase from the options provided that renders each sentence meaningful.

2   Based on the information in the text, match the first part of the sentence with the appropriate ending on the right.

a   People do not argue with gender roles

b   Cars and trucks

c   Gender roles are promoted

d   The stereotypical 'housewife' role changed

e   Men's violence is a result of

f   Gender roles and stereotypes

g   Healthy relationships

1   what the society validates as stereotypical ways to act.

2   due to men's refusal to take up certain jobs after the war.

3   cause inequality in relationships.

4   send messages of stereotypical roles of men.

5   are formed by stepping outside the roles set by society.

6   TV, magazines, war, and commercial advertising.

7   as a means to fit into a society.

8   reflect the influence of a dominant culture.

9   because they grow up considering them fixed standards.

10 limits women from revealing what they can really do.

3   Find words from the text that are similar in meaning to the following:
a   believing
b   qualities
c   authorizes
d   scarcity
e   primary
f   executor
g   even-handed

Interactive oral activity

- In pairs, create a sketch presenting a conversation taking place between males and females about their responsibilities, the stereotypes associated with their roles, and the difficulties or restrictions they face in society.

- Each gender should support his/her argument with adequate and convincing justifications.

- Remember to focus on anglophone cultures.

The personal response

Based on the following stimulus, give a personal response and justify it, using 150–250 words. Choose any text type you have studied so far.

"I'm not convinced that what are traditionally considered to be male energies or qualities or female energies or qualities really have as much to do with gender as many people think they do."   **Andrew Cohen**

Homeschooling & social relationships

Social Skills and Homeschooling Myths and Facts

The Debate

I've heard it a hundred times. If you're thinking about homeschooling, it probably troubles you. "What about socialization?" is the major homeschooling question people have about a homeschooling lifestyle.

Professional educators, who don't fully understand the many styles of homeschooling, often raise this issue. They believe school is the only place children learn socialization skills. But it's just not true!

The socialization myth was born out of a misconception of what it's like to homeschool. Many educators and critics of homeschooling still believe homeschoolers hit the books at 9 a.m., work all day at their kitchen table till 3:00 p.m. or later, and spend their day isolated and alone. This, of course, is ridiculous!

The homeschoolers I know are out and about every day, enjoying museums, beaches, parks, and shows without the crowds. They travel often. The kids participate in Girl and Boy Scouts, 4-H, and sports. They take art, dance, drama, language, and music classes, to name a few.

Dr. Raymond Moore, author of over 60 books and articles on human development, has done extensive research on homeschooling and socialization. His book, The Hurried Child, should be in every homeschooler's library. "The idea that children need to be around many other youngsters in order to socialize" Dr. Moore writes, "is perhaps the most dangerous and extravagant myth in education and child rearing today."

Children often do not respond well to large groups. They become nervous and overexcited by noise and too many people. Learning becomes difficult. Behavioral problems develop. After analysing over 8,000 early childhood studies, Dr. Moore concluded that, contrary to popular belief, children are best socialized by parents – not other children.

What kind of socialization occurs when 20 or 30 kids of the same age are placed in a classroom together day after day? Peer pressure is enormous. Kids feel like they need to look and sound and be like everyone else, at the risk of forgetting or never discovering who they really are. This results in rivalry, ridicule, and competition – hardly the environment for healthy socialization.

A homeschooler who interacts with parents and siblings more than with peers displays self-confidence, self-respect, and self-worth. She knows she's a part of a family unit that needs, wants, and depends on her. The result is an independent thinker who isn't influenced by peers and is self-directed in her actions and thoughts.

Do tests bear this out? You bet!

The Research

In July 2000, the Discovery Institute, a Seattle-based think tank, published an extensive report on homeschooling written by Senior Fellow Dr. Patricia Lines. She describes several controlled studies comparing the social skills of homeschoolers and non-homeschoolers.

The homeschoolers scored as "well adjusted." In one study, trained counselors viewed videotapes of mixed groups of homeschooled and schooled children at play. The counselors didn't know the school status of each child. The results? The homeschooled kids demonstrated fewer behavioral problems. Dr. Lines' conclusion? "There is no basis to question the social development of homeschooled children."

Homeschooling parents know kids need blocks of quiet time alone. Time to dream and grow and find out what it is they love to do. This is something few children enjoy today. They are never alone at school, and their after-school lives are packed full of activities, as well.

If you are considering homeschooling and are still concerned about socialization, I suggest the following:

[1] and strike up friendships. This can be done via the Internet, your place of worship, a food co-op, or library. Put up notices on safe billboards in your community.

[2] like 4-H. 4-H is a youth development organization. Your child can choose one of their many clubs, based on his or her interests (rocketry, crafts, environment, animals, dance, and many more). All are welcome, and it's free.

[3] during school hours, ask them if they homeschool. I know of many friendships that started that way!

[4] available through your local parks and recreation department. Team sports give kids the opportunity to meet peers with common interests.

[5] Visit local nursing homes, shelters, etc. One young homeschooler regularly visited a nursing home with her mom and gave elderly women manicures. Giving unselfishly to one's community sets a good example and develops true socialization skills.

Socialization, like learning and life, takes place every day. How you interact with your kids – and how they watch you interact with the outside world – teaches them all the social skills they'll need to know. Stop worrying about socialization. It's a "problem" that never existed!

Isabel Shaw

1 From the list below, choose the appropriate phrase to fill each of the gaps numbered **[1]–[5]** in the text.

   A Volunteer your services
   B Find out about the sports programs
   C Set a good example to your society
   D Identify common interests among homeschoolers
   E Find other homeschoolers in your area
   F When you meet other families out with kids
   G Invite other kids at school to join your children
   H Join a group

2 Answer the following questions.

   a What does 'this issue' (line 7) refer to?
   b Mention four activities homeschoolers participate in.
   c Find two sentences between lines 7 and 15 that reveal the writer's own strong opposition to the myth surrounding homeschooling.
   d What is the myth that Dr. Moore's book undermines?
   e What does the word 'extravagant' (line 28) mean?
   f Find a phrasal verb between lines 37 and 51 that means 'verify'.
   g According to the text, non-homeschoolers have unhealthy socialization skills. List the **7 factors** given between lines 30 and 43 that contribute to such an environment.
   h Refer to lines 44–64 and list the **6 positive personal traits** that homeschoolers develop.
   i Re-read the text and decide whether it is addressed to potential students, teachers, or parents. What evidence can you find to support your answer?
   j In no more than 100 words, summarize the arguments in favour of homeschooling as presented in the text.
   k What stereotypical image of the homeschooled child does the article present? How does the article break this image?

This short story has been divided into two parts. Read each part and answer the questions.

An Episode of War

Part 1

The lieutenant's rubber blanket lay on the ground, and upon it he had poured the company's supply of coffee. Corporals and other representatives of the grimy and hot-throated men who lined the breastwork had come for each squad's portion.

The lieutenant was frowning and serious at this task of division. His lips pursed as he drew with his sword various crevices in the heap until brown squares of coffee, astoundingly equal in size, appeared on the blanket. He was on the verge of a great triumph in mathematics, and the corporals were thronging forward, each to reap a little square, when suddenly the lieutenant cried out and looked quickly at a man near him as if he suspected it was a case of personal assault. The others cried out also when they saw blood upon the lieutenant's sleeve.

He had winced like a man stung, swayed dangerously, and then straightened. The sound of his hoarse breathing was plainly audible. He looked sadly, mystically, over the breastwork at the green face of a wood, where now were many little puffs of white smoke. During this moment the men about him gazed statue-like and silent, astonished and awed by this catastrophe which happened when catastrophes were not expected – when they had leisure to observe it.

As the lieutenant stared at the wood, they too swung their heads, so that for another instant all hands, still silent, contemplated the distant forest as if their minds were fixed upon the mystery of a bullet's journey.

The officer had, of course, been compelled to take his sword into his left hand. He did not hold it by the hilt. He gripped it at the middle of the blade, awkwardly. Turning his eyes from the hostile wood, he looked at the sword as he held it there, and seemed puzzled as to what to do with it, where to put it. In short, this weapon had of a sudden become a strange thing to him. He looked at it in a kind of stupefaction, as if he had been endowed with a trident, a sceptre, or a spade.

Finally he tried to sheath it. To sheath a sword held by the left hand, at the middle of the blade, in a scabbard hung at the left hip, is a feat worthy of a sawdust ring. This wounded officer engaged in a desperate struggle with the sword and the wobbling scabbard, and during the time of it he breathed like a wrestler.

But at this instant the men, the spectators, awoke from their stone-like poses and crowded forward sympathetically. The orderly sergeant took the sword and tenderly placed it in the scabbard. At the time, he leaned nervously backward, and did not allow even his finger to brush the body of the lieutenant. A wound gives strange dignity to him who bears it. Well men shy from this new and terrible majesty. It is as if the wounded man's hand is upon the curtain which hangs before the revelations of all existence – the meaning of ants, potentates, wars, cities, sunshine, snow, a feather dropped from a bird's wing; and the power of it sheds radiance upon a bloody form, and makes the other men understand sometimes that they are little. His comrades look at him with large eyes thoughtfully. Moreover, they fear vaguely that the weight of a finger upon him might send him headlong, precipitate the tragedy, hurl him at once into the dim, grey unknown. And so the orderly sergeant, while sheathing the sword, leaned nervously backward.

There were others who proffered assistance. One timidly presented his shoulder and asked the lieutenant if he cared to lean upon it, but the latter waved him away mournfully. He wore the look of one who knows he is the victim of a terrible disease and understands his helplessness. He again stared over the breastwork at the forest, and then turning went slowly rearward. He held his right wrist tenderly in his left hand as if the wounded arm was made of very brittle glass.

And the men in silence stared at the wood, then at the departing lieutenant – then at the wood, then at the lieutenant.

1   Answer the following questions.

   a   How are the corporals and other men described in the first paragraph?

   b   What is the significance of the 'puffs of white smoke' (line 25)?

   c   Why is the wood described as 'hostile' (line 40)?

   d   Why has the sword suddenly become 'a strange thing to him'? (line 44)?

   e   What does the phrase 'endowed with' (line 46) mean?

   f   What is the 'desperate struggle' (lines 51–52) the lieutenant is involved in? Find three descriptions that reflect how difficult the struggle was to the lieutenant.

   g   Despite being sympathetic and ready to help, the soldiers do not want to touch the lieutenant's wound. Explain why.

   h   Choose the correct answer from A, B, C, or D.
   1   'This task of division' (line 8) actually refers to
      A   the corporals and representatives lining up around the lieutenant.
      B   the lieutenant distributing the portions of coffee to soldiers.
      C   the lieutenant preparing equal portions of coffee for the men.
      D   the lieutenant calculating how many portions each soldier should take.
   2   The blood on the lieutenant's sleeve is caused by
      A   the sword he carries
      B   a sudden bullet
      C   a personal assault by the man near him
      D   a bullet he had earlier in the battle.
   3   The word 'mournfully' (line 83) means
      A   painfully
      B   gloomily
      C   hysterically
      D   defiantly

2   Copy and complete the following table by indicating to whom or to what the word indicated refers.

In the phrase...	the word/s...	refer/s to...
...and awed by this catastrophe... (line 28)	'this catastrophe'	
...when they had leisure to observe it. (line 30)	'they' 'it'	
...and the power of it sheds radiance... (lines 69-70)	'it'	
...if he cared to lean upon it... (line 82)	'it'	
...but the latter waved him away... (lines 82-83)	'the latter'	

Part 2

As the wounded officer passed from the line of battle, he was enabled to see many things which as a participant in the fight were unknown to him. He saw a general on a black horse gazing over the
5 lines of blue infantry at the green woods which veiled his problems. An aide galloped furiously, dragged his horse suddenly to a halt, saluted, and presented a paper. It was, for a wonder, precisely like an historical painting.

10 To the rear of the general and his staff a group, composed of a bugler, two or three orderlies, and the bearer of the corps standard, all upon maniacal horses, were working like slaves to hold their ground, preserve, their respectful interval, while
15 the shells boomed in the air about them, and caused their chargers to make furious quivering leaps.

A battery, a tumultuous and shining mass, was swirling toward the right. The wild thud of hoofs, the cries of the riders shouting blame and praise,
20 menace and encouragement, and, last the roar of the wheels, the slant of the glistening guns, brought the lieutenant to an intent pause. The battery swept in curves that stirred the heart; it made halts as dramatic as the crash of a wave on the rocks, and
25 when it fled onward, this aggregation of wheels, levers, motors, had a beautiful unity, as if it were a missile. The sound of it was a war chorus that reached into the depths of man's emotion.

The lieutenant, still holding his arm as if it were
30 of glass, stood watching this battery until all detail of it was lost, save the figures of the riders, which rose and fell and waved lashes over the black mass.

Later, he turned his eyes toward the battle where the shooting sometimes crackled like bush-fires,
35 sometimes sputtered with exasperating irregularity, and sometimes reverberated like the thunder. He saw the smoke rolling upward and saw crowds of men who ran and cheered, or stood and blazed away at the inscrutable distance.

40 He came upon some stragglers, and they told him how to find the field hospital. They described its exact location. In fact, these men, no longer having part in the battle, knew more of it than others. They told the performance of every corps,
45 every division, the opinion of every general. The lieutenant, carrying his wounded arm rearward, looked upon them with wonder.

At the roadside a brigade was making coffee and buzzing with talk like a girls' boarding-school.
50 Several officers came out to him and inquired concerning things of which he knew nothing. One, seeing his arm, began to scold. "Why, man, that's no way to do. You want to fix that thing." He appropriated the lieutenant and the lieutenant's

55 wound. He cut the sleeve and laid bare the arm, every nerve of which softly fluttered under his touch. He bound his handkerchief over the wound, scolding away in the meantime. His tone allowed one to think that he was in the habit of being
60 wounded every day. The lieutenant hung his head, feeling, in this presence, that he did not know how to be correctly wounded.

The low white tents of the hospital were grouped around an old schoolhouse. There was
65 here a singular commotion. In the foreground two ambulances interlocked wheels in the deep mud. The drivers were tossing the blame of it back and forth, gesticulating and berating, while from the ambulances, both crammed with wounded, there
70 came an occasional groan. An interminable crowd of bandaged men were coming and going. Great numbers sat under the trees nursing heads or arms or legs. There was a dispute of some kind raging on the steps of the schoolhouse. Sitting with his back
75 against a tree a man with a face as grey as a new army blanket was serenely smoking a corn-cob pipe. The lieutenant wished to rush forward and inform him that he was dying.

A busy surgeon was passing near the lieutenant.
80 "Good-morning," he said, with a friendly smile. Then he caught sight of the lieutenant's arm and his face at once changed. "Well, let's have a look at it." He seemed possessed suddenly of a great contempt for the lieutenant. This wound evidently placed the
85 latter on a very low social plane. The doctor cried out impatiently, "What mutton-head had tied it up that way anyhow?" The lieutenant answered, "Oh, a man."

When the wound was disclosed the doctor
90 fingered it disdainfully. "Humph," he said. "You come along with me and I'll 'tend to you." His voice contained the same scorn as if he were saying, "You will have to go to jail."

The lieutenant had been very meek, but now his
95 face flushed, and he looked into the doctor's eyes. "I guess I won't have it amputated," he said.

"Nonsense, man! Nonsense! Nonsense!" cried the doctor. "Come along, now. I won't amputate it. Come along. Don't be a baby."

100 "Let go of me," said the lieutenant, holding back wrathfully, his glance fixed upon the door of the old schoolhouse, as sinister to him as the portals of death.

And this is the story of how the lieutenant lost
105 his arm. When he reached home, his sisters, his mother, his wife sobbed for a long time at the sight of the flat sleeve. "Oh, well," he said, standing shamefaced amid these tears, "I don't suppose it matters so much as all that."

Stephen Crane

1 Answer the following questions.

   a Briefly describe the four scenes the lieutenant observes on his way to see the doctor.

   b What is 'the war chorus' referred to in line 27?
   Find another phrase between lines 17 and 28 that matches this description.

   c Find a word between lines 17 and 39 that means 'but'.

   d Why does the lieutenant look upon the stragglers 'with wonder' (line 47)?

   e Which phrase between lines 89 and 103 prepares the reader for the amputation of the lieutenant's arm?

   f '*I don't suppose it matters as much as all that*' (lines 108–109). What does really matter for the lieutenant at the end of the story?

2 Choose the correct answer from A, B, C, or D.

   a menace (line 20) means
      A despair
      B discouragement
      C apprehension
      D peril

   b exasperating (line 35) means
      A infuriating
      B astonishing
      C deafening
      D pleasing

   c interminable (line 70) means
      A wounded
      B incessant
      C furious
      D massive

   d disdainfully (line 90) means
      A irritably
      B impudently
      C riskily
      D contemptuously

   e wrathfully (line 101) means
      A angrily
      B briefly
      C scornfully
      D fearfully

3 The five words from question 2 are given again below. Identify each word's part of speech and use it in a meaningful sentence.
   a menace
   b exasperating
   c interminable
   d disdainfully
   e wrathfully

4 Indicate to whom or what the following words or phrases refer in the text.
   a 'his' (line 6)   **c** 'he' (line 78)
   b 'their' (line 16)   **d** 'the latter' (line 85)

5 Scan Parts 1 and 2 of the short story, then collect war-related words and phrases related to:
   ● sounds
   ● sights
   ● smells and tastes
   ● touch.

   In your opinion, what impact do such words and phrases have on the reader?

Beyond the text...

➤ Trace the development of gender roles in both American and British societies over the past 10 years. Can you find any similar patterns in the two cultures?

➤ Analyse the most common stereotypes existing in South Africa and Australia. What is the role of the media in enhancing or removing such stereotypical images?

➤ Find out more about the homeschooling curricula in at least three different anglophone countries. What

differences and/or similarities can you find? What determines the nature of the curriculum used in different countries?

➤ Collect data about the Traumatic Incident Reduction Therapy that was originally developed by Dr. Frank Gerbode in the US. How effective has this therapy been? How does it work? How does it help people who have had traumatic experiences? Is it applied in other English-speaking countries apart from the US?

Interactive oral activity

In groups, explore how a soldier's social relationships and life are gravely affected by war.

'Post-traumatic stress disorder (PTSD) is a real illness. You can get PTSD after living through or seeing a traumatic event, such as war… or a bad accident. PTSD makes you feel stressed and afraid after the danger is over. It affects your life and the people around you.'

Medline Plus, 2012

- Find out more about PTSD experienced after war and read about its effect on social life. You may want to watch the following video: www.youtube.com/watch?v=kNAzSR5SSSo
- Draw examples from English-speaking countries.
- Find a movie, a song, or a documentary that tackles such an issue and use it to initiate discussion.

The HL Written Assignment

Based on *An Episode of War* (pages 218 & 220), complete your written assignment following the guidelines explained earlier in this book.

1 Re-read both parts of the story and summarize each.
2 What is the main theme of the story?
3 Which idea or perspective do you want to reflect on and explore further in your written assignment?
4 Which text type do you want to write? Why?
5 Who is your audience? What is your aim?
6 Discuss ideas with your teacher.
7 Write your rationale (150 words).
8 Write your assignment (400–600 words).

TIP

HL Written Assignment
For the external written assignment, you will base your written assignment on one of the literary works you read in class.

Remember

The purpose of the written assignment is to provide the student with the chance to reflect upon and develop further understanding of one of the literary works read in class, as well as to develop their receptive and productive skills to a higher degree. (Language B Guide Page 41)

Reflection point

- In this chapter, you have explored a wide range of topics related to customs and traditions, communication and media, and social relationships. How inter-related are the sub-topics presented under each?
- What practical solutions are there to curb stereotyping and prejudice in a society?
- How effective is homeschooling? What methods can be adopted to improve existing curricula and procedures?
- What role does the society play in helping alleviate the effects of a traumatic experience?
- What do you have to do to write proposals, formal and informal letters, and emails?

Health

→ How is traditional medicine perceived in your culture?

→ Should traditional medicine practices be regarded as effective as science-based medicine?

→ What does the cartoon below reveal about certain attitudes to herbal medicine?

→ Are alternative medicine, complementary medicine, and traditional medicine synonyms? If not, how do they differ?

→ When do people resort to alternative medicine? What does this show about the relationship between science and belief?

→ What do you think 'old wives' tales' are? Share a couple of old wives' tales in your culture with your classmates.

Traditional medicine

You too can be a medical practitioner

Simply register with the School of Old Wives' Traditional Medicine and we'll give you a big impressive certificate

Do you remember the traditional way to treat burns? Or what [a] **happens / would happen / should happen** to your face if the wind changed? If you think you can answer these questions, why [b] **not / do not / won't**
5 become a registered practitioner of Old Wives' Traditional Medicine?

Tomorrow at 11.30 am [c] **below / inside / outside** the Department of Health in London, a new professional registration scheme for practitioners in the medical tradition of Old Wives' Tales [d] **is launched / will be launched / have been launched**. A group of junior medics and scientists from the Voice of Young Science (VoYS) network [e] **will form / formed / will have formed** the new VoYS School of Old Wives' Traditional
10 Medicine. They will hand out diplomas for people to practise Old Wives' Traditional Medicine, registering members of the public who [f] **have correctly answered / can correctly answer / will correctly answer** questions about traditional cures and advice. The assessment is free of charge and absolutely no medical training or understanding of human physiology [g] **are required / is required / will have been required**.

Hang on a moment. Surely it is better to stop people practising medicine that isn't evidence-based rather than
15 encourage it? Well, according to the Department of Health, to be worthy of a professional registration scheme all that really matters is for practitioners [h] **to be following / to have followed / who have followed** traditional methods. In a Department of Health steering committee report, and a later consultation to [i] **look on/ look at/ look into** how the government should regulate traditional medicine practitioners, a professional registration scheme was proposed.

20 Just like the VoYS scheme, it would register practitioners for everything [j] **including / especially / except** whether a practitioner has medical training or whether the field is based on proper evidence. The VoYS School of Old Wives' Traditional Medicine is delighted with this proposed scheme, as it flatters practitioners just for following traditional methods, and does away with the need for any of that difficult medical training. And while Trading Standards and other schemes already regulate practitioners for standards of hygiene, English fluency
25 and criminal records, a Department of Health stamp of approval is far more glamorous.

But hang on a minute. What if you want little Johnny to be treated by someone with professional medical training? Could that lump that's appeared on the side of his face be indicative of something more serious than the wind changing while he pulled a face?

Sense About Science and a group of professional societies including the Academy of Royal Medical Colleges,
30 the Royal College of Pathologists and the Institute of Biomedical Sciences are [k] **not / somewhat / indeed** concerned about the risks of misdiagnosis, dangerous drug interactions and the problems of blurring the line between what is and what is not medicine.

But the new scheme has the Department of Health's approval, [l] **so / and / however** there can't be anything to worry about, can there? And as the previous health minister Andy Burnham said: "I believe that the introduction
35 of such a register will increase public protection, [m] **additionally / as / but** without the full trappings of professional recognition [n] **whom / which / who** are applied to practitioners of orthodox healthcare."

Dr Tom Dolphin, deputy chairman of the British Medical Association's junior doctors committee, [o] **agrees / states / objects**:

Providing regulation that looks like the kind of regulation that real medicine gets adds an undeserved veneer of
40 respectability to essentially unproven therapies ... If they are proper treatments then they will be covered by the existing medical regulations; if they're not, then there is no benefit to dressing them up as being on a par with actual medical practice."

What a spoilsport. The Department of Health has reassured us, though, that a professional registration scheme that doesn't check for evidence or medical training is the right thing to do.

45 Come and show the Department of Health your enthusiasm for more registration schemes that don't require medical training. Take the test tomorrow, 8 September, between 11.30 and 12.30 at the Department of Health on Whitehall to see if you too can get a diploma in the medical tradition of Old Wives' Tales.

Julia Wilson, *The Guardian,* 2010

1 For each of the gaps marked **[a]–[o]** in the text, choose one word or phrase from the options provided that renders the sentence meaningful.

2 Answer the following questions.

   a What are the Old Wives' Traditional Medicine registration requirements?

   b What is not a requirement for becoming an Old Wives' Traditional Medicine practitioner?

   c Why is the proposed Department of Health scheme well received by the Voice of Young Science?

   d 'does away with' (line 23) is closest in meaning to:

      A eliminate

      B need

      C exhaust

   e What advantage does a Department of Health scheme hold over Trading Standards and other schemes?

   f Give three concerns professionals have regarding the new scheme.

   g Quote a phrase from the text which proves that the author is supportive of the new scheme.

3 Write down to whom or what the following words or phrases refer.

   a these questions (line 4)

   b They (line 10)

   c it (line 15)

   d it (line 20)

   e his (line 27)

   f they (line 40)

Developing writing skills: Blog entry

Re-read the text and

- quote the words or phrases which clarify the author's attitude to the topic she writes about.

- write down whom you think the intended audience of the text is. Be specific and support your answer with evidence from the text.

- find examples of the elements below:

  ▶ Description

  ▶ Fact

  ▶ Narrative voice

  ▶ Direct quotes

  ▶ Emotive language

  ▶ Rhetorical questions

- in pairs, imagine that your school's Journalism Club is interested in alternative medicine and has asked you to make it the topic of the next blog entry which will appear in the Club's electronic magazine. Re-write the text on page 224 with your classmates as your audience. Retain the same information that appears in the text.

- using the HL Paper 2 assessment criteria, critique your neighbouring pair's blog entry. Be prepared to justify your comments.

> **Remember**
>
> **A blog entry** is a form of writing which is read electronically. Its conventions are similar to the diary entry or the magazine article, depending on its topic, audience, and level of formality. The text on page 224 is an example of a newspaper blog entry.
>
> The blog entry uses the same conventions used in the newspaper or magazine article and its audience determines the register the author uses. To revisit the magazine/newspaper article conventions, see page 136.

Writing activity

Imagine that you have visited an alternative medicine practitioner and decided it is an experience worth blogging about. Write a personal blog entry in which you reflect on the visit.

> **Exam tip**
>
> 'A personal blog entry is a type of website, usually written by an individual with regular entries of commentary, descriptions of events, or other material. Entries are often displayed in reverse chronological order. The personal blog is an ongoing diary or commentary by an individual. It often becomes more than a way just to communicate: it becomes a way to reflect on life. Unlike a diary entry, it may contain explanatory words or phrases.'
>
> **November 2010 English B HL Paper 2 Marking notes**

Alternative medicine

CAM practitioners are skilled conmen

Alternative medicine is a con! There are three types of medicine. The first is medicine that has been tested and proven to work, the second is medicine tested and proved not to work. The third is medicine not even tested. Complementary and alternative medicine (CAM) falls into the last two categories.

When medical science was established in the 18th century, gifted scientists began to show how research and experimentation can yield real knowledge which can be used to treat and cure patients. One by one, diseases began to fall, leading to an increase in population. Today every physician is exposed to basic science and clinical research during their training and the links between science and the practice of medicine are strong. Before a physician can prescribe a drug to a patient, that drug must be proven, through many years of stringent research, be safe and effective for specific indications – this is not necessary for CAM.

In the medical community, the activity of all physicians is regulated through licensing, hospital privileges, referrals, and peer reviews. Alternative medicine operates completely outside of this system. Practitioners of alternative medicine can make claims without the burden of scientific proof, and prescribe therapies without any precautions for their safety. There are several journals devoted exclusively to 'Alternative medicine' but they merely advocate unconventional treatments and rarely assess them objectively.

The lack of scientific research means alternative medicine is harmful. Alternative medicine does not go through the testing, research and safety regulations that are required for mainstream science; therefore, consumers may be buying dangerous products. A study of CAM discovered that there have been numerous cases where consumers have suffered from buying medicine from quacks and in some cases proved fatal – one patient with severe skin cancer was treated for 3 months with a buttercup ointment, the cancer spread all over her body and she died a couple of weeks later.

Alternative medicine is harmful to people because practitioners of CAM use the placebo effect, where their patients feel better mentally but not physically.

America has a long tradition of 'medicine shows', 'cure-alls', and 'snake-oil salesmen'. These people are skilled conmen; they know what the public want and give it to them, in a bright attractive package and a shower of dubious testimonials.

It is not the case that mainstream science is against incorporating alternative medicine into their industries, as quite a few therapies originating from alternative medicine have been investigated and proven to be beneficial e.g. osteopaths use massage in the National Health System (NHS). However, this is no longer alternative medicine if it is used by the mainstream science as it is subjected to the normal rules and regulations. What doctors and scientists are against is integrating touch healing or crystallization which are not based on evidence.

But only in Western society there is a choice of science and alternative medicine, and rich people have diverted to CAM because they have the assurance that if something goes wrong, they can be treated in Harley Street.

Ignorance causes problems, whereas reason can solve problems.

Daniel Marshman, for *Culture Wars*

227

1   Find the words in the text which are similar in meaning to the following:

a   talented   f   imposters

b   generate   g   deadly

c   medical doctor   h   questionable

d   harsh   i   adding

e   promote   j   switched

2   From statements **A–J** below, select the five that are true according to the text.

A   The population of the UK decreased in the 18th century.

B   Basing treatment on scientific research increases life expectancy.

C   Without research, doctors are allowed to prescribe drugs.

D   CAM practitioners do not prescribe to the mainstream medicine requirements.

E   Objective assessment of treatment is missing in CAM.

F   Patients treated by CAM are likely to die.

G   CAM patients improve on mental and physical levels.

H   The way CAM treatments are packaged lures patients.

I   Mainstream science is definitely against using CAM practices.

J   Affluent people regularly switch between CAM and medical treatments.

3   Choose the correct answer from A, B, C, or D.

a   The author of the blog

   A   supports the use of alternative medicine.
   B   mildly objects to the use of alternative medicine.
   C   thinks alternative medicine is all fraud.
   D   rejects alternative medicine out of hand.

b   The author believes the only way to gain medical knowledge is through

   A   experimentation.
   B   practice.
   C   collaboration.
   D   education.

c   The author states that alternative medicine

   A   is subject to the same tenets of mainstream medicine.
   B   is practised by charlatans.
   C   is not detrimental to those who use it.
   D   is in need of improvement.

d   According to the author, mainstream medicine

   A   refuses to incorporate alternative medicine into its practices.
   B   needs scientific evidence to incorporate alternative medicine into its practices.
   C   hails crystallization and touch healing as beneficial.
   D   depends on alternative medicine practices which do not include drugs.

e   According to the author, when dealing with health issues, one should not

    A   lack evidence.

    B   lack knowledge.

    C   resort to logical theories.

    D   reject alternative medicine.

Developing writing skills: Opinion essay

The opinion essay has a certain structure. It begins with your opinion, thus its name, which is stated in the introduction. The body of the essay (a minimum of three paragraphs) is devoted to the arguments which clarify or justify your opinion.
You may consider mentioning the opposing viewpoint but do not forget to refute it or rebut it. Restate your opinion in the conclusion.

In pairs:

- Write down the thesis statement in the text on page 227 and all the arguments the author makes regarding the use of alternative medicine.

- Re-write the blog entry on page 227 into an opinion essay. Write between 250 and 400 words. Don't forget to use an eye-catching title.

- How different or similar to the original text (the blog entry) is your essay? Highlight those similarities and differences.

It is of utmost importance to use a number of cohesive devices in an essay. The following linking words, when used appropriately, are considered effective.

- **To add**: and, furthermore, in addition, what is more, to add, moreover, etc.

- **To contrast**: but, although, though, despite, in spite of, however, nevertheless, yet, whereas, while, etc.

- **To give a reason**: because, since, as, due to, owing to, because of, etc.

- **To give a result**: therefore, consequently, so as a result, etc.

- **To show sequence**: firstly, secondly, finally, lastly, last but not least, the former, the latter, etc.

- **To summarize or conclude**: to sum up, in conclusion, in brief, in summary, in a nutshell, in short, to conclude, etc.

In favour of complementary medicine

Most people thought complementary and alternative medicines were to fade back into New Age mysticism. In 1986 they were described as a 'passing fashion', but nowadays

5 these **[a] methods / ideas / descriptions** are still increasing in popularity. One in five adults in Britain has used complementary medicine in the past year and the **[b] infinite / vast / reasonable** majority claim an

10 improvement. Surely thousands of people who use these therapies again and again are not just **[c] applauding / guiding / deluding** themselves.

Practitioners of complementary medicines are

15 not trying to con people – patients are not deceived that a therapy will definitely work. But the fact is, numerous clinical trials have shown that certain complementary treatments can be **[d] effective / preventative /**

20 **suitable** for all these health problems.

I'm sure every single person reading this suffers from, or knows somebody who suffers from health conditions, which could be **[e] deteriorated / stabilized / improved**

25 by using complementary medicines. Clinical tests have shown that things like acupuncture osteopathy, chiropractic and herbal medicine can really make a difference and now these are being **[f] used / practised / sold** within the

30 NHS alongside traditional medicine.

It's true, some of the wackier therapies seem a bit dubious, but a Government report on complementary medicine said – 'mechanisms of action are of secondary importance to

35 efficacy' i.e. the fact that a treatment works is more important than how it works.

Sometimes a mechanism exists but we have yet to find it; an example of this is acupuncture. The traditional explanation was that it worked

40 by affecting energy meridians. This completely contradicts scientific understanding and so acupuncture was **[g] rejected / accepted / opposed** by the mainstream. But as the benefits of acupuncture became clear, research

45 was done, and another quite likely reason has emerged – the effect on the central nervous system and stimulation of endorphin receptors. So if a mechanism for a treatment hasn't been found, maybe it just hasn't been found yet.

50 Some people argue that the effects of complementary medicine are just the placebo effect. But the statement 'just the placebo effect' is a **[h] conceptualization / contradiction / confirmation** in terms,

55 because the placebo effect is very powerful medicine. If everyone reading this article were suffering from a migraine and X gave you all a sugar pill and told you that it was just a sugar pill but it might help you, statistically, one

60 third of you would still feel **[i] worse / well / better** after taking it.

Even if every single complementary medicine were proved to be 'just the placebo effect', they would still help people and so would still

65 be a **[j] formal / official / legitimate** form of treatment. Fundamentally, if it's known to be safe, it would be against clinical freedom to prevent patients from having access to such therapies. Complementary medicine has

70 worked for thousands of people. Established doctors have seen its effect and decided to integrate it into the NHS to improve orthodox medicine.

I believe it would be stupid to ignore such

75 approaches when they can really help people.

Lucie Potter for *Culture Wars*

1   For each of the gaps marked **[a]–[j]** in the text, choose a word from the options provided which renders the sentence meaningful.

2   Answer the following questions.
   a   What does the author mean by 'were to fade back into New Age mysticism' (lines 2-3)?
   b   To which medical system do the majority of the UK inhabitants resort?
   c   According to the author, what could be effective in treating health problems?
   d   What effective alternative medicine treatments are mentioned in the text? Give three.
   e   What does 'maybe it just hasn't been found yet' (line 49) imply?
   f   According to the author, what should happen if a complimentary medicine treatment is proved to be safe?

3   Based on the information in the text, match the first part of the sentence with the appropriate ending on the right.
   a   In the 1980s, many people thought
   b   Alternative medicine patients naturally
   c   The government believes that the mechanism with which a treatment works
   d   The author believes the placebo effect
   e   According to the article, NHS adopted alternative medicine because

   1   believe a therapy will work.
   2   comes second to the placebo effect.
   3   is a treatment on its own.
   4   do not question the suitability of a certain therapy.
   5   treats people better than mainstream medicine.
   6   it is thought beneficial in the development of mainstream medicine.
   7   alternative medicine's boom was temporary.
   8   comes second to its effectiveness.
   9   its effect surpassed that of mainstream medicine.
   10 alternative medicine was there to stay.

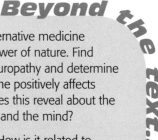
Beyond the text...

➤   The World Health Organization states that people depend on alternative medicine for primary health care in many countries. Do some research and determine whether this statement applies to any Commonwealth nations.

➤   Yoga and acupuncture are two alternative medicine practices. Can you list other practices? Which, do you think, are used the most in anglophone countries?

➤   Look at some sources to find a relationship between lack of good health care and people's use of alternative medicine in anglophone countries. What does this reveal about the role of governments and access to scientific-based health care? Do you think people will shun alternative medicine if they get such access?

➤   Naturopathy is a form of alternative medicine that relies on the healing power of nature. Find more information about naturopathy and determine whether this form of medicine positively affects incurable diseases. What does this reveal about the relationship between illness and the mind?

➤   What is the placebo effect? How is it related to alternative medicine?

➤   *Sicko* (2007) is a documentary that focuses on what the Health Maintenance Organizations in the US lack in comparison to other countries. Watch the film and note down how it presents the HMOs, their strengths and their weaknesses. What, in your opinion, does the US government need to do to improve its public health services?

Developing writing skills: Balanced essay

The balanced essay begins by introducing the topic and proceeds to stating both sides of an argument before it concludes with the author's opinion.

You can approach writing the body of the balanced essay as follows:
AABB = at least two paragraphs in which you state your argument/s for, followed by two paragraphs in which you state your argument/s against the topic.
ABAB = one paragraph for, followed by one against, then another paragraph for, followed by one against.

It is of utmost importance to use a number of cohesive devices in an essay. The following linking words, also mentioned on page 229, when used appropriately, are considered effective:

- **To add:** and, furthermore, in addition, what is more, to add, moreover, etc.
- **To contrast:** but, although, though, despite, in spite of, however, nevertheless, yet, whereas, while, etc.
- **To give a reason:** because, since, as, due to, owing to, because of, etc.
- **To give a result:** therefore, consequently, so, as a result, etc.
- **To show sequence:** firstly, secondly, finally, lastly, last but not least, the former, the latter, etc.
- **To summarize/conclude:** To sum up, in conclusion, in brief, in summary, in a nutshell, in short, in summary, to conclude, etc.

Re-read *CAM practitioners are conmen* and *In favour of complementary medicine* on pages 227 and 230 and follow the steps below to produce a balanced essay.

1   What is the attitude of the authors towards alternative or complementary medicine? Quote at least three phrases from each text which justify your answer.

CAM practitioners are conmen	In favour of complementary medicine
Author's attitude:	Author's attitude:
Justification:	Justification:
1	1
2	2
3	3

2   Using a mindmap like the one below, summarize the main ideas each author provides to clarify his or her opinion and the examples, justifications, anecdotes, or explanations they use to validate their arguments. Be precise and concise.

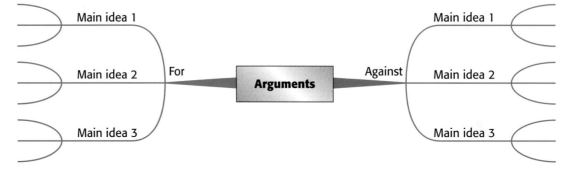

3   How does each blog entry begin? How does it conclude?

4   Now combine the authors' arguments into a balanced essay. Write between 250 and 400 words.

5   Use the HL Paper 2 Section A or the SL Paper 2 assessment criteria to mark a classmate's essay. Be prepared to provide reasons or justifications for the marks you award.

The individual oral (HL/SL)

Work in pairs. Examine the HL/SL assessment criteria and make sure you understand what is expected of the student in the individual oral. Imagine that one of you is the teacher conducting the oral while the other is the student.

Teacher: choose one of the photographs on the right, give it a caption or a title relevant to the Health option and prepare a list of discussion points or questions you would like to ask the student. Make sure your discussion points and questions are relevant to Health and aim to help the student explore the topic in detail and focus on the anglophone culture.

Student: receive your photograph from the 'teacher' and in 15 minutes prepare a 4-minute presentation on the topic. Present your topic to your teacher.

Teacher and student: engage in a discussion on the photograph.

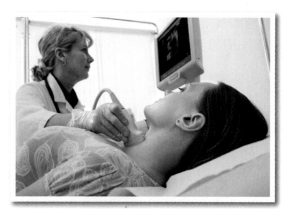

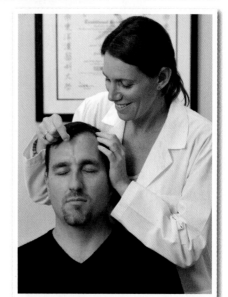

TOK

It is not uncommon for very different approaches to coexist within a single human society. If two competing paradigms give different explanations of a phenomenon, how can we decide which is correct?

Research into one of the following medical controversies:

- Gulf War Syndrome
- Homeopathy
- MMR vaccinations
- The Vitamin C Diet
- The Hearing Voices Movement
- Blood transfusions and Jehovah's Witnesses

For the controversy you have chosen, decide which viewpoint you think is more likely to be true and explain the reasons for your choice.

What is the controversy about?		
What are the main points in the controversy?	Viewpoint A	Viewpoint B
Point A		
Point B		
Etc.		

CAS

Organize a visit to an alternative medicine centre in your area. Interview the therapist and then write an article to be published in your school's magazine based on the interview. Your aim is to present facts; therefore, you may want to consider comparing what the therapist says to a medical practitioner's opinion.

Global issues

BEFORE YOU READ

→ Is drug abuse restricted to being addicted to narcotics?
→ How effective do you think the illustrated pamphlet below is? Do you agree with the information presented? Which of the behavioural changes scares you the most?
→ Should governments play a more positive role in reducing drug abuse? How?
→ How can schools help in raising awareness of the dangers of drug abuse?
→ What can local organizations do to help adolescents avoid substance abuse?
→ What can you do to help?

Substance abuse

Preventing substance abuse

A Proposal

Despite a thirty-five-year war on drug [a] there is evidence that not only is the war far from being won; indeed, it is enlisting
5 younger and younger [b] in ever increasing numbers. Statistically, sixty to sixty five percent of youths who have been jailed have been [c] connected with
10 substance abuse. The age of [d] is estimated to be as early as eleven years old. Once in the "life" the habit of substance abuse is [e] hard to break.
15 Thus it makes sense to try and prevent potential abuse from happening in the first place.

Objectives of this Proposal

In an accurate description of a problem lies an [f] solution.
20 Assuming this statement to be valid, it then follows that the key to successful prevention is the identification of the [g] cause(s) of substance abuse.
25 In my thirty years of professional experience associated with substance abuse, my conclusion is that the central problem underlying substance abuse is
30 the intolerance that the potential abuser has for [h] psychic pain. This psychic pain is commonly referred to as so-called negative feelings including:
35 anxiety, depression, shame, guilt, confusion, weakness, helplessness, hopelessness, ambiguity, complexity, ambivalence, and not knowing. [i]

40 to all is an intolerance of frustration and a frustration about the inevitable experience of frustration. These attitudes render the [j] abuser relatively
45 ineffectual in facing, struggling, and mastering inevitable life problems. In this light, drugs and alcohol are used to [k] the psychic pain associated with
50 these 'unbearable' feelings.

The goal of this project is to provide the potential substance abuser with psychological tools (concepts) for learning how to
55 effectively struggle with struggle, potentially equipping him or her with a necessary self structure for successfully leading a balanced life. Thus, this program aims
60 at providing for each student the know-how in the overly [l] formula: "Just Say No.".

Project Activities

Appropriate time (yet to be specified) will be spent in
65 meeting with administrators, counselors and teachers, to acquaint them with the theory and concepts associated with the workshop.

70 Workshops for adolescents will be given for approximately eight weeks during which they will be primarily focusing on their attitudes when facing
75 unwanted disappointments. The emphasis will be on identifying the presence of negative feelings, attitudes towards these feelings, individual styles of
80 coping or avoiding dealing with these feelings; the introduction of concepts to alter the view of these so-called negative feelings from burdensome to
85 challenging; and the introduction of concepts (tools) utilized as a means of effectively coping with these negative feelings.

To try to objectively measure the
90 effectiveness of the project, each student will be asked to fill out a survey which indicates his or her attitudes towards frustration and the likes. Additionally they will
95 be asked about their attitudes towards drugs and alcohol.

Gibbs A. Williams, Ph.D.

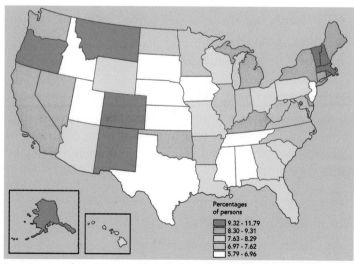

Percentages of persons
9.32 - 11.79
8.30 - 9.31
7.63 - 8.29
6.97 - 7.62
5.79 - 6.96

Percentages of 12–17 year olds in the US who are dependent on illicit drugs

1   Which words go in the gaps **[a]–[l]** in the text? Choose the words from the box below.

abuse	intensify	potential
clear	initiation	recruits
common	intimately	remotely
dealing	known	surprisingly
direct	misguided	underling
embedded	obliterate	underlying
exceedingly	onset	usage
experiencing	optimistic	users

2   Decide whether each of the sentences below is true or false and justify your choice with a relevant brief quotation from the text.

   a   Around two-thirds of young delinquents are associated with drug abuse.

   b   Identifying the causes of substance abuse will not solve the problem.

   c   The main cause of substance abuse is an inability to deal with frustration.

   d   The proposal aims to help people learn how to lead a balanced life.

   e   For approximately eight months, workshop participants will learn how to solve their problems.

   f   A questionnaire will be used to assess the effectiveness of the project.

3   Indicate to whom or what the following words or phrases refer in the text.

   a   'it' (line 4)

   b   'this statement' (line 20)

   c   'my' (line 25)

   d   'all' (line 40)

   e   'them' (line 67)

   f   'which' (line 72)

   g   'their' (line 74)

   h   'these feelings' (lines 78-79)

Developing writing skills: Proposal

Your main goal when writing a **proposal** is to get your suggestions approved. This is why it is very important to determine who your audience is and what action you want your audience to take upon reading your proposal.

To write a convincing proposal, you need to state

- the purpose of the proposal,

- some background information about the topic,

- detailed solutions and outcomes.

In order for your proposal to be effective, use

- short sentences
- language which is easy to understand, although it could be technical at times (depending on the topic of the proposal).

In short, be precise and concise.

1 Re-read the text and answer the following questions.

   a Who is the intended audience of the proposal?

   b What is the main idea in the first paragraph?

   c How does the author present background information?

   d What appears under the 'objectives of the proposal'?

   e Is the language used comprehensible? Does the author use technical terms?

2 In pairs, add one idea which will help control substance abuse to the list proposed in the text.

3 Share your idea with your classmates. Which ideas can be added to the proposal? Which are considered inappropriate? Why?

Interactive oral activity

Imagine that you are a student at a school that is located in an anglophone country. Your school counsellor asked you to present a proposal on one of the problems below to your school's Student Council.

In groups:

1 Choose one of the following problems:
- Binge drinking
- Smoking
- Driving under the influence of alcohol

2 Do thorough research about the topic.

3 Think of solutions.

4 Prepare a presentation in which you outline the problem, the aims of your proposal and your detailed solutions.

5 Present your proposal to your classmates.

TIP

Interactive oral activity guidelines

- The purpose of this exercise is not just to present your solutions; you have to convince your audience that your solutions do address the problem and will help solve it.
- You do not write your solutions in detail in a presentation. You just write summary points and orally explain your solutions.
- Be precise and concise. The topics are too broad and you have to contextualize them. You need to narrow down your topic and focus on the cause(s) and effect(s) of the problem at your school. Remember that you have only 15 minutes to present your proposal and that the more general your solutions are, the less impressive they sound.
- Remember to include specific examples drawn from an English-speaking culture. If you decide to include examples from your own culture, these should be used only to compare how the issue is perceived in your culture compared with your chosen anglophone one.

Drug abuse

Drug Addiction Intervention

Denial is a huge problem

If you are a friend or a family member of someone who is either [a] abusing / using / buying drugs or already
5 addicted, you're probably wondering what you can do to help.

The biggest problem you face is that the abuser or addict [b] will think / is thinking / thinks this is YOUR
10 problem, or you're making a fuss over nothing. "I [c] will / can / do handle it." The last one in the room to know there is a problem is the one who has it.

15 ### There is help
You've seen what's going on and you [d] think / are thinking / have thought of ways to stop the behavior. Maybe you have decided to "get real"
20 with the person you care about and get them help.

The biggest problem you face is
that the abuser or addict believes this is YOUR problem. Therefore, you
25 [e] probably / unfortunately / mostly need the assistance of an interventionist, someone who is trained in drug and alcohol issues.

You are not going to be left out of
30 the loop, as the interventionist will work with the family and friends to plan the best approach to handle the case, based upon his/her history of use. The interventionist will plan according
35 to the user's drug of choice, make the proper analysis and map [f] up / on / out a specific strategy based on the information gathered.

Each drug addiction
40 ### intervention can be different
Interventions will [g] vary / look alike / help, depending on the user's history. For example, if the person is already well into addiction, the interventionist
45 must adjust the strategy. That is where friends and family come in.

[h] Consequently / Moreover / However, the interventionist will understand the approaches
50 to handling alcoholism problems, cocaine abuse, heroin addiction, or those who are abusing inhalants or methamphetamine.

55 Regardless of the drug, [i] trained / good / some professional help is available for a drug addiction intervention. They are the ones who can give an accurate and objective
60 account of the user's behavior. If someone has just moved from being an occasional user to a frequent user, that requires a different approach than the one for a person who is a long-time abuser. Friends and family are vital to
65 this process.

Most people underestimate their problem
People who [j] are caught / caught / have caught in addiction do not
70 realize the severity of their problem. The only thing that matters in their life is getting the drug, regardless of the consequences. Health problems are not considered. Legal problems are not
75 considered.

The person who used to be rational and law-abiding has been swallowed [k] by / with / in the drug. That is why the drug addiction intervention step is
80 so vital.

Don't enable
There is no room for enabling, no room for being the good guy, because the life of the addict may be on the line unless
85 something is done on their behalf. It is sad when family and friends [l] do / no longer / definitely matter. It is even sadder when life does not matter.

Do not be a hero. Get help from
90 a trained professional. That person knows what questions to ask and what information is necessary to make a proper assessment and an effective strategy for battling the problem.

95 ### What is intervention?
Just telling the addict you are concerned for their health and well-being is not going to change the addictive behavior. It is like me telling my dog "Moose" not
100 to chase the rabbits in the back yard. His brain tells him to chase the rabbits.

Depending on the situation, a person might come to the conclusion that their drug use needs to stop and
105 in some cases there is success. But the majority of people cannot [m] often /

frequently / just stop using, so they need help. If you are concerned about a loved one, it is hard for you to be the
110 messenger, because you are too close.

You have an emotional attachment and history with that person. A good example of being too close is found in the wonderful play *The Miracle
115 Worker* when the parents of Helen Keller interfere with the professional help they are receiving from Anne O'Sullivan. Mom and dad feel the therapist is too harsh, or moving too
120 quickly, or too inexperienced, or even too unfeeling.

They are too close to Helen and cannot see the entire situation from beginning to end. They do not know
125 what is in Helen's best interest or how to proceed. They just react emotionally. They are not [n] subjective / objective / reasonable.

If you care, you need help. A trained
130 drug addiction interventionist is your best friend. Where you are likely to fail, the professional will succeed over 90% of the time. Drug addiction is serious and life threatening. If your
135 loved one is addicted, you need to act [o] definitely / emotionally / immediately, for their situation is not going to improve, because addiction has taken over their life and they do
140 not want treatment.

Drug addiction intervention can really help!
Another important point to keep in mind is that an intervention, [p] often /
145 sometimes / however brief, may make all the difference in the world to getting the addict back on track to restoring his/her health.

Even a short encounter with
150 an addiction specialist can prove instrumental in helping someone. Those short visits may lead to putting them into a rehab program, or at least getting them to see a physician.
155 Once in the throes of addiction, addicts will no longer be the person they used to be, and as a result, the intervention stages may be difficult for you to witness. Our affection for the
160 person, our feelings, get in the way and it is difficult for the family member or friend to remain objective.

The interventionist is key to putting the addict back on the right path to a
165 healthy and successful life.

www.Drug-addiction-support.org

1 Choose one word or phrase from the options provided in the text which renders the sentence meaningful.

2 Find the words or phrases in the text which mean the following:

a questioning

b concerned

c problems

d method

e appropriate

f collected

g modify

h irrespective

i precise

j important

k gravity

l sensible

m skilled

n fighting

o controlled

p meeting

q contributory

r observe

s detached

t track

3 Answer the following questions.

a What is the biggest problem a drug addict may face?

b Why does the interventionist need the assistance of the addict's family and friends?

c According to the text, how do interventionists help?

d To whom does 'their' (line 71) refer?

e What is the important thing in an addict's life?

f What does an addict tend to ignore?

g Why does the author recommend that friends or family members not be heroes?

h What will not be effective in changing addictive behaviour?

i How can emotional attachment be detrimental to the help the addict is getting?

j To whom does 'They' (line 122) refer?

k How does visiting an addiction specialist help the addict?

l What effect will addiction have on the addict as stated between lines 149 and 162?

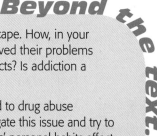

Beyond the text...

➤ In the United States, and under the Controlled Substances Act, one can be imprisoned for 5 to 40 years for possessing certain drugs even in small quantities. However, in India, and under the Narcotic Drugs and Psychotropic Substances Act, the penalty for the same offence is six months. Why do you think there is this huge discrepancy between the penalties? Peruse the laws (both can be found online) and discuss whether they are effective in curbing drug addiction.

➤ *Requiem for a Dream* is one of the films which portray the life of drug addicts. Watch the film and discuss how it represents addiction, what happens to the addicts, and why they resorted to drugs in the first place.

➤ More often than not, people claim they resort to drugs to forget problems. How true is this claim? Do some research about whether drug addicts in an anglophone culture use this claim and note down the problems that they try to escape. How, in your opinion, could they have solved their problems without becoming drug addicts? Is addiction a solution?

➤ Many celebrities are admitted to drug abuse rehabilitation centres. Investigate this issue and try to determine whether celebrities' personal habits affect their fans negatively. Should celebrities be role models?

➤ In Indonesia, Singapore, and Malaysia, the penalty for drug trafficking is death. In your opinion, is this harsh? Why? Why not?

➤ Is there a difference between teenage and adult addiction to drugs?

➤ How is drug abuse and addiction perceived in your culture? How are the laws similar to or different from those applied in anglophone cultures with which you are familiar?

The personal response

Choose one of the following stimuli. Give a personal response and justify it. Choose one of the text types that you have studied in this chapter. Write 150 to 250 words.

- *"The central problem underlying substance abuse is the intolerance that the potential abuser has for psychic pain."*

- *"Drug abuse gives rise to dependence both physical and psychological. This dependence gives rise to mental, emotional, biological or physical, social and economic instability. The effects of drug abuse on an individual therefore form the basis for its cumulative effects on the society."*

- *"Ignorance is still a major factor in drug abuse and so the government must continue to enlighten the youth on the evils of drug addiction and trafficking."*

> **Remember**
>
> In the external examination, you will only get one stimulus.

The SL Written Assignment

Write a proposal to help solve the drug abuse problem in an English-speaking country.

1   Re-read the substance and drug abuse texts on pages 235 and 238.

2   What is the main idea in each text? Summarize the main idea in 30 words. Use your own words.

3   How do the authors support their ideas? List the examples, justifications and/or explanations they use. Use your own words.

4   Choose the general issue that you would like to explore further in your written assignment.

5   Choose the points that will support your argument.

6   Determine who your audience is. This is very important since it determines your style, tone, and register.

7   Discuss your ideas with your teacher.

8   Write your rationale.

9   Write your assignment (300–400 words).

10 Revisit your rationale and include examples from your assignment that support your choice of topic and text type.

> **TIP**
>
> For the written assignment,
> - you will read 3 previously unseen texts chosen by your teacher.
> - it is your responsibility to determine the angle from which you will approach your assignment and the text type you will use.

> **CAS**
>
> Contact your town's police narcotics department and invite them to come to your school and do a presentation on the hazards of substance and drug abuse. In preparation for the presentation, write a one-page informational handout which will help your schoolmates realize how harmful substance and drug abuse is.

Social relationships

→ Is education restricted to the knowledge one gains at school?

→ How is drinking alcoholic beverages perceived in your culture?

→ What is the difference between social drinking and alcoholism?

→ When, in your opinion, can one start drinking?

→ In his letter to Thomas Green in 1789, George Washington wrote: "Refrain from drink which is the source of all evil – and the ruin of half the workmen in this Country." How true or untrue are Washington's words today?

→ Do you think peer pressure affects teenagers' tendency to binge drink?

Education

Mitigate Crime, Poverty and Drug Use through Education

ROCCO BASILE is a gentleman from Brooklyn, New York who has impressed me with regard to his beliefs about how we can all help to make adjustments in our globe these days by means of training.

Rocco Basile mentioned one thing that Gandhi thought: True education consists in drawing the best out of yourself. What much better guide can there be than the book of humanity? (Mahatma K. Gandhi)

"My education taught me to be sympathetic to the desires of others and helped me recognize how that can alter the world. Like Gandhi said it is crucial for us to be the adjustments we want to see in the earth," stated Rocco Basile.

The US Department of Schooling (ED) tagline states, "Promoting academic excellence for all Americans". This organization was founded in 1980 and its mission is "to advertise college student achievement and preparation for worldwide competitiveness by fostering educational excellence and making certain equal accessibility."

Some 500 ED employees and a 0.5 billion spending budget devoted to creating policies on federal monetary assist in training as well as distributing and monitoring the funds, collecting information on America's universities and disseminating studies which focus national attention on essential academic problems, prohibiting discrimination and guaranteeing equal entry to training. For instance, in Brooklyn, New York, gang violence is just a daily occurrence. There are 17 thousand youngster abuse instances in this local community that have been documented. One in each and every household lives beneath the poverty line. There is a 48% dropout rate amongst large school students, so out of the 30 thousand students, 15 thousand are dropouts. Medications, disorder, gang violence, and crime lead to about a thousand fatalities annually. Many men and women have realized that the solution is schooling.

"I really feel my education has authorized me to understand the constructive results it had on my lifestyle. I was educated, and as a result, I was ready to read a lot of guides from every single culture and religion, which inspired me to make positive adjustments," Basile stated. "It has provided me the intuition to see how good adjustment circulates back into my existence."

What transpires to people in society that don't invest in education? Does it make a difference to the total social structure and ultimately influence our economic climate? William Schweke, writer of a book entitled *Wise Funds: Schooling and Financial Development* believes that prevention is almost often less expensive than remedy. He states that if we do not make investments now, we most definitely will shell out later, and discusses the social costs of inadequate academic and workforce planning possibilities, believing that by growing earnings, education can decrease social costs.

Schweke notes that there is a powerful relationship among very low fundamental capabilities and welfare dependency. Sixty percent of out-of-wedlock births between 19 to 23-yr-olds are to individuals who score in the lowest twenty percent on fundamental capabilities tests. About 82 percent of all Americans in prison are substantial college dropouts. Sadly, he also factors out that the United States spends practically ten times more than Western European countries on protection providers, arrest, incarceration and parole, while those countries devote similar quantities on subsidized employment and training.

Many men and women think that educating our youth is the response that will break the cycle of poverty, crime and medication. "Educating our youth is the foundation for prosperity … Financial problems, in flip, exacerbate social difficulties such as crime, drug abuse, gangs, reliance on government help, and loved ones break-ups. To ameliorate these weaknesses in the social material, public money that may well in any other case go toward productive investment are invested rather on crime management, drug treatment and earnings assist programs," says Schweke. "Education positively has an effect on earnings distribution."

There are hundreds of men and women in need of intervention, children in need of education, and families in need of counseling and hope, and Children of the City is an organization generating a big difference. Founded in 1981, the volunteer-based organization mostly connects men and women in need with fundamental providers, educational and employment coaching, wellbeing treatment, counseling, and numerous other personal growth possibilities. People like Rocco Basile are operating via organizations like this.

Kristin Gabriel, 2011

1 Find a word in the right-hand columns that could meaningfully replace each of the words on the left.

a sympathetic (line 16)
b alter (line 18)
c fostering (line 31)
d devoted (line 36)
e disseminating (line 42)
f fatalities (line 61)
g constructive (line 67)
h transpires (line 77)
i remedy (line 88)
j incarceration (line 113)
k ameliorate (line 128)
l generating (line 143)

A adverse
B affecting
C answer
D change
E circulating
F collecting
G cure
H dedicated
I emerges
J encouraging
K faithful
L freedom

M gains
N happens
O imprisonment
P improve
Q insensitive
R losses
S making
T positive
U prohibit
V promoting
W understanding

2 Answer the following questions.

A What is Rocco Basile's life philosophy? Whose philosophy is Rocco Basile's originally?

B According to Ghandi, what do people need to do in order to change the world?

C By distributing studies to the general public, what does the US Department of Schooling aim to achieve?

D Quote the phrase that describes the frequency of gang violence in the city of New York.

E If 17,000 youngster abuse instances have been documented, what does this tell us about violence in New York?

F List two main societal problems in New York as mentioned in the text.

G What effect has Rocco's education had on his life?

H According to the text, how does lack of education affect the American economy?

I How is a significant portion of public money currently spent in the United States?

J What does Children of the City do?

3 From statements A–J, select the five that are true according to the text.

A In order to alter the world, we need to teach people how to understand others.

B Promoting mediocrity is one of the aims of the US Department of Schooling.

C Around one-fifth of New Yorkers live above the poverty line.

D Almost half of the students in New York are dropouts.

E To improve their future, Americans need to believe that prevention is better than cure.

F People should rely on the government to provide help.

G Collectively, European countries spend more than the United States on crime-related issues.

H Monetary problems aggravate social problems.

I Teaching people how to earn their living will reduce societal problems.

J Hope is not one of the needs of many people in New York.

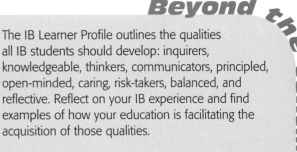

Beyond the text...

➤ Peruse other sources and find examples of educational programmes which focus on helping people realize how beneficial and life-altering education is. What conclusions can you draw?

➤ The IB adopted "Education for a better world" as its slogan. How can education make our world a better world? What problems can education solve?

➤ The IB Learner Profile outlines the qualities all IB students should develop: inquirers, knowledgeable, thinkers, communicators, principled, open-minded, caring, risk-takers, balanced, and reflective. Reflect on your IB experience and find examples of how your education is facilitating the acquisition of those qualities.

TOK

To what extent does the environment (the physical setting) have an impact on the way an additional language is acquired?

How well can a hungry child learn? What happens to the education of a child who is in physical danger? What about a child born to drug addicts? By asking questions like these, American psychologist Abraham Maslow (1908–1970) realized that if successful learning is to take place, humans have certain basic needs which must be fulfilled in order to reduce the overwhelming stress which prevents active learning.

Maslow conceded that the level of basic physical needs must be satisfied before we can start to worry about others. In his theoretical writings he developed a hierarchy of needs demonstrating that basic needs to do with life and death must be satisfied before we can focus on more altruistic activities. Maslow argued that the most fundamental level of needs is related to biological functions of the body. Children need food, water, and sleep in order to function. Without these requirements it is impossible to focus on other less urgent matters.

Maslow also realized that a child's physical safety is essential before students can become effective learners. When students do not live in a safe environment, they are effectively prevented from learning. It may be that there might be communal violence or extreme political turbulence: massive social unrest, criminal activity, or even war. Even in peaceful, prosperous societies, a child who is being victimized or bullied will be prevented from learning. Maslow went on

to say that only when these basic levels of need are satisfied, can we concentrate on developing a higher level need such as the desire to learn. This theory helps to explain why children in unsafe social conditions, such as conflict zones, find it difficult to concentrate on education.

● Do you think Maslow's theory is true for all individuals at all times? Two points to consider:
How do you know when a 'level' has actually been 'satisfied'?
What about individuals who tolerate poor conditions for the promise of future benefits?

● Re-read *Mitigate crime, poverty and drug use through education* on page 242:

1 Imagine setting up an after school English as a second or foreign language programme for teenagers either in Lagos or Brooklyn. What topics would you teach on your course? For example, would you teach only grammar, spelling, and vocabulary? Give reasons.

2 What kind of problems might you have teaching the learners? How would you help them to solve their learning difficulties?

MASLOW'S PYRAMID OF NEEDS

SELF ACTUALIZATION
SELF-ESTEEM
SENSE OF BELONGING
SAFETY NEEDS
PHYSIOLOGICAL NEEDS

 ## The personal response

Based on the following stimulus, give a personal response and justify it. Choose one of the text types that you have studied in class. Write 150–250 words.

> *"My education taught me to be sympathetic to the desires of others and helped me recognize how that can alter the world."*

● Read a classmate's personal response. What do you like about your classmate's response? Why? What do you not like? Why?

● In writing, tell your classmate how s/he can improve his/her personal response. Base your comments on your classmate's performance against the HL P2 Section B assessment criteria.

Exam tip

● Take a clear approach and state your main idea.
● Organize a strongly supported and well-reasoned argument, be it polemic or balanced.
● Use a separate paragraph for each point.
● Write a clear conclusion.

Effects of alcoholism on social relationships

From John Barleycorn: Alcoholic Memoirs

And, ere I begin, I must ask the reader to walk with me in all [a]; and, since sympathy is merely understanding, begin by understanding me and whom and what I write about. In the first place, I am a [b] drinker. I have no
5 constitutional predisposition for alcohol. I am not stupid. I am not a swine. I know the drinking game from A to Z, and I have used my judgment in drinking. I never have to be put to bed. Nor do I [c]. In short, I am a normal, average man; and I drink in the normal, average way,
10 as drinking goes. And this is the very point: I am writing of the effects of alcohol on the normal, average man. I have no word to say for or about the microscopically unimportant excessivist, the [d].

There are, broadly speaking, two types of drinkers. There
15 is the man whom we all know, stupid, unimaginative, whose brain is bitten [e] by numb maggots; who walks generously with wide-spread, tentative legs, falls frequently in the gutter, and who sees, in the extremity of his ecstasy, blue mice and pink elephants. He is the
20 type that gives rise to the jokes in the funny papers.

The other type of drinker has imagination, [f]. Even when most pleasantly jingled, he walks straight and naturally, never staggers nor falls, and knows just where he is and what he is doing. It is not his body but his brain
25 that is drunken. He may [g] with wit, or expand with good fellowship. Or he may see intellectual spectres and phantoms that are cosmic and logical and that take the forms of syllogisms. It is when in this condition that he strips away the husks of life's healthiest illusions and
30 gravely considers the iron collar of necessity welded about the neck of his soul. This is the hour of John Barleycorn's subtlest power. It is easy for any man to roll in the gutter. But it is a terrible ordeal for a man to stand upright on his two legs unswaying, and decide
35 that in all the [h] he finds for himself but one freedom-
-namely, the anticipating of the day of his death. With this man this is the hour of the white logic (of which more anon), when he knows that he may know only the laws of things--the meaning of things never. This is
40 his danger hour. His feet are taking hold of the [i] that leads down into the grave.

All is [j] to him. All these baffling head-reaches after immortality are but the panics of souls frightened by the fear of death, and cursed with the thrice-cursed gift
45 of imagination. They have not the instinct for death; they lack the will to die when the time to die is at hand. They trick themselves into believing they will outwit the game and win to a future, leaving the other animals to the darkness of the grave or the annihilating heats of
50 the crematory. But he, this man in the hour of his white logic, knows that they trick and outwit themselves. The one event happeneth to all alike. There is no new thing under the sun, not even that yearned-for bauble of feeble souls--immortality. But he knows, HE knows,

'The Drunkard's Progress' by Nathaniel Currier, c. 1846

55 standing upright on his two legs unswaying. He is compounded of meat and wine and sparkle, of sun-mote and world-dust, a frail mechanism made to run for a span, to be tinkered at by doctors of divinity and doctors of physic, and to be flung into the scrap-heap
60 at the end.

Of course, all this is soul-sickness, life-sickness. It is the penalty the imaginative man must pay for his friendship with John Barleycorn. The penalty paid by the stupid man is simpler, easier. He drinks himself into
65 sottish unconsciousness. He sleeps a drugged sleep, and, if he dreams, his dreams are dim and inarticulate. But to the imaginative man, John Barleycorn sends the pitiless, spectral syllogisms of the white logic. He looks upon life and all its affairs with the jaundiced eye of
70 a pessimistic German philosopher. He sees through all illusions. He transvalues all values. Good is bad, truth is a cheat, and life is a joke. From his calm-mad heights, with the certitude of a god, he beholds all life as evil. Wife, children, friends – in the clear, white light of his
75 logic they are exposed as frauds and shams. He sees through them, and all that he sees is their frailty, their meagreness, their sordidness, their pitifulness. No longer do they fool him. They are miserable little egotisms, like all the other little humans, fluttering their May-fly life-
80 dance of an hour. They are without freedom. They are puppets of chance. So is he. He realises that. But there is one difference. He sees; he knows. And he knows his one freedom: he may anticipate the day of his death. All of which is not good for a man who is made to live and
85 love and be loved. Yet suicide, quick or slow, a sudden spill or a gradual oozing away through the years, is the price John Barleycorn exacts. No friend of his ever escapes making the just, due payment.

Jack London

1 Which words go in the gaps **[a]–[j]** in the text? Choose the words from the list below.

A	sympathy	**J**	animatedly
B	incomprehension	**K**	vision
C	seasoned	**L**	babble
D	inexperienced	**M**	universe
E	stagger	**N**	universal
F	step	**O**	pathway
G	dipsomaniac	**P**	tactic
H	sober	**Q**	clear
I	numbly	**R**	unclear

> **Remember**
>
> When you come across new vocabulary items, it is not enough to be able to use them to fill in the blank spaces in an exercise. Try to use new vocabulary in your writing. Experiment with words, see how they form meaning, and whether their use in a certain context is appropriate.

2 Answer the following questions.

a About whom is Jack London writing?

b Which word in the first paragraph is closest in meaning to 'extremist'?

c How are some alcoholics described in the second paragraph?

d How is the imaginative drinker different from the unimaginative one?

e What is the only truth in the imaginative drinker's life?

f Why is 'HE' written in block letters in line 54?

g What does 'HE' know?

h 'Good is bad, truth is a cheat, and life is a joke' (lines 71-72). What does this sentence tell us about the kind of days, and nights, the imaginative drinker has?

i What is the price the imaginative drinker pays for drinking?

j Which word in the last paragraph is closest in meaning to 'inadequacy'?

3 The statements below are all true. Give the exact quotes from the text which prove these statements true.

a Alcoholics are prone to fanciful ideas.

b Hardened drinkers understand rules but not their import.

c Imaginative drinkers know they are not immortal.

d Imaginative drinkers have animated but grim dreams.

e To the imaginative drinker, all people are prisoners.

Beyond the text...

➤ In recent years, the UK has suffered from a chronic teenage binge-drinking problem. Peruse some sources to find out more about this problem, its causes and its effects. What, in your opinion, can be done to help British teenagers realise the dangers of binge drinking?

➤ Alcoholics Anonymous (AA) is an aid movement which helps alcoholics battle their addiction and maintain sobriety. Visit the movement's website: www.aa.org to learn more about where the organization works, and which methods are used to help alcoholics. Compare AA's work to that of a similar movement or organization in your culture. How are they similar? How are they different?

➤ Alcoholism has become a universal problem and it severely affects teens. Do some research to find out more about how different anglophone countries are dealing with this problem. What governmental programmes or laws exist? How are private institutions helping?

Interactive oral activity

1 In groups, choose a song which explores an important issue in an English-speaking country, for example:

- Parent/child relationship
- Drug abuse or addiction
- Driving under the influence of alcohol
- Growing up
- Teenage problems
- Ethnicity
- Peer or parental pressure
- Divorce
- Abortion

2 Read the lyrics of the song carefully to identify the angle from · which the problem is projected.

3 Enact a short sketch which clarifies the problem as presented in the song.

The HL Written Assignment

1 Re-read the *Alcoholic Memoirs* text on page 245.

2 What is the main theme in the text? Summarize the main theme in 30 words. Use your own words.

3 Think of a different perspective from which to approach the text and explore the main theme. Write your ideas down.

4 Focus on one idea and think of how you can expand it. This will be your aim.

5 Determine which text type you would like to use in your written assignment. Do not merely choose a text type you would love to write. Think in terms of which text type would best deliver the message you have chosen.

6 After you have chosen your type of text, determine who your audience is. This is very important since it determines your style, tone, and register.

7 Discuss your ideas with your teacher.

8 Write your rationale.

9 Write your assignment (500–600 words).

10 Revisit your rationale and include examples from your assignment that supprt your choice of topic and text type.

> **TIP**
>
> For the written assignment, you will base your writing on one of the literary works you have read in class.

TOK

According to psychologists such as Maslow, self-esteem and self-concept are essential to our educational development. Self-esteem is composed of our beliefs in our own abilities and importance. In addition, it is essential to have a clear self-concept. We can say that our self-concept is defined by our beliefs about ourselves and our identity. A positive self-concept is closely connected to high self-esteem. Both are important for academic and social success.

Establishing an identity (self-concept) is possibly the single most important developmental task during adolescence. Adolescents' self-concept is determined by others' perceptions – especially peers, parents, friends and even teachers. During adolescence, physical changes influence our sensitivity to others' opinions. How many hours do we spend looking at ourselves critically in the mirror in order to look just right to create the exact impression we want to make?

"May I remind you that my core worth as a human being remains constant, and isn't tied to external validation."

Research indicates that self-concept and self-esteem are related to success. Someone with high self-esteem is likely to be able to be more independently minded and able to take bigger risks. Students who take part in class discussions and ask questions are more likely to achieve their aims than students who are crippled by shyness and lack of confidence. Therefore, if you are able to break out of your comfort zone, you are likely to become a better learner. As American writer Mark Twain once said, "Supposing is good, but finding out is better."

How is this related to language learning?

- How do we stop worrying, improve self-image, gain confidence, and perform well in English B? Write a list of tips and advice for younger students in the school.

- When you have finished your list, have a critical look to see if your language learning tips are based on sense perception, logic, or emotions.

- What conclusions do you come to?

Reflection point

- In this chapter, you examined several claims and standpoints about traditional and alternative medicine. What is more, you read about abuse, alcoholism, and how those affect people's relationship with their immediate environment. How related are those topics? What can be done to increase public awareness about addiction and its effects on a person's mental and physical health?
- What is the relationship between culture and acceptance of alternative medicine?
- Why is addiction considered a global issue?
- How is language used to convey meaning? What do you have to do to write an effective essay, a convincing blog entry and a good proposal?

In this chapter, you will continue exploring the English language and anglophone cultures through literature. The following four short stories have all received high acclaim in short story competitions. The stories can be studied and enjoyed by HL and SL students alike, but with a focus on understanding and interpreting literature, some of the suggested activities are aimed at HL students.

Preparatory reading

In groups of four:

- Divide the four stories on pages 254 to 257 among your group so that everyone reads a different story.
- Read your assigned story and make brief notes on the plot.
- You should also make notes on any new vocabulary you come across, as well as literary features in the story. You may find it helpful to use the table on the right to record this information.
- If you prefer to read without interruption, you could complete the table as a post-reading task.

Title of the short story	Exposition	Turning points
Description of characters	Rising action/s	Climax
The setting (time, place, and atmosphere)	Falling action/s	Resolution/s
Imagery	Symbolism	Tone and style
Interpretation of the title	Interpretation, reflection, the theme	

Exploring short stories through visuals

1   Study the four short stories on pages 254 to 257 individually or in small groups. Pay attention to content, language, and literary features.

2   You should decide who is going to work on which story and team up. The teams should then choose how to illustrate their story by using visuals. You may choose from the options below:
  a   a storyboard
  b   a drawing or a series of drawings
  c   a cartoon
  d   a collage (e.g. cut-outs from magazines, brochures, combined with line-drawing and text)
  e   a poster

3   Transform your interpretation of the short story into an illustration in the media of your choice.

4   Reflect on your choices throughout the creative process. For example, which graphics best communicate certain ideas within the story?

5   Write a brief rationale in which you introduce your work and explain the links with the short story. Particular attention should be given to literary features: how are the author's choices and your interpretation shown in your illustrations?

6   To present your stories, organize a gallery-style opening of your work with brief summaries or presentations. You might want to discuss your images and the language used with your peers and ask for their feedback.

Exploring short stories through cooperative learning

Exchanging information through talking and listening

1   In your groups, take turns to give a verbal account of the plot of your story. Without interrupting, the others should listen and make notes of the plot, as well as any details they would like to be clarified.

2   Immediately after the retelling, ask your questions. Discussing the story should be avoided at this point.

3   Choose a representative who retells the plot back to the student who originally read and told the story. The original storyteller pays attention to any changes or alterations and makes notes on these but does not discuss them with the other group members.

4   This process of telling, listening, and re-telling of the plot is repeated so that all four stories are communicated to all group members.

Investigative reading

5   In your groups, read the other three stories your group members told you about earlier.

6   Individually, study the stories carefully and pay attention to how the plot is constructed. Reflect on your initial understanding of the short stories and any changes as a result of reading the text. You should also make notes on any new vocabulary you come across, as well as how literary features are used in the story. You may find it helpful to record your observations in a table like the one on page 249.

Discussion

7   Having studied your short stories, reassemble in your groups to discuss them.

8   Share new vocabulary, structures, and observations on how the stories work as literature.

9   Exchange ideas and give one another constructive feedback based on reflection on your own performance as well as that of your peers. Any deferred questions or clarifications from the telling, listening, and re-telling stage may now be addressed.

10 Reflect on your reading and appreciating the stories. Did the journey you started from the superficial level of reciting the plot, and continued with exploring the language and details of the written text, finally arrive at a more profound understanding of the literary text? Did you encounter any obstacles?

11 Try to build links with the short stories and the core topics and options studied in class.

12 Pool ideas on how these and other short stories can be used in the HL written assignment.

Further stages

- Revisit the stories after some time. Have you made progress in understanding the language and has your interpretation of the stories changed?
- Having studied all four stories, organize a class discussion to vote for your favourite and least favourite story. Justify your choices and reflect on differences in taste.

Exploring short stories in detail (HL)

In pairs or small groups, study the short stories by following the step-by-step instructions below. Make notes at each stage.

1 Look at the title of your story. What does it mean? What does it suggest about the story you are about to read?

2 Look at the information given about the author. How does knowing the gender and place of origin affect your expectations of the story?

3 Look at the first sentence of the story. Break it down to its smallest elements: what happens, where, how, why, to whom? In neutral tone, rewrite the first sentence using the fewest number of words possible, while communicating the core information.

4 Jump to the last sentence of the story. What does the last sentence mean and what does it suggest? How does it link with the first sentence of the story? How does it link with the title of the story? Can you predict what happens between the first and the last sentence?

5 Now read the whole story and pay attention to the twists in the plot from the beginning to the end. Make notes on any significant turning points, surprises, rising and falling actions, etc. Compare your notes with your group members.

6 Identify up to five key sentences between the opening sentence and the end of the story. Again, using a neutral tone and the fewest number of words, rewrite these key sentences.

7 Look at the skeleton of the story: your rewritten opening sentence and your chosen key sentences. Do they represent the story well? Why? Does the last sentence of the story successfully fit as a conclusion to your sentences? Why?

8 Compare the language of your sentences with the original text. What is different? Look at sentence structure and length, vocabulary, style, tone, etc.

9 Try to rephrase your opening line and key sentences while emulating the original language, style, and tone used by the author. Write them down first, and then compare them to the original text. How close did you come?

(HL & SL)

10 You will need up to seven slips of paper. Start by copying the opening sentence of the short story onto a separate slip. Do the same for the last sentence. Next identify up to five key sentences between the opening sentence and the end of the story. Write these onto separate slips.

11 Place your slips in their correct order on the table. Take turns to tell the story using only the slips. Fill in the gaps with your own words, but try to imitate the language, tone, and style of the original story.

12 Jumble the order of the slips and see how the structure and development of the story changes. Are any slips interchangeable? Is the original order the best order or the only order? Why?

13 Collect and pile the slips in a jumbled order. Hand them over to another group or pair working on another story. Tell them the title of your story, and ask them to arrange the slips in the order they deem logical. If you want to help them, indicate which ones are the opening and closing sentences.

   a Observe your fellow students while they are arranging the slips and discussing the order. Compare their interpretation of the story with your own.

   b Give the group members an agreed time limit to finish the task, and then give them feedback. Justify the original order of the slips.

   c Draw the group members' attention to the language of the story. You may illustrate your points by comparing the slips with your rewritten sentences (from step 6).

   d Discuss the title of the story. Concentrate on the relationship you see it has with the rest of the story and its theme.

Developing writing skills

Write 250–400 words on one of the titles below. For each title that mentions 'A short story' you should refer to a specific story that you have read.

- A short story I can identify with
- A short story I cannot identify with
- A short story full of local flavour
- A short story which opened my eyes
- When words fail…
- What unites us/What separates us
- Human relationships in a short story
- How metaphors are used in a short story
- How the plot is developed in a short story

To synthesize the step-by-step activities, organize a series of presentations where each short story is discussed from a different angle. For example, HL students may collate and comment on the literary features used in the short story, or the language may be studied in detail. The written work could also be displayed, submitted for peer feedback, and discussed.

Education for Life

Only a few weeks left, and then Karen's accent would be gone for good. She could hardly wait. She had not enjoyed lessons at school, had not done well in her exams, but each class that she took with Mrs. Melrose excited her more and more: never, she told her tutor, had she learned so much so quickly. Before the first lesson, Mrs. Melrose had
5   made Karen read out a passage from a book, and had recorded her on a cassette as she spoke, which Mrs. Melrose promised to play back at the end of the course. "You won't believe what you hear, Karen!" she had said. "You won't recognise your own voice."

Already, Karen laughed when she remembered the way she used to speak; now, in the audition waiting rooms, she heard the other girls rehearse their lines – "Treat yer
10   'ands, vis win'ah, to rose'ip 'andcream" – "Give 'er somefink special, vis Moverink Sundee" – and she had to hide her smile behind her script. Courage rose in her chest, warm and bright, swelling through her throat and out into her voice: "Treat your hands, this winter..."

With each word she perfected, Karen felt a piece of her old life fall away. Soon, there
15   would be nothing left of the foolish girl she had been, just a trail of dropped consonants and languid diphthongs drying up and disappearing in her wake. Walking, she felt taller, her eyes further from the ground; in the mirror she tilted her head upwards, and practised a smile a mile wide.

"Practise, always practise," Mrs. Melrose said, so Karen spoke whenever she was
20   alone, narrating each action, enunciating each thought. "I am making my breakfast," she said in the kitchenette, "Strawbry – strawberry jam, and a nice cup of tea." Surely, the offers from the auditions would start arriving soon; she dreaded leaving her flat in case the telephone should
ring, and in the evenings she kept the volume on her radio down low, the telephone
25   within an arm's quick reach. She read the news with the newsreader, a beat behind:

"Good evening."

"Good evening." "This is the BBC." "This is the BBC."

Who knew where advertisements on the radio could lead? Television commercials, a small part in an afternoon drama, and why stop there? Karen from the terrace was
30   gone, Karen who had failed her exams; Karen, guaranteed fodder for the typing pool or the factory floor had lost her voice: no one could hear her any more. Karen from the secondary modern, who had saved her paper-round pennies for cheap Rimmel lipsticks that her mother forbade her to wear: she was no more than the flick of a ghost in the mirror, a slip of the tongue.
35   Now, what money Karen had went to Mrs. Melrose, and was money well spent. One day, she thought, decades from now, a plaque would be nailed to the front of her parents' house, on the authority of the Greater London Council, and her grand-daughters would be photographed in Dior beneath it: 'Karen Driscoll, loved by millions, never lived here'.

Anna Lewis, UK
Highly commended, *Commonwealth Short Story Prize*, 2010

Waiting for the Plane

It's the third time now that the plane has gone around and Maggie is feeling her initial euphoria at hearing its engine slowly draining from her heart. Her patient moans softly on the stretcher and Maggie reflexively mumbles some words of comfort, then slumps back against the side of the troopie that doubles as an ambulance. She is so very, very tired and feels something close
5 to hatred towards this lady on the stretcher, this lady who will not leave the drunken husband who beats her and so gets beaten up again tonight, and then comes to Maggie for help with long lacerations down her arms, a broken leg with bones poking out through the skin, puffy lips and her right eye swollen shut, smelling of alcohol and piss, moaning and crying, 'Sister, Sister...' And Maggie, who pulls herself out of bed and inserts intravenous lines, cleans and sutures and above
10 all waits for the plane to get there, can remember a time when her heart would have ached for this pitiful woman, but instead all she can feel is cold fury at being woken.

She tries to feel guilty for this but she cannot even summon the self-discipline to chide herself.

'I am tired and burnt out,' she thinks, as she sags against the troopie and watches the coldly burning stars. High above, the tiny plane attempts a fourth approach at the dirt airstrip. The
15 electric lights will not come on and Jack the policeman is driving manically between the 44 gallon drums that line the airstrip, trying to light the back-up flares before the plane gets too low on fuel and turns back to the city and civilization and drags the last of its hope and light away with it.

It's strange but all that Maggie can remember when she leaves the desert is how beautiful it is. How the colours at dawn and dusk glow in mauve and pastel and how, at night, one can
20 watch the stars and almost hear the earth turning. And when she is away all she remembers of the people are the women who take her digging for yams and laugh hysterically at her attempts to catch goanna; the children who cry out, 'Sister, Sister,' and want hugs from her as she passes. 'Funny,' she thinks, when she's away the flies that gather at their snotty noses and weepy eyes are a reason for her to return and to help them, rather than a reminder of her futility.

25 Right now, though, anxiously waiting as Jack struggles to light another flare, Maggie hates the community. Hates the sounds of people drinking and fighting that she can hear in the distance (for there's money and alcohol in the community tonight) and she hates the desert too, with its huge, imprisoning remoteness.

A memory comes into her head: many years ago, on a holiday in the north of England, she
30 stood atop Hadrian's Wall and stared out across the soft green and grey landscape that was once the outer boundary of the civilized world. She has a sudden surge of empathy for the Roman soldiers who would have been stationed along the wall because the desert and the woman muttering on the stretcher and the distant yells from the community are all alien. The only link with her world is the Royal Flying Doctor plane and even this seems like it is going to desert her.

35 But possibly not. Jack is gunning the engine of his landcruiser as he roars down the runway towards the last flare and Maggie can just make out his silhouette in the headlights of the car as he jumps out and reaches into the drum. With a whoosh, the flare catches and Maggie's satellite phone rings – the flight sister tells her that, yes, they'll be able to come in now. Although she finds him unbearably pompous, Maggie wants to hug Jack as he drives over and jumps out of
40 the cab, stinking of kerosene. Instead she smiles and thanks him and together they watch the plane descend and come to a rapid stop on the short runway. The door opens and the flight sister emerges with a torch that catches the dust hanging in the air. The patient is loaded onto the plane and there are congratulations from the flight sister to Maggie for managing until they arrived. Then the plane turns and takes off again, Jack drives off to break up a fight in the community and
45 only Maggie is left by the runway where she stands, leaning against the troopie, and listening to the last throb of the aeroplane's engines as it disappears into the black night.

Stephanie Davis, Nhulunbuy, Northern Territory, Australia

Winner of the *ABC Short Story Project*, 2007

Shades of Dreaming

Ibrahim arrived to Australia by plane on his 9th birthday. At his new school he settled quietly into the class, one of many students who spoke something other than English at home. At the first lunchtime the other kids asked him "Can you play Cricket?", and Ibrahim learnt to speak a foreign language through the playground rules of sport.

5   While adjusting to school was smooth, he still struggled within himself. Years ago, a drought of happiness had dried up Ibrahim's dreams, and he settled into his new country having only ever slumbered in black inky nothingness.

He asked himself. 'What is a dream? Is it real? Is it a place? What colour is it?'

The sedate pace of the back of the class and of lunchtime balls thwacked for six-and-out

10 eventually restored something to him. A year after he arrived to Australia, on Ibrahim's 10th birthday, he started to dream. He dreamt of riding an aeroplane like a skateboard in the sky, rolling off cloud banks, sliding off skyscrapers. Ibrahim dreamt of spin bowling googlys and yelling "howzaaaaaat!!!!" with one finger raised in appeal.

When Ibrahim woke from a dream it would remain with him. Chunks of fragmented feeling

15 that dissipated as he grasped at them, like smoke from a campfire or bubbles in the bath.

Ibrahim asked his sister "What do you dream of?"

She looked at him over her corn flakes. "I dream of floating in cool water, looking at stars. Sometimes, I dream of Mum."

Ibrahim hated the pain that subject raised, and asked his sister instead "What are dreams?"

20 "I don't know. But now, sometimes I dream in Arabic and sometimes in English. When I wake up I don't remember which language it was. Just the feeling of it."

With the nocturnal tap flowing again, previously buried memories surfaced. Ibrahim's dreams became laced in fear or soaked in longing; lingering nightmares of hard faces and enforced silences. He dreamt of a song that he couldn't quite remember, that was tinged with the smell of

25 rose water and coffee.

Ibrahim asked his father. "Papa, do you dream?"

"Dreams are for nothing. Craziness inside your head." Ibrahim's father grumbled rather than spoke, his voice low to the ground like the yellow cab he drove.

"What is a dream Papa?"

30 "It distracts from the pain of everyday. Your mother would say – 'dreams are for doing' - but she dreamed of changing things back home, not of coming to this place where they look at your university degrees and tell you to go back to driving taxis, or back to your bloody country."

"What colour do you dream in?"

Ibrahim's father looked him in the eye. "My dreams are black with two pinpoints of white.

35 You and your sister."

Two days after his birthday, he spoke to his Grandfather late at night, their voices echoing around the computer headphones like marbles in a jar.

"Grandad, what are dreams?" Ibrahim asked.

Grandad lived far away, but loved Ibrahim and took his questions seriously. "Some

40 people say dreams are nothing important. Others say dreams are messages from God. Some others again say dreams are just your subconscious thoughts, real events jumbled into fantasy."

"Do you dream in colour, or in black and white?"

"My dreams are as bright as the full moon, as silky as the blackest night, all

45 wrapped in Christmas paper." "Do you think Papa dreams?"

"Everyone dreams, my child. But the question is not whether people dream or not. The question is whether someone dreams with their eyes open or with their eyes shut."

Benjamin Rogers, Australia
Highly commended, *Commonwealth Short Story Prize*, 2010

The Perfect Peppersoup

An old man in a faded yellow shirt sat in a windowless room on a raised concrete form, the only source of heat came from somewhere beneath the plastic mattress and the scratchy blanket the blank faced police woman had handed him after taking his thumb prints and swabbing his mouth. He heard voices and a metallic clang as the cell door
5 swung open.

At the front desk a harassed looking sergeant handed the old man back his belongings, his threadbare cap and the Seiko that had stopped working the day his beloved Evelyn died. The policeman dramatically held the blue plastic bag at an arm's length to the old man who took it and made sure its contents were intact: the goat
10 meat, palm oil, leaves and spices. He ignored the bemused expression on the officer's face and signed the document declaring he had been returned the possessions they had taken off him the night before.

No one spoke to him as he shuffled towards the exit.

'Mr Easy-nwa?' He stopped and prayed to the God who now took care of Evelyn
15 to please take him far away from this unhappy place of expressionless faces, clipped accents and people who did not even attempt to pronounce his name right.

'Ezenwa,' He said and looked at a woman with tangerine lips, her name tag said Jessica Harlow, Social Services. 'A bit far from home', she said as she drove fast and with confidence the way Evelyn used to. He wondered if she meant the 50 miles from
20 Toxteth or the 50,000 miles from Enugu. He did not bother replying as this woman had plenty to say about the weather, bad drivers, her daughter's school play…

At last she drew up outside the block of flats where he lived.

'Got here in the end', her cheery tone subsided as she added seriously, 'Really Mr Easy-nwa, if you keep getting lost, we will have to consider moving you into a home'.
25 'No need, I was not lost,' he answered with equal sobriety. He carefully rolled up the sleeves of the oversize bomber jacket he wore and turned on the tap to wash his hands, relieved the pipes were not frozen. In a clean saucepan he placed the chopped pieces of goat meat. The herbs and spices that had taken him three months to track down, the uziza seeds had taken him into the heart of Granby Market in Liverpool, his nchanwu
30 leaves down a shady back alley in Manchester, and yesterday, among other food items, the finest goat meat from a Sierra Leonean Butcher in Birmingham. That had taken some time, so much he missed the last train and when the police found him shivering outside the locked up station, so cold he couldn't answer loudly enough the pink faced burly copper who yelled in his face, 'What's your name sir?' spraying his face with
35 spittle as he did so, leaving them with no choice but to frisk an exhausted, hypothermic old black man and finding him in possession of mysterious condiments including a bag of dried bitter-leaf which could of course be mistaken for anything which resulted in him getting read his rights and charged with… possession???

He lifted the lid of the bubbling broth, the room was suffused with the rich and
40 spicy aroma of his culinary effort. He served two bowls, taking the chipped one and placing the other opposite where Evelyn would have sat. He would tell her about his adventure, it was their anniversary and this was the perfect pepper soup to celebrate.

Ken Onyia, UK (Nigeria)
Highly commended, *Commonwealth Short Story Prize*, 2010

Developing writing skills

Below are some writing exercises based on the short stories you have read.

Education for Life

- An advertisement for Mrs. Melrose's language classes.

- Karen's letter of application to the BBC to become a radio announcer.

- An interview with Karen once she has become a celebrity.

- Karen's diary entry from the time she fails to find a glamorous job.

Waiting for the Plane

- Jack's police report on the disturbances in the community or report of the arrest of the injured woman's husband.

- Maggie's diary entry of the events of the night in the story.

- A magazine feature article on the Flying Doctor service in Australia.

- A brochure for holidays in the Australian desert and outback.

Shades of Dreaming

- A letter from the father to a relative in the homeland retelling the family's escape from political oppression and their arrival in Australia.

- A school report for Ibrahim in which each of his teachers comment on his progress and his English skills.

- A letter from the grandfather to Ibrahim offering him advice on how to settle in his adopted country and retain his identity, culture, and language.

- Ibrahim's blog entry about his dreams and their meaning.

The Perfect Peppersoup

- A newspaper report under the headline "Elderly man arrested for drugs possession released without charge".

- Social worker Jessica Harlow's official report on Mr Ezenwa and her recommendations.

- Mr. Ezenwa's instructions to fellow countrymen for sourcing and preparing Nigerian peppersoup in the United Kingdom.

- A police report on Mr. Ezenwa's arrest and subsequent release.

Beyond the text...

What is the relationship between each short story and the following English B topics?

➤ **Core topic: Social relationships**

'Education for Life' by Anna Lewis

Possible aspects to discuss:

- educational system
- language and cultural identity, or self-identity
- linguistic dominance
- social behaviours and stances
- taboos versus what is socially acceptable

➤ **Option topic: Health**

'Waiting for the Plane' by Stephanie Davis

Possible aspects to discuss:

- drug abuse
- health services
- hygiene
- illnesses, symptoms of good/ill health
- mental health

➤ **Core topic: Global issues**

'Shades of Dreaming' by Benjamin Rogers

Possible aspects to discuss:

- globalization
- international economy
- migration (rural–urban, or international)
- racism, prejudice, discrimination

➤ **Option topic: Cultural diversity**

'The Perfect Peppersoup' by Ken Onyia

Possible aspects to discuss:

- beliefs, values, and norms
- culinary heritage
- how culture is learned
- intercultural assimilation
- migration
- verbal and non-verbal communication

TOK

Compare how each story gives an insight into the character of the protagonist and their method of dealing with a specific issue. How successful are they at tackling the problems they are faced with? Can TOK help us deepen our understanding of these characters? Use the chart below to make judgments and comparisons between the characters and their situations.

The title of the story and the name of the protagonist	What information is given on the background of the protagonist, and what can be deduced about his or her character?	What problems do the characters encounter?	To what extent do the characters use <ul><li>language</li><li>logic</li><li>emotions</li><li>sense perception</li></ul> to solve the issues they are dealing with?
Education for Life Karen Driscoll			
Waiting for the Plane Maggie			
Shades of Dreaming Ibrahim			
The Perfect Peppersoup Mr. Ezenwa			

As a result of this analysis, is it possible to say which characters make the wisest decisions and which ones make the worst decisions?

Dissecting a short story

The following short story on pages 261 to 278 by Alice Munro was first published in 1994 in her collection of short stories titled *Open Secrets*. The story is annotated with one reader's comments and questions which could help you explore and appreciate the story.

The Jack Randa Hotel

On the runway, in Honolulu, the plane loses speed, loses heart, falters and veers onto the grass, and bumps to a stop. A few yards it seems from the ocean. Inside, everybody laughs. First a hush, then the laugh. Gail laughed herself. Then there was a flurry of introductions all
5 around. Beside Gail are Larry and Phyllis, from Spokane.

Larry and Phyllis are going to a tournament of Left-handed Golfers, in Fiji, as are many other couples on this plane. It is Larry who is the left-handed golfer – Phyllis is the wife going along to watch and cheer and have fun.

10 They sit on the plane – Gail and the Left-handed Golfers – and lunch is served in picnic boxes. No drinks. Dreadful heat. Jokey and confusing announcements are made from the cock-pit. *Sorry about the problem. Nothing serious but it looks like it will keep us stewing here a while*
15 *longer.* Phyllis has a terrible headache, which Larry tries to cure by applying finger-pressure to points on her wrist and palm.

"It's not working," Phyllis says. "I could have been in New Orleans by now with Suzy."

Larry says, "Poor lamb."

20 Gail catches the fierce glitter of diamond rings as Phyllis pulls her hand away. Wives have diamond rings and head-aches, Gail thinks. They still do. The truly successful ones do. They have chubby husbands, left-handed golfers, bent on a lifelong course of appeasement.

Eventually the passengers who are not going to Fiji, but on to
25 Sydney, are taken off the plane. They are led into the terminal and there deserted by their airline guide they wander about, retrieving their baggage and going through customs, trying to locate the airline that is supposed to honor their tickets. At one point, they are accosted by a welcoming committee from one of the Island's hotels,
30 who will not stop singing Hawaiian songs and flinging garlands around their necks. But they find themselves on another plane at last. They eat and drink and sleep and the lines to the toilets lengthen and the aisles fill up with debris and the flight attendants hide in their cubbyholes chatting about children and boyfriends.
35 Then comes the unsettling bright morning and the yellow-sanded coast of Australia far below, and the wrong time of day, and even the best-dressed, best-looking passengers are haggard and unwilling, torpid, as from a long trip in steerage. And before they can leave the plane there is one more assault. Hairy men in shorts swarm aboard
40 and spray everything with insecticide.

"So maybe this is the way it will be getting into Heaven," Gail imagines herself saying to Will. "People will fling flowers on you that you don't want, and everybody will have headaches and be constipated and then you will have to be sprayed for Earth germs."

45 Her old habit, trying to think up clever and lighthearted things to say to Will.

* * *

The runway setting points to travelling, which itself could suggest change. The plane's 'actions' are interesting: like something living and feeling, it "loses heart and falters". The unsuccessful plane stops only a few yards from the ocean; not something to laugh at, yet everybody laughs. In sudden anxious situations, strangers often feel united, and "a flurry of introductions are made". Gail is the first name mentioned in the story. Is this her story?

The beginning of the story is a mix of suggested anxiety and light-hearted travelling. Phyllis is planning on cheering her left-handed Larry, and "have fun". No explanation is given as to why Gail is travelling.

The plane is full of couples, united by their cheery-sounding hobby, but Gail seems the odd one out.

The juxtaposition of unease and cheeriness continues.

The first dialogue is between Phyllis and Larry.

Does Phyllis regret coming along?
Is Larry compassionate towards his wife?

Why does Phyllis pull her hand away? Gail's thoughts on wives are interesting and hint that maybe she doesn't see herself as a "truly successful" wife.

Gail and other passengers are deserted to wander about. The wording of how they "find themselves" on another plane emphasizes their passive role.

The long, unpunctuated sentence describes the passengers' long and uncomfortable flight.

The passengers suffer a variety of assaults.

An interesting bout of humour?

Is Gail a sarcastic character? We hear Gail's thoughts and can now confirm the point of view is hers. The name Will is introduced for the first time. Who is he? A friend, family member, a loved one? Gail's thoughts reveal something about her true character and that Will was someone she tried to impress.

The asterisks indicate a new phase in the story. Change of scene, perhaps?

After Will went away, it seemed to Gail that her shop was filling up
with women. Not necessarily buying clothes. She didn't mind this. It
50 was like the long-ago days, before Will. Women were sitting around
in ancient armchairs beside Gail's ironing board and cutting table,
behind the faded batik curtains, drinking coffee. Gail started grinding
the coffee beans herself, as she used to do. The dressmaker's dummy
was soon draped with beads and had a scattering of scandalous
55 graffiti. Stories were told about men, usually about men who had
left. Lies and injustices and confrontations. Betrayals so horrific – yet
so trite – that you could only rock with laughter when you heard
them. Men made fatuous speeches (*I am sorry, but I no longer feel
committed to this marriage*). They offered to sell back to the wives cars
60 and furniture that the wives themselves had paid for. They capered
about in self-satisfaction because they had managed to impregnate
some dewy dollop of womanhood younger than their own children.
They were fiendish and childish. What could you do but give up on
them? In all honor, in pride, and for your own protection?

65 Gail's enjoyment of all this palled rather quickly. Too much
coffee could make your skin look livery. An underground quarrel
developed among the women when it turned out that one of them
had placed an ad in the Personal Column. Gail shifted from coffee
with friends to drinks with Cleata, Will's mother. As she did this,
70 oddly enough her spirits grew more sober. Some giddiness still
showed in the notes she pinned to her door so that she could get
away early on summer afternoons. (Her clerk, Donalda, was on her
holidays, and it was too much trouble to hire anybody else.)

Gone to the Opera.

75 *Gone to the Funny Farm.*

Gone to stock up on the Sackcloth and Ashes.

Actually these were not her own inventions, but things Will used to
write out and tape on her door in the early days when they wanted
to go upstairs. She heard that such flippancy was not appreciated by
80 people who had driven some distance to buy a dress for a wedding,
or girls on an expedition to buy clothes for college. She did not care.

On Cleata's veranda Gail was soothed, she became vaguely hopeful.
Like most serious drinkers, Cleata stuck to one drink – hers was
Scotch – and seemed amused by variations. But she would make Gail
85 a gin and tonic, a white rum and soda. She introduced her to tequila.
"This is Heaven," Gail sometimes said, meaning not just the drink but
the screened veranda and hedged back yard, the old house behind
them with its shuttered windows, varnished floors, inconveniently
high kitchen cupboards, and out-of-date flowered curtains. (Cleata
90 despised decorating.) This was the house where Will, and Cleata
too, had been born, and when Will first brought Gail into it, she had
thought, 'This is how really civilized people live'. The carelessness
and propriety combined the respect for old books and old dishes. The
absurd things that Will and Cleata thought it natural to talk about.
95 And the things that she and Cleata didn't talk about – Will's present
defection, the illness that has made Cleata's arms and legs look like
varnished twigs within their deep tan, and has hollowed the cheeks

---

The tense changes from present to past tense.

The first we learn about Gail and Will is that he "went away". After Will's departure Gail's shop "was filling up with women" who conquer all the space with their presence and spark a change in Gail.

The women talk about men who are both accused of betrayals as well as ridiculed.

Feminist undertones can be read in the women's talk.

Gail loses interest in the women's company.

The women quarrel over something ridiculous. Gail makes a transition from a group of women to "Cleata, Will's mother", and her "spirits grew more sober." Was Will Gail's husband? Where is he now?

The notes she pins to the door reveal her sarcastic sense of humour and how she is feeling after Will's departure.

The witty notes are not Gail's inventions but she is copying them from her and Will's past "when they wanted to go upstairs". Were they lovers or what did they do upstairs?

Gail announces her indifference towards what other people think of her "flippancy".

Gail is soothed by drinking in Cleata's company on her veranda. Heaven is mentioned for the second time in the story.

Cleata's house is described as old, safe, and protected; does the description mirror either of the women or their feelings?

Here the narrative includes both the past (Will and Cleata talking) and the present (Gail and Cleata talking, or indeed not talking) in one sentence. We learn about "Will's present defection"; has he left Gail? We also learn about Cleata's illness.

framed by her looped-back white hair. She and Will have the same slightly monkeyish face with dreamy, mocking dark eyes.

100 Instead, Cleata talked about the book she was reading. *The Anglo-Saxon Chronicle*. She said that the reason the Dark Ages were dark was not that we couldn't learn anything about them but that we could not remember anything we did learn, and that was because of the names.

Avoiding perhaps a difficult topic concerning the present, Cleata talks about history.

105 "Caedwalla," she said. "Egfrith. These are just not names on the tip of your tongue anymore."

Would looking up the names Caedwalla, Egfrith and Aelfflaed help understand and interpret the story?

Gail was trying to remember which ages, or centuries, were dark. But her ignorance didn't embarrass her. Cleata was making fun of all that, anyway.

110 "Aelfflaed," said Cleata, and spelled it out. "What kind of a heroine is Aelfflaed?"

Are women heroines in this story?

When Cleata wrote to Will, she probably wrote about Aelfflaed and Egfrith. Not about Gail. Not *Gail was here looking very pretty in some kind of silky gray summer-pajamas outfit. She was in good form, made*
115 *various witty remarks*... No more than she would say to Gail. "I have my doubts about the lovebirds. Reading between the lines, I can't help wondering if disillusionment isn't setting in…"

Does Gail hope that Cleata would write about her and describe her pretty and witty?

Are the more important, true words left unsaid, or is Gail creating a fantasy in which Will's defection becomes unsuccessful and ridiculous?

When she met Will and Cleata, Gail thought they were like characters in a book. A son living with his mother, apparently
120 contentedly, into middle age. Gail saw a life that was ceremonious and absurd and enviable, with at least the appearance of celibate grace and safety. She still sees some of that, though the truth is Will has not always lived at home, and he is neither celibate not discreetly homosexual. He had been gone for years, into his own
125 life – working for the National Film Board and the Canadian Broadcasting Corporation – and had given that up only recently, to come back to Walley and be a teacher. What made him give it up? This and that, he said. Machiavellis here and there. Empire-building. Exhaustion.

We learn that Will's career had taken a turn, perhaps after disappointments and "exhaustion".

130 Gail came to Walley one summer in the seventies. The boyfriend she was with then was a boatbuilder, and she sold clothes that she made – capes with appliqués, shirts with billowing sleeves, long bright skirts. She got space in the back of the craft shop, when winter came on. She learned about importing ponchos and thick socks from
135 Bolivia and Guatemala. She found local women to knit sweaters. One day Will stopped her on the street and asked her to help him with the costumes for the play he was putting on – *The Skin of Our Teeth*. Her boyfriend moved to Vancouver.

We learn about Gail's youth in the seventies. She comes across artistic, and the narrative refers to many soft, natural elements.

The effect of the new relationship between Gail and Will is revealed in one short sentence.

She told Will some things about herself early on, in case he should
140 think that her capable build and pink skin and wide gentle forehead she was exactly the kind of a woman to start a family on. She told him that she had had a baby, and that when she and her boyfriend were moving some furniture in a borrowed van, from Thunder Bay to Toronto, carbon-monoxide fumes had leaked in, just enough to
145 make them feel sick but enough to kill the baby, who was seven weeks old. After that Gail was sick – she had a pelvic inflammation.

We learn about Gail's baby.

She decided she did not want to have another child and it would have been difficult anyway, so she had a hysterectomy.

Will admired her. He said so. He did not feel obliged to say, What a
150 tragedy! He did not even obliquely suggest that the death was the result of choices Gail had made. He was entranced with her then. He thought her brave and generous and resourceful and gifted. The costumes she designed and made for him were perfect, miraculous. Gail thought that his view of her, of her life, showed a touching
155 innocence. It seemed to her that far from being a free and generous spirit, she had often been anxious and desperate and had spent a lot of time doing laundry and worrying about money and feeling she owed so much to any man who took up with her. She did not think she was in love with Will then, but she liked his looks – his
160 energetic body, so upright it seemed taller than it was, his flung-back head, shiny high forehead, springy ruff of graying hair. She liked to watch him at rehearsals, or just talking to his students. How skilled and intrepid he seemed as a director, how potent a personality as he walked the high-school halls or the streets of Walley. And then the
165 slightly quaint, admiring feelings he had for her, his courtesy as a lover, the foreign pleasantness of his house and his life with Cleata – all this made Gail feel like somebody getting a unique welcome in a place where perhaps she did not truly have a right to be. That did not matter then – she had the upper hand.

170 So why did she stop having it? When he got used to sleeping with her when they moved in together when they did so much work on the cottage by the river and it turned out that she was better at that kind of work than he was?

Was she a person who believed that somebody had to have the
175 upper hand?

There came a time when just the tone of his voice, saying "Your shoelace is undone" as she went ahead of him on a walk – just that – could fill her with despair, warning her that they had crossed over into a bleak country where his disappointment in her was boundless,
180 his contempt impossible to challenge. She would stumble eventually, break out in a rage – they would have days and nights of fierce hopelessness. Then the breakthrough, the sweet reunion, the jokes, and bewildered relief. So it went on in their life – she couldn't really understand it or tell if it was like anybody else's. But the peaceful
185 periods seemed to be getting longer, the dangers retreating, and she had no inkling that he was waiting to meet somebody like this new person, Sandy, who would seem to him as alien and delightful as Gail herself had once been.

Will probably had no inkling of that, either.

190 He had never had much to say about Sandy – Sandra – who had come to Walley last year on an exchange program to see how drama was being taught in Canadian schools. He had said she was a young Turk. Then he had said she mightn't even have heard that expression. Very soon, there had developed some sort of electricity,
195 or danger, around her name. Gail got some information from other sources. She heard that Sandy had challenged Will in front of his

---

We learn about Gail's decision not to have more babies.

We learn about the characteristics Gail admired in Will. We learn that Will admired Gail and her strength.

Gail doesn't see herself the way Will does.

Gail feels she should be grateful that a man accepted her. Gail's feelings towards Will early in the relationship are revealed.

Gail felt like an outsider, undeserving of her place. She did not mind – then, but has the situation changed? What does Gail mean by her having "the upper hand"?

Does the long, unpunctuated sentence reveal possible reasons for Will's leaving? Did it matter that Gail was better at working on the cottage than he was?

Gail does not answer her question. The narrative uses past tense in Gail's self-reflection. Maybe something has since changed?

It seems that somebody had the upper hand, was better at something or went ahead in Gail and Will's relationship.

Gail describes their volatile relationship, but she is not able to assess it herself.

In hindsight, Will was "waiting to meet" someone "alien and delightful". Did Will become tired of safe and familiar?

Gail does not blame Will but depicts him as having lost control over his life.

We learn more about Sandy. Oxford Dictionary defines *Young Turk* as "a young person eager for radical change to the established order". Do Gail and Sandy share something?

Was Will attracted by Sandy's rebelliousness?

class. Sandy had said that the plays he wanted to do were "not relevant". Or maybe it was "not revolutionary".

"But he likes her," one of his students said. "Oh, yeah, he *really likes* 200 her."

Gail got her information about Will and Sandy's developing relationship from someone else.

Sandy didn't stay around long. She went on to observe the teaching of drama in the other schools. But she wrote to Will, and presumably he wrote back. For it turned out that they had fallen in love. Will and Sandy had fallen seriously in love, and at the end of the school 205 year Will followed her to Australia.

Will and Sandy's story is told in a few sentences.

Seriously in love. When Will told her that, Gail was smoking dope. She had taken it up again, because being around Will was making her so nervous.

We learn that Gail had looked for ways to relieve the anxiety caused by Will.

"You mean it's not me?" Gail said. "You mean I'm not the trouble?"

We learn of Gail's relief that Will's "deception" was not her fault. Has she lost her confidence? She sounds very different from the woman she was at the beginning.

210 She was giddy with relief. She got into a bold and boisterous mood and bewildered Will into going to bed with her.

In the morning they tried to avoid being in the same room together. They agreed not to correspond. Perhaps later, Will said. Gail said, "Suit yourself."

215 But one day at Cleata's house Gail saw his writing on an envelope that had surely been left where she could see it. Cleata had left it – Cleata who never spoke one word about the fugitives. Gail wrote down the return address: 16 Eyre Rd., Toowong, Brisbane, Queensland, Australia.

Does Cleata initiate Gail getting in touch with Will?

220 It was when she saw Will's writing that she understood how useless everything had become to her. This bare-fronted pre-Victorian house in Walley, and the veranda, and the drinks, and the catalpa tree that she was always looking at, in Cleata's back yard. All the trees and streets in Walley, all the liberating views of the lake and the comfort 225 of the shop. Useless cutouts, fakes and props. The real scene was hidden from her, in Australia.

Gail has a turning point when she realises the familiar, ordinary is no longer enough. Does she see her life as "cutouts, fakes and props"?

That was why she found herself sitting on the plane beside the woman with the diamond rings. Her own hands have no rings on them, no polish on the nails – the skin is dry from all the work she 230 does with cloth. She used to call the clothes she made "handcrafted," until Will made her embarrassed about that description. She still doesn't quite see what was wrong.

We finally learn the reason why Gail is travelling to Australia.

We return to the present-day Gail, who seems not quite in charge of her actions. Her hands and fingers are bare and natural.

Gail is still affected by Will's views about her.

She sold the shop – she sold it to Donalda, who had wanted to buy it for a long time. She took the money, and she got herself onto a flight 235 to Australia and did not tell anyone where she was going. She lied, talking about a long holiday that would start off in England. Then somewhere in Greece for the winter, then who knows?

Again, the narrative jumps back to Gail's memories and reflection.

Why did Gail lie about her trip?

The night before she left, she did a transformation on herself. She cut off her heavy reddish-gray hair and put a dark-brown rinse on what 240 was left of it. The color that resulted was strange – a deep maroon, obviously artificial but rather too sombre for any attempts at glamour. She picked out from her shop – even though the contents no longer belonged to her – a dress of a kind she would never usually wear, a jacket-dress of dark-blue linen-look polyester with

By stripping her hair of its reddish-gray tones, does Gail deliberately try to make herself unremarkable, someone to blend in?

We learn about Gail's appearance.

245 lightning stripes of red and yellow. She is tall, and broad in the hips, and she usually wears things that are loose and graceful. This outfit gives her chunky shoulders, and cuts her legs at an unflattering spot above the knees. What sort of woman did she think she was making herself into? The sort that a woman like Phyllis would play

250 bridge with? If so, she has got it wrong. She has come out looking like somebody who has spent most of her life in uniform, at some worthy, poorly paid job (perhaps in a hospital cafeteria?) and now has spent too much money for a dashing dress that will turn out to be inappropriate and uncomfortable, on the holiday of her life.

255 That doesn't matter. It is a disguise.

In the airport washroom, on new continent, she sees that the dark hair coloring, insufficiently rinsed out the night before, has mixed with her sweat and it trickling down her neck.

Gail has landed in Brisbane, still not used to what time of day it is
260 and persecuted by so hot a sun. She is still wearing her horrid dress, but she has washed her hair so that the color no longer runs.

She has taken a taxi. Tired as she is, she cannot settle, cannot rest until she has seen where they live. She has already bought a map and found Eyre Road. A short, curving street. She asks to be let out
265 at the corner, where there is a little grocery store. This is the place where they buy their milk, most likely, or other things that they may have run out of. Detergent, aspirin, tampons.

The fact that Gail never met Sandy was of course an ominous thing. It must have meant that Will knew something very quickly. Later
270 attempts to ferret out a description did not yield much. Tall rather than short. Thin rather than fat. Fair rather than dark. Gail had a mental picture of one of those long-legged short-haired, energetic and boyishly attractive girls. Women. But she wouldn't know Sandy if she ran into her.

275 Would anybody know Gail? With her dark glasses and her unlikely hair, she feels so altered as to be invisible. It's also the fact of being in a strange country that has transformed her. She is not tuned into it yet. Once she gets tuned in, she may not be able to do the bold things she can do now. She has to walk this street, look at the house,
280 right away, or she may not be able to do it at all.

The road that the taxi climbed was steep, up from the brown river. Eyre Road runs along a ridge. There is no sidewalk, just a dusty path. No one walking, no cars passing, no shade. Fences of boards or a kind of basket-weaving – wattles? – or in some cases high hedges
285 covered with flowers. No, the flowers are really leaves of a purplish-pink or crimson color. Trees unfamiliar to Gail are showing over the fences. They have tough-looking dusty foliage, scaly or stringy bark, a shabby ornamental air. An indifference or vague ill about them, which she associated with the tropics. Walking on the path ahead of
290 her are a pair of guinea hens, stately and preposterous.

The house where Will and Sandy live is hidden by a board fence, painted a pale green. Gail's heart shrinks – her heart is in a cruel clutch, to see that fence, that green.

Why does Gail choose an unflattering disguise? Why does she want to make herself ordinary?

The present-day Gail reflects on her choices and determines she had made mistakes.

Why does Gail need a disguise going to Australia? We wonder about her plans.

Gail sees the old and the new – or the real and the fake – mixing together.

We learn that Gail is going to see where Will and Sandy live.

Gail lists domestic, everyday items she imagines Will and Sandy buy: detergent for removing dirt, aspirin to kill pain, tampons for a female life.

We learn that Gail knows little about Sandy's appearance.

Does Gail want to be invisible?

Gail has not yet become accustomed to her new surroundings, but she is capable of bolder things than usual.

The description of Eyre Road does not include people or movement, and the hedges and fences protecting houses are unfamiliar and tough.

Gail finds Will and Sandy's house. Why does she react to the colour of the fence?

The road is a dead end so she has to turn around. She walks past
295 the house again. In the fence there are gates to let a car in and out.
There is also a mail slot. She noticed one of these before in a fence in
front of another house, and the reason she noticed it was that there
was a magazine sticking out. So the mailbox is not very deep, and
a hand slipping in, might be able to find an envelope resting on its
300 end. If the mail has not been taken out yet by a person in the house.
And Gail does slip a hand in. She can't stop herself. She finds a letter
there, just as she had thought it might be. She puts it into her purse.

She calls a taxi from the shop at the corner of the street. "What part
of the States are you from?" the man in the shop asks her.

305 "Texas," she says. She has an idea that they would like you to be
from Texas, and indeed the man lifts his eyebrows, whistles.

"I thought so," he says.

It is Will's own writing on the envelope. Not a letter to Will,
then, but a letter from him. A letter he had sent to Ms. Catherine
310 Thornaby, 491 Hawtre Street. Also in Brisbane. Another hand has
scrawled across it "Return to Sender, Died Sept. 13." For a moment,
in her disordered state of mind, Gail thinks that this means that Will
has died.

She has got to calm down, collect herself, stay out of the sun for a
315 bit.

Nevertheless, as soon as she has read the letter in her hotel room,
and has tidied herself up, she takes another taxi, this time to Hawtre
Street, and finds, as she expected, a sign in the window: "Flat to Let."

But what is in the letter that Will has written Ms. Catherine
320 Thornaby, on Hawtre Street?

Dear Ms. Thornaby,

*You don't know me, but I hope that once I have explained myself, we may
meet and talk. I believe that I may be a Canadian cousin of yours, my
grandfather having come to Canada from Northhumberland sometime in*
325 *the 1870s about the same time as a brother of his went to Australia. My
grandfather's name was William, like my own, his brother's name was
Thomas. Of course I have no proof that you are descended from this Thomas.
I simply looked in the Brisbane phone book and was delighted to find there
a Thornaby spelled in the same way. I used to think this family-tracing*
330 *business was the silliest, most boring thing imaginable but now that I find
myself doing it, I discover there is a strange excitement about it. Perhaps it
is my age – I am 56 – that urges me to find connections. And I have more
time on my hands than I am used to. My wife is working with a theatre here
which keeps her busy till all hours. She is a very bright and energetic young*
335 *woman. (She scolds me if I refer to any female over 18 as a girl and she is all
of 28!) I taught drama in a Canadian high school but I have not yet found
any work in Australia.*

Wife. He is trying to be respectable in the eyes of the possible cousin.

Dear Mr. Thornaby,

340 *The name we share may be a more common one than you suppose, though
I am at present its only representative in the Brisbane phone book. You may*

In the context of this story, this sentence could be interpreted as a metaphor.

We learn that Gail takes a letter from Will and Sandy's mailbox. Did she plan to do this?

Ironically, the Canadian Gail is taken for a Texan lady.

Gail examines the letter and finds out it has been returned to Will.

We learn that the recipient of Will's letter has died. Gail is confused.

Having read Will's letter, Gail goes to see where the recipient lived. She finds a sign indicating the flat is empty. Will she take it?

This sentence prepares us to move on from following Gail to reading the letter she found.

Will's thoughts have changed, and he suggests two reasons: his age and unemployment, having less to do than before. We suspect he is feeling lonely too, as his "very bright and energetic" young wife – Sandy – is busy with her theatre work.

We return to Gail's point of view. She assesses Will's voice.

not know that the name comes from Thorn Abbey, the ruins of which are still to be seen in Northumberland. The spelling varies – Thornaby, Thornby, Thornabbey, Thornabby. In the Middle Ages the name of the Lord of the
345 Manor would be taken as a surname by all the people working on the estate, including labourers, blacksmiths, carpenters, etc. As a result there are many people scattered around the world bearing a name that *in the strict sense* they have no right to. Only those who can trace their descent from the family in the twelfth century are the *true*, *armigerous* Thornabys. That is, they *have*
350 *the right* to display the family coat of arms. I am one of these Thornabys and since you don't mention anything about the coat of arms and do not trace tour ancestry back beyond this William I assume that you are not. My grandfather's name was Jonathan.

Gail writes this on an old portable typewriter that she has bought
355 from the secondhand shop down the street. By this time she is living at 491 Hawtre Street, in an apartment building called the Miramar. It is a two-storey building covered with dingy cream stucco, with twisted pillars on either side of a grilled entryway. It has a perfunctory Moorish or Spanish or Californian air, like that of an old
360 movie theatre. The manager told her that the flat was very modern.

"An elderly lady had it, but she had to go to the hospital. Then somebody came when she died and got her effects out, but it still has the basic furniture that goes with the flat. What part of the States are you from?"

365 Oklahoma, Gail said. Mrs. Massie, from Oklahoma.

The manager looks to be about seventy years old. He wears glasses that magnify his eyes, and he walks quickly, but rather unsteadily, tilting forward. He speaks of difficulties – the increase of the foreign element in the population, which makes it hard to find good
370 repairmen, the carelessness of certain tenants, the malicious acts of passersby who continually litter the grass. Gail asks if he had put in the notice yet to the Post Office. He says he has been intending to, but the lady did not receive hardly any mail. Except one letter came. It was a strange thing that it came right the day after she died. He
375 sent it back.

"I'll do it," Gail said. "I'll tell the Post Office."

"I'll have to sign it, though. Get me one of those forms they have and I'll sign it and you can give it in. I'd be obliged."

The walls of the apartment are painted white – this must be what
380 is modern about it. It has bamboo blinds, a tiny kitchen, a green sofa bed, a table, a dresser, and two chairs. On the wall one picture, which might have been a painting or a tinted photograph. A yellowish-green desert landscape, with rocks and bunches of sage and dim distant mountains. Gail is sure that she has seen this before.

385 She paid the rent in cash. She had to be busy for a while, buying sheets and towels and groceries, a few pots and dishes, the typewriter. She had to open a bank account, become a person living in the country, not a traveller. There are shops hardly a block away. A grocery store, a secondhand store, a drugstore, a tea shop.
390 They are all humble establishments with strips of colored paper

Whose letter are we reading? The real Catherine Thornaby was previously reported as deceased.

The tone of the letter is strict, polite but hostile. *Armigerous* means "a person entitled to heraldic arms".

The abrupt end does not invite further communication.

We learn that Gail, who wrote the letter, is now living in Catherine Thornaby's flat.

We learn about the real Catherine Thornaby.

Again, Gail is mistaken for someone from USA, but this time she gives a different answer. Why not Texas?

Do we hear the manager's voice here?

In order to continue impersonating Catherine Thornaby, Gail offers to deal with the Post Office.

The picture on the wall does not depict people or movement.

Gail settles in, and must "become a person living in the country".

Gail's surroundings are described as humble, limited, scarce, ordinary, yet they may be "of special value or significance."

hanging in the doorways wooden awnings over the sidewalk in front. Their offerings are limited. The tea shop has only two tables, the secondhand store contains scarcely more than the tumbled-out accumulation of one ordinary house. The cereal boxes in the grocery
395 store, the bottles of cough syrup and packets of pills in the drugstore are set out singly on the shelves, as if they were of special value or significance.

But she has found what she needs. In the secondhand store she found some loose flowered cotton dresses, a straw bag for her
400 groceries. Now she looks like the other women she sees on the street. Housewives, middle-aged, with bare but pale arms and legs, shopping in the early morning or late afternoon. She bought a floppy straw hat too, to shade her face as the women do. Dim, soft, freckly, blinking faces.

405 Night comes suddenly around six o'clock and she must find occupation for the evenings. There is no television in the apartment. But a little beyond the shops there is a lending library, run by an old woman out of the front room of her house. This woman wears a hairnet and gray lisle stockings in spite of the heat.
410 (Where, nowadays, can you find gray lisle stockings?) She has an undernourished body and colorless, tight, unsmiling lips. She is the person Gails calls to mind when she writes the letter from Catherine Thornaby. She thinks of this library woman by that name whenever she sees her, which is almost every day, because you are only
415 allowed one book at a time and Gail usually reads a book a night. She thinks, There is Catherine Thornaby, dead and moved into a new existence a few blocks away.

All the business about armigerous and non-armigerous Thornabys came out of a book. Not one of the books that Gail is reading now
420 but one she read in her youth. The hero was the non-armigerous but deserving heir to a great property. She cannot remember the title. She lived with people then who were always reading *Steppenwolf*, or *Dune*, or something by Khrisnamurti, and she read historical romances apologetically. She did not think Will would have read
425 such a book or picked up this sort of information. And she is sure that he will have to reply, to tell Catherine off.

She waits, and reads the books from the lending library, which seem to come from an even earlier time than those romances she read twenty years ago. Some of them she took out of the public library in
430 Winnipeg before she left home, and they seemed old-fashioned even then. *The Girl of the Limberlost. The Blue Castle. Maria Chapdelaine.* Such books remind her naturally, of her life before Will. There was such a life and she could still salvage something from it, if she wanted to. She has a sister living in Winnipeg. She has an aunt there, in a
435 nursing home, who still reads books in Russian. Gail's grandparents came from Russia, her real name is not Gail, but Galya. She cut herself off from her family – or they cut her off – when she left home at eighteen to wander about the country, as you did in those days. First with friends, then with a boyfriend, then with another
440 boyfriend. She strung beads and tie-dyed scarves and sold them on the street.

How did Gail stand out before she makes herself look like the other women? Why does she want to blend in?

Gail meets a woman who becomes her image of Catherine Thornaby. Gail, pays attention to the woman's "gray lisle stockings".

We learn that Gail is a keen reader.

We learn that Gail's taste in books has changed. With historical romances read apologetically, Gail remembers how she stood out from the other people. Did – or does – she feel inferior?

Did Gail plant the word *armigerous* in her letter as a bait to evoke an angry reaction from the annoyed Will?

We learn about the books Gail reads to spend her evenings. They remind her of her life before meeting Will.

We learn that Gail's taste in books has changed.

Does Gail want to "salvage" something from how she lived before Will?

Gail's family is mentioned for the first time. She was "cut off" from her family due to her behaviour. Yet, did she stand out from her peers, after all? The remark "as you did in those days" appears to claim otherwise.

Dear Ms. Thornaby,

I must thank you for enlightening me as to the important distinction between the armigerous and the non-armigerous Thornabys. I gather that you have
445 *a strong suspicion that I may turn out to be one of the latter. I beg your pardon – I had no intention of* treading on such sacred ground or of wearing the Thornaby coat of arms on my T-shirt. *We do not take much account of such things in my country and I did not think you did so in Australia, but I see that I am mistaken.* Perhaps you are too far on in years to have noticed
450 the change in values. *It is quite different with me, since I have been in the teaching profession and am constantly brought up, as well, against the energetic arguments of a young wife.*

My innocent intention was simply to get in touch with somebody in this country outside the theatrical-academic circle that my wife and I seem to be
455 absorbed in. *I have a mother in Canada, whom I miss. In fact your letter reminded me of her a little. She would be capable of writing such a letter for a joke but I doubt whether you are joking.* It sounds like a case of Exalted Ancestry to me.

When he is offended and disturbed in a certain way – a way that is
460 hard to predict and hard for most people to recognize – Will becomes heavily sarcastic. Irony deserts him. He flails about, and the effect is to make people embarrassed not for themselves, as he intends, but for him. This happens seldom, and usually when it happens it means that he feels deeply unappreciated. It means that he has even
465 stopped appreciating himself.

So that is what happened. Gail thinks so. Sandy and her young friends with their stormy confidence, their crude righteousness might be making him miserable. His wit not taken notice of, his enthusiasm out-of-date. No way of making himself felt amongst them. His pride
470 in being attached to Sandy gradually going sour.

She thinks so. He is shaky and unhappy and casting about to know somebody else. He has thought of family ties, here in this country of non-stop blooming and impudent bird life and searing days and suddenly clamped-down nights.

475 *Dear Mr. Thornaby,*

Did you really expect me, just because I have the same surname as you, to fling open my door and put out the "welcome mat" – as I think you say in America and that inevitably includes Canada? You may be looking for another mother here, but that hardly obliges me to be one. By the way you are quite wrong
480 *about my age – I am younger than you by several years, so do not picture me as an* elderly spinster in a hairnet with gray lisle stockings. *I know the world probably as well as you do. I travel a good deal,* being a fashion buyer for a large store. *So my ideas are not so out-of-date as you suppose.*

You do not say whether your busy energetic young wife was to be a part of
485 *this familial friendship. I am surprised you feel the need for other contacts. It seems I am always reading or hearing on the media about these "May– December" relationships and how invigorating they are and how happily the men are settling down to domesticity and parenthood. (No mention of the* "trial runs" *with women of their own age or mention of how those women*
490 *are settling down to their* lives of loneliness!*) So perhaps you need to become a papa to give you a "sense of family"!*

Another jump to a letter, this one from Will.

His tone is very different from the first letter.

Gail predicted that Will would have to tell Catherine off.

Will reveals something about his relationship with Sandy.

The sarcasm gives in a little when Will writes about her mother. Cleata seems to appear throughout the story and in both Will and Gail's thoughts.

Gail is able to recognize the effect Will's hurt feelings have on his behaviour.

Gail assumes something has forced a change in Will. She makes assumptions on Will and Sandy's relationship.

Unable to impress them, Will is fading behind her energetic wife and her young friends.

Gail thinks Will is writing to Catherine Thornaby to relieve his loneliness and feelings of alienation.

By now, we are used to the shifts between the narration and the letters.

In her letter, Gail presents herself as younger, wittier, more modern, and worldlier than Will.

To us, the remark about gray lisle stocking is ironic.

Would the real Gail like to be a fashion buyer?

Gail cunningly asks about Sandy.

When writing about relationships between young women and older men, her tone is ironic. Is she thinking of herself?

Gail is surprised at how fluently she writes. She has always found it hard to write letters, and the results have been dull and sketchy, with many dashes and incomplete sentences and pleas of insufficient
495 time. Where has she got this fine nasty style – out of some book, like the armigerous nonsense? She goes out in the dark to post her letter feeling bold and satisfied. But she wakes up early the next morning thinking that she has certainly gone too far. He will never answer that, she will never hear from him again.

500 She gets up and leaves the building, goes for a morning walk. The shops are still shut up, the broken venetian blinds are closed, as well as they can be, in the windows of the front-room library. She walks as far as the river, where there is a strip of park beside a hotel. Later in the day, she could not walk or sit there because the verandas of
505 the hotel were always crowded with uproarious beer-drinkers, and the park was within their verbal or even bottle-throwing range. Now the verandas are empty, the doors are closed and she walks in under the trees. The brown water of the river spreads sluggishly among the mangrove stumps. Birds are flying over the water, lightning on the
510 hotel roof. They are not sea gulls, and their bright white wings and breasts are touched with pink.

In the park two men are sitting – one on a bench, one in a wheelchair beside the bench. She recognizes them – they live in her building, and go for walks every day. Once, she held the grille open
515 for them to pass through. She has seen them at the shops, and sitting at the table in the tearoom window. The man in the wheelchair looks quite old and ill. His face is puckered like old blistered paint. He wears dark glasses and a coal-black toupee and a black beret over that. He is all wrapped up in a blanket. Even later in the day, when
520 the sun is hot – every time she has seen them – he has been wrapped in this plaid blanket. The man who pushes the wheelchair and who now sits on the bench is young enough to look like an overgrown boy. He is tall and large-limbed but not manly. A young giant, bewildered by his own extent. Stong but not athletic, with a stiffness,
525 maybe of timidity, in his thick arms and legs and neck. Red hair not just on his head but on his bare arms and above the buttons of his shirt.

Gail halts in her walk past them, she says good morning. The young man answers most inaudibly. It seems to be his habit to look out at
530 the world with majestic indifference, but she thinks her greeting has given him a twitch of embarrassment or apprehension. Nevertheless she speaks again, she says, "What are those birds I see everywhere?"

"Galah birds," the young man says, making it sound something like her childhood name. She is going to ask him to repeat it, when the
535 old man bursts out in what seems like a string of curses. The words are knotted and incomprehensible to her, because of the Australian accent on top of some European accent, but the concentrated viciousness is beyond any doubt. And these words are meant for her – he is leaning forward, in fact struggling to free himself from
540 the straps that hold him in. He wants to leap at her, lunge at her chase her out of sight. The young man makes no apology and does not take any notice of Gail but leans towards the old man and gently

We learn what Gail thinks of her skills in writing letters.

Gail is clearly affected by what she reads.

Gail's confidence is fleeting.

Do her outside surroundings reflect how Gail is feeling inside?

Why is she afraid of the beer-drinkers?

Does the notion that the birds are not sea gulls bear a significance?

The description of the two men is detailed. Will they become important in Gail's story?

The young man is red-haired, like Gail.

Gail initiates communication with the men and perseveres despite lack of encouragement from the men.

A connection is made between the birds and Gail's real, "childhood", name. What are Galah birds like?

Why does the old man react so strongly against Gail?

pushes him back, saying things to him which she cannot hear. She sees that there will be no explanation. She walks away.

The young man does not defend or protect Gail.

To what do the last two sentences refer?

545 For ten days, no letter. She cannot decide what to do. She walks every day – that is mostly what she does. The Miramar is only about a mile or so away from Will's street. She never walks in that street again or goes into the shop where she told the man she was from Texas. She cannot imagine how she could have been so bold, the 550 first day. She does walk in the streets nearby. Those streets all go along ridges. In between the ridges, which the houses cling to, there are steep-sided gullies full of birds and trees. Even as the sun grows hot, those birds are not quiet. Magpies keep up their disquieting conversation and sometimes emerge to make menacing flights at 555 her light-colored hat. The birds with the name like her own cry out foolishly as they rise and whirl about and subside into the leaves. She walks till she is dazed and sweaty and afraid of sunstroke. She shivers in the heat – most fearful, most desirous, of seeing Will's utterly familiar figure, that one rather small and jaunty free-striding 560 package, of all that could pain or appease her, in the world.

Gail is desperately waiting for Will's reply. She does not seek company, which makes her encounter with the two men more important.

Gail records a change since arriving in Australia. Are the ridges, steep-sided gullies and persistently noisy birds metaphors?

What is the connection between the "foolishly" crying and unsettled Galah birds and Gail?

Gail's feelings towards Will are increasingly confused.

Dear Mr. Thornaby,

This is just a short note to beg your pardon if I was impolite and hasty in my replies to you, as I am sure I was. I have been under some stress lately, and have taken a leave of absence to recuperate. Under these circumstances one does 565 *not always behave as well as one would hope or see things as rationally…*

Gail breaks her waiting with another letter. Her tone is different from before. What has brought about the change? Is she feeling guilty, ashamed?

One day she walks past the hotel and the park. The verandas are clamorous with the afternoon drinking. All the trees in the park have come out in bloom. The flowers are a color that she has seen and could not have imagined on trees before – a shade of silvery 570 blue, or silvery purple, so delicate and beautiful that you would think it would shock everything into quietness, into contemplation, but apparently it has not.

Gail observes the new shades of colour in the park and is surprised they have not "shocked everything into quietness, into contemplation". Is the vibrancy of her surroundings in contrast with how she feels?

When she gets back to Miramar, she finds the young man with the red hair standing in the downstairs hall, outside the door of the 575 apartment where he lives with the old man. From behind the closed apartment door come the sounds of a tirade.

The young man smiles at her, this time. She stops and they stand together, listening.

Gail is stopped by the young man's smile.

Gail says, "If you would ever like a place to sit down while you're 580 waiting, you know you're welcome to come upstairs."

Gail is friendly towards the young man.

He shakes his head, still smiling as if this was a joke between them. She thinks she should say something else before she leaves him there, so she asks him about the trees in the park. "Those trees beside the hotel," she says. "Where I saw you the other morning? 585 They are all out in bloom now. What are they called?"

The man refuses Gail's offer, but somewhat incongruously, continues to smile.

Gail asks about the trees in bloom.

He says a word she cannot catch. She asks him to repeat it. "Jack Randa," he says. "That's the Jack Randa Hotel."

Does the man answer Gail's question?

Dear Ms. Thornaby,

I have been away and when I came back I found both your letters waiting for 590 *me. I opened them in the wrong order, though that really doesn't matter.*

Now a letter from Will.

My mother has died. I have been "home" to Canada for her funeral. It is cold there, autumn. Many things have changed. Why I should want to tell you this I simply do not know. We have certainly got off on the wrong track with each other. Even if I had not got your note of explanation after the first letter
595 *you wrote, I think I would have been glad in a peculiar way to get the first letter. I wrote you a very snippy and unpleasant letter and you wrote me back one of the same. The snippiness and unpleasantness and readiness to take offense seems somehow familiar to me. Ought I to risk your armigerous wrath by suggesting that we may be related after all?*

600 *I feel adrift here. I admire my wife and her theatre friends, with their zeal and directness and commitment, their hope of using their talents to create a better world. (I must say though that it often seems to me that the hope and zeal exceed the talents.) I cannot be one of them. I must say that they saw this before I did. It must be because I am woozy with jet lag after that horrendous*
605 *flight that I can face up to this fact and that I write it down in a letter to someone like you who has her own troubles and quite correctly has indicated she doesn't want to be bothered with mine. I had better close, in fact, before I burden you with further claptrap from my psyche. I wouldn't blame you if you had stopped reading before you got this far…*

610 Gail lies on the sofa pressing this letter with both hands against her stomach. Many things have changed. He has been in Walley, then – he has been told how she sold the shop and started out on her great world trip. But wouldn't he have heard that anyway, from Cleata? Maybe not, Cleata was close-mouthed. And when she went into the
615 hospital, just before Gail left, she said, "I don't want to see or hear from anybody for a while or bother with letters. These treatments are bound to be a bit melodramatic."

Cleata is dead.

Gail knew that Cleata would die, but somehow thought that
620 everything would hold still, nothing could really happen there while she, Gail, remained here. Cleata is dead and Will is alone except for Sandy, and Sandy perhaps has stopped being of much use to him.

There is a knock on the door. Gail jumps up in great disturbance, looking for a scarf to cover her hair. It is the manager, calling her
625 false name.

"I just wanted to tell you I had somebody here asking questions. He asked me about Miss Thornaby and I said, Oh, she's dead. She's been dead for some time now. He said, Oh, has she? I said, Yes, she has, and he said, Well, that's strange."

630 "Did he say why?" Gail says, "Did he say why it was strange?"

"No. I said, She died in the hospital and I've got an American lady in the flat now. I forgot where you told me you came from. He sounded like an American himself, so it might've meant something to him. I said, There was a letter come for Miss Thornaby after she was dead,
635 did you write that letter? I told him I sent it back. Yes, he said, I wrote it, but I never got it back. There must be some kind of mistake, he said."

Gail says there must be. "Like a mistaken identity," she says.

"Yes. Like that."

What effect has opening the letters in the wrong order had on Will?

Will writes about change.

Will's tone becomes personal and reflective; he reveals a lot about himself as well as his relationship with his wife.

Will feels like an outsider.

Is Will feeling sorry for himself and asking to be pitied?

Is Will trying to manipulate Gail?

Is Will suspecting something?

The motif of change has become apparent.

How does Gail feel about the fact that Will could have guessed Gail is in Australia?

Cleata's death startles Gail who thought life stood still during her time in Australia.

Is Gail feeling sorry for Will? Is she hoping Sandy will not be able to console Will in the new situation?

Gail's thoughts are suddenly interrupted.

The manager's line recreates the dialogue between him and somebody asking about Miss Thornaby.

Does Gail suspect it was Will asking the questions?

Another reference to a mistaken identity.

273

640 *Dear Ms. Thornaby*

> *It has come to my attention that you are dead. I know that life is strange, but I have never found it quite this strange before. Who are you and what is going in? It seems this rigmarole about the Thornabys must have been just that – a rigmarole. You must certainly be a person with time on your*
645 *hands and a fantasizing turn of mind. I resent being taken in but I suppose I understand the temptation. I do think you owe me an explanation now as to whether or not my explanation is true and this is some joke. Or am I dealing with some "fashion buyer" from beyond the grave? (Where did you get that touch or is it the truth?)*

Oxford English Dictionary defines *rigmarole* as "a lengthy and complicated procedure".

Is Will addressing the real Gail?

650 When Gail goes out to buy food, she uses the back door of the building, she takes a roundabout route to the shops. On her return by the same back-door route, she comes upon the young red-haired man standing between the dustbins. If he had not been so tall, you might have said that he was hidden there. She speaks to him but he
655 doesn't answer. He looks at her through tears, as if the tears were nothing but a wavy glass, something usual.

Why is the young man there, with tears in his eyes? What does this predict for the story?

"Is your father sick?" Gail says to him. She has decided that this must be the relationship, though the age gap seems greater than usual between father and son, and the two of them are quite unlike in
660 looks, and the young man's patience and fidelity are so far beyond – nowadays they seem even contrary to – anything a son customarily shows. But they go beyond anything a hired attendant might show, as well.

What do Gail's thoughts tell about her take on family relationships?

"No," the young man says, and though his expression stays calm, a
665 drowning flush spreads over his face, under the delicate redhead's skin.

Lovers, Gail thinks. She is suddenly sure of it. She feels a shiver of sympathy, an odd gratification.

Is she thinking about herself?

Lovers.

670 She goes down to her mailbox after dark and finds there another letter.

> *I might have thought that you were out of town on one of your fashion-buying jaunts but the manager tells me you have not been away since taking the flat, so I must suppose your "leave of absence" continues. He tells me*
675 *also that you are a brunette. I suppose we might exchange descriptions – and then, with trepidation, photographs – in the brutal manner of people meeting through newspaper ads. It seems that in my attempt to get to know you I am willing to make quite a fool of myself. Nothing new of course in that…*

Unlike the previous letters, this one has no opening. Are we reading an excerpt or have all pretenses been dropped between Will and Gail?

Will's tone is sarcastic; has he been offended?

680 Gail does not leave the apartment for two days. She does without milk, drinks her coffee black. What will she do when she runs out of coffee? She eats odd meals – tuna fish spread on crackers when she has no bread to make a sandwich, a dry end of cheese, a couple of mangos. She goes out into the upstairs hall of Miramar – first
685 opening the door a crack, testing the air for an occupant – and walks to the arched window that overlooks the street. And from long ago a feeling comes back to her – the feeling of watching a street, the visible bit of a street, where a car is expected to appear,

Does Gail feel threatened or ashamed? Surely she cannot hide forever.

or may appear, or may not appear. She even remembers now the
690 cars themselves – a blue Austin mini, a maroon Chevrolet, a family
station wagon. Cars in which she travelled short distances, illicitly
and in a bold daze of consent. Long before Will.

She doesn't know what clothes Will be wearing, or how his hair is
cut, or if he will have some change in his walk or expression, some
695 change appropriate to his life here. He cannot have changed more
than she has. She has no mirror in the apartment except the little
one on the bathroom cupboard, but even that can tell her how much
thinner she has got and how the skin on her face has toughened.
Instead of fading and wrinkling as fair skin often does in this climate,
700 hers has got a look of dull canvas. It could be fixed up – she sees
that. With the right kind of make-up a look of exotic sullenness
could be managed. Her hair is more of a problem – the red shows at
the roots, with shiny strands of gray. Nearly all the time she keeps it
hidden by a scarf.

705 When the manager knocks on her door again, she has only a second
or two of crazy expectation. He begins to call her name. "Mrs.
Massie, Mrs. Massie! Oh, I hoped you'd be in. I wondered if you
could just come down and help me. It's the old bloke downstairs,
he's fallen off the bed."

710 He goes ahead of her down the stairs, holding to the railing and
dropping each foot shakily, precipitately, onto the step below. "His
friend isn't there. I wondered. I didn't see him yesterday. I try
and keep track of people but I don't like to interfere. I thought he
probably would've come back in the night. I was sweeping out the
715 foyer and I heard a thump and I went back in there – I wondered
what was going on. Old bloke all by himself, on the floor."

The apartment is no larger than Gail's, and laid out in the same way.
It has curtains down over the bamboo blinds, which make it very
dark. It smells of cigarettes and old cooking and some kind of pine-
720 scented air freshener. The sofa bed has been pulled out, made into
a double bed, and the old man is lying on the floor beside it, having
dragged some of the bedclothes with him. His head without the
toupee is smooth, like a dirty piece of soap. His eyes are half shut and
a noise is coming from deep inside him like the noise of an engine
725 hopelessly trying to turn over.

"Have you phoned the ambulance?" Gail says.

"If you could just pick up the one end of him," the manager says. "I
have a bad back and I dread putting it out again."

"Where is the phone?" says Gail. "He may have had a stroke. He may
730 have broken his hip. He'll have to go to the hospital."

"Do you think so? His friend could lift him back and forth so easy. He
had the strength. And now he's disappeared."

Gail says. "I'll phone."

"Oh, no. Oh, no. I have the number written down over the phone in
735 my office. I don't let any other person go in there."

Gail revisits a feeling from "long before
Will", perhaps from the days of her wild,
"illicit" youth.

Gail admits she does not know everything
about Will's present life.

She recognizes her own change.

Could this reflect Gail's change; has her life
become an empty canvas to be adorned?

Does Gail not want to look after herself, or
remove the sullenness?

Gail's help is summoned.

The elderly manager's frailty is obvious.
What connection does this have with Gail
or her story?

Where has the young man gone?

The old man is vulnerable and needs help.

Gail springs to action.

Is the manager unable to see that the
situation has changed?

Left alone with the old man, who probably cannot hear her, Gail says, "It's all right. It's all right. We're getting help for you." Her voice sounds foolishly sociable. She leans down to pull the blanket up over his shoulder, and to her great surprise a hand flutters out, searches
740 for and grabs her own. His hand is slight and bony but warm enough, and dreadfully strong. "I'm here, I'm here," she says, and wonders if she is impersonating the red-haired young man, or some other young man, or a woman, or even his mother.

The ambulance comes quickly, with its harrowing pulsing cry, and
745 the ambulance men with the stretcher cart are soon in the room, the manager stumping after them, saying, "… couldn't be moved. Here is Mrs. Massie came down to help in the emergency."

While they are getting the old man onto the stretcher, Gail has to pull her hand away, and he begins to complain, or she thinks he
750 does – that steady involuntary-sounding noise he is making acquires an extra *ah-unh-anh*. So she takes his hand again as soon as she can, and trots beside him as he is wheeled out. He has such a grip on her that she feels as if he is pulling her along.

"He was the owner of the Jacaranda Hotel," the manager says. "Years
755 ago. He was."

A few people are in the street, but nobody stops, nobody wants to be caught gawking. They want to see, they don't want to see.

"Shall I ride with him?" Gail says. "He doesn't seem to want to let go
760 of me."

"It's up to you," one of the ambulance men says, and she climbs in. (She is dragged in, really, by that clutching hand.) The ambulance man puts down a little seat for her, the doors are closed, the siren starts as they pull away.

765 Through the window in the back door then she sees Will. He is about a block away from the Miramar and walking towards it. He is wearing a light-colored short-sleeved jacket and matching pants – probably a safari suit – and his hair has grown whiter or been bleached by the sun, but she knows him at once, she will always know him, and will always
770 have to call out to him when she sees him, as she does now, even trying to jump up from the seat, trying to pull her hand out of the old man's grasp.

"It's Will," she says to the ambulance man. "Oh, I'm sorry. It's my husband."

775 "Well, he better not see you jumping out of a speeding ambulance," the man says. Then he says, "Oh-oh. What's happened here?" For the next minute or so he pays professional attention to the old man. Soon he straightens up and says, "Gone."

"He's still holding on to me," says Gail. But she realizes as she says
780 this that it isn't true. A moment ago he was holding on – with great force, it seemed, enough force to hold her back, when she would have sprung towards Will. Now it is she who is hanging on to him. His fingers are still warm.

When she gets back from the hospital, she finds the note that she is

---

Who is Gail consoling?

Gail is taken by surprise when the man reaches for her.

The contact between Gail and the man cannot be broken.

The trees were Jacaranda, not Jack Randa.

We learn what the old man used to be, "years ago". How does this concern Gail or her story?

Unable to resist or make a decision to let go, Gail is dragged in (by the man she hardly knows).

Keep the ambulance man's words in mind until the end of the story.

In this dramatic situation Gail spots the man who occupies her mind most. She cannot resist making a connection with the most familiar figure in her life, detaching her from the present situation.

Gail is not the only one fighting her emotions.

Gail still calls Will her husband.

The tension rises at the moment Gail is trying to decide between the men, and the old man dies.

Who is Gail referring to? Could the statement apply to Will's hold of Gail? Gail's grasp almost changes direction: who is hanging on to whom?

The intense moment is over. We jump to when Gail returns from the hospital. She did not leave the old man.

785 expecting.

Gail. I know it's you.

Hurry. Hurry. Her rent is paid. She must leave a note for the manager. She must take the money out of the bank, get herself to
790 the airport, find a flight. Her clothes can stay behind – her humble pale-print dresses, her floppy hat. The last library book can remain on the table under the sagebrush picture. It can remain there, accumulating fines.

Otherwise, what will happen?

What she has surely wanted. What she is suddenly, as surely, driven
795 to escape.

Gail, I know you're in there! I know you're on the other side of the door.

Gail! Galya!

Talk to me, Gail! Answer me. I know you're there.

I can hear you. I can hear your heart beating through the keyhole and your
800 *stomach rumbling and brain jumping up and down.*

I can smell you through the keyhole. You. Gail.

Words most wished for can change. Something can happen to them, while you are waiting. *Love – need – forgive. Love – need – forever.*
805 The sound of such words can become a din, a battering, a sound of hammers in the street. And all you can do is run away, so as not to honor them out of habit.

In the airport shop she sees a number of little boxes, made by Australian aborigines. They are round, and light as pennies. She
810 picks out one that has a pattern of yellow dots, irregularly spaced on a dark-red ground. Against this is a swollen black figure – a turtle, maybe, with short splayed legs. Helpless on its back.

Gail is thinking, A present for Cleata. As if her whole time here had been a dream, something she could discard, going back to a chosen point, a beginning.

815 Not for Cleata. A present for Will?

A present for Will, then. Send it now? No, take it back to Canada, all the way back, send it from there.

The yellow dots flung out in that way remind Gail of something she saw last fall. She and Will saw it. They went for a walk on a sunny
820 afternoon. They walked from their house by the river up the wooded bank, and there they came on a display that they heard about but never seen before.

Hundreds, maybe thousands, of butterflies were hanging in the trees, resting before their long flight down the shore of Lake Huron and
825 across Lake Erie, then on south to Mexico. They hung there like metal leaves, beaten gold – like flakes of gold tossed up and caught in the branches.

"Like the shower of gold in the Bible," Gail said.

Will told her that she was confusing Jove and Jehovah. On that day,

---

A dramatic note from Will.

Gail is preparing to leave. She is prepared to leave her Australian life – her disguise, perhaps – behind.

Gail is still unable to control her emotions and make informed decisions.

Are we hearing Will's voice? Why is the text in italics, as the letters were?

Why is Will using Gail's real name?

Are these sentences a culmination of the change or development taking place in Gail?

Does Gail offer here an explanation to her own fleeing or that of Will earlier in their relationship?

From reflection, a jump to an airport setting.

Does Gail feel helpless, or could she be thinking of Will?

Gail is still holding on to a chance of withdrawing recent events.

Seeing certain colours creates another bridge between Gail's present and past with Will.

Gail's remark was ridiculed by Will. Looking back, Gail can see that change had already started. What deceits is Gail referring to? Were the earlier words in italics imagined by Gail?

830 Cleata had already begun to die and Will had already met Sandy. This dream had already begun – Gail's journey and her deceits, then the words she imagined – believed – that she heard shouted through the door.

Love – forgive

835 *Love – forget*

Love – forever

Hammers in the street.

What could you put in a box like that before you wrapped it up and sent it far away? A bead, a feather, a potent pill? Or a note, folded up

840 tight, to about the size of a spitball.

Now it's up to you to follow me.

How do these thoughts feature in the story?

Why are a bead, a feather, and a potent pill given as options? What could they represent?

What does the note suggest about Gail? What is the outcome of her recent journey?

How does the note conclude the story? What questions remain about Gail?

To conclude

What does the story say about change, relationships, identity, self-discovery, past and present, real and fake?

The HL Written Assignment

Have you ever been in a situation, where:
- your life or a relationship with someone important to you has taken a sudden turn?
- you have not been able to make up your mind about someone?
- you have had second thoughts about a decision you previously made?
- you have struggled with your feelings towards someone?
- you have changed your appearance or gone undercover because of someone?

Having studied the short story by Alice Munro, you could:
- re-write the story from the man's point of view.
- continue the short story: what happens after the last note?
- write a further series of letters between Gail and the man, to be inserted at a place of your choice (this should be justified in the rationale).
- write an inspirational speech given by Gail at a seminar for women.

Reflection point

- What did you find easy or difficult about the story? Why?
- How did the story make you feel? Why?
- Can you identify with the situation Gail finds herself in? Why?
- Which linguistic elements did you find difficult to understand?
- Make a list of new vocabulary and structures.
- What skills did you need to interpret the story?
- How did the guiding questions and notes help you understand the story?
- What does this short story evoke in the reader?
- What literary features are you now familiar with? Make a list of them with examples from the short story.
- How does Munro's story link with the core topics of communication and media, global issues, and social relationships?
- Draw a mindmap to illustrate the links between the story and core topics.
- How does Munro's story relate to the options you have studied: cultural diversity, customs and traditions, health, leisure, and science and technology?

Reading

Choose another short story and practise your skills of reading fiction in English.

1   Read the story once and then jot down your first impressions.
    a   What is the short story about?
    b   What is the language like?
    c   How does the story make you feel?

2   Re-read the story, and annotate the text or make notes as you read.
    a   Underline new, interesting, or difficult vocabulary and language structures.
    b   Circle the use of literary features.
    c   Observe how your understanding of the theme is starting to emerge.

3   Collate your annotations and observations and transform them into a list of questions. Your questions may follow the order of the text, or you may want to put the questions in order of difficulty; sometimes it is easier to start with simple questions dealing with the surface details or the plot before moving to interpretation.

4   Check your questions and devise short sample answers. Reflect on the range and difficulty of your questions: do they help the reader gain a thorough understanding of the story?

TIP

If you are a visual learner, you could use different colours for metaphors, symbolism, imagery, foreshadowing, etc.

If you identify yourself as an auditory learner, why not record an audio version of the story with your classmates. How do different voices affect your understanding and interpretation of the story?

If you learn best by doing something physical, put your kinaesthetic learning traits into action: act out certain parts of the story with your classmates or adapt the whole story into a play.

5   Ask a friend to read the short story and then present him or her with your questions.

6   Paying particular attention to how literary features affect your interpretation of the theme, discuss the story with your friend. Reflect on any different interpretations you may have of the most important features of the text.

CAS

- All four stories on pages 254 to 257 involve descriptions of social issues such as health, migration, education, and language. Two of the stories communicate the need to uphold the rights of various groups in society, and the other two stories deal with human rights. Think of social issues in your own community that need highlighting. Write your own short story to illustrate the social issue of your choice.

- Set up a short story reading group or a 'Literature Café' to present, share, and discuss fiction in English. Explore original, creative writing by students or selected texts from the anglophone world which will promote togetherness within your school community.

- Design posters which marry fiction with visual arts and show them around the school. Could images and words brighten up a dull corner? Can an uplifting poem elevate a corridor? Will the cafeteria become more inspiring with a well-chosen quotation?

- You could also organize a poetry slam to showcase contemporary poetry. How about mixing poetry and music, or preparing an interdisciplinary performance combining poetry, music, and movement?

Paper 2 (HL)

SECTION A

Complete *one* of the following tasks. Write 250 to 400 words.

1 Cultural diversity

You read an article about "Universal concept of beauty" in your local newspaper and decided to write the editor a letter in which you explain how beauty standards differ across cultures. Write your letter to the editor.

2 Customs & traditions

Dress codes are a blessing to students. In class, you are asked to give a speech to your classmates either agreeing or disagreeing with this statement. Write your speech.

3 Health

As a member of the Student Council, you have been asked to produce a set of guidelines for 15 and 16-year-old students on how to follow a healthy diet. Write your guidelines.

4 Leisure

How does travelling enhance social interaction? You have been asked to write an article on this topic to be published in your school magazine. Write your article.

5 Science & technology

Scientists are expected to follow a set of ethical standards when doing research. Write an email to the manager of a research centre in an English-speaking country in which you explain the code of ethics expected while conducting scientific researches. Write your email.

SECTION B

Based on the following stimulus, give a personal response and justify it. Choose any text type that you have studied in class. Write 150–250 words.

"If advertisers spent the same amount of money on improving their products as they do on advertising then they wouldn't have to advertise them."

Source: http://thinkexist.com

Leisure

→ How do you spend your leisure time?

→ When you go on holiday, what determines where you want to spend your holiday? What do you look for? What do you avoid?

→ What is the difference between a journey, a trip, and a holiday?

→ How does tourism affect a country both positively and negatively?

→ How do natural disasters affect tourism in the short term and in the longer term?

→ Henry Miller once said: "One's destination is not a place, but a new way of seeing things". Do you agree? How is this quote related to travelling and to life in general?

Travel & recreation

Wildlife safaris in India – Tips from the expert

1 Taking a jungle safari is an exhilarating experience if done properly. To fully enjoy and experience nature, the visitor needs to be extremely sensitive to his surroundings and display a large measure of patience and self-discipline.

2 India has more than five hundred national parks and wildlife sanctuaries and more than half of them have adequate infrastructure for the tourist. For those willing to put up with a certain amount of physical discomfort, the sky is the limit.

3 A safari can be best described as a sojourn into the wild and there are many ways to do so. Most parks offer jeep rides into the park and these are one of the best ways to see the park. The advantage of a jeep ride is that one is able to cover a lot of ground in the shortest possible time, thus maximizing one's chances of seeing wildlife. However, most jeep safaris turn out to be just mindless driving in the forest. One needs to stop every now and then, especially near ecological features that attract game, like waterholes, etc. A discerning guide is necessary on any safari and he should not be pressured to show animals, as no one is a magician able to conjure up game. Sounds play an important role, and one must be willing to stop and spend time listening.

4 An elephant safari is probably the best way to get up close and personal with nature and in certain habitats, such as the tall elephant grass habitats, it is the only way to go about. The advantages of elephants are that wildlife accepts them as animals and does not associate them with an alien presence. The other advantage is that there is no noise pollution and one can get to listen to the jungle sounds, which are usually drowned out in the roar of a jeep engine. The elephant also gives you a vantage point and visibility is much improved, adding to the overall experience.

5 Trekking in protected areas is discouraged and rightly so. The average tourist does not possess the skills required to survive in the forest and is thus most vulnerable while on foot. Fitness levels and the ability to climb trees play an important role in escaping danger while on foot, and as these are hard to assess, it is best to avoid going into the forest on foot.

6 Water-based safaris are on offer in certain parks that have large water bodies within them. A boat safari can be quite an enjoyable experience at the right time of the year and is certainly the most comfortable and relaxing way to do a safari. For the avid bird watcher, a boat is one of the best ways to get close to certain species of birds.

7 A machan, or a hide, situated close to a waterhole during the heat of summer is probably the best way to view game. However, this demands a lot of patience. Most parks have machans built close to waterholes and with prior permission one can get to use them. Make sure to check on the availability of these before you visit a park the next time.

8 To derive maximum pleasure from a safari, one must go properly prepared. A pair of good binoculars is the most important piece of equipment to carry on safari. A pair of 8X magnification is [a] for the mammals but for watching birds a 10X magnification is required to bring out details of [b] for correct identification. One should carry a pair that has an adequate diameter of lens as it helps in capturing more light. A ratio of 1:5 (magnification to diameter) is the norm.

9 A good camera is an asset to jog your memory later; however, one should not get [c] with taking the perfect picture, as the effort tends to distract from the experience. Large and cumbersome lenses add to the discomfort, and it is best to restrict your photography when using hides or machans. Most resorts allow photographers to hire jeeps for their exclusive use for an extra charge, and if photography is your purpose, it is recommended that you do so. A good field guide that is easy to carry can be an invaluable asset.

10 Dress for comfort. Cotton fabrics in neutral or dull colours are most suitable. Avoid synthetic fabrics and those made of vinyl as they reflect UV light that is visible to animals. Use detergents that do not contain brighteners for the same reason. A wide brimmed hat is useful in summer and dark glasses are a strict no-no.

11 Smells play an important role in the wild; therefore, do not use strong deodorants and avoid insect [d] and sunscreens that have powerful scents.

12 Your behaviour and [e] are extremely important. Do not get excited on seeing wildlife, take care to speak in hushed tones and do not make any sudden or violent gestures. Try not to break the profile of the jeep by standing up.

13 Leave the forest as you find it. Do not [f]; it can be fatal for wildlife. Resist the temptation to pluck flowers and fruit. Do not leave anything behind and do not take anything away except [g].

14 In addition, give yourself time. Nature cannot be hurried. She does not respond to deadlines. If you wish to get a better understanding, you must be prepared to be patient. The more time you spend, the better your chances of seeing wildlife. The more time you spend watching wildlife, the more you learn about them.

15 [h] follow the local rules that may vary from place to place and listen to your guide. In the forest, he is also your minder and teacher. Respect him and respect wildlife. Wildlife can be dangerous and therefore it is best to avoid cheap thrills. Do not under any circumstances encroach upon an animal's private space – it can be fatal.

16 If you strictly observe these guidelines, you can have one of the most [i], experiences of your life. A word of caution – wildlife safaris can be highly addictive!

Vikram Nanjappa

1 Read the text and use a table like the one below to outline the advantages and disadvantages (where necessary) of the following:

	Advantages	**Disadvantages**
Jeep rides		
Elephant safaris		
Boat safaris		
Trekking		
Using a machan		

2 Complete the following sentences.

  a To fully enjoy nature, one should... and ....

  b In paragraph 3, another word for 'vacation' is ....

  c In paragraph 3, another word for 'perceptive' is ....

  d In paragraph 4, another word for 'foreign' is ....

  e In paragraph 5, a phrase which means that a person is in a position which gives him/her a good view is... .

  f Another word given in the text for 'machan' is ....

  g In paragraph 9, another word for 'sidetrack' is ....

3 Answer the following questions.
  a Give a drawback to Indian national parks and wildlife safaris.
  b Which sense is important if you want to observe animals in their natural environment?
  c Which phrase in paragraph 5 shows that the author supports forbidding walking in protected areas?
  d Which skill plays a crucial role in a tourist's ability to survive in a forest?
  e Which bird is best watched from a machan?
  f Which attribute should a tourist possess to watch birds?
  g What should a tourist do to ensure his/her ability to use a machan?
  h Which piece of equipment is most important to enjoy a safari?
  i In "as the effort tends…" (paragraph 9), to what does 'the effort' refer?
  j What type of guide is recommended by the author?
  k Based on your understanding of paragraph 14, explain "Nature cannot be hurried. She does not respond to deadlines" in your own words.

4 For spaces **[a]-[i]**, choose one word or phrase from the options below which renders each sentence meaningful.

awarding	litter	plumes
blasé	memories	repellents
clutter	memoirs	restraints
gestures	nods	rewarding
inappropriate	obsessed	strictly
leniently	plumage	suitable

Grammar

- Re-read the sentence around the missing word. Can you work out the missing word from the context of the sentences around it?

- Look at each potential answer. Is it a verb, noun, adjective, or adverb? Do some words have more than one function? How does this information help you to find the correct answer?

5 The writer gives the reader a number of 'Dos' and 'Don'ts' in paragraphs 8-15. Use a table like the one below to list them and to explain them.

Advice	Justification

Beyond the text...

➤ Investigate how teenagers in an English-speaking country spend their leisure time. How is it similar to or different from the way you spend your leisure time?

➤ While it is true that air travel made travelling times shorter, it is said that we spend more time in airports than we do actually travelling. Do you agree?

➤ To enjoy free time, some people attend concerts while others watch films or read. How do you enjoy your time indoors? Do different cultures have different indoor and outdoor activities?

➤ Travel writing is a genre which provides accounts of different places. Look into travel writing, its conventions, and what it offers its audience. Find examples of English-speaking travel writers and the places they have written about.

➤ 'Travelogs' or travel blogs are online travel journals. How similar are travel blogs to magazine travel articles? How are they different?

Developing writing skills: Letter of application

1 A travel course combines traditional learning with travelling and aims to enrich students' educational experiences through travelling. One of your local universities decided to offer summer travel courses in biology, economics, history, and English. In pairs write a brochure in which you encourage students to enrol in the summer travel courses and describe the benefits they will gain from taking part in these courses.

2 Exchange your brochure with another pair. Read the brochure and then individually write an application letter to the university in which you describe why you want to take part in one of the travel courses described in your classmates' brochure.

Before you write your letter, do a basic electronic search to find out which phrases, sentences, and expressions are usually included in a letter of application. You could organize your findings into a table like this one:

Beginning	Body	End

A letter of application is usually written when you apply for a job or a course.

The register used in a letter of application is formal and a university application letter is structured as follows:

● Begin by clearly stating your reason for writing: mention the course you are applying for and where you have learned about it.

● In the body of the letter, explain your interests and your qualifications: Why have you chosen this course and this university? What benefit can the university gain from your enrolment?

● Conclude the letter by mentioning how you will apply the knowledge you gain from the course in your future life. Remember to include information about where and when you can be reached and an invitation for the university to request further information if needed.

Recreational dangers

Australian snorkeler snatched by shark

A snorkeler [1] to have been snatched by a shark as he [2] last weekend with his son at a beach south of Perth. Witnesses reported seeing a dorsal fin and thrashing in the water before the sea turned red and the man vanished at the scene on Australia's west coast.

Father of three Brian Guest, 51, who [3] for many years for the protection of sharks, had been looking for crabs yesterday morning with his 24 [a] year-old son when he [4] about 30 metres from the shore.

Luke Tubbs told how a witness ran to his house in shock and screaming for help [b] "He just saw a big splash and then the shark roll over in the water with the guy and then [he saw] no body or anything. [c]

Daniel Guest, who [5] six metres away at the Port Kennedy beach, heard his father's screams but did not see the attack. He [6] to shore when he saw blood in the water. His father's shredded wetsuit was found later, and aerial searches spotted a five-metre great white shark swimming in the area.

In Sydney, some hours later, a kayaker survived a terrifying ordeal after [7] from his craft by a great white shark. That encounter, endured by 29-year-old Steve Kulcsar, occurred less than a mile off Australia's east coast, at Long Reef, and [8] by a fisherman in a small boat nearby. The video footage apparently showed the shark circling Kulcsar after bumping him off his kayak.

Kulcsar said: "I knew it was there, but my first thought was to just get back in the kayak as quick as possible."

For 10 minutes [d] the shark is seen lurking around him and two other kayakers before losing interest and swimming away.

The two great white encounters sparked panic and closed a number of beaches across Australia.

Bondi beach [9] yesterday after a shark was spotted close to shore. Swimmers were also evacuated from a Queensland holiday island after sharks were spotted in waist-deep water.

During an aerial search on the West Australian coastline for Guest's body, sharks were spotted, forcing the closure of two beaches.

45 The attack on Guest was the second by sharks in Australia this year. A 16-year-old surfer, Peter Edmonds, died after being attacked by a shark near Byron bay, on the New South Wales coast, in April.

On average there are 15 shark attacks a year 50 in Australia [e] with about one death each year. Swimmers [10] more likely to die of a lightning strike than be taken by a great white shark.

Yesterday Daniel Guest recalled how his father had spoken of the risks of sharks and how he had [f] loved 55 and respected the ocean environment [g].

Brian Guest wrote on the Western Angler website forum in 2004: "I have always had an understanding with my wife that if a shark or ocean accident caused my death then so be it, at least it was doing what I 60 wanted. Every surfer [h] fisherman and diver has far more chance of being killed by bees, drunk drivers, teenage car thieves and lightning. Every death is a tragedy – regardless of the cause – but we have no greater claim to use of this earth than any of the other 65 creatures [we] share it with."

His son said he viewed his father's death as a random event that should not make people fear the water [i] and said he would eventually go back into the sea [j] "When I'm ready ... I'll do that."

Ellen Conolly, *The Guardian,* 2008

1 For the gaps **[a]–[j]** in the text, choose the appropriate punctuation mark from the table below which renders the sentence meaningful:

,	.	;	-
:	!	?	"

TIP

Refer to Chapter 6 for a reminder on punctuation.

2 Choose the verb from the table below which best fits each of the gaps marked **[1]-[10]** in the text.

are	having knocked
being knocked	is believed
believes	raced
campaigned	swam
closed	was attacked
filmed	was closed
had attacked	was filmed
had campaigned	was racing
had swum	was swimming
has been swimming	were

Beyond the text...

➤ Many incidents involving 'killer beasts' have been made into horror films. Go online and find some examples of films which emphasize how dangerous some leisure activities can be.

➤ Many travel websites highlight the importance of immunisation before one travels to a new country. Why do you think this is the case? What other precautions should one consider before travelling?

➤ Another recreational activity is playing computer games. Find examples in the English-speaking media of the effects of video gaming. Is the issue fairly presented? What benefits are gained from playing computer games? What are the drawbacks?

➤ Hooliganism is a negative, disruptive behaviour that is associated with sports fans. What are the origins of hooliganism? How are hooligans and hooliganism in British society portrayed in the media?

➤ What is graffiti? Look at the photographs below: Is graffiti an act of vandalism or a form of art?

➤ Look into the work of some famous street artists like Banksy. Is there a specific message the artist tries to get across through his art?

Developing writing skills: News report

1 Re-read the text then answer the following questions.
   a Which main tense is used in the news report?
   b Which point of view is used in the news report?
   c How long are the paragraphs? Why?
   d Does the reporter use direct and indirect quotes? Give examples.

2 The news report *Australian snorkeller snatched by shark* on page 302 appeared in a mainstream newspaper. In pairs, electronically search for the similarities and differences between mainstream and tabloid news reports. Write your findings in a table like the one below.

	Mainstream	Tabloid
Similarities	* * * *	* * * *
Differences	* * * *	* * * *

3 Now change the news report *Australian snorkeller snatched by shark* from a conventional news report to a sensational report from a tabloid. Make sure you use the same facts.

Writing activity

Choose a set of key words from the options below to plan a newsworthy story. Choose when, where, how, and to whom the story happened and plan the remainder of the story based on the rules you learned in this unit for writing a news report. Do not forget to decide whether your news report will appear in a mainstream newspaper or a tabloid.

1	suicide	skyscraper	love
2	fatalities	safari	elephants
3	demonstrations	green vacationing	university students
4	wedding	celebrities	Hawaii
5	football match	Australia	riot

Remember

A **news report**, presents newsworthy information. It is 'designed' in a way which will make it possible for the reader to gain the essential information even though the whole report may not be read. This is why a news report presents information chronologically in the following manner:
- Headline
- The lead paragraph: Who? What? When? Where? Why?
- Explanatory paragraphs: further details including statements and direct quotes.
- Final paragraphs: similar incidents, least important information, etc.
- Refer to Chapter 5 for further advice on how to write a news report.

Interactive oral activity

Look at photographs A, B, C, and D and in small groups:

- write an appropriate caption or title linked to the option of Leisure for each photograph.

- write a minimum of five questions you would like to ask about the topic.

- prepare a 4-minute presentation on one of the photographs in which you describe the photograph and link it to Leisure in an anglophone country.

- having listened to your colleagues' presentations, ask the group to clarify or justify any points which you felt could have been explained more clearly.

A

B

C

D

→ What is ecotourism?
→ What, in your opinion, are the characteristics of a responsible traveller? What are the characteristics of the irresponsible traveller or tourist?
→ Sustainability is defined as the "conservation of an ecologic balance by avoiding depletion of natural resources" (*Oxford Dictionaries Online*). What do you think the relationship between ecotourism and sustainability is?
→ How can ecotourism be promoted in your country?

Responsible travelling

Eco-friendly vacationing

A green vacation is more than just an idea these days, now it's a whole industry. Just type "green vacation" into a search engine and peruse thousands
5 of links to companies offering eco-friendly vacations neatly packaged and ready to go. But you don't need to buy into a marketing ploy in order to have an environmentally friendly vacation.
10 Instead, use common sense and make extra effort to be an eco-friendly traveller. To get you started, here are ten tips you can use the next time you go on vacation.

15 **[1]**
All of those three day weekends really make your carbon footprint skyrocket. With shorter vacations you produce more CO_2 because you travel more. If
20 you think about it, this is really neither relaxing nor eco-friendly. Instead of travelling often, for short periods of time, lump your vacation time together and take life slow for a while. This way
25 you'll come back truly relaxed, and you'll have wasted far less fuel.

[2]
Part of green vacationing 101 is learning to buy credits to offset your
30 carbon footprint. When you travel, you produce CO_2, and the Earth needs trees to transform that CO_2 into oxygen for us humans. When you buy carbon credits, you basically fund the
35 purchase of those trees. Many travel sites now conveniently allow you to buy carbon credits on their sites.

[3]
The less weight a plane has to carry
40 into the air, the less fuel it will use. This is the reason why many airlines have started charging for bags over a certain weight. Do your pocketbook and the environment a favor by packing only
45 what you need. Chances are you can wash your clothes wherever you are going, and you'll have more room for souvenirs on the way back.

[4]
50 A train produces one third of the emissions a plane does, and half that of a car. Train travel is truly the choice method of transportation for green vacationing. The US is currently lacking
55 in fast train services, but Europe and New Zealand both have lovely trains that get you to your destination on time and in comfort.

[5]
60 Of course, you don't have to fly halfway around the world to have a vacation. Why not enjoy the wonders around you? Camping is a great way to have a green vacation and to enjoy
65 the outdoors as well.

[6]
Before you leave for your destination, check out the public transportation options available. Urban areas
70 especially usually have a bus or train system that you can buy a pass for. It may seem daunting and scary at first, but by using public transportation you'll really get a taste of local life.

75 **[7]**
Many large chains are now offering green vacationers the chance to opt for a hybrid rental car. Not only will you save gas money while on vacation, but
80 you'll also greatly reduce your carbon emissions. Can't get a hybrid? Do the next best thing and go for an economy sized car. Not only will it cost you less, it will also use less fuel than its luxury
85 counterparts.

[8]
In the US eco-friendly hotels are either marked with the Green Seal or are LEED certified by the US Green
90 Building Council. Don't fall for any "ecotourism" labels, only the hotels that have these approvals are the real deal. In Canada, look for hotels marked by the Green Leaf Eco-Rating Program.

95 **[9]**
In most hotels, the staff will wash your sheets and any towels left on the floor on a daily basis, eating up enormous amounts of electricity and water. To
100 have a green vacation, forgo the extra washing, hang your towels up and ask the staff to wash your sheets when you leave.

[10]
105 Some people think that they need to see every tourist attraction within a hundred miles when they go on vacation. Instead of driving everywhere and seeing everything, why not take it
110 slow? Plan a few activities interspersed throughout your vacation in the local area, and then leave the rest of the days open for exploration and relaxation. If you push yourself too
115 hard, you won't feel like you had a vacation at all.
    A green vacation can not only save the environment but also your pocketbook and perhaps your sanity.
120 Next time you travel, remember these handy tips, and you'll have helped contribute to a healthier world.

SuperGreenMe

1   The paragraph headings have been removed from the text.
    Choose the heading below which best describes each of the paragraphs **[1]–[10]**.

   A   Consider buying a different car
   B   Make sure you know how much CO_2 you produce
   C   Buy credits to offset your carbon emissions
   D   Don't travel by plane
   E   Consider staying local
   F   Don't have your hotel launder your towels or linens daily
   G   Keep your sheets clean
   H   Look for appropriate hotels
   I   If you must rent a car look into a hybrid

   J   Look for hotels with the green seal
   K   Take one suitcase
   L   Pack light
   M   Be slow
   N   Slow down
   O   Don't travel a lot
   P   Take fewer, longer trips
   Q   Choose a better means of transport
   R   Take the train
   S   Walk
   T   Use public transport when possible

2   To whom or to what do the following words or phrases refer?
   a   an idea (line 2)
   b   this (line 20)
   c   their (line 37)
   d   that (line 51)
   e   it (line 83)
   f   these approvals (line 92)

3   Re-read the text. Identify the tips the author gives on having an eco-friendly vacation. Using the ideas in the text and your own words, write a short set of instructions on 'How to have an eco-friendly holiday'.

Beyond the text...

Welcome to responsible-travel.org

In an age where the opportunity to travel has never been so easy, international travel is no longer a luxury.

Tourism is now the world's fastest growing industry. With this proliferation of travel comes a heavy
5   responsibility on all travellers to ensure that the heritage and environment of those nations we seek to explore do not disintegrate under the rapid influx of new visitors.

Tourism accounts for over six percent of the world's
10   gross national product, providing up to ten percent of the world's total employment. Yet the vast majority of tourists come from only 20 predominantly Western countries.

No longer the preserve of the elite, since the 1960s,
15   tourism as an international industry hasn't looked back thanks to the package holiday and dropping flight prices. Today few areas are beyond the reach of the average Western citizen.

Now every corner of the globe is a Sunday supplement
20   photo shoot, or next season's hot destination.

Travel as a lifestyle, to a greater extent, has led to the commodification of many areas of the world, creating a hyper-reality of very real destinations with equally real fragile environments, cultures, and economies.

25   There is an argument that to not travel is the most responsible form of travel. Guaranteed minimum impact.

Responsible-travel.org disagrees. Travel is all the enlightening, life changing clichés it promises to be.
30   In 1967, International Year of the Tourist, the United Nations recognised that tourism is "a basic and most desirable human activity, deserving the praise and encouragement of all peoples and all governments". We agree.

35   Quite simply, if you do travel, be aware that the choices we make while away do have an impact.

Please browse the advice and articles herein, and stay a responsible traveller.

With the opportunity to travel, however, comes a
40   new responsibility to all travellers to ensure that their activities do not upset or destroy the very cultures and environments we choose to visit.

> The message above appears on responsible-travel. org homepage. The message highlights several issues that people need to take into consideration when travelling. Peruse websites like www.responsibletravel. com, www.sustainabletravelinternational.org, www. ecotourismcesd.org or any other website which aims to help people become responsible travellers. Do all those sites highlight the same issues?

> Synthesize the information available on the sites you examined above and write your own definition of a responsible traveller.

Developing writing skills: Interview

1 Imagine that you have just interviewed the person who provided the tips in *Eco-friendly vacationing* on page 307. Write the transcript of the interview.

2 Exchange your transcript with the person sitting next to you. Write an article that would be published in your local newspaper based on your classmate's interview transcript.

Writing activity

1 Choose one of the people below and interview him or her. Your interview should focus on this person's interests and how this person spends his or her leisure time.

- school principal
- teacher
- parent
- classmate
- local policeman
- doctor
- local politician
- school nurse

2 Write an article based on the interview to be published in your school magazine.

3 Share your article with your classmates. Which article do you think best fulfilled the requirements of a magazine article based on an interview? Why?

TIP

Writing an **interview** is not easy. The interview should be well structured and coherent. The questions and answers used in an interview should help the reader understand the topic and should not leave him/her wondering if s/he has missed something.

When writing an interview, you have to remember that it is essentially a dialogue. This does not mean that you have to stick strictly to the question and answer format. Your ability appropriately to use cohesive devices, inject humour into the dialogue and make it read as authentic an interview as possible determines your mark.

Sometimes, you may not be asked to write an interview but to embed it in a magazine article. Such a task requires that you use the format of the magazine article. However, you need to remember that unlike regular articles, this one is based on the interview; therefore, the information you present summarizes the interview to an extent and focuses on its most important parts. The use of direct quotes in those parts is essential.

TOK

- In what ways might CAS be said to promote ethical education?
- Do International Baccalaureate students have ethical responsibilities?

At the American International School Dhaka in Bangladesh, one of the students embarked on an ambitious project to teach English at a local children's home. This is what she said in her journal:

One of the three aspects of CAS is Service, where IB Diploma candidates find ways to give back to the community and surroundings they live in. AISID has already provided us with one opportunity to do this, which is the Service Learning program, yet I feel like its requirement is taking away the feeling of accomplishment; your own goodwill should in fact be the driving force for your aid to others. I felt I wanted to be more passionate about service and found that this would happen best if I found something to do myself outside of school.

Rica Duchateau

- Do you agree with Rica? Is service to others, in whatever form, a moral obligation?
- Is preserving our environment an ethical responsibility?

CAS

Many IB schools are situated in places where people live in inferior living conditions and have fewer life chances than many IB Diploma students. In such communities, learning English is an essential tool for a variety of reasons. These reasons could include:

- Gaining access to education
- Finding employment
- Improving living conditions
- Gaining access to better medical services

As one of your CAS activities, you decided to teach English to people in your local community. Before you embark on this project, consider the following:

- Who will you choose to teach?
- Who will you enlist to help?
- How will you approach teaching English? Reflect on the strategies you deem useful and outline the difficulties you think your 'students' will face.

Global issues

• •

BEFORE YOU READ

→ How green (environmentally responsible) are you?

→ It is claimed that human actions and behaviours have had a negative effect on nature. Do you agree? Can human beings also have a positive impact on nature?

→ How do you approach environmental issues in your country?

→ In your opinion, how aware are people of environmental issues like water scarcity, deforestation, and pollution? What can be done to preserve our natural resources?

→ What role should the media play in increasing environmental awareness?

→ Look at the cartoon below. Is 'wireless data pollution' real?

Impact of man on nature

The environmental impacts of kayaking – is it dangerous?

Kayaking is an activity enjoyed by many people of all ages. It requires little or no experience and nearly anyone of any skill level can participate. It's most popular as a summertime sport, but is also a great activity during the winter. Kayaking also seems relatively friendly to the environment; more so than speed boating or water skiing. Because a kayak doesn't create large or frequent waves, require fuel, or disperse hazards into the air, it is indeed a fairly safe activity for humans and wildlife alike.

Kayaking on freshwater lakes and streams creates little turbulence and therefore does not disturb fish or other aquatic life. Actually, the gentle paddling and movement of the kayak helps to bring kelp and seaweed to the surface, making for convenient snacking to the fish. However, there is a downside to kicking up an all-you-can-buffet for your fishy friends. In addition to bringing food to the surface, kayaking also stirs up litter that's been lurking beneath the waters. Most fish will not eat the trash that rises to the top, but other aquatic animals will mistake it for food. This could cause the animals to choke on the indigestible litter, leading to death. As hazardous as this sounds, it isn't very likely for such an event to take place. Most litter in lakes and streams is found along the shoreline and settles in the sand and dirt, and isn't likely to drift away to the main body of water.

Unlike boats operated by motor and fuel, kayaks pose little or no harm to the fish swimming beneath. Kayaks don't move at a rapid pace, and the fish swimming below have ample time to move out of the boat's way. And because kayaks do not have a motor, fish have no risk of getting caught underneath the boat.

One potential hazard that results from kayaking is human waste. This depends solely on where you plan to kayak, and if there are resources available (such as campsites) along the shoreline. When there are no facilities in sight, you're paddling in the middle of a lake, and nature calls, then often you are given no choice but to expel your waste in the middle of the water. While human waste is considered biodegradable, it can be harmful when ingested by fish. The only preventative measure is to avoid using the water as a restroom, but again, this can't always be helped. Some public lakes and streams have taken steps to preserve the quality of the water by requiring permits for kayaking. This won't eliminate a human waste problem, but does help regulate entry into the lake and prevent it from becoming overcrowded.

An important factor to remember when kayaking is that you are a guest in someone else's home. You may not be greeted by anyone or be able to kick up your feet and watch TV, but the water is home to many aquatic animals and wildlife. Just as you would not throw trash on the floor or destroy the home of another, you shouldn't do it outdoors either. Keep all trash with you in your kayak and properly dispose of it after you return to shore. Don't dump anything in the water, and try to avoid expelling human waste if at all possible. By doing your part, you will help keep kayaking a safe and enjoyable activity for yourself and the environment.

Forest Schellenberg

1   From statements A to J, select the five that are true according to the text.
   A   Young people's enjoyment of kayaking exceeds that of other people.
   B   Usually, kayaking is practised in the summer.
   C   Water skiing negatively affects the environment.
   D   Kayaking facilitates the finding of food for fish.
   E   Kayaks could be a little dangerous to aquatic life.
   F   Kayaks hardly ever harm the fish swimming under them.
   G   Human excrement rarely poses a problem to aquatic life.
   H   Public water bodies have taken preventative measures to control human waste problems.
   I   Potential harm to aquatic life increases when public lakes get swarmed with kayaks.
   J   When kayaking, it is important to consider nature your home.

2   Answer the following questions.
   a   Who can take part in kayaking?
   b   Why is kayaking considered a green activity to an extent?
   c   Name one drawback to kayaking.
   d   To what does 'this' (line 44) refer?
   e   Why isn't kicking up buried litter considered a significant problem when kayaking?
   f   Why is the lack of a motor in a kayak considered positive?
   g   Human waste is a problem under two conditions. Name them.
   h   When is human waste considered dangerous?
   i   According to the text, what shouldn't you do when kayaking?
   j   In your opinion, is kayaking enviromentally friendly? Why?

3   For each of the words below, choose a word from the box that could meaningfully replace it.
   a   relatively (line 10)   **e**   ample (line 58)
   b   disperse (line 16)   **f**   solely (line 67)
   c   convenient (line 29)   **g**   biodegradable (line 79)
   d   hazardous (line 44)   **h**   eliminate (line 90)

correct	handy	some
dangerous	only	somewhat
environmentally harmless	partially	sufficient
eradicate	safe	undo
extremely	scatter	unsophisticated

4   The article proves that kayaking, if done properly, does not harm the environment. However, from the text, we infer some ways in which the environment suffers from the actions of man. For example, if a kayak does not create large or frequent waves and therefore does not disturb aquatic life, we infer that any device which creates large and frequent waves disturbs aquatic life. What other harmful actions that humans perform do we infer from the text?

Interactive oral activity

It is Earth Day, and your school is celebrating it by organizing a number of events to help raise awareness about environmental issues. You decide to do a presentation about one of the following topics:

- Melting glaciers
- Global warming
- Green living
- Desertification

1   Prepare your presentation. Remember to concentrate on how the issue you are tackling affects an English-speaking country or how it is perceived in that country.

2   Present your topic to your classmates and be prepared to answer questions after the presentation.

The personal response

Based on the following stimulus, give a personal response and justify it. Give a talk to your classmates using 150 to 250 words.

"The earth we abuse and the living things we kill will, in the end, take their revenge; for in exploiting their presence we are diminishing our future."   **Marya Mannes**, *More in Anger*, 1958

> **Remember**
>
> A talk is similar to a speech (revisit pages 33-34), but it is at times less formal. Of course, formality – or the lack of it – is determined by your audience and the topic.

Environmental awareness

What can you do to help the environment?

A well-known, ancient proverb says:

"We do not inherit the Earth from our ancestors; we borrow it from our children."

In essence, what this proverb is saying is that we need to be
5   respectful of our children and our homes, by safeguarding their
futures with what we do today.

There are three things we desperately need to live: oxygen, water,
and sunlight. Food is important too but oxygen, water, and sunlight
are imperative to life. A man can live longer with food than he can
10   with a lack of water.

Tearing down trees, useless waste, pollution, using plastic instead
of paper, and a general lack of knowledge are just a few of the
things that are contributing to the demise of the three core matters
we need to live. When we read the doom and gloom in the media about our earth, we often feel
15   overwhelmed and confused, wondering what it is that we can do to make a difference.

There are ways for you to take action. There are things you can do each and every day to lessen
the negative impact on the environment, starting right now.

Here are some things you can do to take action and start making a more proactive impact on the
environment.

20   **Start a compost bin** for kitchen scraps, grass clippings, leaves, and paper. It is not nasty – it is
wise living.

Use vinegar, lemon, essential oils, and baking soda to clean your house – Essential oils like tea
tree oil, lemons, and vinegar all have antifungal and disinfectant properties. No need for bleach.

Use Reusable Bags – How often does a typical family shop each month? If you kept reusable
25   bags in your car for your storing items from your shopping trips, you would make a huge difference
in the number of plastic bags that end up in landfills, all of which will still be around when your
great-grandchildren are alive. If you look around your home, you may have several cloth bags
already that would be suitable. Many stores like Target, CVS, Trader Joe's and Whole Foods sell
attractive reusable grocery bags at reasonable costs.

30   **Go Digital!** Could you read an e-book instead of a paper version? Do online banking instead of
getting a statement in the mail? Pay bills online instead of using an envelope? Get your favorite
reading materials digitally delivered. Reconsider having the newspaper delivered to your home
every day and see if you can read it online instead. Subscribe to magazines that offer digital
subscriptions and read your favorite magazines online.

35   **Shop used first** – When looking for new clothes, try hosting swap party with friends and neighbors
to see if you can exchange clothing instead of buying new all the time. Go to a thrift store in your
area and try to go on a day when the prices are cut in half. You would be surprised at the treasures
you find in a thrift store.

The key to success in the fight to save the environment is to set goals and commit to making
40   changes slowly. This way, good habits of stewardship for the care our planet are more likely to stick
and become permanent lifestyle choices.

GreenEarthTraveler.org, 2008

1   Find the words in the text which have the same meaning as the
    following:
    a   at the core
    b   protecting
    c   vital
    d   termination
    e   astounded
    f   effect
    g   positive
    h   basic
    i   sensible
    j   saving

2   Based on the information in the text, match the first part of the
    sentence with the appropriate ending on the right.

    a   Lack of water   **1**   costs less.
    b   Several factors   **2**   ensures an early demise.
    c   By doing a few things   **3**   help endanger our planet.
    d   Swapping clothes with friends   **4**   is a proactive way to help preserve the environment.
    e   Commitment to set goals   **5**   is as important as food.
                                               6   is key to saving the environment.
                                               7   means we care about the environment.
                                               8   play a role in the disappearance of core materials.
                                               9   we can safeguard our planet.
                                               10   we contribute to the environment.

3   Choose the correct answer from A, B, C, or D.
    a   In order to save the environment, we need to
            A   respect it and preserve it.
            B   make sure our children do not disrespect it.
            C   keep it safe for our children.
            D   encourage our children to respect it.

    b   When reporting environmental issues, media reports are
            A   pessimistic.
            B   optimistic.
            C   disastrous.
            D   true.

    c   To avoid using synthetic material, use
            A   essential oils.
            B   reusable bags.
            C   plastic bags.
            D   compost bins.

    d   To preserve trees,
            A   stop cutting them down.
            B   recycle material.
            C   buy electronic softcopies.
            D   read material in a digital, rather than print, format.

Beyond the text...

➤ In 2010, a huge oil spill in the Gulf of Mexico caused the poisoning of many living organisms, created toxic waste zones and invoked a huge environmental concern. Look into the issue of this and similar incidents which affected an anglophone country. Whose fault is it that such incidents happen? How can similar incidents be prevented?

➤ In 2011, Nigeria suffered from an incident similar to that of the Gulf of Mexico. Nigeria's disaster, however, did not make the same news. Why do you think this is the case? What does this show about bias in the media?

➤ 'Greentech' is one way of conserving natural resources. Investigate 'greentech' to learn more about the latest developments in the field and how it promotes sustainable development.

➤ Environmental issues and sustainable development have been addressed at many conferences worldwide. Examine the issue in an English-speaking country. How are environmental issues addressed? What role does education play in raising environmental awareness?

➤ Many political speeches include references to global warming, sustainable development, and green living. Look into some speeches which were given in an anglophone country and note down how the speaker addresses the aforementioned environmental issues. What, in addition to addressing environmental issues publicly, should politicians do to raise environmental awareness?

"News, sports, weather, comics, advice, politics, opinion — it's the Internet in a biodegradable, easily recycled format. The latest thing in green technology!"

Interactive oral activity

1 In groups of three, choose one of the ways to help save the environment that are mentioned in the text on page 314 and plan a short sketch in which you clarify to your audience how this particular way can be beneficial.

2 Act your sketches out in front of your classmates.

3 Which sketch best delivered its message? On what basis will you decide which sketch has the most effective message?

The SL Written Assignment

1 Re-read *The environmental impacts of kayaking* on page 312 and *What can you do to help the environment?* on page 314. What is the main idea in each text? How do the authors support their ideas?

2 Choose the idea that you would like to explore further in your written assignment.

3 Determine who your audience is. Identifying your audience is very important, for it determines your style, tone, and register.

4 Discuss your ideas with your teacher.

5 Write your rationale.

6 Write your assignment (300–400 words).

7 Revisit your rationale and include examples from your assignment that support your choice of topic and text type.

TOK

It is not unusual for very different opinions to coexist within the social sciences. This is particularly true of environmental issues. If two or more competing schools of thought offer different explanations for a problem, how can we decide which is correct? In sensitive environmental matters, academics, politicians, the business community, and local community experts can be publicly divided. What effect does a highly sensitive political context have on objectivity? How do we know who is right or wrong? Look into one of the following controversies:

- Gulf War Syndrome
- Homeopathy
- MMR vaccinations
- The Vitamin C Diet
- The Hearing Voices Movement
- Blood transfusions and Jehovah's Witnesses

What do you notice? How are the four ways of knowing used to drive public opinion?

CAS

With your classmates, present your principal with a proposal to make your school a green school. You have to plan your proposal to the smallest detail, outlining the conversion process from beginning to end. Take into consideration the following:

- Your school's vision and mission
- Financial issues
- Support from your classmates, teachers, parents, the school administration and the local community

Once your proposal is ready, discuss it with your CAS coordinator and your principal, and then modify it as per their recommendations before you begin the implementation phase.

For this exercise, you are asked to write an official report on green living.

What is the main purpose of an **official report**? What are you trying to communicate to your audience?

An official report aims to present information to a person or a group of people in a coherent, formal manner. It includes explanation and summarizes findings, descriptions, recommendations, etc.

An official report begins by providing essential background information about the subject of the report. You will then have to present your findings and explain the main or most important ones through providing facts, statistics and details. The report concludes with a short summary of the ideas which were presented in the body of the report.

Remember

When writing an official report, you have to organize your ideas clearly under subheadings and use clear features like bullet points.

A **report to the police** or a **witness statement** also fall under the general umbrella of the official report.

Communication & media

BEFORE YOU READ

→ Watch a film which promotes an environmental cause, like Al Gore's *An Inconvenient Truth*. How do you think the film will help you change your perception about the effect of man on nature?

→ Should the media take a more ethical stance when tackling environmental issues?

→ Should harming the environment, in your opinion, be punishable by law?

→ How many science fiction films and TV series have you watched? How believable is the science fiction genre? Think in terms of how Jules Verne's science fiction novels which were written in the 19th century became ordinary occurrences in the 20th century. Do you think ideas depicted in todays science fiction will someday cease to be classified as science fiction?

How the media can be used to promote environmental issues

3 | News

In a world left silent, one heart beeps

The first 40 minutes or so of *Wall-E* – in which [a] any dialogue is spoken, and almost no human figures appear on screen – is a cinematic poem of such [b] and beauty that its darker implications may take a while to sink in. The scene is an intricately rendered city, bristling with skyscrapers but [c] of any inhabitants apart from a battered, industrious robot and his loyal cockroach sidekick. Hazy, dust-filtered sunlight [d] a landscape of eerie, post-apocalyptic silence. This is a world without people, you might say without animation, though it teems with evidence of past life.

We've grown accustomed to expecting surprises from Pixar, but *Wall-E* surely breaks new ground. It gives us a computer-generated cartoon vision of our own potential [e]. It's not the only film lately to engage this sombre theme. As the earth heats up, the vanishing of humanity has become something of a hot topic, a preoccupation shared by directors like Steven Spielberg *(A.I.)*, Francis Lawrence *(I Am Legend)*, M. Night Shyamalan *(The Happening)* and Werner Herzog. In his recent documentary "Encounters at the End of the World" Mr. Herzog [f] that "the human presence on this planet is not really sustainable," a sentiment that is voiced, almost [g], in the second half of *Wall-E*.

Not that *Wall-E* is all gloom and doom. It is, undoubtedly, an earnest (though far from simplistic) ecological parable, but it is also a [h] sweet and simple love story, Chaplinesque in its emotional purity. On another level entirely, it's a bit of a sci-fi geek-fest, [i] to everything from *2001* and the *Alien* pictures to *Wallace and Gromit: A Grand Day Out*. But the movie it refers to most insistently and overtly is, of all things, *Hello, Dolly!*, a worn videotape that serves as the title character's instruction manual in matters of choreography and romance.

That old, half-forgotten musical, with its Jerry Herman lyrics crooned by, among others, Louis Armstrong, is also among Wall-E's mementos of, well, [j]. He is a dented little workhorse who, having [k] his planned obsolescence, spends his days in the Sisyphean, mechanical labor of gathering and compacting garbage. His name is an acronym for Waste Allocation Load Lifter- Earth Class. But not everything he finds is trash to Wall-E. In the rusty metal hulk where he and the cockroach take shelter from dust storms, he keeps a carefully sorted collection of treasures, including Zippo lighters, nuts and bolts, and a Rubik's Cube.

Wall-E's tender regard for the material artifacts of a lost civilization is understandable. After all, he too is a

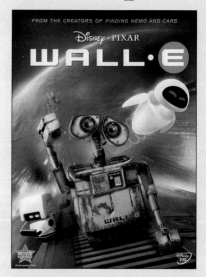

product of human [l]. And the genius of *Wall-E*, which was directed by the Pixar mainstay Andrew Stanton, who wrote the screenplay with Jim Reardon, lies in its notion that creativity and self-destruction are sides of the same coin. The human species was driven off its home planet – Wall-E eventually learns that we did not die out – by an economy consecrated to the manufacture and consumption of ever more stuff. But some of that stuff turned out to be useful, interesting, and precious. And some of it may even possess something like a soul.

Observing Wall-E's surroundings, the audience gleans that, in some bygone time, a conglomerate called BnL (for "Buy N Large") filled the earth with megastores and tons of garbage. Eventually the corporation loaded its valued customers onto a space station (captained by Jeff Garlin), where they have evolved into fat, lazy leisure addicts serviced by a new generation of specialized machines. One of these, a research probe named Eve (all of the robot names are acronyms as well as indicators of theoretical gender) drops to Earth and wins Wall-E's heart.

Their courtship follows some familiar patterns. If *Wall-E* were a romantic comedy, it would be about a humble garbage man who falls for a supermodel who also happens to be a top scientist with a knack for marksmanship. Wall-E is a boxy machine of the old school, with creaks and clanks and visible rivets, his surface pocked with dents and patches of rust. He is steadfast, but not always clever or cool. Eve, shaped like an elongated egg, is as cool as the next iPhone and whispers quietly, unless she's excited, in which case she has a tendency to blow things up. She and Wall-E communicate in chirps and beeps that occasionally coalesce into words. Somehow their expressions – of desire, irritation, indifference, devotion and anxiety, all arranged in delicate counterpoint – achieve an otherworldly eloquence.

Rather than turn a tale of environmental cataclysm into a scolding, self-satisfied lecture, Mr. Stanton shows his awareness of the contradictions inherent in using the medium of popular cinema to advance a critique of corporate consumer culture. The residents of the space station, accustomed to being tended by industrious robots, have grown to resemble giant babies, with soft faces, rounded torsos and stubby, weak limbs. Consumer capitalism, anticipating every possible need and swaddling its subjects in convenience, is an infantilizing force. But as they cruise around on reclining chairs, eyes fixed on video screens, taking in calories from straws sticking out of giant cups, these overgrown space babies also look like moviegoers at a multiplex.

They're us, in other words. And like us, they're not all bad. The paradox at the heart of *Wall-E* is that the drive to invent new things and improve the old ones – to buy and sell and make and collect – creates the potential for disaster and also the possible path away from it. Or, put another way, some of the same impulses that fill the world of Wall-E – our world – with junk can also fill it with art.

A.O. Scott, *New York Times*, 2008

---

1 Which words go in the gaps **[a]-[l]** in the text? Choose from the table below.

alluding	easily	ingenuity	us
approximately	extinction	lacks	verbatim
barely	existence	light	we
bereft	gloomily	lived	will
darkens	highlighting	muses	wit
disarmingly	illuminates	outlasted	wonders

2 Answer the following questions.
   a Who are the main characters in *Wall-E*?
   b Which phrase between lines 1 and 15 shows the reader that there is plenty of evidence that life existed on Earth in *Wall-E*?
   c What does 'this sombre theme' (line 21) refer to?
   d Whose films is *Wall-E* compared to in lines 25–28?
   e Which word between lines 43–48 shows that *Wall-E* clearly refers to *Hello, Dolly!*?
   f To which film does 'That old, half-forgotten musical' (line 49) refer?
   g What does Wall-E stand for?
   h What items does Wall-E collect?
   i Why is *Wall-E* considered brilliant?
   j Why did the human beings in *Wall-E* leave planet Earth?
   k How is Wall-E a 'boxy machine of the old school' (line 105)?
   l Which word between lines 108–120 is closest in meaning to 'combine'?
   m To whom are the human beings living on the space station compared in lines 121–140? What does this show about the corporate consumer culture?
   n What is *Wall-E*'s main theme?

3 Refer to lines 84–151. The sentences below are either true or false. Choose the correct response and then justify it with a relevant brief quotation from the text.
   a In *Wall-E*, the audience is told about BnL.
   b *Wall-E* is a romantic comedy.
   c Wall-E is committed and intelligent.
   d Eve is not always calm and quiet.
   e Consumer capitalism has the power to make people act like babies.
   f The human world is similar to *Wall-E*'s world.

➤ Al Gore's *An Inconvenient Truth* is not the only documentary that highlights environmental concerns. Find other documentaries which discuss the issue in an anglophone culture and note down the similarities and differences in how the documentaries address environmental issues. How are the same issues addressed in your culture?

➤ The media are used to support a number of issues other than environmental ones. Listen to Martina Mcbride's *Concrete Angel*, Susan Vega's *Luka*, and Babyface's *How Come, How Long*. Which social issue do these songs emphasize? Can you think of other songs in English which highlight other social issues?

➤ Documentaries are powerful tools with which to raise public awareness. Morgan Spurlock's *Super Size Me* and Michael Moore's *Sicko* are two examples of documentaries which address health issues. Watch the documentaries (both can be found on *YouTube*). What issues do the documentaries highlight?

Developing writing skills: Informal correspondence (letter or email)

1 Watch *Wall-E* and then write your own film review.

2 Write a letter or an email to a friend of yours in which you tell him or her about *Wall-E* and recommend that your friend watch the film.

3 Exchange your email or letter with that of the person sitting next to you. How does this letter or email compare to the review you have previously written in terms of: tone, register, style, and sentence structure? Write your observations down.

4 Write a set of instructions to be distributed to your classmates on how to write a review in a letter or an email. You may consult online sources but remember to cite the sources you consult.

The personal response

Based on the stimulus, give a personal response and justify it. Choose any text type you have studied in class. Write 150–250 words.

'Consumer capitalism, anticipating every possible need and swaddling its subjects in convenience, is an infantilizing force.'

Before you write,

- determine the communicative purpose of your response. Are you writing to inform, describe, persuade or analyse?
- decide on the approach you will adopt to respond to the stimulus. Will you adopt the one-sided, the balanced but undetermined, or the analytical approach?
- choose the type of text which will best communicate your purpose.

Interactive oral activity

Watch another film which discusses ecological problems and in groups, discuss the film.

- What ecological themes does the film portray? How does the film present its themes?
- Is the cast suitable?
- How successful (or not) are the cinematographic techniques like backlighting, camera angle, flash-forward, etc.? (You may need to look into cinematographic techniques before you discuss the film.)

> **Remember**
>
> The informal letter and the informal email are similar in their style: their tone and register are similar, for they both depend on the nature of the relationship between the addresser and the addressee. Nevertheless, the letter and the email have different layouts: When writing an informal letter, write your address at the top right-hand corner of the page. This should be followed by the date. When you write an email, make sure you give the 'From, To, Subject and Date' fields, even though those are automatically generated when one writes an email.

BEFORE YOU READ

→ Many teenagers nowadays have Facebook and Twitter accounts. How do you think this is affecting their lives both positively and negatively?

→ What are the dangers associated with social networks?

→ What is the difference between a regular user of the Internet and an addict? Do you think people who spend a long time sitting in front of a computer screen are aptly called addicts?

→ Do you think children are robbed of a normal childhood because they spend a lot of time playing computer or video games instead of spending their time outside playing 'normal' games?

Social networking

A few poems about Facebook

By Heather Grace Stewart

Dear Friend I've Never Met (The Facebook Poem)

Once upon a time
in the social network race
you and I met
in Cyberspace.

5 Divided by lines:
longitude, latitude;
we've typed and texted
tears, gratitude.

Now we're closer than neighbors;
10 in tune like a song.
(and your dog never leaves
doodoo on my lawn.)

Some say it's not real.
How can it be?
15 How can you trust
what you can't see?

But you sense when I'm down.
This is holy. Sublime.
(Alright, not exactly.
20 But it makes a good rhyme.)

You've read me at my worst.
You've read me at my best.
You've loved me all the same;
forgiven typos, and the rest.

25 You're a microbyte of madness,
and sunshine, and fresh air.
(And faster than FedEx,
so I know you really care.)

I know you'll reply
30 whenever I hit "send".
I know this is real—
you're my Forever-friend.

Lolita

Her name is Lolita.
She's got Double D's.
She's bold and she's beautiful;
She's eager to please.

5 She's got five hundred friends;
She's charming and wise.
They flock to her photos;
She's so easy on the eyes.

Oh so lovely, dark, mysterious.
10 But that's not just a fake tan.
That's one fake old photograph.
That's one smart old man.

A "Dear Facebook" Letter

Dear Facebook:
It's over.
This time it's for good.
Cool! A Fan Page for
5 Boyz n da Hood!

Dear Facebook:
I'm taking
a cyber-vacation.
(Just let me check
10 that notification.)

Like a moth to the flame,
it's always the same.
Leaving's not easy;
weekly won't do.
15 You're using me;
I'm using you.

Dear Facebook:
Deletion.
I think that it's best.
20 (Why do I have to
submit a request?)

Dear Facebook:
Not fair!
Guilt's not very nice.
25 "Your friends will miss you"
made me think twice.

Like a moth to the flame,
it's always the same.
Leaving's not easy;
30 weekly won't do.
You're using me;
I'm using you.

Dear Facebook:
I'm sorry.
35 You win this fight.
Twitter meant nothing!
It was one night!

I'm socially blind–
it's like an abyss–
40 no viral videos;
no urban myths.

Dear Facebook:
You've got me.
We'll never be done.
45 I'd miss all my friends–
and Bieber(RealOne).

Dear Friend I've Never Met (The Facebook Poem)

1 Which word in the first stanza shows that the two friends had a virtual meeting?

2 What have the two friends shared?

3 Why do you think that the relationship between the poet and her friend is deemed 'unreal'?

4 How does the poet describe the way her friend senses her moods?

5 In lines 21-22, the poet says 'You've read me…'. Why does the poet use the verb 'read' instead of 'known'?

6 How does the poet describe her relationship with her friend? What does this show about how the poet regards virtual communication?

Lolita

7 From statements **A** to **H**, select the four that are true according to the poem.
   A Lolita has a good figure.
   B Lolita is coy.
   C Lolita's friends do not like her photos.
   D Lolita has many virtual friends.
   E Lolita has a fake tan.
   F Lolita's photos have been tampered with.
   G Lolita's photos are not the photos of the Facebook account user.
   H Lolita is friends with an old man.
   I Lolita is an old man.

A "Dear Facebook" Letter

8 The poem is a letter to Facebook highlighting the poet's desire to control her 'Facebook addiction'. Copy the table below and fill in the blank spaces with the reasons why the poet is not able to control this addiction.

Reasons why Facebook addiction is not controlled:	
A	There is a new fan page for Boyz n da Hood.
B	
C	
D	
E	

9 What is the significance of the moth and the flame (line 11)?

10 The poet repeats 'You're using me; I'm using you' twice. How is Facebook using the poet?

11 What does the poet mean by 'I'm socially blind–it's like an abyss–' (lines 38 & 39)?

12 To what does '(RealOne)' (line 46) refer?

13 Having read the poems, list all the potential dangers of social networking mentioned in the poems.

➤ Many successful platforms like Facebook and YouTube have been created by young, creative people. Watch *The Social Network*, which describes how Mark Zuckerberg developed Facebook. In the film, how is Mark Zuckerberg portrayed as being very different from other young people his age? In what ways is he typical of his generation?

➤ Look into how social networking platforms like MySpace or Twitter were created. Can you draw any similarities between their creation and that of Facebook? What conclusions do you draw?

➤ In addition to being a means of communication, social networks are used for a number of other purposes nowadays. In fact, you can read your favourite newspaper on Facebook and your 'timeline' would show your friends exactly which article you have read and at what time. In your opinion, is this an invasion of privacy? Use a search engine to find out what teenagers in anglophone countries think about invasion of privacy.

➤ In addition to being a useful invention, inappropriate use of the Internet can be very dangerous. Use a search engine quickly to find out what kinds of internet-related crimes were committed in an anglophone country last year. Do all those crimes fall under the same category? What do your findings suggest?

➤ The letter on the right appears in a *Boy Scouts of America* comics book which highlights responsible use of the Internet. Internet technology is changing so rapidly. How relevant is the advice given in the letter? Is it already out of date? If so, why?

➤ What can be done to promote responsible use of the Internet?

Dear Parents,

The internet offers to us and to our children a wealth of information and opportunities to communicate with people from all over the world instantly. The Internet attracts more users each day to enjoy the benefits that this technology offers. Many internet users are children, and while the Internet offers children many benefits, there is also a lot of information on the Internet that is not suitable for children. In addition, the Internet offers a degree of anonymity to individuals seeking access to children for inappropriate reasons.

To let our children enjoy the benefits of the Internet while protecting them from the dangers that may be found there requires parents to participate in their children's Internet experiences. Communication is the key to helping your child use the Internet safely.

One thing parents can do is ask their children about their Internet sessions. Questions such as "What did you do on the Internet today?" or "Did you come across anything that bothered you?" are helpful. It is also important to establish some house rules so your children understand the boundaries for their Internet use. Make sure your children know how to turn off the computer, how to exit a website, and to tell you when they come across information they find upsetting.

While software filters can limit access to websites, there is no substitute for your active interaction with your child about his or her Internet use.

Here are some suggested Internet safety activities for children:

• Create a poster with Internet safety rules and post it by your computer to remind you to be safe while on the Internet.

• With your parents, practise leaving a website, turning off the monitor, and shutting down the computer.

• Choose something you would like to know more about and do a search to find information on that topic.

For more information about Internet safety, try the following Web sites:

• ██████████████████ Site with a lot of information for family Internet safety

• ██████████████████ A web site maintained by the National Center for Missing and Exploited Children with information and activities broken down by age groups and a section for parents and educators

• ██████████████ A booklet for parents published by the Federal Bureau of Investigation, available in both English and Spanish

Writing activity

A young member of your family has recently opened a Facebook account. Write an email to your family member in which you explain to him or her both the benefits and the dangers of children using Facebook.

The personal response

Based on the stimulus below, give a personal response and justify it. Choose any text type you have studied in class. Write 150 to 250 words.

> 'Human beings are human beings. They say what they want, don't they? They used to say it across the fence while they were hanging washing. Now they just say it on the Internet.'
>
> **Dennis Miller**

Interactive oral activity

In pairs, choose one of the following contexts and enact a scenario reflecting your understanding of responsible behaviour on the Internet. Remember that your setting is an English-speaking one, and therefore any examples used need to be drawn from an English-speaking culture or country.

Context 1:
Mother and daughter discuss daughter's latest uploaded photographs on Facebook.

Context 2:
Persuade a person who has no idea about Twitter that they should get an account and use it.

Context 3:
A talkshow host interviews a teenage Facebook user who has started a campaign at school to make young people aware of the dangers of cyberbullying.

The HL Written Assignment

1 Re-read the three poems about Facebook on pages 321 and 322 .

2 What is the main theme in each poem? Summarize the main theme in 30 words. Use your own words.

3 Think of a different perspectives from which to approach the poems and explore these perspectives further. Use mindmapping techniques to expand your ideas.

4 Focus on one major idea that comes from your reading of the poems and think of how you can expand it. This will be your aim.

5 Determine which text type you would like to use in your written assignment. Do not merely choose a text type you would love to write. Think in terms of which text type would best deliver the message you have chosen.

6 After you have chosen your type of text, determine who your audience is. Identifying your audience is very important, for it determines your style, tone, and register.

7 Discuss your ideas with your teacher.

8 Write your rationale. How will the text type, topic, and the audience affect the language of your text? How will the choice of text type affect the structure of your text?

9 Write your assignment (500–600 words).

10 Revisit your rationale and include examples from your assignment that support your choice of topic and text type.

TOK

The artistic process can be used as a means of expression, communication, and education. This creativity extends to the production of media texts which often contain very powerful specific messages for specific audiences. Media texts like advertisements, brochures, and leaflets can be used to create powerful and informative messages which can assist people in their daily lives. However, media products can also be very biased and used for propaganda and indoctrination purposes. Media texts can be used for political purposes or to sell specific products and services. In Media Studies, texts are not simply neutral. They are created objects that can be interpreted by the audience or readers. Often the way we read such a text depends on our cultural and social background. Consequently, different audiences will interpret the same text in different ways.

Stuart Hall, Professor of Media Studies, developed a theory of encoding and decoding media texts. According to Professor Hall's theory, audiences can have three different reactions to a media text, whether it be a film, documentary, or newspaper:

1 Dominant, or Preferred, Reading – how the director/creator wants the audience to view the media text.

2 Opposition Reading – when the audience rejects the preferred reading, and creates their own meaning of the text;

3 Negotiated Reading – a compromise between the dominant and opposition readings, where the audience accept parts of the director's views, but have their own views on parts as well.

For example, the poster on the right was produced by the United States Navy as propaganda during the Second World War. What do you think the preferred reading of the creators of the advertisement was? How might people find an opposition reading to the advert as a comment on gender roles in the 1940s? Can you find other, negotiated, readings of the advertisement?

This ambiguity is also true of photographs. In English B, for example, the photographs you are asked to interpret for your individual oral all have captions. These captions help you to interpret a photograph in a certain way.

How might you interpret this photograph if the newspaper caption was:

1 Mindless rioting hits London (dominant/preferred reading).

2 Striking a blow for freedom (oppositional reading).

3 Frustrated youth protest against the wrong targets (negotiated reading)

How do the different captions change your perspective on the events in the photograph?

On a wider TOK note, who creates the meaning of a photograph: the photographer or the viewer?

Reflection point

- In this chapter you have looked at travel, recreational activities, eco-friendly vacationing, the effect of man on nature, how the media can be used to promote ecological problems and social networking. What has this section taught you about how related the topics you have explored are?
- What role do the media play in shaping our understanding of certain issues? How can the media be used to lend support to certain causes?

- Are human beings affected by what the media project? Or do the media reflect our cultural and behavioural stances?
- How is language used to communicate a message? What should you take into consideration when writing a letter of application, a news report, an interview, an article based on an interview, a proposal, a personal letter or an email?
- What new vocabulary have you learned in this chapter? How will your expanded vocabulary repertoire be of use to you when speaking or writing?

Science & technology

BEFORE YOU READ

The world is moving slowly, some would say too slowly, away from the use of fossil fuels. Scientists have been investigating alternative sources of energy for most of the 20th and 21st centuries.

→ Why is there an increasing sense of urgency to do so?

→ What are the most important types of alternative and renewable energy sources being investigated and put into practice? Make a list and investigate the advantages and disadvantages of each.

→ What about your country? What efforts are governments, organizations and individuals making to introduce new forms of energy?

As part of these investigations, look up biofuels.

→ What are biofuels? Are there different types?

→ Where and how are they produced? Who benefits from their production and use?

→ The text below is titled *The advantages of biofuels*. Can you predict what advantages will be discussed in the text?

Renewable energy

12:43 PM 99%

The advantages of biofuels

Oil prices have a great impact on everyone. Every time there's an increase, people feel it, even if they don't drive a car. Some suggest we use biofuel to lessen the impact of the rising fuel costs.

5 But what is biofuel, and how does it differ from fossil fuel?

Biofuel is produced from recycled elements of the food chain, and from plants. It is used in vehicles, and is considered a sustainable and renewable source of energy, as compared to the majority of liquid and gas fuels used today. Conventional

Los Angeles: Is this where we are heading?

10 fuels are fossil-based, and there are limited sources available. These sources are depleting fast, and if we don't find a good replacement, one day our cars will basically stop running.

Types of Biofuels

Biofuels can be used in their pure forms, or they can be blended with other fossil fuels. There are two basic types: biodiesel, and bioethanol. These are currently available on

15 the market and most engines are compatible with them. There is no need to modify one's existing engine in order to use them.

Biodiesel

This type of biofuel is created using a process that combines oil with alcohol, in the presence of a catalyst, to produce either methyl or ethyl ester. The alcohol used can

20 either be methanol or ethanol. The esters are then blended with the standard diesel fuel, or can be used in their pure forms (100% biodiesel). Biodiesel can replace diesel or can be combined with it in such a way that it helps run diesel engines with little or no modifications required. Biodiesel is said to be better for the environment because it produces less in terms of emissions, while at the same time being made from renewable

25 supplies.

Bioethanol

Bioethanol is made by oxygenating various agricultural stocks, such as sugar and starch crops. It can be used in existing engines, although a small amount of conventional fuel is needed for cold starting. Vegetable ETBE (ethyltertbutyl ether) is used at present, as a fuel

30 additive that can enhance octane rating. The vegetable ETBE is a replacement for MTBE (methyl tertiary butyl ether) which is made from unsustainable sources.

Controversy

Biofuel might appear to be a promising renewable energy solution, but there are still some issues that need to be addressed regarding its use. While its use may lower the level

35 of carbon emissions on the planet, the production of biofuel has caused debate. The concern is whether crops should be used for fuel or be reserved for use as food. Hopefully these problems can be resolved. Biofuel might be an inexpensive and renewable source of energy, but people certainly shouldn't starve because of it.

www.livingclean.com, 2009

1   Answer the following questions.
    a   Who is the potential target audience of this text?
    b   Which phrases in the introductory paragraph (lines 1-4) indicate the readership?
    c   What is the purpose of the text?
    d   What has caused the need for alternative forms of fuel for road vehicles?
    e   According to the text what are the advantages of biofuel
    •   for drivers?
    •   for the general public?
    f   What is controversial about the increased use of biofuels?
    g   Which phrase between lines 30 and 37 indicates the writer's uncertainty as to whether the problems caused by biofuels can be resolved?

2   For each of the following words or phrases from the text, choose a word or phrase from A, B, or C that could meaningfully replace it.

a sustainable (line 8)
   A continuous
   B renewable
   C reliable

b depleting (line 10)
   A extending
   B running out
   C altering

c compatible with (line 15)
   A adapted to
   B attuned to
   C well-suited for

d catalyst (line 19)
   A method
   B agent
   C converter

e blended (line 20)
   A mixed
   B moulded
   C reacted

f modifications (line 23)
   A revisions
   B settlements
   C adjustments

g emissions (line 24)
   A secretions
   B discharge
   C production

h conventional (line 28)
   A predictable
   B usual
   C humdrum

i enhance (line 30)
   A boost
   B maintain
   C alter

3   Re-read the paragraph entitled *Types of Biofuels* and then copy and complete the following table.

	Biodiesel	Bioethanol
Properties		
Advantages		
Disadvantages		
Solutions to disadvantages		

4   By looking at the diagram below and by using information from the text, write a paragraph to explain how biofuels are produced.

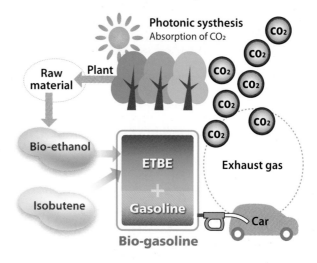

Beyond the text...

➤ Explore the need for finding alternative sources of energy in an anglophone culture and in your own. Why is this an important issue? Or do you believe that the situation has been grossly exaggerated? At the same time, look into the advantages of biofuels and other forms of alternative energy for road transport. How do you think such issues will affect transport, for example, in Great Britain, Canada, Australia, or the United States? How will it affect transport in your country? How do you think you will be affected in your lifetime?

The individual oral

1   Choose one of the photographs below and prepare to talk about it. Before you start, answer the following questions:

  a   Can you identify the English B option and its aspect or subtopic?

  b   What vocabulary do you need to name the objects that seem significant in the photograph?

  c   What can you say about the caption that goes with the image?

2   Present your picture to your classmates.

Biofuels have the power to transform the world!

> ### Remember
>
> For more information about how to interpret a photograph, go to page 141 in Chapter 5

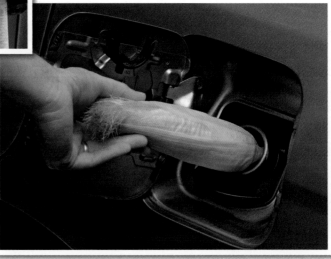

A new source of fuel from the farm to the freeway!

Ethics & science

BEFORE YOU READ

On the face of it, biofuels seem to be a great source of clean and renewable energy. In reality, as we have seen previously, there are serious drawbacks and many experts are very sceptical about their overall benefits.

→ In the research you carried out about the topic earlier, what disadvantages have you found? Which, in your opinion, are the most serious? Which issues do you think might be mentioned in the following text in which one such expert voices her deep misgivings about the current production and use of biofuels?

RUNNING CARS ON BIOFUELS CAN BE 'UNETHICAL'

Green targets to run our cars on plants are in danger of driving slavery, world hunger and climate change, according to a damning new report into the ethics of biofuels.

5 Biofuels could drive deforestation if not properly monitored.

The UK is currently signed up to European targets that dictate that by 2020, 10 per cent of transport fuels must come from biofuels like 10 sugar cane, corn or palm oil.

But an independent study by the Nuffield Council on Bioethics said the target is already back-firing because the crops are taking land away from food production and therefore driving 15 up food prices.

Production of cheap biofuels in developing countries is also driving slave labour and human rights abuses.

Worst of all, biofuels are failing to bring 20 down greenhouse gases, even though the policy was designed to fight climate change because production is so energy intensive.

At the moment, the UK gets 3 per cent of transport fuels from biofuels, but only a third is 25 from certified 'ethical sources'.

The Nuffield study said there must be a compulsory certification scheme for all biofuels imported into and sold in Europe in order to ensure that the 2020 target actually helps the 30 planet rather than causing worse problems.

Professor Ottoline Leyser, of the University of Cambridge, said the targets would be 'unethical' if they are met without ensuring biofuels are produced in a sustainable way.

35 She suggested more biofuels should be produced in Britain from waste products, straw, 'energy grass' or willow. There should also be more research into 'second generation' biofuels, for example algae grown in tanks in the desert, 40 that are better for the environment and do not take land away from food.

"Doing nothing is actually an immoral position. We need to address these issues urgently," she said.

Louise Gray,
The Daily Telegraph, **2011**

1 Answer the following questions.

a How does the attitude of the writer of this text differ to that of the writer of *The advantages of biofuels* on page 328?

b Find two phrases between lines 1 and 6 which clarify the writer's attitude to biofuels.

c What event triggered the writing of the article?

d What is the meaning of the phrase 'the target is already back-firing' (lines 12-13)?

e According to the text, what are the two biggest ethical problems with biofuel
- for consumers?
- for agricultural workers?

f In the context of the text, why is the UK increasing its use of biofuels for road transport?

g What is paradoxical about the increased production of biofuels?

h What is an 'ethical source' of biofuels?

i What is the meaning of a 'compulsory certification scheme' (line 27) for imported biofuels?

j According to Professor Leyser, what is potentially unethical about the continued import of biofuels?

k Which alternative products does Professor Leyser suggest for use as raw materials for biofuel?

l What solutions does Professor Leyser offer to this controversy?

2 Re-read the texts *The advantages of biofuels* and *Running cars on biofuels can be 'unethical'* on pages 328 and 331. Copy and complete the following table. What is the attitude of each author to the issues mentioned in the chart? To what extent does each text offer a solution?

Issues	Attitude: The advantage of biofuels	Solutions: The advantage of biofuels	Attitude: Running cars on biofuels can be 'unethical'	Solutions: Running cars on biofuels can be 'unethical'
Energy scarcity				
Economic issues				
Environmental issues				
Ethical issues				
Other?				

The individual oral

Study the following photgraphs.

Biofuel is the future: It's green, safe and environmentally friendly.

We need solutions now! Anything is better than this!

Is this a sustainable future?

Cycling - The green alternative?

Can solar power offer an alternative?

Wind turbines - Are they the way forward?

1 Study the photographs and choose one to present to your classmates. Your presentation should not exceed 4 minutes.

2 Begin by identifying the English B option and the subtopic illustrated by the photographs, and jot down ten points on what is important (or most difficult) to remember. Remember that your opinion is important and it should be heard; therefore, do not rely solely on being informative. State your viewpoint and defend it.

3 Be spontaneous: do not try to memorize your points.

4 Evaluate a classmate's presentation against the IB Individual Oral Assessment Criteria (Language B Guide, p. 55). What advice would you offer your classmate to improve his or her presentation?

Beyond the text...

➤ Biofuels are just one alternative energy source that science is examining as a potential replacement for fossil fuels. Research other alternative sources of energy. These include: tidal power, wave power, solar power, wind power, hydroelectricity, radiant energy, geothermal power, biomass, compressed natural gas, and nuclear power. What are the advantages of each? Can any or all of these replace our limited supply of fossil fuels?

➤ Go to the following website: www.ted.com By typing 'Steven Cowley: Fusion is energy's future' into the Search bar, you will find a video of a provocative presentation about another possible energy source: Fusion. Do you think fusion will replace fossil fuels in the future?

➤ On the same website, search for a video called: 'Saul Griffiths: Kites as the future of renewable energy'. Watch the video and research other sources to see if wind power is already being used as an energy source in some anglophone countries. Why? Why not?

TOK

Ethics is the study of morality. Morality in general is concerned with what is 'right' and what is 'wrong'. In the case of arguments for and against biofuels, how can we know what is 'right' and what is 'wrong'?

Developing writing skills: Essay

What is an essay?

An essay is a piece of writing in which you can state your organized thoughts on a topic. The essay is an essential tool in school and an invaluable cross-curricular skill. Well-written, well-organized essays receive good marks. Therefore, you should communicate your ideas clearly and persuade your audience that your opinions and facts are reliable.

Structure

All essays have four essential components:

- A question or stimulus

- An introduction with a thesis

- Body paragraphs with topic sentences

- A concluding paragraph containing a final thought.

Here are some essay titles based on texts *The advantages of biofuels* and *Running cars on biofuels can be 'unethical'* on pages 328 and 331.

Write 250–400 words.

1   Which are greater: the advantages or the disadvantages of biofuel?

2   Can opponents realistically oppose the use and development of biofuels?

3   A world without alternative energy sources is doomed.

4   Scientists never agree so we can never know who is right and who is wrong.

5   When debating the fuel crisis, which comes first: economics or ethics?

Remember

Some further pointers and tips

- Does your opening paragraph contain a thesis statement? The thesis is your main idea and can take the form of the answer to the question you are about to answer.
- Is your work arranged in paragraphs? Does each paragraph contain a topic sentence? Do the paragraphs follow one another in logical order?
- Do you give clear, justified examples for each point you make?
- Have you used cohesive (linking) devices such as 'therefore', 'consequently', 'on the other hand', to make logical links between the paragraphs?
- Does your final thought clearly relate to your thesis statement?

TIP

By underlining your thesis statement, topic sentences, and conclusion, can you summarize your argument? If you can, the chances are your essay is coherent.

BEFORE YOU READ

→ There have been many examples in literature, particularly science fiction, in which scientists experiment with the creation (and destruction) of human life. One of the earliest and most famous examples is *Frankenstein* by Mary Shelley. What other books and films deal with similar issues?

→ What are stem cells? Why is embryonic stem cell research so controversial? What ethical arguments are used in favour of and against this research? What scientific arguments are used by defenders and opponents of the research?

→ The article below is titled *Top 10 arguments against stem cell research*. What do you think some of these arguments might be?

Mary Shelley
Frankenstein

OXFORD WORLD'S CLASSICS

Top 10 arguments against stem cell research

Embryonic stem cell research has been in the [a] focus for many years and has gathered a lot of [b] to stem cell research from the public and religious groups. Some believe that there's a lot of [c] in the embryonic stem cell research as only this cell has the [d] or repairing damaged nerves, organs and tissues, and curing hundreds of deadly diseases. On the other hand, a lot of people [e] their arguments against stem cell research and believe it's highly [f] and even murderous to destroy a human embryo for a [g] possibility of finding a cure or helping someone in need. Here's a list of the top 10 arguments against stem cell research:

1 Destruction of a human embryo that has a potential to grow into a baby is necessary to receive a portion of stem cells, which is inhumane in itself.

2 There has been virtually no real successful cure or even a potential for cure found to support destroying the beginning of life. There's no evidence that a destroyed human embryo will help someone.

3 Stem cells for research can be successfully obtained from other sources like umbilical cord stem cells, amniotic fluid or adult stem cells.

4 By allowing therapeutic cloning or genetic engineering of human organs, tissues or embryos we open up a door to research programs with devastating consequences.

5 Embryonic stem cell research is a costly and unethical way to obtain scientific accomplishments; it takes away funding from more ethical and successful research programs.

6 Adult stem cells are far more effective in treating disease-affected tissue than embryonic cells, as the latter have a possibility of being rejected by the body or later develop into a tumor mass.

7 Another strong set of arguments against stem cell research is that some believe that an embryonic stem cell is not stable and might on a DNA level carry a possibility of genetic disorders in itself.

8 Stem cell therapy treatments have not been thoroughly studied and could result in the evolution of even more dangerous and deadly diseases still unknown to humanity.

9 Multiple animal studies in the stem cell therapy have proven to be ineffective and dangerous and do not justify the cost of a human embryo.

10 The actual cost of such treatments is simply too high to be implemented on a large scale.

www.healtharticles101.com

1   Some of the words have been removed between lines 1 and 19. From the box below, choose the word which best fits each of the gaps labelled **[a]-[g]**. Do not use the same word more than once.

| average | controversial | defend | faint | flexibility |
| opposition | negative | potential | research | unethical |

2   Answer the following questions.

  a   What is the main argument given in favour of embryonic stem cell research?

  b   According to the text, what is the main argument against embryonic stem cell research?

  c   To what does the phrase 'in itself' (lines 24-25)?

  d   In line 42, what does the phrase 'open up a door to' suggest?

  e   To what does the phrase 'the latter' (line 54) refer?

  f   In what ways could the title be seen as inaccurate or misleading?

The individual oral

In pairs, discuss the photographs below. Which one would you prefer to receive for your individual oral? Why?

Outline the points you would want to emphasize should you get a similar photograph in your individual oral.

Discuss your points with your partner. Which would you keep and expand? Which do you deem too dry or irrelevant? Why?

TOK

Re-read *Top 10 arguments against stem cell research* on page 336 and put the arguments 1-10 in order from the strongest to the weakest.

Justify the reasoning behind your list.

Hint: Can you use the TOK ways of knowing to help you make decisions about the order in which you place the 10 arguments from the text?

Follow up: Share your findings with the rest of the class and work out collectively which seem to be the strongest and which the weakest arguments. Do you feel you have sufficient information to make an informed decision about all of the arguments? If not, how would you proceed?

Is it right just to look at one side of an argument or should you find out what the supporters of stem cell research say before you consider its rights and wrongs?

All scientific research benefits mankind in the long run

Stem cell research - A moral dilemma?

Beyond the text...

  ➤   In the US, the pros and cons of embryonic stem cell research have gained a lot of attention due to President Barack Obama lifting a ban imposed by the previous American administration. Why has the issue been so controversial in the US?

  ➤   Given the arguments you have read in the text on page 336, do you think an opposing argument is valid? Is the same controversy being raised in your own country? What arguments are used by the opposing sides of the argument? On what TOK ways and areas of knowledge do they base their arguments?

Scientific research

Sci-fi brought to life as spray allows scars to heal themselves

A cosmetic clinic has become the first centre in Scotland to use stem cell therapy to help heal burns and scars.

5 Sculpta Clinic in Glasgow is one of just six in the UK to use the treatment, dubbed "spray-on skin", which uses the body's own ability to heal itself.

10 The treatment can also be used to treat vitiligo (a disorder that causes depigmentation of patch acne and burns scarring), say clinicians.

15 The Glasgow centre is the only one in Scotland to be part of a roll-out of the treatment, which was originally used to treat those burned in fires.

20 It is most effective in those patients where only the upper layers of skin are damaged.

Dr Mohammad Ahmad, clinical director at the Sculpta Clinic, 25 said: "It really is the next generation of treatment and brings the magic of science fiction to life. Thanks to the technology involved, patients 30 suffering from debilitating burns, horrific scarring, vitiligo, pigmentation and aged appearance are now able to heal properly, leaving them 35 with no traces of the previous affliction."

The technique uses a sample of skin cells from a concealed area of the body, usually from 40 behind the ear, in a biopsy of around 2mm in size. These are then placed in a special enzyme solution to loosen critical cells which are then harvested.

45 The patient's skin is then treated with a laser to remove the top "dead" layers of skin to create a fresh surface to boost uptake of the solution.

50 A solution of stem cells in a suspension is then sprayed on to the treatment area and it is covered with a dressing for seven days.

55 The clinic says results of a one-off treatment are seen within weeks, with scars "virtually" gone within a year. But Dr Ahmad admitted the therapy 60 was not an instant solution – it takes time as it is simply a catalyst for the natural healing process of the skin. He said: "So far we have had two patients 65 use the treatment and even within just a few weeks they are happy with the way their skin is healing and are looking forward to seeing how the 70 area improves over the coming weeks and months."

Treatments are not cheap at £3,500 a time, but are ethical as the method of using a 75 patient's own cells – and only on them – is not seen as controversial.

Dr Kieren Bong, a cosmetic doctor who runs Essence clinic 80 in Glasgow, said: "I have heard of stem cell research being used for burns victims.

"It's a very new technology with very promising signs. 85 Studies have been very encouraging.

"But it is something that is not completely understood and we need more long-term data 90 before we can say it is safe for everyone.

"We need more long-term data on the effects of using new cells generated from stem cells."

Fiona Macleod, 2011

www.scotsman.com

Case study 1:
Treatment has given me my life back

By FIONA MACLEOD

Jacqueline Gemmel from Glasgow spent years hiding indoors after suffering burns caused by a steroid cream her GP prescribed for a skin rash in 2003.

5 She said: "It was horrific; it looked as if I had been branded. It was dreadful, swollen and weeping and felt like it was on fire. My esteem went through the floor and I went into hiding."

After researching on the internet for years to 10 find a solution she stumbled upon ReCell.

With the financial help of her family, she was able to undergo treatment at the end of March. She said: "What put me off at first was whether it was ethical because it could be embryonic 15 cells and the fear of rejection. But it's your own cells and that means there is no rejection."

She added: "It was a little uncomfortable, but not as much as I thought it would be. There was no pain afterwards and already my eyes 20 are definitely better and I don't have a rash anymore. It's given me my life back."

Case study 2:
I have my life back

RUSSELL Turnbull is one of those who have already benefitted from the treatment.

Mr Turnbull, was on a bus on 1994 when he intervened in a fight and was sprayed in the eye 5 with ammonia.

Doctors told him the attack had damaged stem cells in his cornea, leaving him with severely impaired vision – as though he was 'looking through Perspex'.

10 "It completely ruined my life," he said, "It was as though everything was on hold, I was a very active person and cycled and jet-skied but I couldn't do that anymore."

Mr Turnbull, from County Durham, spent 12 15 years in 'a living hell' before he was asked to take part in the trial.

Now the 38-year-old's sight is almost as good as it was before the attack.

"I'm working, I can go jet-skiing again and I 20 also ride horses," he said, "I have my life back thanks to the operation."

1 The sentences below are either true or false. Choose the correct response, and then justify your answer with a relevant brief quotation from the text.

   a Spray-on skin is a chemical treatment.

   b Spray can be used to treat several types of damaged skin.

   c The treatment leaves some scars.

   d The technique uses the sufferer's own skin cells.

   e The skin cells are placed in direct contact with the damaged skin.

   f The healing process lasts only a day or so.

   g The medical treatment is very cheap.

   h Most doctors believe the spray-on skin treatment is safe.

   i Jemma Gemmell was immediately certain that the treatment would be ideal for her.

   j Jemma's treatment has only been partially successful.

2 Copy the sentences and fill in the blank spaces below with the relevant information from the text.

   a Skin cells are usually taken from …………………..

   b Doctors undertake a ………………….. in order to …………………..

   c The cells are placed in a special enzyme solution so that …………………..

   d This ………………….. the cells.

   e The doctors can then …………………..

   f A laser ………………….. a layer of damaged skin.

   g A fresh surface of skin …………………..

   h A spray is used to …………………..

   i The doctors must then …………………..

   j This enables the cells …………………..

3 Answer the following questions.

   a What disability was stem cell treatment originally designed for?

   b On which patients is stem cell treatment most successful?

   c Name two advantages of stem cell treatment.

   d What mechanism actually heals the damaged skin?

   e What role does the stem cell treatment play in the healing process?

   f Why is this kind of stem cell treatment considered ethical?

   g Why does the treatment give grounds for optimism?

   h Why does the treatment give grounds for caution?

   i What is the practical advantage of using the patient's own cells?

   j What is implied by the headline 'Treatment has given me my life back'?

Beyond the text...

Cloning pets

Here is another scientific breakthrough you might like to ponder:

The world's first cloned dog was an Afghan hound named Snuppy in 2005. Since then, several others have been created including copies of police sniffer dogs, but this is the first commercial success. Cloning arouses furious opposition. Critics argue that not enough is known yet about the effects on an animal's lifespan, or physiology. Of the species cloned so far, some have suffered from faulty immune systems and many have died prematurely. Opponents are also appalled at the sheer number of embryos that have to be destroyed or are spontaneously aborted.

With pet cloning there are concerns that people genuinely believe they will be getting their dead animal back. It is not pet resurrection. It may look like the deceased and, genetically speaking, it is effectively a later-born identical twin, but it is not the same animal. Behaviour and character are the result of a complex interplay of factors: nutrition, environment, and perception of the world, for example. It is not a perfect copy of the original. Cloning companies insist they are offering a valuable service, citing anecdotal evidence of behavioural similarities between clone and original in cats.

Pet cloning looks like it is here to stay. There is also a large market of potential customers who are unwilling to accept the fact that their precious animal has left the planet and cannot be brought back. It appears they would prefer a clone rather than the much cheaper option of buying a new pet.

How do you feel about this issue? Is science going too far? Will the cloning of humans be the next scientific development?

What next?

Developing writing skills: Speech

Writing to a specific audience

When writing a persuasive speech, you must first decide which side you wish to take on the topic under discussion. You will also have to consider your audience and how you are going to convince them of your point of view. (Revisit Aristotle's modes of persuasion in chapter 2 on page 34 and the information on the following page. Therefore, you need to consider the angle you will take. Be clear about your purpose: is it to persuade, inform, demonstrate, or entertain? Or should your speech combine some of these functions? Whatever your angle, make sure you connect with your audience. Use direct address, 'you', but be careful with the use of the pronouns. How you address your audience can radically affect your relationship with them. For example, there are two meanings of 'we': "We will solve this together" suggests partnership. On the other hand, "We give you the choice" suggests a distance and difference between you and your audience with you having more power. Which form of address is appropriate for your speech?

Four approaches to the persuasive speech

Below are four basic methods of arranging the body of your speech. Choose the one most appropriate for your needs.

- **Thesis**: You have a point of view that you wish to prove.
- **Cause and effect**: You show that event *A* happened, so event *B* occurred. This results in *C*.
- **Problem and solution**: You state that the problem is *X* and the solution is *Y*.
- **Advantage and disadvantage**: You examine the positive and negative aspects of an idea or event.

Concluding

Your conclusion might contain a summary of your key ideas. You can do this by re-stating your thesis statement or question, and then restating your key ideas from the body of your speech. Remember to restate the benefit of your ideas to your audience. End with a bang, not a whimper! The final sentence should be a clincher or call to action.

> *"The 21st century awaits us. Let us confront its challenge with confidence, and together give our children the future they deserve."*
> (**Tony Blair**, British Prime Minister, 26 November, 1998)

TOK

Biotechnology is radically changing the world: genetically modified food, biofuel technology, stem cell research and cloning are examples of these rapid changes. To what extent is it true to say that these technological advances change our moral values? Are there any areas of scientific knowledge which are still morally unacceptable?

Using rhetorical devices in speeches

If the purpose of your speech is to persuade your audience, you must convince them that your ideas are correct.

Personal commitment or experience

"I went to segregated schools, swam in segregated swimming pools, sat in all-white sections at the movie... By the grace of God, I had a grandfather... who taught me it was wrong."
(*Bill Clinton, US President, San Diego, June 1997*)

Statistics

"In 1960–61, the per capita Government spending on African students at State-aided schools was estimated at R12.46. In the same year, the per capita spending on white children in the Cape Province was R144.57."
(*Nelson Mandela, Rivonia trial, 1942*)

Another method of persuasion is to appeal to the audience's emotions. To make your ideas seem more persuasive, put rhythms and patterns into your language.

Lists of three

"Friends, Romans, countrymen, lend me your ears."
(*Julius Caesar, William Shakespeare, Act 3, Scene 2*)

"I have nothing to offer you but blood, sweat and tears."
(*Winston Churchill, 1940*)

"There are three kinds of lies: lies, damned lies, and statistics."

(Attributed to Benjamin Disraeli)

Repetition

Repeated sentence patterns suggest almost identical situations and lead to a climax or point.

"I have a dream that one day this nation will rise up and live out the true meaning of its creed... I have a dream that one day on the red hills of Georgia the sons of former slaves... I have a dream that my four little children... I have a dream today."

(*Dr. Martin Luther King Jr., Washington, 28 August 1963*)

CAS

Organize a poster campaign in school on the subject of ethical responsibility in science. Ask your science, IT, and TOK teachers what some of the most urgent issues in areas of knowledge such as biology, chemistry, information technology, environmental science, and physics are. Find out what the ethical and moral issues surrounding each contentious issue are and conduct further research into them. You could create posters to illustrate these various scientific and moral dilemmas. The posters could either represent the issue graphically, or summarize opposing viewpoints. You could 'take the moral temperature' of your school by asking members of the school community to vote for one of the sides in each of the issues. Publish your results in your school magazine.

Writing activity

SL and HL (250–400 words)
- Write a speech either defending or opposing stem cell research.
- Write a speech to your school council on the ethics of using biofuels.
- Write a speech to parents of young children arguing either for or against restricting access to Facebook for under tens.

Communication & media

BEFORE YOU READ

→ The following article examines some of the rapid developments in the use of mobile phones in Africa and south Asia. In her report, the writer uses technical jargon to highlight these advances in mobile phone technology. Make a list of all the technical vocabulary you know which is related to mobile phones and their uses.

→ The writer also describes the ways in which access to mobile phone networks has benefited consumers and small businesses in rural communities. Which benefits do you predict might be mentioned in the article?

→ The writer also highlights some of the remaining barriers to business growth. What do you think might be some of the biggest problems?

The Internet

Cell phones and sustainable development: The future is mobile

On April 12, internet analyst Mary Meeker from Morgan Stanley gave a presentation on Internet trends. Meeker's reports on the "State of the Internet" have long been recognized as important indicators for the present and future directions of Internet and web
5 technology trends. The assertion from Meeker's latest report: the future is mobile. Meeker predicts that in the next five years, mobile Internet will outstrip desktop Internet usage. She contends that 3G coverage has reached a global inflection point. In other words, it will be available to over 20% of the world's cell phone users.

10 Although this ranges depending on location – from 54% coverage in Western Europe to 96% coverage in Japan, from 7% coverage in Central and South American to 12% in Africa – there is little doubt that the push towards mobile technology and mobile Internet access will have profound impacts on the entire world.

15 According to some figures, more than 80% of the world's population now lives within range of a cellular network, a figure that has doubled in the past ten years. As Johanna Hoopes wrote in November, there are more than 4 billion cell phones now in use around the globe, and 75% of them are located in developing
20 countries. Hoopes's article notes the opportunities for both entrepreneurs and end-users: the growth of the mobile operator industry, the development of mobile money transfers.

With the advent of text-messaging and low-cost calls and cheaper phones, mobile technologies have been embraced by
25 consumers, investors, and governments in the developing world. The construction of cellular networks allows for the bypass of government-run telecommunication systems, which can be beneficial in terms of difficult bureaucracies and non-existent infrastructures. It is often easier and cheaper to build and maintain
30 cell towers in remote areas than it is to integrate them into pre-existing telecom networks.

Research has shown that
35 cellphone access helps spur economic growth in the developing world. Cellphones are a powerful communication device in areas that have often been without access
40 to regular telecom service. They allow users to access information, whether for business, medical, or educational purposes. For those without fixed addresses and without bank accounts, a cellphone gives them a place where they can be contacted and a means by which they can pay bills. Unlike other forms of communication,
45 including most web technologies, cellphones do not require literacy (although they can play a role in its development).

There are still many barriers to the spread of mobile technology in the developing world. The cost of phones is still too high for some. Many areas still do not have cell phone coverage. And most
50 importantly, perhaps, many areas do not have the power necessary to recharge the phones. It may be that the pressures to expand mobile technology into the developing world can press forward other sustainable energy projects, such as solar-charging mobile phone stations.
55

Audrey Watters, 2010
www.justmeans.com

1   Read the first paragraph of the text and match each of the words given (**a-j**)
    with the word closest in meaning from the right-hand column (**1-14**).

    a   analyst (line 1)
    b   trends (line 2)   **1**   accelerate   **8**   exposure
    c   assertion (line 5)   **2**   argues   **9**   flexible
    d   mobile (line 6)   **3**   changeable   **10**   forecaster
    e   outstrip (line 7)   **4**   changes   **11**   overtake
    f   contends (line 7)   **5**   claim   **12**   serious
    g   ranges (line 10)   **6**   crisis   **13**   superficial
    h   coverage (line 10)   **7**   decisive   **14**   vary
    i   push (line 13)
    j   profound (line 14)

2   The sentences below are either true or false. Choose the correct
    response and then justify it with a relevant brief quotation from the text.

    a   The majority of people on earth now own a mobile phone.
    b   The number of mobile phone owners has increased rapidly.
    c   There are around 1 billion cell phones in the developing
          world.
    d   Only business owners are benefiting from increased mobile
          phone ownership.
    e   Mobile phone networks need to use government
          communication networks.
    f   Mobile phone networks are integrated into existing networks.
    g   Mobile phones can accelerate economic development.
    h   People without fixed home or bank accounts have better
          economic prospects.
    i   Mobile phones are now universally affordable.
    j   There is no limit to the spread of mobile phone use in Africa.

A new technology for a new economy?

3   Copy and complete the following table by indicating to whom or to
    what the underlined word refers.

In the phrase...	the word	refers to
'75% of <u>them</u>' (line 19)	'them'	
'<u>which</u> can be beneficial' (lines 27–28)	'which'	
'to integrate <u>them</u>' (line 31)	'them'	
'<u>They</u> allow users' (line 40)	'They'	
'in <u>its</u> development' (line 46)	'its'	

4   Answer the following questions.
    a   How is mobile phone technology making banking easier?
    b   How has mobile phone technology helped to avoid unnecessary
          paperwork?
    c   Why are network companies building cell towers in remote parts of
          Africa?
    d   Why do mobile phones assist people who follow a nomadic lifestyle?
    e   What additional advantage do mobile phones have over traditional
          written forms of communication?
    f   Name three potential barriers to the development of mobile phone
          technology in remote parts of Africa.
    g   Which technological innovation might assist the continued expansion of
          mobile phone use?

Interactive oral activity

Imagine working for a telecom company which installs new cell towers in a remote part of an English-speaking country.

You only have the financial means to install one new tower this year. Area A is easily accessible and already has partial network coverage. Area B is remote with no coverage at all. Do you put the tower in Area A or Area B?

This is an opportunity to take some risks in front of an audience and explore different values and ideas. You could have two groups: one supporting the interests of Area A, the other supporting Area B. The rest of the class can be the arbiters and final decision makers.

Area A	Area B
Easily accessible (300 km from the capital)	Remote (1000 km from the capital)
Enjoys partial coverage	No coverage at present
Population speaks the national language	Population speaks a minority language
Community stable	Community vulnerable to external political influence
25% of population own mobile phones	3% of the population own a land line
Some literacy	Population largely illiterate
Small dense population (50,000)	Large widely scattered population (300,000)
High levels of urban poverty	Farming community with low levels of poverty
Few natural resources	Unexploited natural resources
Some bank branches	No banks
Some opportunities for increasing small business	Many opportunities for new businesses
Low cost of installation of a new cell tower	High cost (twice the cost of Area A) of installation of cell tower

The personal response (HL)

Based on the following stimulus, give a personal response and justify it using 150 to 250 words. Use any text type you have studied in class.

> *"I'll admit sometimes I do miss the simple life before mobile phones existed. Being connected to the world at all times comes with an incredible number of perks, but it has huge disadvantages too."*

Telephone

BEFORE YOU READ

The metaphor 'silver bullet' refers to any simple solution which is very effective. In the context of the following text, the idea is that new technological developments will easily cure an existing problem. One problem for many small businesses in Africa is the cost of setting up a business with very little capital.

→ Study the photograph. What do the photograph and the caption suggest about the way people without offices can do business by using a mobile phone?

You can do business anywhere and at any time you like

3 | News

Are mobile phones Africa's silver bullet?

Whether it's checking market prices of crops, transferring money or simply making a call, mobile
5 phones are transforming Africa. But could this new technology end up bypassing the poorest?

The mobile phone is
10 turning into Africa's silver bullet. Bone-rattling roads, inaccessible internet, unavailable banks, unaffordable teachers, unmet medical
15 needs – applications designed to bridge one or more of

these gaps are beginning to transform the lives of millions of Africans, and Asians, often
20 in a way that, rather than relying on international aid, promotes small-scale entrepreneurship.

While access to a fixed
25 landline has remained static for a decade, access to a mobile phone in Africa has soared fivefold in the past five years. Here, in one of
30 the poorest parts of the globe, nearly one in three people can make or receive a phone call. In Uganda, almost one in four has their
35 own handset and far more can reach a "village phone", an early and successful microfinance initiative supported by the Grameen
40 foundation.

One recent piece of research revealed how phone sharing, and the facility for phone charging,
45 has been an engine of this small-business revolution. Particularly in rural areas, a small investment in a phone can first create a business
50 opportunity, then maximize its reach by overcoming the possible limitations of real or technological illiteracy – because the phone operator
55 can make sure the call gets through, and can cut off the call at exactly the right moment to avoid wasting any part of a unit. And what
60 a difference a phone call can make.

Often the mere fact of being able to speak to someone too far away to

347

meet can be a transforming experience. For fishermen deciding which market is best for their catch, or what the market wants them to fish for, a phone call makes the difference between a good return on the right catch or having to throw away the profit from a wrong catch. For smallholders trying to decide when or where to sell, a single phone call can be an equally profitable experience.

But establishing market conditions is just the start. Uganda has pioneered cash transfers by phone through the innovative Me2U airtime sharing service, which allows a client to pay in cash where they are and transmit it by phone to family or a business associate hundreds of miles away. They receive a unique code that they can take to a local payment outlet to turn into cash.

But the market leaders are M-PESA, a mobile money system set up by Safaricom, in its turn an affiliate of Vodafone, in Kenya (although it operates in Uganda now too). Less than three years old, it has 7 million customers and, according to some sources, processes as much as 10% of Kenya's Gross Domestic Product.

At an International Telecommunications Union session held recently, Nokia's Teppo Paavola pointed out that there are 4 billion mobile phone users and only 1.6 billion bank accounts. The huge scope for providing financial services through mobile phones represented by that differential is a tempting prospect for the big players.

One British contender, Masabi, has developed a secure mobile payment system like their *Street Vendor* - which works on old handsets and in most scripts – and another to deal with the international financial regulators that police cross-border cash flows. Masabi has worked with another UK company, Kiwanja.net, that aims to help NGOs and other not-for-profit organisations use mobile technology.

Ken Banks, founder of Kiwanja.net (Kiwanja means "earth" in Swahili) has pioneered a two-way texting system called FrontlineSMS that allows mass texting from a single computer-based source to which individual subscribers can reply.

So, for example, health workers attached to a hospital in Malawi can "talk" to their base to seek advice, pass on news of patients' progress or ask for drug supplies. The data can be centrally collected and managed. All that's needed is a mobile signal – far more available than an internet connection.

The only barrier to even greater mobile use, apart from international financial regulations, is the taxes levied by national governments that can make the cost prohibitive. According to one recent report, despite exponential growth in countries like Uganda, there is growing evidence that what for millions is a life-changing technology risks leaving out the poorest.

**Ann Perkins,
14 January 2011**

1   Answer the following questions.

   a   According to the article, what is the connection between the growth in mobile phone use and the growth of small businesses in Africa?

   b   Why is there a much greater number of users of mobile phones than subscribers?

   c   How can owning a mobile phone create a small business opportunity?

   d   How does the mobile phone assist fishermen and farmers to make a better profit?

   e   How has the mobile phone improved banking services?

   f   Why do some banks see Africa as a huge business opportunity?

   g   Name **two** potential barriers to the development of mobile phone technology that Masabi had to overcome.

   h   What is the unique feature of FrontlineSMS?

   i   How does FrontlineSMS benefit the medical profession?

   j   What is the greatest internal barrier to access to mobile phones among the poorest sections of society?

2   Copy and complete the following table by indicating to whom or to what the underlined words refer.

In the phrase...	the word(s)...	refer to...
...maximize <u>its</u> reach... (lines 50–51)	'its'	
...avoid wasting any part of a <u>unit</u>... (lines 58–59)	'unit'	
...in <u>its</u> turn... (line 97)	'its'	
...and <u>another</u> to deal with... (line 126)	'another'	
<u>The data</u> can be centrally collected... (lines 149–150)	'The data'	
...make <u>the cost</u> prohibitive... (lines 160–161)	'the cost'	

Give explanations for these items of jargon in the text.

   a   'a microfinance initiative' (line 38)

   b   'technological illiteracy' (line 53)

   c   'establishing market conditions' (lines 80–81)

   d   'a local payment outlet' (line 92)

   e   'market leaders' (line 94)

   f   'an affiliate' (line 98)

   g   'a tempting prospect' (line 118)

   h   'the big players' (lines 118–119)

   i   'cross-border cash flows' (lines 128–129)

   j   'exponential growth' (line 163)

> **Remember**
>
> To find the meaning of phrases, you may need to scan carefully the sentences that precede them. The system by which words relate to earlier ideas in a text is known as anaphoric reference.

> **Remember**
>
> For some of the jargon, you may need to consult a dictionary or even an Internet search engine

4   The title refers to a 'silver bullet'. Look at the table and, using the information in the text, fill in as much detail as possible. Some information you may need to infer from the text.

Existing problem	Technological 'silver bullets'	Benefits	Example
Poor communications, schools and healthcare	Greater access to mobile phones		
No increase in land lines	Increased use of mobile phones		
Illiteracy	Mobile phone use for business		
Low prices for produce and products	Long distance communications with markets		
No access to banking	Me2U mobile money system		
Small number of bank accounts	More mobile phone financial services		
Many cannot afford new phones	*Street Vendor* technology		
Poor communications in community health care programmes	FrontlineSMS Two-way texting and mass texting from a single computer		
Difficult to keep health records	Centrally collected data		
High costs	Even greater mobile phone use in the future		

The personal response (HL)

Based on the following stimulus, give a personal response in the form of a speech and justify it. Write 150–250 words.

> *"(The) taxes levied by national governments can make the cost (of mobile phones) prohibitive (....) Despite exponential growth (....) there is growing evidence that (....) a life-changing technology risks leaving out the poorest."*

Interactive oral activity

* Create a presentation on some aspect of mobile phone technology in developing English-speaking country.
* Discuss some of the main features of the technology, its uses, and the advantages and disadvantages for personal and business opportunities.
* Follow this presentation up with a discussion or debate on the merits and demerits of the technology and speculate how the mobile phone will develop in the future.

Developing writing skills

Here are some topics related to mobile phones in Africa.
Write 250–400 words on each.

1   Write an interview with a family of Kenyan farmers or fishermen on how the mobile phone is transforming their lives.

2   Write a speech entitled 'How mobile phones are transforming rural economies'.

3   Look again at the interactive oral activity on page 350. Write an official report recommending one of the areas to receive a cell tower to transmit a mobile phone signal.

4   Using the same stimulus, write a formal letter from a community leader asking a mobile phone signal provider to build a cell tower to serve your community.

5   Write an advertising blurb for a telecom company in an African country mentioning all the benefits and opportunities mobile phone ownership can bring.

6   Write a feature article on the use of mobile phone technology in your own country.

TOK

More and more people have access to mobile phones and the Internet. Does this growth lead to more information or more knowledge? Is the same answer valid for a farmer in Tanzania with access to a community phone and an IB Diploma student in an international school?

Beyond the text...

A great deal of progress is being made in mobile phone access and there are grounds for optimism. However, there remains much to be achieved.

The good news

➤   There is undoubtedly a huge growth in mobile phone access in the developing world.

➤   The developing world's share of mobile phone subscriptions increased from 53% in 2005 to 73% in 2010.

➤   Mobile phone subscriptions increased by 16% in the developing world in 2010, as opposed to 1.6% in the developed world.

➤   Innovations in mobile banking and mobile health are just two areas where new services are transforming people's lives.

The not so good news

➤   Gender and income disparities mean that by no means is everybody able to reap the benefits of the growth in mobile penetration.

➤   While there is excellent signal coverage in the most populated areas, there are vast expanses of almost every African country where there is no signal at all.

➤   In South Asia, Africa, and the Middle East, men are much more likely to have access to mobile phones than women.

➤   In Sub-Saharan Africa, where the 'mobile divide' is slightly smaller than in the other two regions, a woman is 23% less likely to own a mobile phone than a man.

➤   Women are less likely to receive information via mobile phone, relying more in interpersonal communication.

➤   Unequal educational opportunities present another divide. For example, 93% of Kenyans with formal education have access to a mobile phone, as opposed to 50% of those without.

➤   Even when people have mobile phones they may not be able to take advantage of access to a range of information services if they cannot read (despite the existence of projects that use mobile phones to promote literacy).

➤   Despite the advance of cheap mobile banking, in parts of Kenya making a money transaction using the MPESA mobile banking service costs the same as a bag of maize.

Explore these issues further and see what solutions you can offer to the problems mentioned.

Advertising

The following text advertises micro-banking. Conduct some preliminary research on micro-banking and find answers to the following:
→ Who are the potential customers?
→ What services does micro-banking provide?
→ What is the main benefit derived from micro-banking services?
→ Find out more about the Grameen Foundation.

Micro-Banking
Branch-less banking for the un-banked

A simple gap has emerged globally in recent years: the difference between mobile penetration and banking penetration!

5 In most countries, a large number of people do not have access to banking & financial services, whereas they either have a mobile phone or have access to a mobile handset & service. Mobile Wallets can bring low-cost banking & remittance services to millions of 10 such people, especially in developing countries where banking services are not readily available or easily accessible, but the mobile telephony infrastructure is well developed. This offers enormous potential to open new markets and business opportunities for service 15 providers, banks, mobile operators & merchants!

Our technology converts a mobile into a Debit Card, and enables low cost banking to be made available at retail outlets

- Banking agents & customers use mobiles for all
20 transactions

- Deposit, withdraw and transfer funds using mobile phone

- Easy to use; menu driven interface

- Fully secure

25 Benefits:

- Makes low cost, relevant banking services easily available everywhere

- Financial inclusion: anyone with a mobile & ID can get access to low cost banking

30 • Secure way to save money for the un-banked

- Banks extend reach without relying on traditional banking infrastructure

- Significantly increases bank brand & visibility

- Opens new 'bottom of pyramid' segment for banks

35 **Employers can deposit salary directly into micro-banking account.**

Open Account, Deposit & Withdraw Cash,
40 *Check Balance, Transfer Money, Make Payments, Get Statement*

www.esteltelecom.com

1 Answer the following questions.
  a Who is the advertisement written for?
  b What is the purpose of the advertisement?
  c What technology allows the electronic banking system mentioned in the text to function?
  d Give **three** reasons why this represents a great business opportunity for investors.
  e In what ways is the language of the first section (lines 1–15) different from that used in the remainder of the advertisement?
  f In what ways is the layout of the first paragraph different from that used in the remainder of the advertisement? Justify your answer.

2 Who or what are:
  a mobile penetration
  b mobile wallets
  c remittance services
  d telephony
  e menu-driven interface
  f the un-banked
  g reach
  h banking infrastructure
  i bank visibility
  j bottom of the pyramid segment

3 Copy and complete the following table explaining the benefits of the three partners on the micro-banking scheme. In some cases, more than one group may benefit from a single item.

	Advantages to banks	Advantages to customers	Advantages to investors
There is enormous potential to open new markets and business opportunities			
Bank services are readily available and easily accessible			
The technology converts a mobile into a Debit Card			
The system enables low cost banking to be made available at retail outlets			
It is possible to use a mobile for all transactions			
The system is fully secure			
The service makes banking easily available everywhere			
Anyone with a mobile and ID can get access to low cost banking			
It is a secure way to save money			
Customers do not have to rely on a traditional banking infrastructure			
The system significantly increases bank brand and visibility			
It opens a new 'bottom of pyramid' segment of the market			
Employers can deposit salaries directly into micro-banking accounts			
It is easy to open an account, deposit, and withdraw cash,			
It is easy to check a bank balance and get a statement			

Writing activity

1 As a community leader, write a letter to Estel telecom praising the micro-banking scheme they have developed.

2 Write an advertisement aimed at potential 'un-banked' clients and community groups who you would like to encourage to join the micro-banking scheme.

3 Write a feature article for a travel magazine describing the changes that the mobile micro-banking scheme has made to the life of a community.

4 Write an official report by a government official discussing the changes that the mobile micro-banking scheme has made to the life of a community and recommend ways in which the government can help.

Interactive oral activity

In groups, and using the information in the texts from this **communication and media** section, create a presentation on micro-banking and mobile phone banking to be shown to potential customers. Make your presentation as persuasive as possible. Be prepared to answer your classmates' queries.

The personal response (HL)

Based on the following stimulus, give a personal response and justify it using 150 to 250 words. Use a text type you have studied in class.

"This is the moment when we must build on the wealth that open markets have created, and share its benefits more equitably. Trade has been a cornerstone of our growth and global development. But we will not be able to sustain this growth if it favors the few, and not the many."

Barack Obama

To complete the personal response successfully, you may want to consider the following approach:

Brainstorming

• Find reasons for agreeing and reasons for disagreeing with the statement.

• Find evidence (the more concrete the better) to justify your argument. You could put all your information into a table like the one below:

Reasons for agreeing	Evidence	Reasons for disagreeing	Evidence

Assessing the argument

• Which ideas (for or against) seem most valid?

• How strong is the supporting evidence? Is the evidence based on logic, emotions, or sense perception, or more than one of these?

• Note any points on both sides which are only opinions, or where there is little or no supporting evidence or examples.

Approach

Which of the following approaches will you adopt:

- The 'one-sided' approach
- The 'balanced but undecided' approach
- The 'analytical' approach?

Writing

- Take a clear approach and state your main idea.
- Organize a strongly supported and well-reasoned approach.
- Use a separate paragraph for each point.
- Write a clear conclusion.

The SL Written Assignment

Re-read the texts from this section, then choose one of the following:

- A leaflet from a mobile phone network company aimed at potential customers for its micro-banking service.
- A feature article about a family whose life has been transformed by the mobile phone.
- An interview with a health worker explaining how she uses the mobile phone to help her patients.
- A speech about the need for more investment in rural Africa.
- A set of instructions on 'How to set up your own business with just one mobile phone'.
- A blog entry in which you reflect on the changes you have witnessed as a gap year student in Kenya as a result of new technology coming in.

Remember

- Manage your time wisely. Remember that the three to four hours includes time to read the three texts, find a focus and text type, discuss your ideas with your teacher, write an outline, a rationale, and a first draft, and review what you have written. You must also leave time to write your final draft and your rationale.
- Remember to stay on topic. Base your writing on the three written sources selected by your teacher. Do not use more information more than necessary to link your text to the source material.
- Proofread, proofread, and then proofread again. One practical tip is to read your work out loud. If you stumble over a word or phrase, there is probably something wrong.

Beyond the text...

Find examples of the following advertising techniques in the text on page 352:

Argument

An argument is a proposition aimed at the intended audience. It is used to justify the advertiser's viewpoint of the product. There are four main types of argument:

- factual (using facts and statistics)
- definitive (defining the issue)
- evaluative (giving a value judgment)
- advocative (suggesting a solution)

Which types of argument are used in the text?

To what extent are the arguments used in the text based on emotions, sense perception, logic, or language?

Caption

The caption in print advertisements serves to 'anchor' the meaning of the advertisement. The function of anchorage is to reinforce the intended meaning.

What is the caption in the text? Is it effective?

Hyperbole

Hyperbole is the use of deliberately exaggerated language to create emphasis or effect.

What examples of hyperbole can you find in the text?

Register

Register is the deliberate use of a variety of English to create a relationship between the seller and the buyer of the product. Register can change according to the context, purpose of the advertisement, and the relationship between the participants.

What register is used in the advertisement? Find examples.

Why is this particular register used? Which audience is being addressed?

Layout

The organization of text and graphics on the page.

Global communication

BEFORE YOU READ

As the Internet and mobile phone usage increase across the world, more inventors and business people are seeing new ways in which banking, new media, and Information Communication Technology (ICT) can help in the developing world. Many non-governmental agencies are now helping to set up micro-banking schemes.

The following text looks at some of the most recent innovations created by social business entrepreneurs. What could these innovations be? Here are some categories to think about:

→ Building and construction
→ Agriculture
→ Water and sanitation
→ Energy generation and uses
→ Transportation

→ Health care
→ Food preparation and storage
→ Finance
→ Information and communication technologies

Top 5 Mobile Innovations for Social Causes

There are over 3 billion cell phone subscribers in the world, the last billion having been added in just the past two years — largely due to explosive growth in India, Africa, Latin
5 America, and Asia, reports Boston.com. Many new phone subscribers exist in impoverished areas and many entrepreneurs are using mobile technology to help them grow their communities economically. Here are some of
10 the latest innovators in the mobile space that are helping those in need, whether it's an individual, community or the non-profit itself:

RUMA: Business-in-a-Box
Indonesia has incredible cell phone penetration
15 rates and three-quarters of the population live in poverty. The RUMA organization aims to combine the two to empower individuals to emerge from poverty. RUMA sends a 'business-in-a-box' to qualified franchises for
20 $23. The individuals are equipped with a phone, promotional materials and an operating manual to set-up kiosks and sell prepaid airtime to their community. The enterprise has taken off with support from the Grameen Foundation and
25 Qualcomm. RUMA sent over 1,600 micro-franchises in its first five months. The 'business-in-a-box' enables and empowers impoverished individuals to dig their way out of poverty.

Sparked
30 Just as Kiva and the Grameen Foundation revolutionized social cause fundraising through micro-loans, Sparked aims to take that concept and apply it to volunteerism. Sparked's, The Extraordinaries, enables users to micro volunteer
35 by donating only a few minutes of time here and there. Sparked's site lets nonprofits post requests (called 'challenges') that are then routed to volunteers that have the skills to complete the task. Then, when volunteers have a spare
40 moment or two, they jump onto the Sparked mobile app to complete a given task.

Free2Work
As consumers, we vote with our dollar and sometimes that dollar goes to corporations
45 that outsource their labor to manufacturers that abuse employees through humiliation, starvation and rape. Free2Work's new iPhone app aims to educate consumers by rating products, from Apple's iPad to Hasbro's Beyblades,
50 based on the labor practices. The app has a barcode scanner that consumers can use to scan products and while the list of brands and products is limited at the time, Free2Work is building more and more products into its
55 database. Free2Work hopes consumers will put pressure on corporations that have loose morals when it comes to how their products are made.

CCBRT

Mobile banking is surging in Africa, with
60 innovators like FrontlineSMS and PayPal taking
the lead. The Comprehensive Community Based
Rehabilitation in Tanzania clinic (CCBRT) has
created an app that leverages mobile technology
to provide healthcare to women in rural Tanzania
65 using micro-payments. Using Vodafone's M-Pesa
service, "the clinic can send transport grants
directly to patients to cover the average USD 60
cost of a round-trip from rural Tanzania," reports
Springwise. Like CCBRT, there are numerous
70 small startups in Africa that are revolutionizing
communities through mobile devices in highly
targeted and need-based ways.

MoVirtu

More than four billion people do not own a
75 mobile device. And as we've explored, mobile
phones can offer access to healthcare, banking
and entrepreneurship to those that wouldn't
otherwise have access. Movirtu's aim is to
provide mobile services to those four billion
80 without mobile devices through "the cloud."
Movirtu's cloud-based service, called MXShare,
creates cloud phone numbers for anyone
without a phone, so one community could
have one cell phone, but each member of that
85 community could have access to individual
mobile accounts.

Ethan Lyon

1 The sentences below are either true or false. Choose the correct response and then justify your answer with a relevant brief quotation from the text.

a Growth in mobile phone use is restricted to developing countries.

b Internet companies benefit local communities more than businesses.

c In Indonesia poverty is related to mobile phone ownership.

d RUMA employs 'Business-in-a-Box' technology.

e Sparked deploys volunteers to help not-for-profit organisations.

f Free2work informs consumers about workers' rights.

g CCBRT uses existing mobile phone technology to provide healthcare.

h MoVirtu has created shared community phone numbers.

2 Find a word or phrase in the column on the right that could meaningfully replace each word or phrase on the left.

a	subscribers (line 1)	**1**	vast
b	explosive (line 4)	**2**	accelerating
c	franchise (line 19)	**3**	licence to run a business
d	impoverished (line 27)	**4**	hard-up
e	volunteerism (line 33)	**5**	clients
f	nonprofits (line 36)	**6**	philanthropic organizations
g	outsource (line 45)	**7**	influence
h	surging (line 59)	**8**	new companies
i	leverage (line 63)	**9**	subcontract
j	startup (line 70)	**10**	declining
		11	contract
		12	helping for free

3   Answer the following questions.
   a   In what ways are mobile phones being used other than for
       communication?
   b   According to the article, what is paradoxical about mobile phone
       ownership in Indonesia?
   c   How does a 'business-in-a-box' allow franchise holders to make a
       living?
   d   How can volunteers use Sparked services to help nonprofit
       organizations?
   e   How does Free2work empower its target audience?
   f   What is the business relationship between CCBRT and Vodafone?
   g   How does MoVirtu use 'cloud' technology to benefit its customers?
   h   Of the five inventions which do you think is the most useful? Give
       reasons.

4   Copy and complete the following table by indicating to whom or to what
     the word underlined refers.

In the phrase...	the word(s)...	refer(s) to...
...to help them grow their communities economically...(lines 8-9)	'their'	
...whether it's an individual, community or the non-profit itself: (lines 11-12)	'it'	
The RUMA organization aims to combine the two... (lines 16-17)	'the two'	
...when it comes to how their products are made... (line 57)	'their'	
...FrontlineSMS and Paypal taking the lead... (lines 60-61)	'the lead'	
And as we've explored... (line 75)	'we'	

Interactive oral activity

1 Research further into the organizations quoted in *Top 5 Mobile Innovations for Social Causes* on pages 356 & 357. Create a series of presentations showing the work of each organization in detail. Your presentations could be aimed either at customers or potential investors and donors. One way of doing this would be to re-read the information given about each scheme and then represent it in the form of a diagram. You may need to look into each company in more detail. Here are the web addresses to get you started:
   - **RUMA: www.ruma.org.uk**
   - **Sparked: www.sparked.com**
   - **Free2Work: www.free2work.org**
   - **CCBRT: www.ccbrt.or.tz**
   - **MoVirtu: www.movirtu.com**

2 Use the research material from the text on page 356 to present a debate in which five teams, representing each of the five companies mentioned in the text, compete for the prize of 'Social Entrepreneur of the Year'.

Through discussion each group creates a speech for their company describing:
   - its vision
   - its target audience
   - its methods of working
   - the technological background
   - its current successes and future goals.

The class can discuss the merits of each presentation and vote to find which is the most persuasive one and the most convincing product.

The personal response (HL)

Using the quote below as a stimulus, write a personal response to one of the issues dicussed in this chapter and justify it using 150 to 250 words.

"A pessimist sees the difficulty in every opportunity; an optimist sees the opportunity in every difficulty."

Winston Churchill

TOK

24 October is United Nations Day. For the occasion, organize a display to raise awareness of the use of alternative technology and its power to transform lives. You might wish to contact community organizations that are helping people to gain access to mobile phones and examine the economic, educational, and health benefits. You might also want to point out what measures still need to be taken to improve the opportunities of the most vulnerable in the community.

Please read the following text from the RUMA website and then look at the questions below.

RUMA in Numbers

We have over **8,000** micro-entrepreneurs

... who serve more than **800,000** clients.

The number of micro-entrepreneurs we serve is growing **20.4%** per month.

63.7% of our micro-entrepreneurs made less than **$2.5/day** before joining Ruma.

... **10.2%** survived with only **$1.25/day**.

And **90%** are women.

Collectively, they sell **$4,500** worth of prepaid minutes per day.

... which translates to **$1.8/day** additional income.

That may seem small, but it's enough to put **2 kids** through school.

... or 3 meals per day for **2 people**.

After completing the IB Diploma, what will you do in life?
Will you make a difference?

Reflection point

In this chapter, you have explored renewable energy sources and their pros and cons. You also learned about how mobile phones can be used to do business or improve banking services. How related are these topics?

- In this age of technological advancement, what predictions can be made about the future of the Internet?
- How has the Internet affected people's social life?
- Considering everything you have learned about how to write an effective essay or speech, what rules do you have to keep in mind when writing those types of texts?

The written assignment – Standard Level

Below is a sample of an SL written assignment and its rationale. The sample is annotated and commented on by an English B examiner.

Before completing the assignment, the student had studied three texts provided by the teacher, all dealing with the topic of child abuse. The source texts included the lyrics of a contemporary song, an article exploring myths and facts of child abuse and neglect, and two short blog entries discussing child abuse.

Rationale

The aim of this entry is reveal the consequences of child abuse on the society or other members in the public. Taking into considaration the magnitude of this problem, I decided the writer to be a social worker in the US Internal Affairs Department – Social complications branch. This social worker decides to resign since she made a mistake, or rather was deceived by an abusing father. The child dies after the alcoholic father beats him to death.

A diary entry is the most appropriate in revealing the emotions of the writer. Furthermore, the diary is the only 'thing' that now knows the truth behind the whole incident; her boss regards it as a 'simple tragedy'. This worker reveals all of her feelings of the Department's incompitance in dealing with this matter.

The audience of course is the writer herself. Again, this is to show how cases of abuse are generally hidden from the public.

Overall style is similar to that of a normal diary. There are numerous questions to reveal the writer's confusion and state of anger.

177 words.

The assignment does not achieve this; the focus remains on the individual.

This is not related to the aim of the assignment. How does the social worker's resignation demonstrate the consequences of child abuse on society? Needs further explanation to clarify the link between the two: does the resignation of the social worker fall under the consequences of child abuse on other members in the public?

Good justification for the text type.

Why is this significant, especially if the objective is to convey the consequences?

Good, the student shows awareness of how the audience affects the writer's choices.

Some awareness of knowledge gained from reading the source texts.

What is a "normal" diary? The student needs to include examples from the diary to describe the style.

The student shows awareness of style and justifies some aspects of his text.

Dear Diary,   June 22, 1999

I don't actually know if you're 'dear' to me anymore... You know all my vulnerabilities, my secrets, and above all, the fragilness that hides within the rigid mask society forces me to wear. As you know, the past 2 weeks have been the worst in my long 50 years in this cruel world... I've made my decision, one I should have made long ago... I'm going to resign.

Basic conventions of the text type observed.

Relevance?

Sounds like a diary.

Needs explanation; this aspect is not included in the rationale.

Do you remember that child, John? Such an angel he was. I remember him so vividly, playing joyfully in my office... Well, now he's dead. Do you believe that?! Dead. And it's all my fault! I'm the one who was deceived by that wicked and abusing father of his, claiming he has fully recovered from his rage attacks and has become sober again... His blood is in my hands; it's all my responsibility...

I should have noticed! I am the social worker who's duty is to guarantee the safety of the abused children! But what did I do? I sent him back thinking the father has recovered and is now fit to be a loving parent... Huh, a loving parent...

How can I still go on with my life, knowing that I've caused the death of another? How can I escape these constant, haunting images of little John being beaten to death with a hammer? I have failed... And now I'm going to free society of my incompetance, maybe it'll become a better one. I cannot bear this burden anymore... This world is just beyond my understanding and capabilities.

How relevant is this to the aim of the assignment? How does the social worker's resignation highlight the consequences of child abuse?

Do you know what my supervisor said? That idiot claimed it was an "unpredictable situation, simply a tragedy beyond our reach". What did he mean 'simply a tragedy'? Is this loss, this viscous murder a simple act beyond our reach?! If it's not within the US Social Department's reach, who's reach is it within? How can society simply regard this murder a tragedy? I know he's being prosecuted, but that's not enough. Pleading insanity! Well, the judge would be insane if he falls for that...

Some evidence of using the source texts.

And now, my dear friend, my only friend, my career is finished. No more, no more of this pain, no more of this constant incessant pain! Tomorrow I'll complete my letter of resignation. Tomorrow I'll be free of the cruelness of child abuse... A new chapter begins upon the end of this one...

The solution applies to the individual only.

Examiner's comments

Criterion A: Language
With exactly 400 words the diary entry follows the prescribed length. Despite some inaccuracies in spelling and grammar, this SL student uses language fairly effectively. A fairly good range of vocabulary, and some complex structures are used accurately and effectively.

Criterion B: Content
The diary entry focuses heavily on the emotions felt by the social worker, and the topic of child abuse could be generally replaced with any other topic causing distress. It is, at times, difficult to assess the student's understanding of the three source texts as there are few apparent links. The student has missed the opportunity to explore the topic in-depth; for example, the short reported dialogue between the social worker and her supervisor could have been exploited to include information rather than fairly superficial and emotional comments.

Criterion C: Format
The conventions of writing a diary entry are observed. The entry is personal and somewhat reflective.

Criterion D: Rationale
The rationale lacks detail in clarifying the aims and how they have been achieved. The student clearly justifies his/her choice of type of text, but the rationale does not appear to be directly linked to the source texts.

The written assignment – Higher Level

Below is a sample of an HL written assignment and its rationale. The sample is annotated and commented on by an English B examiner.

Rationale

Option to which the task is linked: Literary work, 'Pygmalion' by George Bernard Shaw (1912)

Title: Letter from Mrs. Pearce to her sister

Type of text: A letter ———————————————— A personal letter.

Purpose: Mrs. Pearce wants to share her concern over the bet that Mr. Higgins was placing with her sister. ——— Is this a typo or a case of carelessness?

I wrote the poem in the style that would reflect the time period that Mrs. Pearce was living in. I found it important to show Mrs. Pearce's emotion as it is not portrayed in the play and is only mentioned however not acted upon. Although she is Mr. Higgins' servant, she is portrayed to have a natural instinct that allows her to appear wiser than Higgins himself, "I still find myself worried about the girl". I introduced Mrs. Pearce in the letter to appear as a busy caring woman, "for this I deeply apologise".

> Should be explained; which emotion(s)?
>
> Good justification.
>
> Shows good knowledge and understanding of the work.
>
> This could be explained further. Also, how does the quotation clarify this?

I introduced and put the letter in context in the first part of the second paragraph by having Mrs. Pearce introduce the situation to her sister, "Mr. Higgins has a new client... plans to transform her to a duchess" because the cause of the letter is addressed early on in the letter the rest of it can focus on Mr. Higgins feelings which the reader never has access to in the play. Mrs. Higgins is able to predict the feelings and the consequences that arise from the bet Higgins has placed. She first predicts that Eliza when the bet is won "will not fit in anywhere" and "will have nowhere to go". This is one of the main conflicts that arise in the end of the play.

> The quotations could be integrated better.
>
> Good insight to the literary work.
>
> Mrs. Pearce?
>
> Good evidence of understanding of the play.

Other problems that Mrs. Pearce foreshadows are the fact that Mr. Higgins is "caught up in the fantasy of being the best" and that Mr. Higgins falls in love with Eliza, this is written in the subtext of the play however in the letter I wrote that "he will probably be dreaming of her every night".

Words: 324

My Dearest Sister,

How have you been, the time really does go very fast now a days and I feel as though I have not written to you in quite some time, for this I deeply apologize. I hope all is well with you, at the moment I have been quite preoccupied with work, as always and have recently found myself wondering, how those who are so intellectual can be so naïve? I found that they are probably more ignorant and cannot fathom the idea that there is a consequence to their brilliant ideas.

> Style agrees with the objectives stated in the rationale.

> Mrs. Pearce's qualities as 'a busy caring woman' are highlighted.

Mr. Higgins has a new client and it has become his own little project. She is not the usual foreign client with plenty money to spare, she sells flowers on a street corner. However she did not even ask for his help. The poor girl is part of a bet and he plans to transform her to a duchess. I have no doubt that he can do it, yet I still find myself worried about the girl. What is she to do once the bet is won?

> Interesting choice of pronoun.

> Mrs. Pearce shows concern and empathy.

I even find myself helping Mr. Higgins; I teach her manners that Mr. Higgins does not have the capacity to teach. I realize that I act as a mother to him. I am fond of him and care for him; I make his coffee, and his bed. Despite this I cannot influence him. He will not listen to my advice for at the end of the day, I am only his servant in his eyes, not someone to advise him. I find that the only woman who has ever been able to influence him is his mother.

> In line with the rationale; Mrs. Pearce appears "wiser than Higgins himself".

What am I to do? I wonder if I am overreacting, but at this point I feel like Mr. Higgins is deluded. He is caught up in the fantasy of being the best. At the same time he feels like he is doing her a favor. He knows she would never have been given an opportunity like this. He considers her fortunate, he sees himself as her hero, the man who pulled her from the gutter, the man who saved her from her reality. I often find myself thinking he does not know her reality at all. I have always trusted Mr. Higgins's intelligence and judgments, but he is a selfish man. He always has been. Not in the sense of money of course, just in the sense of pride. In spite of this I think he actually cares for her, as she is different from his other clients. Does he really not understand that once she is taught everything that he knows she will not fit in anywhere?

> UK spelling? When trying to emulate a certain style, consistency is important!

> Apparent knowledge of the work.

> Clever foreshadowing.

I need someone outside of all this to give me some perspective and to help me gather my thoughts. I really appreciate you listening and hope you understand how important and helpful you have been towards me all these years. I hope everything is going well for you and send my best regards to the rest of the family. I love you and miss you terribly and hope to hear from you soon.

> Conventions of personal letters observed; focus on Mrs. Pearce's caring nature.

Love, your sister

> Usually the name or the signature appears on a separate line.

Wimple street, London October 3rd 1913

> Another typo? The name of the street is Wimpole Street.

Examiner's comments

Criterion A: Language
With 529 words the letter follows the prescribed length. The language is fluent, sufficiently varied and complex and with very few significant errors interfering with communication. The attempted style of 'early 1900s' English is not consistent though this is not severely penalized.

Criterion B: Content
The letter is successful in revealing the student's insight of the play. Having Mrs. Pearce voice her concerns in a letter to her sister is a sophisticated way to present the student's understanding and interpretation of the literary work. The connection with the text is obvious, but some of the points could be explained further as the letter, to a certain degree, relies on the reader's prior knowledge of the play.

Criterion C: Format
The student demonstrates good awareness of letter writing conventions, appropriate to the chosen task, but perhaps the letter could include more interaction throughout.

Criterion D: Rationale
Although the rationale occasionally lacks clarity, it successfully introduces the letter and justifies its connection with Shaw's work. The aims of the letter are equally well described as well as some of the choices made by the student in his/her assignment.

Exam practice 3: Paper 1 (SL)

Text booklet
Text A

Ecotourism Australia launches 2011/12 Green Travel Guide

"Ecotourism Australia celebrates its 20th Birthday this year, and this year's Green Travel Guide Australia is a tribute to the growth of responsible and sustainable tourism
5 in Australia," Ms Kym Cheatham, CEO of Ecotourism Australia said. "The 2011/2012 Green Travel Guide Australia features over 1,000 Australian tourism experiences that offer responsible, ethical and sustainable tourism
10 experiences."

The Green Travel Guide Australia 2011/2012 also features the newly launch Eco Lodges of Australia brand, a marketing initiative of Advanced Ecotourism Certified
15 accommodation experience in Australia.

"Australia is globally recognised for outstanding ecotourism experiences. Eco Lodges of Australia offers the ECO-conscious traveller responsible, ethical and sustainable
20 ECO experiences in Australia's most amazing natural locations," Ms Cheatham said.

The Green Travel Guide Australia 2011/2012 also highlights tourism operators who have been ECO certified for 10 years or more,
25 under the logo of the Green Travel Leaders of Australia.

Ms Kym Cheatham said, "Long before most people were thinking about green issues, these businesses saw the importance of creating
30 minimal impact experiences by linking conservation and tourism, and ensuring they behaved in a responsible, ethical and sustainable way."

The Green Travel Guide is the definitive
35 consumer and industry guide to the best in **[X]** responsible tourism experiences in Australia. It is available in **[5]** number of hard copies and **[6]**, which sees nearly 8,000 copies downloaded every year.

40 Ecotourism Australia is celebrating its 20th year this year and its **[7]** programs were announced by the Federal Tourism Minister as one of the first to be included in the **[8]** formed National Accreditation framework, TQUAL on
45 2 April 2011. Ecotourism Australia introduced the world first ECO certification program in 1996 and now has more than 1,000 tourism products certified **[9]** their programs.

www.travelweekly.asia, 2011

Text B

My relationship with my parents

I truly value my relationship with my parents. The role of my parents and my siblings in my life can hardly ever be overstated. To begin with, I should state that my parents
5 have always provided me with support. Their opinion has always played a significant role in my decision making process. Whenever I had a problematic situation over the course of my life, I would necessarily talk to my parents about an
10 issue that generated a seemingly irresolvable dilemma. I could go talk to my father about almost anything. When I was in high school and actually all my way through college, my parents used to give me valuable advice as to what kind
15 of men I should choose for relationships, what classes I should take and what clothes I should put on. They always taught me something. I cannot say that I necessarily followed their advice. The ultimate source that I always
20 refer to when I have to make an important decision is my own brain. I believe that I am smart enough as well as experienced enough to make my own decisions. However, it is always important to consult my parents simply because
25 they might give me a different perspective that I would never think of on my own. Even though their opinion might not be exactly what I am looking for at a particular point in my life, their contribution is extremely valuable. It is hard to
30 explain, but sometimes when I get in a really complex position and I feel that I know the answer to a question that torments me, I go talk to my parents anyway. Most of the time I am totally positive that I will not take their advice
35 and that my own decision is the one that I will take eventually, but it is just important for me to have my parents hear my story and contribute to my decision. In other words, there are times when I need someone to talk to. My parents
40 and my siblings are the only people that I will select for that role.

My parents and siblings provide a great deal of moral support at times of trouble. However, the role of those people in my life is not confined
45 to comforting me when I cannot find a way out of a complex situation. My relationship with my brother and sister is somewhat different. Of course my brother and sister support me

a lot in almost any situation, and I am sure
50 that they are the people that I can count on in case I have a dilemma to deal with. However, there has always been tremendous competition among us in the family. It was always vital for me to outdo my siblings in almost every aspect
55 of life. Back when I was a high school student, I felt like I needed to pick better grades in all the classes that we took together. When it was time for me to pick a university to apply to, I always had to know what schools my brother and
60 sister applied to so that I could apply to a better one. That ultimate desire to be the best in the family has always dominated my personality. At this point I cannot say for sure whether it is a good or bad thing. Sometimes I happened
65 to excel in something and that brought me enormous satisfaction. Other times I would sustain a considerable failure and that would just devastate me completely. Nevertheless, now that I can take a look back at my entire
70 life and consciously evaluate everything I ever did, I can confidently state that I would not have accomplished most of the things that I have ever done in my life had I not had my siblings. They were the source of my energy
75 and my drive, which motivated and inspired me to persevere and keep going even when a situation was bleak and hopeless. My brother and sister are the people that I have to thank for almost everything that I have achieved over
80 the course of my life. I did not realize that when I was younger. Now I can clearly see their role in my life.

Tim Johnson, 2006

Text C

Using online social networking to grow your business

There once was a time when "tweet" was only something birds did and MySpace referred to your apartment. These days, however, those terms have a whole new meaning with the latest trend in communication and marketing
5 called 'social networking'.

What started as a simple way for friends to stay in touch with sites like MySpace and Facebook has merged into the corporate world, quickly becoming a standard in how businesses communicate and market.

10 *How does social networking work?*
Social networking is basically a conversation arena that takes place. Depending on the network you join you might be able to do a daily or weekly update of any news or events taking place within your company. Many social
15 networks also offer interest groups within the network that you can join and talk to others about the topic of interest. This presents a bit of an icebreaker and gives members common ground to start a conversation and take it from there.

20 **[19]**
According to Katie Hellmuth, a New York City-based social networking expert, "Social networking can help your business in unexpected ways. While some believe that it is free-form and without strategy, I believe that there
25 are, at the very least, small, calculated efforts you can make to strengthen brand awareness or alert customers about events and movements within your business. Social networking is people-based. Treat it that way, and residual effects may happen for your business. These
30 effects can include finding an employee, developing a relationship for a future partnership, attracting traffic to your website, announcing a product or sale, and more. The possibilities are up to you."

[20]
35 It depends on your goals and your business. I normally suggest that people join two to four general networks and then possibly one or two that are specific to their industry. This gives people the opportunity to network with others about their business and also to learn from
40 and share ideas with others in their own industry. The idea is to do what is comfortable to you and not over-join since it can be too time consuming to keep up with more than a few.

[X]
Getting started is easy. Once you decide which networks
45 you'd like to join, all you need to do is sign up for an account. In most cases it is free to join although some networks offer members the option of paying a monthly or annual fee for a premium membership to have access to special features or resources on the site that may
50 benefit their businesses.

Once you sign up, you are normally asked to fill out a profile with your name, a picture or logo, website address and other information you want people to know about you and your business. Typically, there is an option
55 that allows you to receive email notifications if someone is trying to contact you or if someone responds to something you have posted. Any time your information changes, simply update that information in your profile.

Oftentimes you can do a search for people you know or
60 import email contacts to see if they are a member of the network. When you find people you know, you can send them an invitation through the network to become one of your contacts. You can use contacts you already know as a starting point and build your network from there.

65 **[21]**
Social networking can be a useful tool in driving traffic to your blog or website. By mentioning your website or blog URL in your networking, people will visit them to get more information about you and your business. One
70 helpful tip is to sign your name with your website or blog address each time you post a question or an answer when networking online. Search engines pick up on the postings which can help your search engine rankings as well as traffic.

75 **[22]**
Social networking can be time consuming but well worth it. If you simply cannot find the time, you could outsource. Many Virtual Assistants and other consultants offer social networking to their clients and will go in
80 as you and create updates for you. They can keep you updated on new contact requests as well as what is happening in the network.

To get the hang of social networking, practice is required but once you do, you'll find you have new contacts, new
85 ideas and possibly even new customers – all without leaving your office.

www.officearrow.com

Text D

Overrun by Nature!

Over the last century, there have been several waves of disaster movies pitting mankind against all sorts of natural forces, aliens, and even giant worms living under the Earth's surface. With only so many ways to end the world, disaster movies tend to explore similar themes and they tend to arrive in waves on the heels of real-life disasters. One of the most prominent themes in disaster movies is man vs. nature. The totally awesome power of tsunamis, earthquakes, and tornadoes to not only endanger but completely overrun and eradicate civilization fascinates us collectively.

As the threat of some sort of legitimate Earth-ending natural disaster becomes more real, natural disaster movies give us something important. They give us a way to conceive of, and face the possibility of, such realities in the safety of a movie theater or living room. Natural and all disaster movies give us a cathartic chance to confront harsh realities.

So in light of the Tsunami in Japan, and the soon to arrive next wave of disaster movies, here are my completely unscientific and biased top man versus nature movies of the last 20 years.

The Day After Tomorrow
This movie places a simple father/son narrative in the middle of a cataclysmic super freeze that hits the entire Northern Hemisphere. This was the first serious disaster movie released after 9/11, receiving a lot of conflicted reviews due to the generous destruction scenes set in New York. What redeems this movie, for the naysayers, is the fact that those scenes are treated with a lot of sincerity and sensibility. There is something very knowing in the message of this movie.

The Perfect Storm
One of the best ways to dramatize the man vs. nature struggle is to make us care about both the man and the natural event. *The Perfect Storm* pits George Clooney and Mark Walhberg against some epic waves. This movie is a little slow to launch, with fishermen down on their luck, looking for a good catch, but as the storm systems come together, so does the movie.

Armageddon/Deep Impact
While no two movies about a life threatening asteroid hitting the earth could be more different, in my mind *Armageddon* and *Deep Impact* are essentially the same movies, just packaged differently for different audiences. Both movies are indulgent, *Armageddon* because of the overblown and over-the-top aspect to pretty much everything, and *Deep Impact* because of how long and drawn out it is. With these two, which both came out in 1998, you get both sides of the coin. *Armageddon*, whose action takes place over 18 days, gives you the shoot from the hip, Hail-Mary, "Oh my god what are we going to do?" feelings of sudden doom. *Deep Impact*, which follows a wider cast over a much longer period of time, lets you experience more of not "What are we going to do?" but "How are we going to deal?".

Greg jensen, 2011

Question and answer booklet

Text A: Ecotourism Australia launches 2011/12 Green Travel Guide

Answer the following questions.

1 On which occasion is the *Green Travel Guide Australia* published?

....

2 Why are the 1,000 tourism experiences highlighted in the *Green Travel Guide Australia*?

....

3 According to the text, what is Australia reputable for?

....

4 Which phrase between lines 27 and 33 is similar in meaning to 'least effective'?

....

Which words go in the gaps **[5]–[9]**? Choose the words from the list and write them below.

certification	by	limited	online	ethically	through
recent	figures	authorization	environmentally	plenty	newly

Example [X]: ....*environmentally*........

5 ....

6 ....

7 ....

8 ....

9 ....

10 Choose the correct answer from A, B, C, or D. Write the letter in the box provided.

The purpose of the article is to

A highlight the extraordinary natural locations in Australia.

B promote the newly founded Ecotourism Australia company.

C promote the recently issued *Green Travel Guide Australia*.

D raise awareness about responsible and ethical tourism.

Text B: My relationship with my parents

11 From statements A to H, select the **three** that are true according to text B. Write the appropriate letters in the answer boxes provided. *(3 marks)*

Example [A]

A The writer highly regards her family's role in her life.

B There are no restrictions to what the writer would discuss with her parents.

C The writer has never failed to follow her parents' advice.

D The writer is fully confident of her ability to make the right decisions.

[ ]

E One reason why the writer resorts to her parents is their ability to make her look at things differently.

[ ]

F According to the writer, siblings are less important to consult than parents.

G The only time the writer seeks help is upon facing unsolvable dilemmas.

[ ]

H The on-going competition between the writer and her siblings has always led her to success.

Answer the following questions.

12 Which phrase between lines 1 and 10 is similar in meaning to 'not exaggerated'?

....

13 What does the word 'it' refer to in 'whether <u>it</u> is a good or bad thing' (lines 63 and 64)?

....

14 Find a sentence between lines 45 and 60 that reveals the writer owes who she is now to her siblings.

....

Find the word in the right-hand column that could meaningfully replace each of the words on the left.

Example: generated (line 10) [F]

15 torments (line 32) [ ]

16 tremendous (line 52) [ ]

17 sustain (line 67) [ ]

18 bleak (line 77) [ ]

A	gigantic
B	mysterious
C	depressing
D	tortures
E	create
F	caused
G	remarkable
H	founded
I	regrets
J	maintain

Text C: Using online social networking to grow your business

Match the headings with the paragraphs in the text. Write the appropriate letter in the boxes provided.

Example: [X]   [H]

19	☐	**A**	What types of social networks should I join?
		B	How can I have more time to social network?
20	☐	**C**	I'm so busy, I just don't have time.
		D	How is traffic driven to my blog or website?
21	☐	**E**	How can social networking help my business?
		F	How do I sign up for a network?
22	☐	**G**	How can you recruit employees using social networks?
		H	How do I get started?
		I	How many social networks should I join?
		J	I already have a website and a blog - Why do I need to social network too?

Find the correct phrases in the text to complete the sentences.
Base your answers on information from the text, which appears between lines 35 and 50.

23 The writer does not recommend joining many social networks because

....

24 In some social networks, members pay money when

....

Complete the following table by indicating to whom or to what the word/s underlined refer/s.

In the phrase...	the word/s...	refer/s to...
Example: ...those terms have a whole new meaning... (line 3)	'those terms'	*Tweet and MySpace*
25 This presents a bit of an icebreaker... (line 17)	'This'	
26 ...believe that it is free-form... (lines 23–24)	'it'	
27 ...build your network from there. (line 64)	'there'	
28 They can keep you updated...(line 80)	'They'	

29 From statements A to D select **two** benefits of social networking as mentioned in the text. Write the appropriate letters in the boxes provided.   *(2 marks)*

   A Social networking is the only standardized way for businesses to thrive.   ☐

   B Social networking promotes a member's blog and website.

   C Sharing experiential knowledge is a possibility when social networking.   ☐

   D Social networking allows males and females to find their future partners.

Text D: Overrun by Nature

The sentences below are either true or false. Tick ✓ the correct
response and then justify it with a relevant brief quotation from the
text. Both a tick ✓ and a quotation are required for one mark.

Example: Man's struggle with nature has been notably tackled in movies.

Justification: ...One of the most prominent themes in...
...disaster movies is man vs. nature....

True ✓ False

30   The dangers of natural disasters on civilization are far from reality.

Justification: ....

31   Disaster movies aim to distract our attention from the severe effects
of natural disasters.

Justification: ....

32   *The Day After Tomorrow* was received with a unanimous positive
reaction.

Justification: ....

33   What characterizes *The Perfect Storm* is the quick pace of events
maintained throughout.

Justification: ....

34   *Deep Impact* tackles possible means to deal with natural disasters.

Justification: ....

Answer the following questions.

35   According to information given between lines 1 and 10, mention
two disasters threatening the existence of humankind. (*2 marks*)

....

....

36   Which phrase between lines 33 and 39 proves the writer's
subjectivity in the text?

....

....

Choose the correct answer from A, B, C, or D. Write the letter in the box provided.

37   The word 'prominent' (line 13) is closest in meaning to

    A   thrilling

    B   realistic

    C   well-known

    D   recurrent

38   The word 'conceive' (line 26) is closest in meaning to

    A   envision

    B   handle

    C   solve

    D   replace

39   *The Day After Tomorrow*

    A   is based on 9/11 events.

    B   includes unrealistic destruction scenes.

    C   follows a simple, predictable line of events.

    D   is considered an authentic representation of a disaster.

40   It can be inferred that *Deep Impact* and *Armageddon*

    A   present different natural disasters.

    B   complement each other.

    C   are considered the best disaster movies.

    D   fail to convince the different audiences targeted.

41   In general, the writer believes that disaster movies are

    A   overrated

    B   misleading

    C   unrealistic

    D   significant

Paper 2 (SL)

Complete *one* of the following tasks. Write 250 to 400 words.

1 Cultural diversity

After watching a movie about migration, you have decided to write a blog entry reflecting upon the difficulties migrants face upon moving to a new country and how they manage to successfully cope with each. Do not forget to mention the name of the movie. Write your blog entry.

2 Customs & traditions

Understanding customs and traditions results in better relationships between cultures and countries. Write an article to be published in your school magazine in which you highlight the importance of customs and traditions to create harmony between different cultures. Write your article.

3 Health

It is anti-bullying day at school. The student council has asked you to prepare a leaflet in which you highlight how bullying can affect the mental and physical health of young people, and how parents and teachers can help students avoid such problems. Write your leaflet.

4 Leisure

You are participating in a class debate on how leisure activities can shape one's personality more than academic studies. Write a speech either agreeing or disagreeing with this motion.

5 Science & technology

You have bought a new mobile phone, but shortly afterwards discovered it has several flaws. Write a letter of complaint to the general manager of the company explaining the problem and suggesting solutions. Write your letter.

Exam practice 3: Paper 1 (HL)

Text booklet

Text A

Playing football for hope

Sixteen-year-old Neo Malema and his brothers and sister live with their grandmother in the impoverished Alexandra Township in Johannesburg. Despite his poor background, Malema dreams of playing football one day for the country's national squad, Bafana Bafana. Football for Hope, a Non-Governmental Organization (NGO) that aims to take children from disadvantaged communities around the world and develop them into future leaders for their communities, has given him the chance to realise his dreams.

"Football for Hope has changed my life. I used to be so naughty, I would wander around playing football in the streets. One day a coach found me and put me in his team. I have been playing for four years. Now I know that if you work hard, you can achieve your dreams," Malema said.

Malema and eight other young football players are part of Team Alexandra, which will represent South Africa at the FIFA Football for Hope festival in Alexandra.

The Football for Hope initiative was established in 2007 by FIFA and Streetfootballworld to use football as a tool for enhancing global peace and social development. The movement relies on the universal appeal of football to achieve its mission, and so far 1.5 million youngsters have benefited from the programme.

Speaking at the official opening launch of the event in Alexandra, managing director of Streetfootballworld said that the aim of the event was to encourage young people to take responsibility for their own lives. "The participants were chosen to show the world that they are young leaders so that when they are talking about themselves and where they are going, you yourself become inspired," he said.

Thirty-two teams from disadvantaged communities from all over the world will participate in the exciting event. The delegates come from over 40 countries and some teams comprise of players from more than one country.

But each of the 12-minute games will be played without official referees. So all disagreements will be resolved through dialogue, a method which organisers hope will enhance mutual understanding and personal development in the young players.

The players will also participate in activities which promote the exchange of ideas and life experiences, including talks on issues like HIV/AIDS and football coaching workshops.

Also speaking at the launch, the chief executive of the local organising committee for the FIFA 2010 World Cup said that the upcoming World Cup was not only about the famous football stars that are coming to South Africa for the event but also about the youngsters participating in the Football for Hope Festival. "It is a World Cup of hope, a World Cup of change, a World Cup of opportunity, a World Cup that focuses on the young people and their ambitions and their dreams," he said.

Malema has a passion for soccer and helping other disadvantaged youths. He hopes to one day manage an organisation like Football for Hope. "Football has brought me back to the right path; it taught me that when you work hard, you will definitely achieve your dreams," said Malema.

Zukiswa Zimela, 2010

Text B

The Social Network

By now you know there's a movie about the origins of Facebook. It's called *The Social Network*. I saw it a few days ago. It is the best movie I have ever seen.

5 Pause to digest that.

I'm not saying you'll like it as much as I do. Art is personal. And you might wonder how I can put one movie above all others, even on my own personal list. Actually, I couldn't do that until I 10 saw this movie. It grabbed me in the first minute, and hasn't released me yet, several days later. It's actually getting better as it ages in my mind.

To begin, I appreciate the movie for what it did not do. It did not rely on special effects in a way that 15 was obvious to the viewer. It wasn't in 3D. There was no violence. There was no car chase scene. If you make a list of all the elements that can make a movie predictable and lame, this movie had none. That's at least partly because the story is inspired 20 by reality.

If you have ever studied the art of script writing, you might know that movie studios expect scripts to fit a fairly specific sort of formula. For example, you have an "event" that changes someone's life 25 early in the movie, you have the so-called "third act" where things appear impossible to fix, and your main character needs to "change" as a result of his/her experiences. There are a number of other story requirements, but you get the idea. 30 Normally, a writer pushes these must-do elements right in your face. For example, how many movies open with loved ones dying?

The Social Network hits all of the required story 35 elements, but with a subtlety that can only come from reality plus extraordinary writing skill. It was only after the movie was over that I realized all of the elements were in place. Normally, the writer's craft is so obvious that it buries the art. When the 40 art buries the craft, you have something special.

Speaking of reality, the fact that much of the story is real – it's not clear how much – added the extra level of fascination to put it over the top for me. I enjoy non-fiction more than fiction, and this had 45 just the right mix of both.

The movie's writer, Aaron Sorkin, is one of the best writers of this era. And he's at the top of his game with this movie. If you can find an online betting site that takes bets on who will win the 50 Academy Award for Best Writer, this is easy money. And I say that without even seeing the other movies that will get nominated. If you're one of the other contenders, you're feeling pretty bad that your movie came out in Sorkin's year.

55 There has been much curiosity about the degree to which the story is accurate, and how the main character, Facebook founder, Mark Zuckerberg, feels about his portrayal. Apparently, some moviegoers feel the script treats Zuckerberg 60 poorly. I didn't see it that way. All I saw was massive respect from a genius in one field (Sorkin) to a genius in another. The story was as close to self-love as you can get. As written, the Zuckerberg character does change, a little, but he 65 does so in a context of changing the social fabric of the entire world. It is almost as if the world was broken, and Zuckerberg fixed it, like a super hero with a hoodie. He can't be too unhappy about that.

70 Someone once told me that when a movie works, you believe all of the elements were excellent at the same time even if that wasn't true. I suspect the writing elevated the other elements in this case, but even so, the directing, casting, and acting 75 came across as superb. Place your second bet for an Academy Award on the casting director.

Scott Adams, 2010

Text C

Help your children feel special

Do you ever wonder, "Will my children suffer because they have a working mother? Will they be deprived?" The answer: That
5 **[X]** and what you do.

Let's begin with your beliefs. It is a myth that children who have a working mom are automatically more deprived than children who have a
10 stay-at-home mom. Many stay-at-home moms are just as busy as you are. However, children usually adopt the attitudes of their parents – **[16]** in areas of weakness. If you are feeling
15 guilty and fearful that your children will be deprived, chances are they will feel deprived. They may develop a victim mentality, or they may play on your guilt for special privileges. On the
20 other hand, if you have an optimistic, courageous attitude, your children will be influenced and will learn from you.

Give up the belief that you have to make it up to your child for being a
25 working mother.
Present your circumstances with a positive attitude: "**[17]**, and we are going to benefit from how it is."

The greatest gift you can give
30 your children is to **[18]** no matter what your circumstances – and all circumstances, no matter how difficult, offer opportunities to learn and grow. **[19]** of your present opportunities as
35 a working mom to help your children feel special. Following are five possibilities.

Take time for hugs. No matter how busy you are, there is always
40 time for a three-second hug. That is a substantial hug that can lift spirits and change attitudes – yours and your child's. Sometimes a hug can be the most effective method to
45 stop misbehavior. Try it the next time you are feeling frazzled or your child is whining and see for yourself. Give hugs in the morning, right after work,

several during the evening, a longer
50 one just before bed. You will both feel very special.

Hold weekly family meetings. Twenty to thirty minutes a week is a small investment of time with huge
55 payoffs. Children feel very special when they are listened to, taken seriously and have their thoughts and ideas validated. That is the immediate payoff. The near future payoff is that
60 you can solve many daily hassles during a family meeting. Your kids can help you create morning and bedtime routines and come up with creative ways for handling chores. It is amazing
65 how much more willing children are to follow rules and plans they have helped create. The long-term payoff is that children learn important life skills such as communication skills
70 and problem-solving skills. Think of the benefits to their future jobs and relationships. It takes much less time to hold weekly family meetings where children learn to cooperate and solve
75 problems than the time it takes to nag, lecture, and scold. During busy times, parents often find relief or create a diversion from a problem by simply inviting the child to put the problem on
80 the family meeting agenda. Everyone learns to trust that a respectful solution will be found soon.

Ask for help. Children need to feel needed. It is much different when

85 you ask for help in an inviting manner instead of lecturing and scolding. "I would appreciate anything you can do to spruce up the family room before dinner," usually invites much
90 more cooperation than, "How many times have I told you not to leave all your stuff all over the family room!" Children feel special when they are helping. They don't feel special when
95 they are being scolded and put down.

When you run a short errand in the car, ask one of your children to ride along – just so you can spend as much time as possible
100 together. You might make a big deal of this by creating a chart during a family meeting so you can check whose turn it is. During these rides be a closet listener (don't ask questions).
105 You may be surprised at how much your children may open up and start talking when there is no "inquisition" that invites them to clam up. Simply let them know how glad you are to
110 have a few minutes to be with them, and share special moments from your own life or day. Kids feel special when you share yourself.

Helping your child feel special is a
115 matter of planning and habit, not a lack of time. The fringe benefit of making it a habit to help your child feel special is that you will feel like a special mom or dad.

Dr Jane Nelson Ed.D., 2010

Text D

'The Freedom Fighter' by Sean Gilpatrick

No one wore yellow.

She had asked, with a quote under her picture in the play program two, maybe three years earlier, that everyone wear yellow to
5 her funeral. No one did.

There was no doubt she would have left in the summer, probably right before the turn to autumn.

I thought of a hand-painted 1965
10 Volkswagen Split Window Van careening through heavy turns surrounded by the divinely painted autumn leaves in a thousand and one New England towns, and it was clear she intended to leave in late
15 summer.

I don't like talking about someone in the past tense, no matter how appropriate, but with the wake two days after I got home, and the funeral the following morning, I
20 couldn't understand how the girl kept such a complete record of her life. She had made the transition from is to was better than anyone I ever knew. A diary of her day-to-day life, a schedule updated weekly, a list of
25 goals (short term and long term, with labels for each), and one very detailed itinerary complete with globes, charts, and maps, all left behind.

And they really were the best-laid plans.

30 So, on that morning, I sat between my mother and father, next to her mother and father while our parish's priest spoke about the only thing that Brienne Allison Hale still does in the present tense. Here lies Brienne
35 Allison Hale: daughter, sister, and neighbor. Two speeches later, 'here lies' her first boyfriend on how they broke up amicably and how he will always remember her. He somehow forgot to mention the fights they
40 had, and how I could hear her crying on the phone from across her yard.

Every time Brie had an important phone call to make, she'd climb up the rotted and waterlogged boards to the tree house her
45 father built her after she was first diagnosed. Somehow, this is not included in her first boyfriend's speech. Or anyone else's.

I can't pretend that I was the shoulder she would cry on, but that tree house is only
50 four or five non-noise canceling feet from my bedroom window, so I guess I'm the shoulder she cried near.

I wasn't close to her like her ex-boyfriend was close to her. Or like her brother DJ was
55 close to her. Or a few of her friends from school. But we did talk, hell, we talked a lot, mostly through the four or five non-noise canceling feet between her safety tree and my windowsill. There's something I can't just
60 let go about firing questions and opinions into the dark to have them returned from summer-wet, hunter green tree branches.

And we had our summers, the most notable of which culminating in a poorly executed,
65 half spontaneous kiss from my lips to hers.

And we had our winters. Like when we didn't talk about those summer nights.

But we weren't like that. Well, we weren't some unfulfilled romance. We were not
70 star-crossed lovers who just couldn't get the timing right; we were friends who stumbled through the 'convenience meets attraction' phase of adolescence. We were great friends, though that never seemed to extend outside
75 our yards. It's not that we ignored each other in school, we just ran in different circles, my circle being slightly smaller. I guess our relationship needs clarification; we were friends and neighbors, not lovers and 'best
80 friends forever', and I guess we were most of the former and a mix of the latter if the latter was ever more appropriate than the former.

Text E

6 tips for creating 'sticky' social relationships

Every day, around 30 new people follow me on Twitter. Then around the exact same number of people usually 'un-follow' me. They're apparently upset that I haven't
5 blindly reciprocated their "friendship" despite the fact that they've never even said "hi" or interacted with me. They're so obsessed with the numbers' game that they don't seem to understand the most basic social networking
10 principle, where you have to be *sociable and personally interact with people before you win their trust and friendship.*

Social relationships evaporate quickly. Personal interaction is the "glue" that holds
15 them together. Take a moment to think of the *"people online you actually care about"*. Usually, the *important* folks are those who have taken the time to personally interact with you or acknowledged you (recently). These are
20 people you're willing to help out and stand up for. When you're under pressure or pressed for time, *the people who haven't interacted with you become second-class "nobodies" who are incredibly easy to ignore and forget*... no
25 matter how cool or famous they are.

Here are 6 tips for cultivating authentic, long-term, "sticky" personal connections – and maintaining them:

1.   [X]
30 Don't just blindly add people without interacting with them. A quick, personalized friend request note that says *"We met last week at the Social Media Meet up, enjoyed discussing design with you. Let's keep in touch?"* is enough to
35 make a strong, personal impression. Then most people will take a moment to check you out or take your request seriously.

2. Leave a quick comment on friends' blogs every time you stop by.
40 If you're already wasting two minutes to check out a blog post, why not go *all the way* and take another 30 seconds to leave a quick comment? This will transform you from an anonymous nobody to a *friend* and *supporter*,
45 who is a valuable and unforgettable part of their online social community.

3.   [42]
Don't be totally self-centered. Link out to what other people have to say about topics
50 you're interested in. Re-tweet content you feel is worth sharing or endorsing. Forgetting to do this is the online equivalent of going to a cocktail party and launching into an endless monologue about yourself.

55 **4.   [43]**
The deeper you get into the social web, the more "requests" will start to show up in your inbox. Try to get back to everyone who sends you a heartfelt request.

60 **5. Never pitch someone [XX] getting to know them.**
An essential, but widely **[50]** marketing principle is to give before you try and get. At the very least, before you pitch someone with
65 a **[51]** that will benefit you – *you need to take a few minutes and get to know (about) the person you're asking.*

6. Be grateful and explicitly thank people.
70 When someone does something for you – like promotes your content or links to you – don't forget to thank them! A little recognition creates a powerful **[52]** for more positive action – and it goes a long way **[53]** making sure that
75 person doesn't forget you.

[44]
If you want to build a potent, responsive social network, the most important thing is to be social and show that you're a real human.
80 Communicate, comment, and show concern and care for people – and pace yourself to keep doing it. It's not easy, but it's the only way to build real trust and long-term social **[54]**.

Brett Borders, 2009

Question and answer booklet

Text A: Playing football for hope

Answer the following questions.

1 What is South Africa's national football team called?

    ....

2 What helped Neo Malema fulfill his ambition of playing football?

    ....

3 What is Malema's next big endeavour?

    ....

4 Which phrase between lines 55 and 65 is similar in meaning to 'include'?

    ....

5 Which two social and personal areas are improved through the use of dialogue during games?   (*2 marks*)

    ....

    ....

6 From statements A to J, select the **four** that are true according to text A. Write the appropriate letters in the answer boxes provided.   (*4 marks*)

    A Football for Hope targets young men from all social backgrounds.

    B Malema believes that perseverance leads to success.

    C Football for Hope's mission statement reflects the necessity to spread peace worldwide.

    D Participants from underprivileged communities in 40 countries will participate in the Alexandra Festival.

    E Each game during the Hope Festival in Alexandra lasts for less than 15 minutes.

    F During the games, referees will be consulted to settle disagreements.

    G Young men's participation is restricted to football games during the festival.

    H Some teams might represent a variety of geographical locations.

    I Malema's future plan is to help young people achieve what he himself has managed to fulfil.

    J Football for Hope mainly prepares young people to become legendary football players.

Example: | C |

☐

☐

☐

☐

Text B: *The Social Network*

Answer the following questions.

7 Which phrase between lines 1 and 12 proves that the writer of the review is still influenced by the movie?

....

8 According to the writer, what makes a film predictable? Give **two**. *(2 marks)*

....

....

9 What contributes to the subtlety of *The Social Network*?

....

Complete the following sentences with information from the text. Refer to lines 45–68.

10 Any other Oscar nominee would feel insecure because

....

11 The highest debate about *The Social Network* revolves around

....

....

12 Who is the second genius referred to by 'to a genius in another' (line 61)?

....

Choose the correct answer from A, B, C, or D. Write the letter in the box provided.

13 What mostly fascinates the review writer about *The Social Network* is that it is
   A based on a true story.
   B includes all the must-do elements required.
   C mixes reality with fiction.
   D won two Academy Awards.

14 What Zuckerberg 'can't be too unhappy about' (line 67) is
   A not being portrayed poorly in the movie.
   B how accurate his character's depiction in the movie is.
   C the money gained upon releasing the movie.
   D his ability to make a change in the world.

15 The word 'elevated' (line 72) is closest in meaning to
   A exceeded
   B raised
   C promoted
   D demeaned

Text C: Help your children feel special

Which phrases go in the numbered gaps **[16]–[19]**? Choose the phrase from the list on the right and write the letters in the boxes provided.

Example: [X] ☐ D

16 ☐

17 ☐

18 ☐

19 ☐

A	have a hopeful outlook on life
B	focus on how you can make the best
C	and rebel against you
D	depends on what you believe
E	we have so many choices
F	give no attention to
G	determines how they will behave
H	this is how it is
I	or learn to manipulate
J	have an open mind when dealing with them

Find the appropriate advice given in the text for each of the following. Base your answers on information that appears in lines 38–95.

Example: End misconduct .... *Give regular hugs* ....

20 Work out regular annoyances...

21 Focus on finding a solution ....

22 Develop collaboration ....

Choose the correct answer from A, B, C, or D. Write the letter in the box provided.

23 Children are more at ease when
   A somebody tells them what to do.
   B they are given total freedom to run daily chores.
   C they listen to someone's instructions.
   D someone listens to them in an attentive manner. ☐

24 The text implies that parents who fail to make their children feel special
   A are constantly busy.
   B do not adopt a habitual pattern.
   C reject the suggestions made.
   D have not felt special themselves. ☐

Find the word in the right-hand column that could meaningfully replace one of the words on the left. Write the letter in the answer box provided.

A	annoyed
B	suggested
C	chore
D	improve
E	rebuking
F	fatigued
G	edge
H	raise
I	yelling
J	approved

Example: lift (line 41) ☐ H

25 frazzled (line 46) ☐

26 validated (line 58) ☐

27 scolding (line 86) ☐

28 errand (line 96) ☐

Text D: 'The Freedom Fighter'

Answer the following questions.

29 What does the comparison given between lines 9 and 15 actually refer to?

....

....

30 Based on the information given between lines 1–47, what are the two things everyone failed to do for Brie?   (*2 marks*)

....

....

Choose the correct answer from A, B, C, or D. Write the letter in the box provided.

31 'There was no doubt she would have left in the summer' (lines 6–7) suggests that
  A Brie prefers summer to other seasons.
  B Brie chose summer to end her life.
  C everyone knew Brie was dying.
  D Brie told everyone she was dying.

32 Judging by the description of the diary between lines 20 and 29, Brie seems to be
  A artistic
  B paranoid
  C omniscient
  D organized

33 From the text, one understands that Brie's death is attributed to
  A the falling off the tree house.
  B having suffered from a fatal disease.
  C her first boyfriend's maltreatment.
  D her having isolated herself for a long time.

34 The word 'amicably' (line 37) is closest in meaning to
  A agreeably
  B violently
  C justifiably
  D abruptly

35 Brie and the writer
  A always hesitated to speak to each other.
  B fell in love during the summer.
  C attended the same school.
  D were best friends.

36 The word 'culminating' (line 64) is closest in meaning to
  A excluding
  B proving
  C strengthening
  D concluding

Complete the following table by indicating to whom or to what the word/s underlined refer/s.

In the phrase...	the word/s...	refer/s to...
Example: So, on <u>that morning</u>, ... (line 30)	'that morning'	*the morning of her funeral*
37 ... <u>she</u>'d climb up the rotted and waterlogged boards ... (lines 43 and 44)	'she'	
38 But <u>we</u> did talk... (line 56)	'we'	
39 ...to have <u>them</u> returned from summer-wet... (lines 61 and 62)	'them'	
40 ...though <u>that</u> never seemed to extend... (line 74)	'that'	
41 ...if <u>the latter</u> was ever more appropriate... (lines 81 and 82)	'the latter'	

Text E: 6 tips for creating 'sticky' social relationships

Match the headings with the paragraphs in the text. Write the appropriate letter in the boxes provided.

Example: [X]   ☐ F

42 ☐

43 ☐

44 ☐

A	It's a jungle out there. Be human.
B	Respond to everyone who reaches out. Don't drop the ball.
C	It's difficult out there. Never give up.
D	Make a strong impact to let people remember you.
E	Invite friends to follow you and comment on your blogs.
F	Send a quick personal note every time you follow/fan/friend someone.
G	Re-tweet, link to and talk about what other people have to say.
H	Accept all the requests you receive. Don't ignore any.
I	Have an open mind when dealing with them.

The sentences below are either true or false. Tick ✓ the correct response and then justify it with a relevant brief quotation from the text. Both a tick ✓ and a quotation are required for one mark.

Example: The people un-following the writer have been unsociable.

	True	False
Justification: <u>they've never even said "hi" or interacted with me</u>	✓	☐

45   The writer responds to any person's tweet by following him/her.

Justification: ....   ☐   ☐

46   You can remain acknowledged even if you fail to interact with others.

Justification: ....   ☐   ☐

47   Personalizing request notes is usually unproductive.

Justification: ....   ☐   ☐

48   Posting frequent comments makes you an asset in a virtual environment.

Justification: ....   ☐   ☐

49   By isolating yourself from others, you end up having a small number of followers.

Justification: ....   ☐   ☐

Which words go in the gaps **[50]–[54]**? Choose the words from the list and write them below.

before	proposal	reinforcement	capital	interaction	without
recognized	post	overlooked	relationship	for	towards

Example: [XX] ...._without_........................

50 ....

51 ....

52 ....

53 ....

54 ....

Paper 2 (HL)

SECTION A

Complete *one* of the following tasks. Write 250 to 400 words.

1 Cultural diversity

You are participating in a class debate on how non-verbal communication can be louder than verbal communication. Write your speech either agreeing or disagreeing with this motion.

2 Customs & traditions

Your friend plans to study in an English-speaking country and asks you to send him/her details about the most important customs that he/she needs to be aware of to avoid any embarrassing situations. Write your letter.

3 Health

You have noticed that your school lacks the necessary hygiene required to provide a healthy environment for students and staff members. In a proposal sent to your school principal, highlight how significant this issue is and suggest ways to improve hygienic conditions on the premises. Write your proposal.

4 Leisure

Your school is organising an international youth festival during the winter break holiday. Your teacher asks you to produce a brochure describing the purpose of this festival, its importance and impact on the youth as well as the activities involved. Write your brochure.

5 Science & technology

It is predicted that some technological devices will soon become outdated. Write an article to be published in your local magazine to explain why this would happen and what types of devices will be out of use. Write your magazine article.

SECTION B

Based on the following stimulus, give a personal response and justify it. Choose any text type that you have studied in class. Write 150 to 250 words.

> *"I think the environment should be put in the category of our national security. Defense of our resources is just as important as defense abroad. Otherwise, what is there to defend?"*

Robert Redford
Source: http://greenquotes.html

Extended Essay in Group 2

The English B Extended Essay

Introduction

The 4,000 word extended essay in English B is suitable for those who wish to gain deeper understanding of a topic related to the English Language, English Literature, or an aspect of culture in English-speaking societies.

What is the purpose of the extended essay?

Such a task introduces you to the type of independent study required at university. **The IB Diploma extended essay is a research paper, not a descriptive essay.** Therefore, the extended essay should be seen as an exercise in using research and presentation skills.

Examples of successful extended essay titles in Group 2

In Group 2, extended essays must fall into one of the following three categories:

- **Category 1: Language**. This could be an analysis of some aspect of the English language: for example, anglophone national language policies, the nature of bilingualism in an anglophone culture, the way the English language is formed to convey meaning, etc.

- **Category 2: Culture and society.** This essay requires an analysis of some aspect of a social issue within an English-speaking society. This category is divided into two sections:

  A: Essays of a sociocultural nature with an impact on the language
  If you are attempting this essay, your focus should be on how a cultural or social issue affects the use of the English Language. For example, you may want to explore how immigration policies in the United States affect the use of English, or how Internet jargon has seeped into Standard English.

  B: Essays of a general cultural nature based on specific cultural artifacts
  If you are attempting this type of essay, you have to base your analysis on a specific artifact, like a film, a newspaper article, some photographs, or a certain work of art to name a few. For example, you may want to investigate how some pop songs (specify the songs) portray a certain social issue like parent/child relationship, or how a film represents cultural minorities in an anglophone country, etc.

- **Category 3: Literature**. This essay focuses on the literary analysis of one or more literary texts originally written in English.

Here are some examples of successful extended essay titles:

- How is 'Singlish' used in advertisements in Singapore? A linguistic analysis.

- To what extent are the female protagonists in *The Woman Warrior* by Maxine Hong Kingston and *Wild Meat and the Bully Burgers* by Lois-Ann Yamanaka able to find a balance between the differing Asian and American cultures and, thus, ascertain their identities?

- How does a character analysis assist an understanding of Kazuo Ishiguro's novels *A Pale View of Hills* and *The Remains of the Day*?

- What effects are achieved by the language used in editorials from *The Washington Post* and *The Nation* on the events in the United States on 11 September, 2001?

Note

You have to be very careful when choosing your English B extended essay topic, for English is a global language and you may be tempted to discuss this globalization without focusing on an English-speaking society. For example, while the topic 'Will the spread of English cause death to the mother tongue in Senegal?' is quite interesting, it is not a suitable English B essay since the focus of the essay is on Senegal, which is not an English-speaking country.

The process of writing an extended essay in English B

Choosing a topic for the extended essay

Before writing the essay, you will undertake hours of research and planning. Here are some general comments on how to proceed:

1 Find a topic that interests you. Discuss your initial ideas with your supervisor to see if they are suitable for an English B extended essay.

2 At this point, it might be a good idea to find source material and skim read it. If you find the subject does not interest you or you cannot find enough source material to work with, it is a good idea to start again.

3 If you are making good progress, find a focus or specific idea that you want to investigate within the topic and formulate a research question. At this point, you should be in a position to assemble your source material and start your reading and note-taking in earnest.

Reading and planning

Once you have chosen your topic, formulate an essay plan including the scope, shape, and direction of the essay. For example, the mindmap on the following page outlines several possible areas of discussion connected to how school shootings are portrayed in the media in an English-speaking country. The purpose of the mind map is to help the researcher narrow down ideas and determine the **scope** (which country, which media, etc.), the **shape** (Will it be an analysis of language used by/in the chosen media, or a discussion of the effect of such portrayal on the chosen society? Which data should be used under which main headings? etc.), and the **direction** (Will the essay try to prove a relationship? How will a conclusion to the essay be reached?).

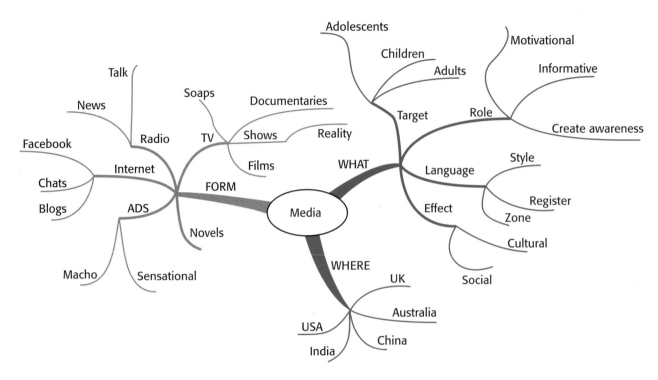

After you narrow down your research question, try to outline the major areas for discussion. Remember to look at your research question and make sure your essay plan enables you to answer the question.

At this point, you have to peruse the sources you have identified earlier and try to find more specific ones. As you begin to read, it is a good idea to identify and note the sections worth re-reading and which will be useful for core information. Here are some useful questions to guide you:

- Does the information I am reading seem useful?

- If so, why is it useful? How does the information relate to my essay plan?

- How does the new information relate to what I already know?

- Does the new information confirm or contradict the information I already have?

It is important to differentiate between **primary sources** and **secondary sources** at this stage. Primary sources are either the literary work itself if you have chosen a Category 3 essay, or actual research which was carried out on your topic for Category 1 and Category 2 essays. Secondary sources are the ones which discuss a literary work and research done by others. In other words, a successful essay is based on your own observations and conclusions rather than a summary of previous research done by academics and other professionals. **Do not plagiarise**. Once you have read a section of a text, such as a chapter of a novel, summarise the information you have read in your own words. Look at your research question and categorise what you have written. You may find it extremely useful to create visuals such as concept maps, diagrams, or charts of your outlined essay structure, mindmaps, or anything else that helps you to understand both the topic and your response to it. It is a good idea to go back to the main headings of your essay. Do remember to make an exact list of all useful sources. This will help you later.

Writing an initial draft – exploratory writing – writing to think

The purpose of exploratory writing is to help you know what you think. At this point, you are not yet writing for your examiner. However, an initial draft will help you to sketch out your ideas and come to some general conclusions about your research question. It does not have to be written in full sentences – note form is perfectly acceptable. The initial draft will also help you to know if you have mastered your material or if there is information which is still missing.

You should sketch out all your paragraphs including the introduction with headings, and then you can add detail to each. Draw an essay plan: write your research question and section headings. You may not yet have a clear conclusion; do not worry too much if you are still working on your conclusion as it may only come once you have finished thinking through your ideas. Plan the individual paragraphs with supporting details. At the end of the process, write down your thoughts and conclusions. Now is a good time to see your supervisor again to make sure that your conclusion relates clearly to your research question and that your provisional essay structure is clear and logical. Once you have clarified your ideas, you should be in a position to write a first draft for your supervisor.

Writing a thesis statement

A thesis statement states the broad answer to the research question. A good thesis statement can make all the difference between a sound extended essay and a simple listing of facts and opinions. Therefore, it is worth spending time making sure that you get your thesis statement just right. If, for example, your research question were 'Will the spread of English cause death to the mother tongue in Mauritius?', your thesis statement should declare quite clearly whether you **think** the answer is 'yes', 'no', or 'to some extent'. If you need to modify your research question and your thesis, now is the time to do both. **A general rule for the extended essay is that the narrower and more specific the research question, the easier it is to prove the thesis statement.**

Planning the first draft – writing to communicate

Draw up your essay plan. This should now consist of:
- your research question
- your thesis statement
- section headings
- paragraphs
- conclusion.

Plan the individual paragraphs with supporting details. Make sure that you have enough concrete detail and commentary in each paragraph. Ask yourself, 'Have I got the big picture?' A clear essay will have a clear research question and a clear thesis statement. Make sure that you have enough concrete detail and commentary in each paragraph. Above all, always remember to reference properly each time you quote source material. A good extended essay will also have organized paragraphs that support the thesis statement or at least structure the way your argument is leading. This means each paragraph should have a clear topic sentence that relates to your thesis statement. Your paragraph structure and paragraph links will help your audience understand the logic of your arguments. In addition, do not simply jot down quotes and explain them. Synthesize instead: use the points you highlighted in your reading to support your argument or analysis

Write your first draft. Proofread carefully what you have written. As this draft will be read by your supervisor, you should make sure you have communicated your ideas clearly and accurately.

Have you read your work carefully? One trick is to read your paper aloud. As you go along, check for spelling, vocabulary, grammar, punctuation, and overall logic. A word of warning: a spellcheck will not catch everything and grammar checks are sometimes wrong! Double-check all sources and references. What about referencing and documentation? Have you credited all sources? Have you used a proper referencing system? Once you are completely satisfied with this first draft, show it to your supervisor and discuss its strengths and weaknesses. Do not believe that you have finished. Your first draft will almost certainly need serious revision and your supervisor can help you to remodel your essay. Do remember to discuss this first draft with your supervisor, for he or she will not read another complete draft before you officially submit your extended essay.

Writing a second draft

In your second (and third and possibly fourth) draft you will almost certainly need to work on your introduction, sections, paragraphing, topic sentences, concrete details, and conclusion. At this point, you can think about adding a title page, an abstract, a contents page, bibliography, and appendices. Proofread again and double-check for grammar, expression, coherence, and logic. Re-check for concrete detail and commentary in each paragraph. You may still need to refine your research question, thesis statement, and conclusion. Treble-check all sources and references. Make sure you know the assessment criteria for marking the extended essay and that you have met the requirements per criterion.

Writing your conclusion

You can have a heading such as 'Conclusion' and continue with a sentence like, 'The following conclusions were reached:…' Alternatively, you can elaborate on your thesis statement to explain your ideas in detail. However, **do not introduce new ideas into your conclusion**. Instead, in the concluding part of your essay you may want to suggest ideas for further research or investigation.

Writing the abstract

Once you have completed the extended essay you will need to write an abstract of not more than 300 words. The abstract serves as an overview and allows your examiner to understand quickly the contents of your extended essay. In your abstract include your research question, your thesis, how you went about your investigation (the scope of your extended essay/a summary of your supporting points) and your conclusion(s). The abstract comes immediately after the title page.

Remember

You have to cite any ideas which are not originally yours, be they direct quotes or paraphrases. What is more, you have to be consistent when using a certain documentation style.

The following are examples of acceptable documentation styles:

- American Political Science Association (APSA)
- American Psychological Association (APA)
- Chicago/Turabian
- Council of Biology Editors (CBE)
- Harvard citation and referencing
- Modern Language Association (MLA)
- Numbered references

Here are a few links to online citation guides which will help you understand how to cite and reference your sources:

- www.wisc.edu/writing/ Handbook/Documentation. html
- www.library.uq.edu.au/ training/citation/harvard. html
- www.citationmachine.net

Use the following checklist to make sure that you have not forgotten anything:

	Extended Essay Checklist	Yes	No
1.	I have included a title page on which the title of my essay and its category are clearly stated.		
2.	My abstract includes my research question, scope of investigation, and conclusion.		
3.	I have included a table of contents right after the abstract.		
4.	My research question is clear and focused.		
5.	My research question and thesis are clearly stated in the introduction.		
6.	My argument is coherent, organized and clearly presented.		
7.	Sections have headings and, where appropriate, subheadings.		
8.	My conclusion is clearly marked.		
9.	My conclusion is clear, relevant to my topic, and lends itself to further research.		
10.	Appendices are attached (where necessary).		
11.	References are appropriately listed.		
12.	The pages are numbered.		
13.	My candidate number appears on every page.		
14.	I have used formal, academic English.		
15.	Direct quotations appear inside quotation marks and are properly cited.		
16.	I have properly and consistently cited paraphrased ideas.		

Some further advice

- Here are a few webpages which may help you with writing an extended essay:

  http://owl.english.purdue.edu/workshops/hypertext/ResearchW/notes.html

  http://managementhelp.org/businessresearch/planning.htm

  http://writing.wisc.edu/Handbook/PlanResearchPaper.html

  http://literacy.kent.edu/Oasis/Pubs/0200-08.htm

- Always keep a backup copy! Even better, keep two backup copies!

- Keep everything in perspective. An extended essay, may be worth only one or two points, but passing it is integral to obtaining the Diploma. Therefore, plan your time carefully and try to find some balance between working on your extended essay and meeting the requirements of your other subjects. You should only spend about 40 hours on this project in total. Do not spend hours worrying or going round in circles.

- When in doubt, see your supervisor.

- Do not rely on memory alone. Keep a notebook for ideas and brainwaves. Log visits to your supervisor so you both know how much time you have spent on the project.

The viva voce

Once you have completed your extended essay, your supervisor will have to write a report on your efforts. The viva voce is a short interview about your extended essay between yourself and your supervisor.
It is also an opportunity for both of you to reflect on successes and difficulties you have encountered in the research process and to reflect on what you have learned from the exercise. Your supervisor may also check that the work is your own and there is no plagiarism.

Good luck!

Appendix

• •

Answers
Exam Practice 1 (SL)

Page 113

Paper 1

TEXT A: Clean water campaign

1. C, G, H   (in any order)   *(3 marks)*
2. False
    Justification: (Students should write) a 300 to 500-word essay.
3. False
    Justification: (The essay must include) why both water quality protection and water conservation are important.
4. True
    Justification: (Students must also explain) how they would begin making a difference (in their communities).
5. prevent
6. promote / further
7. communicate
8. C
9. each
10. an

[Total: 12 marks]

TEXT B: Foods of the Irish

11. D
12. A
13. B
14. C
15. Irish bakers
16. Tea
17. The Irish value hospitality
18. when
19. often
20. however

[Total: 10 marks]

TEXT C: Proper etiquette of social networking

21. D, E   (in any order) *(2 marks)*
22. False
    Justification: (One golden rule everyone must abide by is that) social media doesn't tolerate spam.
23. True
    Justification: (Social media is) a walled paradise.

24. True
    Justification: posting about gifts.
25. True
    Justification: (You can also) modestly advertise by showing yourself to be an expert.
26. F
27. C
28. They are time-wasting
29. more importantly

[Total: 10 marks]

TEXT D: Blue blood
30. C
31. A
32. D

	Author's view	Is the author's comment positive (P) or negative (N)?
33.	Less than royal / Like any accommodation that a regular student would lodge in	N
34.	Somewhat dated	N
35.	Unreal / (I wonder why) the women don't stand up for themselves / Why don't they ever think they will get discarded?	N
36.	What a cheek!	N
37.	Not a good movie / Good editing is vital	N

38. somewhat
39. something
40. drastic
41. haphazard
42. one-dimensional

[Total: 13 marks]

Paper 1 total: 45 marks

Paper 2

1. **Cultural diversity**
   A good answer
   • will look like a blog: the name of the blog is clearly laid out; it may be divided into sections with titles and subtitles; it may have (imagined) hyperlinks, etc.
   • will adopt an informal register
   • will adopt a subjective view
   • will describe the author's visit to the restaurant and give details on the evening.
   What was the restaurant like?
   What was the food like?
   What made the visit an evening to remember and why was it a culinary adventure?

2. **Customs & traditions**

A good answer

- will adopt a semi-formal register
- will look like an article: it has a title and an author; it may have subheadings; it may have (imagined) illustrations
- will describe the fashions and trends teenagers were wearing (e.g. the types of clothing, colours, materials, accessories)
- may have an element of comparison with the fashion and trends in the student's hometown
- may be either objective or subjective (but not biased).

3. **Health**

A good answer

- will adopt a formal register
- will look like a letter: it is dated, addressed to the recipient, has a greeting and a closing, and it is signed by the author
- will provide justified and sufficiently detailed arguments for continuing the nurse's post
- may provide examples of incidents when the nurse is needed or what would happen if the school did not have a resident nurse
- will ask for funding for the nurse's post.

4. **Leisure**

A good answer

- will look like a proposal: it is titled and addressed to the company, it may be signed by the author and include his details
- will adopt a semi-formal to formal register
- will propose how the money will be used to promote students' sports activities and how this will improve their physical well-being
- may make detailed references to the students and the school community.

5. **Science & technology**

A good answer

- will adopt an informal to semi-formal register
- will look like an email
- will make reference to the bet and the outcome of it
- will describe the week spent without IT and give an account of personal experiences (e.g. difficulties, challenges, revelations encountered)
- may be reflective and/or humorous in tone.

Answers
Exam Practice 2 (HL)

Page 281

Paper 1

TEXT A: Educating dads may help protect babies from abuse
1. *Pediatrics*
2. Vulnerable
3. Shaking babies to death often because of crying
4. Home visiting **AND** hospital-based
    educational programs   *(2 marks)*
5. Any **two** of the following:
    blindness, brain damage, other injuries   *(2 marks)*
6. D, F, H, J (in any order)   *(4 marks)*
7. B

[Total: 12 marks]

TEXT B: Google plus social network forecast to hit the 400m mark
8. The world may well seem to be your oyster
9. Google's performance
10. Clocked up
11. G
12. E
13. C
14. G
15. E
16. I
17. B
18. B
19. B

[Total: 12 marks]

TEXT C: Harp seals on thin ice after 32 years of warming
20. To highlight and examine the increasing deaths of the North
    Atlantic harp seals and seal pups due to the decreasing ice
    covers.
21. The thickest, oldest ice packs
22. The North Atlantic
23. Harp seals
24. Period from 1950 to 2000
25. Johnston / W. Johnston
26. East Greenland / Gulf of St. Lawrence or off Newfoundland
27. False
    Justification: since 1979, when satellite records of ice conditions
    in the region began.
28. False
    Justification: each February and March
29. False
    Justification: may not be well adapted to absorb the effects of
    short-term variability combined with longer-term climate change

30. True
    Justification: but thousands still return each year to traditional breeding grounds
31. False
    Justification: It may take years

[Total: 12 marks]

TEXT D: From *The Storyteller* by Saki

32. All stories are dreadfully alike no matter who told them.
33. Bertha was 'horribly good'/ The use of 'horribly good' to describe Bertha / Describing Bertha as 'horribly good' carries an element of truth missing from other stories.
34. She did not expect the Bachelor to provide a convincing answer for Cyril's question.
35. 'a murmur of approval' **AND** 'immediate quickening of interest'   *(2 marks)*
36. B
37. D
38. B
39. A
40. C
41. B

[Total: 11 marks]

TEXT E: Illegal South African rhino killings hit record high

42. The country was still losing its war against poachers.
43. Eight rhinos were killed at Kruger National Park on one day when usually it was one rhino every 20 hours.
44. As a post-partying cleanser **AND** a cure for cancer.   *(2 marks)*
45. Any **two** of the following:
    helicopters / silent tranquilizers / body armour / night-vision equipment / mercenaries experienced in rhino tracking

    (2 marks)
46. extinction
47. into
48. fatally
49. escape
50. legalized
51. B
52. C

[Total: 13 marks]

Paper 1 total: 60 marks

Paper 2

Section A

1. **Cultural diversity**
   A good answer
   • will adopt a serious tone and a formal register
   • will make the viewpoint clear by focusing on how beauty differs from one culture to another
   • will provide examples to support viewpoint

- will adopt the elements of a formal letter to the editor
- may refer to the original article read.

2. Customs & traditions

A good answer

- will adopt a semi-formal to informal register
- will use the appropriate elements of a speech
- will address the audience and maintain contact with them throughout
- will make the writer's viewpoint clear
- will focus on either agreement or disagreement with the statement
- will provide supporting details for the agreement or disagreement
- may refer to the opposing viewpoint
- may draw examples from personal experience.

3. Health

A good answer

- will adopt a semi-formal to an informal register
- will provide specific, clear guidelines
- will present points using (sub)headings / bullet points, etc.
- will address the target audience
- will adopt a convincing and persuasive tone.

4. Leisure

A good answer

- will adopt a semi-formal register with probably some flashes of informality
- will have an eye-catching title and the name of the author
- will have an appropriate introduction
- will make the writer's viewpoint clear
- will provide clear examples to support how travelling enhances social interaction.

5. Science & technology

A good answer

- will adopt a formal to semi-formal register
- will adopt a serious tone
- will adopt a formal email format (address(es), the date, greetings, closing salutation, etc.)
- will clarify the purpose of the email at the beginning
- will explain in detail what is ethically expected from scientists upon conducting research
- will provide examples to support the argument
- will <u>not</u> use textese (e.g. 4 instead of for / u instead of you, etc.).

Section B

A good answer

- will make the writer's viewpoint clear
- may personalize the issue by providing examples drawn from the candidate's own experience
- may draw comparisons (similarities and differences) between practices in an anglophone culture and the candidate's own culture.

Answers
Exam Practice 3 (SL)

Page 365

Paper 1

TEXT A: Eco-tourism Australia launches 2011/12 Green Travel Guide

1. Ecotourism Australia's 20th birthday anniversary / celebration
2. They offer responsible, ethical, and sustainable tourism experiences.
3. Its outstanding ecotourism experiences
4. Minimal impact
5. limited
6. online
7. certification
8. newly
9. through
10. C

[Total: 10 marks]

TEXT B: My relationship with my parents

11. B, D, E (in any order)   (3 marks)
12. hardly ever be overstated
13. being dominated with the ultimate desire to be the best
14. I would not have accomplished most of the things that I have ever done in my life had I not had my siblings.
15. D
16. G
17. J
18. C

[Total: 10 marks]

TEXT C: Using online social networking to grow your business

19. E
20. A
21. J
22. C
23. It is too time consuming to keep up and will prevent you from learning from and sharing ideas with people in the same industry.
24. They want to access special features or more resources to help their business.
25. Social networks offering interest groups
26. Social networking
27. Using contacts you already know
28. Virtual assistants and other consultants
29. B, C (in any order)   (2 marks)

[Total: 12 marks]

TEXT D: Overrun by nature!
30. False
    Justification: becomes more real
31. False
    Justification: they give us a way to conceive of, and face the possibility of, such realities
    OR give us a cathartic chance to confront harsh realities
32. False
    Justification: receiving a lot of conflicting reviews
33. False
    Justification: This movie is a little slow to launch.
34. True
    Justification: lets you experience more on an existential level
    OR but "How are we going to deal?"
35. Any two from:
    natural forces (tsunamis, earthquakes, and tornadoes) / aliens / giant worms living under the Earth's surface   *(2 marks)*
36. my completely unscientific and biased
37. C
38. A
39. D
40. B
41. D

[Total: 13 marks]

Paper 1 total: 45 marks

Paper 2

1. **Cultural diversity**
   A good answer
   • will be reflective
   • will describe the problems faced by immigrants and how they can be handled successfully
   • will adopt an informal register appropriate for a blog entry
   • will mention the name of the movie.

2. **Customs & traditions**
   A good answer
   • will adopt a semi-formal register with probably some flashes of informality
   • will have an eye-catching title and the name of the author
   • will have an appropriate introduction
   • will make the writer's viewpoint clear
   • may refer to specific countries or cultures
   • will provide convincing supporting details.

3. **Health**
   A good answer
   • will adopt a semi-formal to formal register
   • will adopt a leaflet format (eye-catching title, short paragraphs, headings/sub-headings, use of bullet points, and numbers, etc.)

- will mainly focus on the effects of bullying on the mental and physical health of young people
- will provide parents and teachers with specific suggestions
- will adopt a serious but friendly tone.

4. **Leisure**

   A good answer
   - will use the appropriate elements of a speech
   - will address the audience and maintain contact with them throughout
   - will make the writer's viewpoint clear
   - will focus on either agreement or disagreement with the motion
   - will provide supporting details for the agreement/ disagreement
   - may refer to the opposing viewpoint
   - may draw examples from personal experience.

5. **Science & technology**

   A good answer
   - will adopt a formal register
   - will adopt a friendly but serious tone
   - will adopt a formal letter format (address, the date, greetings, closing salutation, etc.)
   - will clarify the purpose of the letter at the beginning
   - will state the complaint and provide justifications
   - will provide clear suggestions of what should be done.

Exam Practice 3 (HL)

Page 375

Paper 1

TEXT A: Playing football for hope

1. Bafana Bafana
2. Football for Hope / Football for Hope's mission statement
3. He will be part of Team Alexandra, representing South Africa at the FIFA Football for Hope festival in Alexandra.
4. comprise of
5. Mutual understanding **AND** personal development *(2 marks)*
6. B, E, H, I (in any order) *(4 marks)*

[Total: 10 marks]

TEXT B: *The Social Network*

7. hasn't released me yet
8. Any **TWO** of the following:
   relying on special effects / being in 3D / having violence / including car chase scenes *(2 marks)*
9. Having a real-life story written in an extraordinary way / Real-life story with extraordinary writing skills
10. ...it will be difficult to compete with Aaron Sorkin, one of the best writers of this era.

11. ...how accurate the story is and how Zuckerberg feels about his portrayal.
12. Mark Zuckerberg
13. C
14. D
15. A

[Total: 10 marks]

TEXT C: Help your children feel special
16. I
17. H
18. A
19. B
20. Hold weekly family meetings
21. invite the child to put the problem on the family meeting agenda
22. ask for help in an inviting manner
23. D
24. B
25. F
26. J
27. E
28. C

[Total: 13 marks]

TEXT D: The Freedom Fighter
29. Brie is compared to an old Volkswagen Van staggering because of her illness and trying to survive.
30. Wearing yellow to her funeral as she requested **AND** mentioning in the speeches the tree house her father built her (after she was first diagnosed and which she used to climb up whenever she had an important call).   (*2 marks*)
31. C
32. D
33. B
34. A
35. C
36. D
37. Brie
38. The writer and Brie
39. The questions and opinions (fired into the dark)
40. Brie and the writer being great friends
41. Brie and the writer not being lovers and 'best friends forever'

[Total: 14 marks]

TEXT E: 6 tips for creating "sticky" social relationships
42. G
43. B
44. A
45. False
     Justification: I haven't blindly reciprocated their "friendship".

46. False
   Justification: incredibly easy to ignore and forget
47. False
   Justification: is enough to make a strong, personal impression **OR** most people will take a moment to check you out or take your request seriously
48. True
   Justification: a valuable and unforgettable part
49. True
   Justification: The deeper you get into the social web, the more 'requests' will start to show up in your inbox.
50. overlooked
51. proposal
52. reinforcement
53. towards
54. capital

[Total: 13 marks]

Paper 1 total: 60 marks

Paper 2

Section A

1. **Cultural diversity**
   A good answer
   - will use the appropriate elements of a speech
   - will address the audience and maintain contact with them throughout
   - will make the writer's viewpoint clear
   - will focus on either agreement or disagreement with the motion
   - will provide supporting details for the agreement/disagreement
   - may refer to the opposing viewpoint
   - may draw examples from personal experience.

2. **Customs & traditions**
   A good answer
   - will adopt an informal register
   - will adopt a friendly but serious tone
   - will adopt an informal letter format (address, the date, greetings, closing salutation, etc.)
   - will clarify the purpose of the letter at the beginning
   - will mention the English-speaking country the friend is studying at
   - will refer to more than one custom and explain their significance
   - will provide examples to support argument
   - will not use text speak (e.g. 4 instead of for / u instead of you, etc.).

3. **Health**

    A good answer
    *   will adopt a formal register
    *   will adopt a serious tone
    *   will adopt the format of a proposal (the use of headings, short clear paragraphs, sections identified by numbers/letters, etc.)
    *   will mention why the issue of hygiene is of extreme significance
    *   will explain the current hygienic conditions and why they need to be improved
    *   will offer suggestions to improve the existing conditions and explain why they are better alternatives.

4. **Leisure**

    A good answer
    *   will adopt a semi-formal register
    *   will adopt a brochure format (eye-catching title, short paragraphs, heading/sub-headings/use of bullet points and numbers, etc.)
    *   will mention the name of the international youth festival
    *   will clearly state when and where the festival will be held
    *   will explain how the festival is going to benefit students
    *   will detail the activities involved.

5. **Science and technology**

    A good answer
    *   will adopt a semi-formal register with probably some flashes of informality
    *   will have an eye-catching title and the name of the author
    *   will have an appropriate introduction
    *   will make the writer's viewpoint clear
    *   will mention specific technological devices that are predicted to be outdated.

Section B

A good answer
*   will make the writer's viewpoint clear
*   may personalize the issue by providing examples drawn from the candidate's own experience
*   may draw comparisons (similarities and differences) between practices in an anglophone culture and the candidate's culture.

Index

The authors and publisher are grateful for permission to reprint from the following copyright material:

Scott Adams: Review of *The Social Network*, 7 .10.2010, www.dilbert.com, reprinted by permission of Scott Adams.

David Amerland: 'Google Plus Social Network Forecast to Hit the 400m Mark', www.technorati.com, 30.12.2011, reprinted by permission of the author.

Craig Anderson: extracts from an interview given to a group of students on the subject of Video Game Violence published at www.psychology.iastate.edu, reprinted by permission of Craig Anderson.

Laurie Halse Anderson: extract from 'Welcome to Merryweather High' from *Speak* (Farrar, Straus & Giroux, 1999), copyright © Laurie Halse Anderson 1999, reprinted by permission of Farrar, Straus & Giroux LLC.

Iain M Banks: extract from *Surface Detail* by (Orbit, 2010), reprinted by permission of Little Brown Book Group Ltd.

Adriana Barton: 'Scrap the teen stereotypes' an interview with Reginald Bibby, *Globe and Mail*, 26.5.2009, copyright © The Globe and Mail Inc, reprinted by permission of The Globe and Mail Inc. All Rights Reserved.

Brett R Borders: '6 Tips for Creating "Sticky" Social Relationships', www.socialmediarockstar.com, 24.8.2009, reprinted by permission of the author.

William Boyd: 'Not Yet, Jayette' from *On the Yankee Station* (Penguin, 1998), copyright © William Boyd 1981, reprinted by permission of the Curtis Brown Group Ltd, London on behalf of William Boyd.

Jasbir Chatterjee: 'The Delhi Metro', published on www.poemhunter.com, copyright © Jasbir Chatterjee 2011, reprinted by permission of the author.

Sylvia Chidi: 'Round and Round the London Underground', published on www.poemhunter.com, copyright © Sylvia Chidi 2005, reprinted by permission of the author.

Laura Clark: 'Cartoon violence "makes children more aggressive"', *Daily Mail*, 6.3.2009, reprinted by permission of Solo Syndication, Associated Newspapers Ltd.

Arthur C Clarke: extract from 'Superiority' by from *The Collected Short Stories of Arthur C Clarke* (Gollancz, 2000), reprinted by permission of David Higham Associates Ltd.

Ellen Connolly: 'Australian snorkeller snatched by shark', Guardian.co.uk, 28.12.08, copyright © Guardian News & Media Ltd 2008, reprinted by permission of GNM Ltd.

Andy Coghlan: 'Thank climate change for the rise of humans', *New Scientist*, Issue 2824, 5.8.2011, copyright © 2011 Reed Business Information UK, distributed by and reprinted by permission of Tribune Media Services International. All Rights Reserved.

Stephanie Davis: 'Waiting for the Plane', ABC Short Story Project 2007, copyright © ABC 2007, reprinted by permission of the Australian Broadcasting Corporation and ABC Online. All rights reserved.

Kathy Ennis: 'Are dress codes in the workplace necessary?', 6.7.2009, www.kathyennis,co.uk, reprinted by permission of the author, kathy@kathyennis.co.uk.

D J Enright: 'Poem on the Underground', from *Collected Poems 1948-1998* (OUP, 1998), reprinted by permission of Watson, Little Ltd.

Hanna Gersmann: 'Public supports geoengineering, survey finds', Guardian.co.uk, 24.10.2011, copyright © Guardian News & Media Ltd 2011, reprinted by permission of GNM Ltd.

Louise Gray: 'Running cars on biofuels can be "unethical"', *The Daily Telegraph*, 14.4.2011, copyright © Telegraph Media Group Ltd 2011, reprinted by permission of TMG Ltd.

Karen Jennings: 'From Dark', Commonwealth Foundation short story competition 2010, reprinted by permission of the author.

Jonathan Jones: 'Book Festivals bring out the brains in Britons', Guardian.co.uk, 8.8.2010, copyright © Guardian News & Media Ltd 2010, reprinted by permission of GNM Ltd.

Anuradha Kumar: 'The First Hello', Commonwealth Foundation short story competition 2010, reprinted by permission of the author.

Maxine Hong Kingston: extract from 'Song from a Barbarian Reed Pipe' in *The Woman Warrior: Memoirs of a Girlhood Among Ghosts* (Vintage, 1989), copyright © Maxine Hong Kingston 1976, reprinted by permission of Random House, Inc.

Lauraine Leblanc: *Pretty in Punk: Girl's Gender Resistance in a Boy's Subculture* (Rutgers, 1999), copyright © Lauraine Leblanc 1999, reprinted by permission of Rutgers University Press.

Anna Lewis: 'Education for Life', Commonwealth Foundation short story competition 2010, reprinted by permission of the author.

Ethan Lyon: 'Top 5 Mobile Innovations for Social Causes', 25.2.2011, www.sparxoo.com, reprinted by permission of the author and of Sparxoo, a branding agency based in Tampa, Florida.

Claude McKay: 'Subway Wind' from *Complete Poems* (University of Illinois Press, 2004), copyright © Claude McKay 2004, reprinted by permission of The Schomberg Center for Research in Black Culture, The New York Public Library, Astor, Lenox and Tilden Foundations, as the Literary Representative for the Works of Claude McKay.

Emmanuel Makeri: 'Help Children maintain their mother tongue in foreign environments', *Daily Monitor*, 20.3.2011, reprinted by permission of Monitor Publications Ltd (Uganda).

Fiona McLeod: 'Sci-fi brought to life as spray allows scars to heal themselves', *The Scotsman*, 25.4.2011, and case study from *The Scotsman*, 26.4.2011, reprinted by permission of Scotsman Publications Ltd.

Iona Roumeliotis (Massey): 'Grandma Makes Meatballs', Commonwealth Foundation short story competition 2010, reprinted by permission of the author.

Shazia Mirza: 'The Courage to Change', first published in *Asian Woman*, 1.9.2008, and also on the author's website at www.shazia.mirza.com, reprinted by permission of Vivienne Smith Management on behalf of the author.

Kwesi Mugisa: 'Ignoring the Bananas - How John Barnes tackled racism in English Football', *The Jamaica Gleaner*, 2.3.2008, copyright © The Gleaner Company Ltd 2008, reprinted by permission of The Gleaner Company Ltd.

Alice Munro: 'The Jack Randa Hotel' from *Open Secrets* (Chatto 1994/Vintage 1995), reprinted by permission of the publishers, The Random House House Group Ltd, McLelland & Stewart Ltd (Canada) and Random House, Inc.

Edward R Murrow: extract from convention speech before the Radio News Directors Association (RNDA) 'Wires and Lights in a Box', 15 October 1958, reprinted by permission of the Radio Television Digital News Association (RTDNA).

Seth Mydans: 'As English's dominance continues, linguists see few threats to its rule', *International Herald Tribune*, 29.4.2007, copyright © The New York Times 2007. All rights reserved. Reprinted by permission of PARS International Corp and protected by the Copyright Laws of the United States. The printing, copying, redistribution, or retransmission of this content without express written permission is prohibited.

Vikram Nanjappa: 'Wildlife Safaris in India - Tips from the Expert', www.ecotourdirectory.com, 2007, reprinted by permission of the author.

Dr Jane Nelsen: extract from 'Seven Ways Busy Parents Can Help Their Children Feel Special', 11.9.2010, www.store.positivediscipline.com, reprinted by permission of Positive Discipline.

David Ronald Bruce Pekrul: 'Our Lives On A Chip', from www.myhiddenvoice.com, reprinted by permission of the author.

Anne Perkins: 'Are mobile phones Africa's Silver bullet?', Guardian.co.uk, 14.1.10, copyright © Guardian News & Media Ltd 2010, reprinted by permission of GNM Ltd.

Daniel Pope: extracts from 'Making Sense of Advertisements' on *History Matters: The U.S. Survey Course on the Web*, published in June 2003, reprinted by permission of American Social History Productions, Inc.

Mark Potterton: 'Unique vs. Uniform', *Mail & Guardian* (South Africa), 28.1.2011, reprinted by permission of the author, National Director, Cathotic Institute of Education.

Benjamin Rodgers: 'Shades of Dreaming', Commonwealth Foundation short story competition 2010, reprinted by permission of the author.

Feroz Salam: 'I don't understand the words', *Denizen* Magazine, denizenmag.com, 12.4.2011, reprinted by permission of the editor, Denizenmag.com.

Mary Schmich: 'Wear Sunscreen' from 'Advice, Like Youth, Probably Wasted on the Young' *Chicago Tribune*, 1.6.1997, copyright © Chicago Tribune 1007. All rights reserved. Reprinted by permission of PARS International Corp and protected by the Copyright Laws of the United States. The printing, copying, redistribution, or retransmission of this Content without express written permission is prohibited.

A O Scott: extract from film review of *Wall-E*, 'In a World Left Silent, One Heart Beeps', *New York Times*, 27.6.2008, copyright © The New York Times 2008. All rights reserved. Reprinted by permission of PARS International Corp and protected by the Copyright Laws of the United States. The printing, copying, redistribution, or retransmission of this Content without express written permission is prohibited.

Isabel Shaw: 'Social Skills and Homeschooling: Myths and Facts', copyright © Pearson Education 2000-2012, reprinted by permission of Pearson Education, publishing as Family Education Network. All Rights Reserved.

Julia Sherstyuk: 'Singlish: Broken English or Badge of Identity', *103rd Meridian East* Magazine, Is. 3 (Autumn 2009), copyright © Julia Sherstyuk 2009, reprinted by permission of the author.

David Simpson: 'I've seen the future and it's Goth', *The Guardian*, 21.3.2006, reprinted by permission of GNM Ltd.

Paul Sims & Jenny Hope: extract 'I have my life back' from 'Stem cell treatment allows the blind to see again', *Daily Mail*, 23.12.2009, reprinted by permission of Solo Syndication, Associated Newspapers Ltd.

David Smith: 'Illegal South African rhino killings hit record high', Guardian.co.uk, 12.1.2012, copyright © Guardian News & Media Ltd 2012, reprinted by permission of GNM Ltd.

Heather Grace Stewart: 'Dear Friend I've Never Met' (The Facebook Poem), 'Lolita', and 'A "Dear Facebook" Letter', © Heather Grace Stewart, reprinted by permission of the author.

Liz Szabo: 'Educating dads may help protect babies from abuse', *USA Today*, 27.7.2009, copyright © 2009 USA Today, a division of Gannett Co, Inc, reprinted with permission, via Copyright Clearance Center.

Bob Tedeschi: 'App Smart: 'Quick Access to Poetry in the Age of Technology", *New York Times*, 18.8.2010, copyright © The New York Times 2010. All rights reserved. Reprinted by permission of PARS International Corp and protected by the Copyright Laws of the United States. The printing, copying, redistribution, or retransmission of this Content without express written permission is prohibited..

David Toomey: extract from 'Eco-Friendly Vacationing', www.supergreenme.com, reprinted by permission of David Toomey, Founder, SuperGreenMe.

Arthur Waley: 'Falling Leaves and the Sadness of the Cicada's Song', translation of the poem 'Li Fu-jen' by Wu-ti, from *The Book of Chinese Poems* (G Allen & Unwin, 1946), reprinted by permission of Antonia Robinson for The Arthur Waley Estate.

Audrey Watters: 'Cell Phones and Sustainable Development: The Future is Mobile', 19.4.2010, www.justmeans.com, reprinted by permission of 3BL Media/Justmeans

Anna Vera Williams: 'The Advantages of Biofuels', www.livingclean.com,13.3.2009, reprinted by permission of the author.

C K Williams: 'On the Metro' from *Collected Poems* (Bloodaxe, 2006), first published in *Poetry Magazine* September 2005, copyright © C K Williams 2006, reprinted by permission of the publishers, Bloodaxe Books and Farrar, Straus & Giroux, LLC.

Gibbs A Williams: 'Preventing Substance Abuse: a proposal', published at www.gibbsonline.com reprinted by permission of Dr Gibbs A Williams.

Julia Wilson: 'You too can be a medical practitioner', Guardian.co.uk, 6.9.2010, copyright © Guardian News & Media Ltd 2010, reprinted by permission of GNM Ltd.

Lois-Ann Yamanaka: extract from *Wild Meat and the Bullyburgers* (Farrar, Straus & Giroux, 1996), copyright © Lois-Ann Yamanaka 1996, reprinted by permission of Farrar, Straus & Giroux, LLC.

Benjamin Zephaniah: 'Neighbours' from *Propa Propaganda* (Bloodaxe, 1996), copyright © Benjamin Zephaniah 1996, reprinted by permission of Bloodaxe Books; 'The British (serves 60 million)' and 'We Refugees' from *Wicked World!* (Puffin, 2000), copyright © Benjamin Zephaniah 2000, reprinted permission of Penguin Books Ltd.

Zukiswa Zimela: 'Playing Football for Hope', IPS, 29.3.2010, reprinted by permission of IPS/Inter Press Service, North America Inc.

and to the following for permission to reprint copyright material

Aberdeen City Events Office for 'Aberdeen's Homecoming Tartan Day' flyer (August, 2009).

The Academy of Ideas Ltd for entries on Alternative Medicine to their Debating Matters Competition 2002, by Lucie Potter (Graveney School) and Daniel Marshman (JFS).

The Associated Press via YGS Group for 'English won't dominate as world language', AP, 26.2.2007 copyright © The Associated Press 2004, 2012. All Rights Reserved.

Drug Addiction Support for 'Drug Addiction Intervention', copyright © 2012 Mission Enabled, www.drug-addiction-support.org.

Duke University's Nicholas School of the Environment for extract from press release 'Harp seals on thin ice after 32 years of warming', 4.1.2012, a study by David Johnston, Matthew Bowers, Ari Friedlaender and David Lavigne.

Gale, a part of Cengage Learning, Inc, www.cengage.com/permissions for extract from UXL *Junior Worldmark Encyclopedia of Foods and Recipes of the World* edited by Karen L Hanson, copyright © Gale 2002.

Government of South Australia, Southern Adelaide Local Health Network for 'What are gender roles and stereotypes?', *Keep Safe Stay Cool* program, 2008, www.keepsafestaycool.com.au.

IB Organization for definition of a personal blog from marking notes for *English B Higher Level Paper 2, November 2010*, (IB Publications, 2010).

Media Awareness Network, Ottawa, Canada, for extracts from 'Beauty and Body Image in the Media', copyright ©2011 Media Awareness Network, www.media-awareness.ca.

*Metropolitan North Georgia Water Planning District for Clean Water Campaign webpage giving entry details for the 2011 Essay Contest

Military Schools US for 'Why Schools should maintain the use of school uniforms in Arkansas', 9.1.2011, www.militaryschools.com.

Moviexclusive.com for review by B S Lokman of the film *Mad About English* from www.moviexclusive.com.

National Geographic Society for extract from article on Global-Warming published at www.environment.nationalgeographic.com .

Nolly at Nollywoodforever for review of *Blue Blood* (2010), nollywoodforever.com.

Oxford University Press for Dictionary definitions from the *Oxford English Dictionary Online*: www.oxforddictionaries.com.

The Joe Raposo Music Group, Inc for lyrics of 'It's Not Easy Bein' Green', music and lyrics by Joe Raposo, copyright © 1970 Jonico Music Ltd, US © renewed 1998 Green Fox Music, Inc.

Although we have made every effort to trace and contact all copyright holders before publication this has not been possible in all cases. If notified, the publisher will rectify any errors or omissions at the earliest opportunity.